We Always Had a Union

THE WORKING CLASS IN AMERICAN HISTORY

Editorial Advisors
James R. Barrett, Thavolia Glymph, Julie Greene, William P. Jones,
and Nelson Lichtenstein

For a list of books in the series, please see our website at www.press.uillinois.edu.

We Always Had a Union

The New York Hotel Workers' Unions, 1912–1953

SHAUN RICHMAN

© 2025 by the Board of Trustees
of the University of Illinois
All rights reserved
1 2 3 4 5 C P 5 4 3 2 1
♾ This book is printed on acid-free paper.

Library of Congress Cataloging-in-Publication Data
Names: Richman, Shaun, author.
Title: We always had a union : the New York hotel workers'
   union, 1912–1953 / Shaun Richman.
Description: Urbana : University of Illinois Press, [2025] |
   Series: The working class in American history | Includes
   bibliographical references and index.
Identifiers: LCCN 2024047606 (print) | LCCN 2024047607
   (ebook) | ISBN 9780252046445 (cloth) | ISBN 9780252088537
   (paperback) | ISBN 9780252047756 (ebook)
Subjects: LCSH: Hotels—Employees—Labor unions—New York
   (State)—New York—History—20th century. | New York (N.Y.)—
   Economic conditions—20th century. | Labor unions and
   communism—New York (State)—New York.
Classification: LCC HD8039.H82 U675 2025 (print) |
   LCC HD8039.H82 (ebook) | DDC 331.7/6164794097471—
   dc23/eng/20250103
LC record available at https://lccn.loc.gov/2024047606
LC ebook record available at https://lccn.loc.gov/2024047607

For Michael J. Obermeier (1892–1953) and Michael Simo (1946–2012), two Presidents of Local 6 who were robbed of the long, comfortable retirements they so richly deserved.

Contents

Acknowledgments ix

Abbreviations xi

Introduction 1

1. The Unsafest Proposition in the World, 1912–1913   11
2. Bolsheviki Methods, 1913–1918   33
3. Practical Trade Union Tactics, 1919–1924   49
4. Strange as It May Seem, 1925–1929   61
5. Political Sentimental Giddiness, 1929–1934   75
6. An Industry Has Been Freed, 1934–1938   104
7. Status Quo, 1938–1939   127
8. Only the Question of Final Alliances Remains, 1939–1941   150
9. We Cook, Serve, Work for Victory, 1941–1945   169
10. In Normal Order, 1945–1947   190
11. The Crack, 1947–1950   215
12. Trusteeship, 1950–1953   239

Afterword 261

Notes 267

Sources 309

Index 317

Acknowledgments

I want to thank my wife, Kate, and my daughters, Audrey and Bernadette, and our families for their support.

I am deeply appreciative of the many librarians whose daily work makes projects like this book possible. Archivists who stand out for their sleuthing include Eirini Melena Karoutsos at the New York City Municipal Archives; Sarah Lebovitz at Wayne State University; Steven Calco and Melissa M. Holland at the Kheel Center for Labor-Management Documentation & Archives at Cornell University; and Malia Guyer-Stevens, Michael Koncewicz, and Shannon O'Neill at the Tamiment Library and Robert F. Wagner Labor Archives at New York University.

Annemarie Strassel and D. Taylor were instrumental in making the scanned archives of *Mixer & Server* and *Catering Industry Employee* fully available on HathiTrust, which was a lifesaver during the COVID lockdown. Thanks as well to Craig Becker and Liz Shuler for making the American Federation of Labor's publications similarly available. I especially want to thank Samantha Klein, John Ruben, and most of all, Richard Maroko for opening the Local 6 and Hotel Trades Council offices and files to me and generally for being so supportive of this project.

I'd also like to thank my deans at SUNY Empire for fostering a conducive environment for research and writing. I've had a depressingly large number of them in the last five years, but Nicola Marae Allain and Lynne Dodson stand out for being particularly supportive.

I used my union-negotiated tuition benefit to enroll in the university's Liberal Studies master's program to help structure my thinking and give me access to a few colleagues who had to read my early drafts because it was literally their job. Thanks to Susan Forbes, Sabrina Fuchs-Abrams, Diane Gal,

Anastasia Pratt, and especially Mark Soderstrom who read several iterations and offered consistently useful advice and a bit of cheer.

Sean Guillory was gracious with his time and resources, helping me navigate the Communist Party microfilm, Comintern archives, and their many finding aids and legends, and connecting me with a crackerjack research assistant in Moscow: Vladislav Tiurin.

Faith Bennett, Dorothy Sue Cobble, Jacob Remes, Zach Schwartz-Weinstein, and David Whitford have been a friendly little community of Hotel Employees scholars.

Similarly, I'd like to thank Alan Cage, Peter Cole, Otoniel Figueroa-Duran, Steve Lawton, and John Wilhelm for being early readers.

Erik Loomis, who talked me out of my imposter syndrome as a historian and gave me early advice (while we walked around a cemetery, natch) and gave me enormously helpful feedback on a version of my "final" draft, is doing his level best to democratize labor history.

I want to thank Alison Syring Bassford and everyone at the Press for getting this book in your hands (or on your screen).

Abbreviations

ACPFB	American Committee for the Protection of the Foreign Born
AFL	American Federation of Labor
AFW	Amalgamated Food Workers
B&C	Bakery & Confectionery Workers International Union
BSEIU	Building Service Employees International Union
CIO	Committee for Industrial Organizing / Congress of Industrial Organizations
CP	Communist Party
CPLA	Conference for Progressive Labor Action
FWIU	Food Workers Industrial Union
GEB	General Executive Board (of HRE)
HRE	Hotel and Restaurant Employees' International Alliance and Bartenders' International League
HUAC	U.S. House Un-American Activities Committee
IBEW	International Brotherhood of Electrical Workers
IFWHR	International Federation of Workers in the Hotel and Restaurant Industry
IHWU	International Hotel Workers Union
ILGWU	International Ladies Garment Workers Union
INS	Immigration and Naturalization Service
IWA	Industry Wide Agreement
IWW	Industrial Workers of the World
JAFRC	Joint Anti-Fascist Refugee Committee
LJEB	Local Joint Executive Board
NWLB	National War Labor Board

NYHTC	New York Hotel Trades Council
OEIU	Office Employees International Union
RILU	Red International of Labor Unions (Profintern)
RWDSU	Retail, Wholesale, and Department Store Union
SLRB	New York State Labor Relations Board
TUEL	Trade Union Education League
TUUL	Trade Union Unity League
TWU	Transport Workers Union
ULP	Unfair Labor Practice
WSB	Wage Stabilization Board
WTUL	Women's Trade Union League

We Always Had a Union

Introduction

In the late spring of 1953, a letter arrived via airmail from Munich, Germany, to the Times Square office of New York Hotel Trades Council president Jay Rubin. "It's over a half a year now, since we stood on that ship to say good by," the letter began. "You asked me to write and I promised to do so." The writer was Michael J. Obermeier, the former president of Hotel & Club Employees Union Local 6 and for decades a close friend, comrade, and organizing partner of Rubin's before he was arrested at union headquarters and deported as an "undesirable alien" during the Red Scare.

"To tell you the truth I hesitated because I did not want to be carried away with my feelings," Obermeier wrote, though proceeded to be. "I was a very disappointed man," he confessed, because of the way that ex-comrades turned on him in his last days in the union and about "ratting" that came from within the Hotel and Restaurant Employees International Union. Mostly, he complained about the lack of respect he felt and the fact that he would not receive a pension. "I can always take care of myself as you said but it is an irony that I fought far far back for pension and security, I had it on the old *Hotelworker* program in 1917 and now I have such a tight squeeze," he wrote. "Those were 20 years before [Local] 6 and we always had a Union."[1]

Indeed, the hotel workers of New York City *had* had a union—several of them—for decades before Local 6 and the Hotel Trades Council enrolled tens of thousands of members in some of the largest Communist-led affiliates of the American Federation of Labor. They had a union decades before their collective bargaining was protected by law, regulated by the state, and endorsed by leading politicians like New York Mayor Fiorello La Guardia and Governor Thomas E. Dewey. They had their union long before AFL leaders embraced their radical local leadership during the Popular Front era, and they continue to have a union decades after the international union attempted to purge the Communists during the Cold War. For the four decades covered in this book, New York's hotel workers maintained a militant union, experimented with forms of union organization, and evolved from one radical ideology to another—emerging by the 1950s with a durable framework of industry-wide collective bargaining and progressive leadership in the mainstream of the postwar labor movement. It is a history that broadly corresponds to the wider labor movement's evolution during this time period, although it is a rare example of how the Communist Party's power and influence were so clearly and explicitly *negotiated* within an AFL union.

The hotel workers union can trace its roots back to a seemingly spontaneous strike of waiters and cooks in the fancy dining rooms of New York's most prestigious hotels in the spring of 1912. The official union for the hotel industry, the AFL's Hotel and Restaurant Employees International Alliance and Bartenders International League, was a bartenders union at the time, and its leadership was nativist and closed off to newcomers. So an independent union organized and agitated among the immigrant workers in the hotels and sparked the strike. It was briefly a cause célèbre, owing in part to the novelty of servants standing up for themselves and mildly inconveniencing their high-class patrons, but it ended in failure after a few weeks.

The hotel workers regrouped, and the Italians among them appealed to the Industrial Workers of the World to lead a new strike. The 1913 strike, which began with a dinnertime walkout on New Year's Eve, has been described by Melvyn Dubofsky as a "fiasco," an example of the IWW's "emphasis on direct action, sabotage, and violence-suffused rhetoric."[2] The press and polite society watched the strike's conduct with alarm. Acts of sabotage and property destruction were reported almost daily, and the workers lost much of their public support when one IWW strike leader, in a widely watched public address, seemingly threatened to poison the hotels' rich clientele.

The hotel workers regrouped again after that loss. There would be more strikes, in 1918, 1923, 1929, 1934, and beyond. Some of them would target specific employers; some waged across entire sectors of the hospitality industry. And there always would be a union. Among the unions were the International Hotel Workers Union, the International Federation of Workers in the Hotel and Restaurant Industry, the Amalgamated Food Workers, the Food Workers Industrial Union, and the union that remains today, the New York Hotel Trades Council.

From 1912 until 1936, this was a "dual union" competitor to the AFL's Hotel & Restaurant Employees union. After that, its largest affiliate was and still is Local 6 of the union that today goes by the acronym UNITE HERE, but during the period discussed in this book, it shortened its name to HRE.

The standard account of HRE remains Matthew Josephson's *Union House, Union Bar* (Random House, 1956). An officially commissioned history, it offers a broad history of the international union to that point. It remains one of the best books of its kind, although the author treads lightly around the issues of corruption and communism that were in the union's recent past. Josephson's narrative was shaped by Jay Rubin and Michael J. Obermeier's self-published *Growth of a Union: The Life and Times of Edward Flore* (The Historical Union Association, Inc., 1943). It is best treated as a primary source that shows how the union leaders tried to craft their own historical narrative. Morris A. Horowitz's *The New York Hotel Industry: A Labor Relations Study* (Harvard University Press, 1960), a postwar profile of a mature collective bargaining relationship between the union and the Hotel Association, offers some history, and once again shows how this union shaped its own historical narrative.

In *Dishing It Out*, Dorothy Sue Cobble provided a critical reappraisal of the international union, showing how its approach to craft unionism carved out a space for the inclusion and empowerment of women workers—primarily waitresses—in the early 20th century. In doing so, she argued that old HRE offered potential models for the 21st-century labor movement to "appeal to the growing female-dominated service work force."[3] Waitresses were less of a factor in the New York unions' success. Aside from being briefly employed as strikebreakers in 1918, women were shut out of work in hotel banquet halls. These were seen as physical, masculine jobs and the workers who performed them were the backbone of the union. Although the strikes of 1912 and 1913 were led by women—Rose Pastor Stokes and Elizabeth Gurley Flynn, respectively—they were outside agitators. When the union won a neutrality agreement to organize hotel workers in all departments—from the front of the house to the back, from the basement to the elevators—it faced the daunting task of appealing to the women who worked in the housekeeping and laundry departments. Again the union turned to outsiders—Helen Blanchard of the Women's Trade Union League and Gertrude Lane, a young Communist who was one of the more effective organizers for the Trade Union Unity League—to integrate the women into the union. Their story adds to our understanding of the early days of organizing women workers in the service sector.

This story also helps complicate the narrative around the AFL during labor's great upsurge of the 1930s and '40s. Most of the published history of this era rightly focuses on the unions of the Congress of Industrial Organizations, where major breakthroughs were made in the mass production industries and the dominant paradigms in unionism and collective bargaining were established. But, as Priscilla Murolo reminds readers in *From the Folks*

Who Brought You The Weekend, once the AFL—prodded, in no small part by the crusading efforts of HRE—fully embraced the industrial union model, its affiliates quickly eclipsed the organizing gains of the CIO, rising "from 3.4 million in late 1937 to over 4 million in late 1939, surpassing the CIO by more than half a million by the end of 1940."[4] In New York's HRE locals, and others in the Painters and Service Employees unions affiliated with the Hotel Trades Council, we see a radicalism and a militancy most often associated in the popular imagination with the CIO. Similarly, while the public imagination commonly associates the wave of organizing victories and strikes with factory workers, longshoremen, teamsters, and other stereotypically masculine jobs, the organizing demands of service sector workers made HRE the third-largest affiliate of the AFL by the end of this volume, on the eve of the AFL-CIO merger. The Hotel Employees union has always been one of the most important unions in the labor movement.

In *Restoring the Power of Unions*, Julius Getman explored how today's Hotel Employees union developed its effective organizing model, which has enabled the union to grow at a time when many other unions are losing. Coming out of campaigns led by former UNITE HERE President John Wilhelm and Organizing Director Vincent Sirabella, the union builds rank-and-file organizing committees and trains members to shut down anti-union captive audience meetings. Local 6 and the Hotel Trades Council stood aloof from the international union's renaissance, insisting, as HTC President Peter Ward commented in that book that the organizing model, "has been going on here when Vinnie was in diapers." Hired into an entry-level position while Jay Rubin was still President, Ward was only the third leader of the Trades Council. So he knows what he's talking about when he says certain organizing strategies "have been institutional parts of this union since the thirties" and passed down through oral tradition. Wilhelm, who ceded a large amount of autonomy to Local 6, also acknowledged its organizing prowess, chalking it up to a "legend" that the Communists prevailed over the Socialists because they "were tough enough to fight the gangsters," and that's what got New York's hotel industry organized in the 1930s. Interestingly, one of Wilhelm's early predecessors, HRE President Hugo Ernst, who was a Socialist that one might expect would relish an opportunity to purge the Communists from the union, was instead a stalwart defender of Local 6. He bucked AFL leaders who wanted him to clean house and backed Michael J. Obermeier in his efforts to fight for his freedom, harming his own leadership prospects within the AFL in the process. Because of Peter Ward's standoffishness, the New York story is largely missing from Getman's book, and his predecessors' wariness about similar inquiries has detracted from UNITE HERE's contemporary understanding of its own history. The full story, in this book, is both more fascinating and occasionally less fantastic than the legend.[5]

How these unionists who spent decades competing with HRE wound up inside it was explored by Howard Kimeldorf in *Battling for American Labor*, in which he highlighted how this was one of two unions that had their roots in the IWW in the 1910s that ended up affiliating with historically craft-oriented AFL unions in the 1930s, a time when one might expect them to find the CIO a better match. Challenging the thesis of "proletarian conservatism"—which holds that left-wing workers in the 20th century ultimately abandoned their radicalism for the stability of predictable wage increases, grievance procedures, and no-strike/no-lockout agreements—he argued that "the victorious AFL unions came to embrace many of the same practices that defined the rival organizations" that preceded them.[6] It's true that the union maintained an industrial structure and retained a predilection for Wobbly-style direct action of quickie strikes and even sabotage, but the hotel workers' transition from the IWW to the AFL can be more fully explained by their leaders' embrace of the Communist Party, which was more complete than Kimeldorf appreciated. Therefore, part of this story is how syndicalists became Communists and how both ideologies melded within the CP in the 1920s and '30s.

The orthodox historians of American Communism have depicted the Party—largely composed of immigrants in foreign language federations—as isolated from the mainstream labor movement until the Popular Front upsurge of the Great Depression years placed young Communists into positions of influence as hired organizers within the CIO. Of the Party's 1922 turn towards "boring from within" the mainstream unions of the AFL to contest for power and leadership, Theodore Draper wrote, "Communist contact with this organized body of workers was very slight among the rank and file and almost nonexistent among the leadership."[7] Draper's *The Roots of American Communism* and *American Communism and Soviet Russia* remain the essential accounts of the Party's first decade.[8] With the opening of the Comintern and CPUSA files in Moscow, as well as the Federal Bureau of Investigation files, and the unions' own archives, we are afforded richer detail on the push-and-pull development of American Communist strategy.

This book joins Edward P. Johanningsmeier's *Forging American Communism: The Life of William Z. Foster*, James R. Barrett's *William Z. Foster and the Tragedy of American Radicalism,* and Bryan D. Palmer's *James P. Cannon and the Origins of the American Revolutionary Left 1890–1928* as using the Moscow files—and their own words—to center American union activists in their own story and show a more complicated process of negotiation over the so-called "orders from Moscow."[9]

Because the hotels' culinary workforce was largely immigrants, many of these workers were early converts to Communism; some joining well before the Workers (Communist) Party was founded in 1921. During the sectarian fights, which were quippingly dismissed in the movie *Reds* as "the fine distinction of which half of the left of the left is recognized by Moscow as the real Communist Party in America," they joined John Reed's Communist Labor Party.[10] The changing CP line had a real impact on this union that had over 15,000 members at its 1920s height and could call more out on strike. When the Party directed the policy of "boring from within" the AFL, they were an independent union—the Amalgamated Food Workers—and were building a national federation of independent "amalgamated" unions—the United Labor Council of America—that promised to be a viable successor to the IWW. They resisted the command to shut their union down and join the HRE, and won for themselves an exception to Party policy, while agreeing to shut the Labor Council down. *American Communism and Soviet Russia* is the only book to record the United Labor Council (also called the Labor Unity League). Because it is not a labor history, per se, Draper does not treat it as the significant "road not taken" that it was. This book sees this negotiation of the Party line on independent unionism as a key transition from syndicalism to Communism.

When Leon Trotsky was secretly censured in Moscow by the Politburo in 1924, in order to keep it quiet, Trotsky's "most intimate American friend" was expelled from the Party for invented misdeeds.[11] Ludwig Lore, in addition to being editor of a German language newspaper for workers and a Party founder, was an activist in the AFW. "Loreism," the Party's Aesopian epithet and the first effort to "exploit the possibilities of amalgamating the factional struggle in the Russian party with the factional struggle in the American party," has been depicted by Draper and others as having little meaning outside of a small handful of Party insiders.[12] But, as a bewildering attack on a loyal union member, it roiled the AFW. It drove one breakaway faction into HRE, with new chartered locals of their own, and fateful and fatal consequences when their tiny membership (but strategic position within the cutthroat world of the post-Prohibition restaurant industry) left them vulnerable to underworld predation.

When Stalin's "Third Period" called for Party members to abandon work within the established unions and form new pure "red" unions in the TUUL, again the Party line caused a split in the AFW; this time with Michael J. Obermeier leading Communist cadres and the workers who followed them into the Food Workers Industrial Union. For half a decade, AFW, FWIU, and the corrupted HRE locals vied for dues-paying members and leadership of the workers—culminating in an industry-wide strike in 1934 that hotel owners could not get settled and which forced them to first consider a neutrality agreement to win labor peace. James P. Cannon's memoir, *History of American Trotskyism*, portrayed the 1934 strike as an almost exclusively Trotskyist project.[13] It *was* theirs to lose, and history is written by the winners. Missing from Josephson's and Kimeldorf's narratives, the Trotskyists are restored—within reason—in this story.

The 1934 strike was technically a failure, but the workers emerged from it with clear leadership in Jay Rubin and new momentum for union recognition. That development, and the Party's Popular Front strategy, impelled Rubin to negotiate mergers, first between the AFW and FWIU and then HRE. Of the Party's controversial 1929–1935 experiment in forming competing radical unions in the TUUL, Harvey Klehr claims in *The Heyday of American Communism: The Depression Decade* that in their dissolution only some of the unions managed "to negotiate entry into the federation as a unit, their leaders obtaining union positions or some limited autonomy in exchange for bringing several thousand dues-payers with them," while the dozens of capable organizers that the Party had trained "would be fully utilized only when John L. Lewis had to find people able to build new industrial unions." He speculates that the CP "deliberately held back" Obermeier and Rubin from bolting to the CIO in 1937.[14] But here we see that long decades of activist leadership, punctuated by periods of messy competition, combined with public pressure and employer preference for orderly collective bargaining made the hard-won unity within the AFL an inviolable principle by 1937.

With Rubin and Obermeier at the helm, HRE's Local 6 organized tens of thousands of hotel and restaurant workers into the union. But they did it in astonishing and confounding ways. Forming the New York Hotel Trades Council as a coalition of AFL craft unions, they made good and regular use of New York State's labor-management mediators and conciliatory bureaucracy. They incorporated a form of tripartite dispute settlement into a collective bargaining agreement that endures to this day. They formed a labor-management partnership with the Hotel Association that replaced predatory employment agencies with an industry employment office, acknowledging seniority and providing job protections. As they negotiated successor agreements, wages continued to rise, pensions were won, and healthcare benefits took the form of a miniature system of socialized medicine with group practice healthcare clinics run by the union and the Association.

The union continued to employ strikes and boycotts in the 1940s and beyond, but they were targeted against outlier employers who either resisted the terms of industry-wide peace or advocated hard-bargaining to restrain workers' demands within that system. In its militant defense of structured and predictable industry-wide collective bargaining and its loyalty to politicians who enabled and protected its contract gains, New York's hotel workers made a similar transition from radicalism to postwar left-liberalism that many unions made—albeit, on their own terms.

This union retained Communist leadership into the 1950s. Many labor histories deal with the 1948 purge of the CP-led affiliates of the CIO and narratively leave the Communists for dead. But Hugo Ernst refused to purge HRE's Communists as a matter of principle, and anyway, the Hotel Trades Council was not chartered by any of its constituent unions. It could not be placed under trusteeship; it answered to its members and constituent affiliates alone. And because hotels fell under state labor law instead of the Taft-Hartley Act, anti-Communists were deprived of an easy path to decertifying it.

Maurice Isserman's *Which Side Were You On?* is the definitive account of the CP's war fateful period, and the story of New York's hotel workers largely conforms with his narrative.[15] David A. Shannon's orthodox account, *The Decline of American Communism*, gets the timeline right but seems motivated by a spirit of name and blame.[16] Joseph Starobin's *American Communism in Crisis* offers a much more nuanced, sympathetic, and well-informed account of the Party's tailspin.[17] The story of the final crack between NYHTC leaders and the CP, told in this book's last chapters, offers an intimate narrative that complements Starobin's.

Unions like District 65, Local 1199, and the Farm Equipment Workers survived a stint in the wilderness, fought off enough decertifications, and eventually negotiated their way back into the CIO through mergers, but only after their leaders made a clean break with the CP. The historians of these unions make clear that such breaks happened, but only Toni Gilpin in *The Long Deep Grudge* even glancingly delves into the facts of that split.[18] In Local 6, we have a detailed story of comrades trying to maintain unity in leadership under pressure of controversial CP policies demanding support for pro-Soviet causes. The pressure created a "crack" in unity that became a split when the Party tried to oust Jay Rubin from union leadership.

This is also a criminal justice story, or, rather, several stories of injustice. In 1935, Thomas E. Dewey, a politically ambitious prosecutor, put the notorious Dutch Schultz gang on trial for the cafeteria racket that had ensnared the HRE locals. As Mary M. Stolberg has detailed in *Fighting Organized Crime*, his goals were to generate headlines and to roll a series of racketeering convictions into a case that would allow him to put the Democrats' Tammany Hall machine out of business.[19] In his expediency, Dewey allowed the violent gangsters who ran the racket to escape justice while some of the unionists that he blamed appeared more like victims of a criminal conspiracy than perpetrators of one.

Many labor radicals were similarly railroaded towards jail and deportation during the Second Red Scare. Jennifer Luff's *Commonsense Anticommunism* provides a good explanation of the whys and hows of the AFL's anti-Communist activities and the creation of the House Un-American Activities Committee.[20] In *Threat of Dissent*, Julia Rose Kraut offers a comprehensive history of how U.S. immigration laws were repeatedly amended to provide for the denaturalization of citizens and deportation of immigrants who advocate the "overthrow by force or violence of the Government of the United States," with ten years of retroactivity and diligent efforts to prove that participation in Communist and front organizations met that definition.[21] In this narrative, we will see how the House Un-American Activities Committee, the Federal Bureau of Investigation, and a slew of ex-comrade informants nursing grudges over the twists and turns in the Party line—including Ludwig Lore—built the case against Michael J. Obermeier over the course of a decade. Obviously, Obermeier lost his case. That is why he was writing from Germany in 1953. He would die in exile seven years later, the same week that the union was hosting one of its periodic dinner dances to raise funds to support him. Despite changes in Local 6's leadership, the radicals who had long organized the union continued to lead it with the same principles and tactics.

Readers of this book are probably familiar with unions that in their organizational form and strategy, approach to the law, bargaining priorities, and boilerplate contract language have not changed substantially in over a half-century. And all the while, the labor movement has struggled to adapt to a 21st-century economy. What is fascinating about New York's hotel workers unions in the four decades this book covers is that they constantly changed. They adapted to their times, experimented with different strategies, and made substantial changes in how they organized, how they governed their unions, and how they related to and affiliated with other unions and federations. They tried negotiating closed shop recognition and then spent years stubbornly refusing to sign any kind of contract at all. They engaged in sabotage and wanton acts of picket line violence, then embraced mediation and tripartite arbitration. Yet to this day, they still have a penchant for quickie job actions and puckish acts of subversion. For a while, they competed with each other for shop floor leadership of the workers, leading to a dynamic that made labor peace impossible for the bosses. Then, they unified the workers under one multi-union coalition that guaranteed employers long periods of labor peace.

Today, as unions continue to struggle with organizational change and search for strategic breakthroughs, the history of New York's hotel unions contains some valuable lessons. Similarly, as a new generation of radicals engage in the labor movement as an organized bloc, the Communist Party in the latter three decades covered in this narrative remains the widest-scale example of such a project that the United States has previously seen. We have the benefit of the Party archives in Moscow, the Federal Bureau of Investigations' surveillance of Party activities, the unions' own voluminous records, and decades of journals and newspapers to reconstruct these workers' experiences as union members and activists within the Communist Party as well as dissidents and critics outside of it. Communists' role within the labor movement has been mythologized, romanticized, and vilified. What's far more interesting is taking them on their own terms, and their own words. The story of New York's hotel workers unions shows an activist group navigating a changing political and legal context and adapting their strategy, accepting or rejecting the advice and assistance of potential allies and enemies, and always persevering to fight another day. As such, it retains lessons for trade unionists of any generation.

1

The Unsafest Proposition in the World
1912–1913

At a quarter past seven on the evening of May 8, 1912, just after the oyster course had been served at New York's Belmont Hotel, a union organizer pulled a whistle from under his shirt and blew the alarm that announced the start of a job action. "Pardon me," one waiter said, "but I beg to inform you that there is a waiters' union now, and by that whistle which you have just heard we have been ordered to strike."[1]

Though short-lived, this strike led to an ongoing organizing campaign in the city's hotels and fancy restaurants. That campaign and the strike that followed on New Year's Eve were guided and inspired by the Industrial Workers of the World. Some of the Wobblies' most legendary organizers would take part in the campaign. The conflict aroused a tremendous amount of press attention and middle-class sympathy. Partly, this was because of the novelty of watching the rich and powerful be personally inconvenienced on a grand scale. And partly because the workforce seemed the least likely to sign up for class warfare; servility was supposed to be an essential part of their craft.

The 1913 strike is most often recorded as a blip during a period that saw some of the IWW's most storied strikes and organizing campaigns. To the extent that the strike is remembered today, it is usually an object lesson in how the IWW of this period was more interested in spontaneous action and careless talk about sabotage than being a practical trade union.

Although the Wobblies left no lasting organization of their own, IWW principles and strategy would remain a profound influence on the workers in New York's hotel industry for decades to come.

Luxury Everywhere

There have been inns and public houses since before there was a republic, but these were small establishments—usually a room or two in the proprietor's home. The expansion of railroad travel, following the Civil War, gave rise to a new class of hotel that could house and feed over 200 guests—requiring the employment of a small industrial workforce. The growth of a new class of super-rich customers created the market for evermore luxurious palatial hotels, and a workforce trained in European culinary traditions and obsequious deference to the nouveau bourgeoisie.

New York's hotel industry changed forever when the 13-story, 450-room Waldorf Hotel opened in 1893. Located at Fifth Avenue and 33rd Street in what was then a residential neighborhood of millionaires' townhouses, it had been the private estate of the hotel's owner, William Waldorf Astor. Hotel operator George C. Boldt's strategy was to "cater to the First Families of New York, draw them from their mansions to dine in comparative luxury in a place that would lend luster to the occasion." He hired the head of catering at the legendary Delmonico's restaurant, Oscar Tschirky, to be the Waldorf's maître d'hôtel. "Make the Waldorf so convenient and comfortable," he commanded, "they will never go to another place." Tschirky exclusively hired waiters who could at least speak French, German, *and* English for a cosmopolitan flair and enforced Boldt's dictum "that every order is obeyed with military discipline."[2] It was a fast success, with its ballrooms, banquet halls, and grills packed with guests each night, and the hallway connecting them a "Peacock Alley" where Gilded Age ladies strutted in their evening wear finery. Tired of his family mansion's loss of privacy due to his new next-door neighbor, John Jacob Astor decided in 1897 to build a 17-story hotel to rival his cousin's. Boldt prevailed on Astor to allow him to manage the Astoria and to permit the two buildings to be adjoined. The new Waldorf-Astoria had the distinction of becoming the first hotel to take up an entire city block. This added 550 guest rooms to the hotel plus a new bar, a 1,500-capacity ballroom, new cafes, restaurants, room service, Turkish baths, laundry rooms, a legendary wine cellar, and more entertainment space on the roof. The hotel had more than 1,000 full-time employees and seasonally required hundreds of additional banquet waiters.

Others soon followed. John Jacob Astor spent $5.5 million to build "the finest hotel in the world." Opened in 1904, the 18-story 650-room St. Regis advertised "luxury everywhere," including a large restaurant, tearoom, palm garden, and grand ballroom. Astor hired management away from London's Ritz hotel, and got a special law passed in Albany allowing the restaurants to serve alcohol within 200 feet of a church.[3] Astor also invested in the Hotel Knickerbocker, a 550-room, 15-story Beaux Arts building in Times Square that opened in 1906. Its main restaurant could accommodate 2,000 guests and was augmented by a bar and grill, a separate elevator system for room service, and two kitchens "so that nothing can go wrong from the duplicate service."[4] It opened for business in 1906. That same year, the Hotel Belmont went up at 42nd Street and Park Avenue, boasting that its 27 stories made it the world's tallest hotel. Another five sub-basements were carved into the city's bedrock to make room for laundry and other hotel workers to toil out of sight from the guests. Built by the same architect as the Grand Central Terminal railroad station across the street, it had a direct underground connection to the city's new subway system, 700 guest rooms, multiple dining rooms, and room service.[5] In 1905, William Waldorf Astor began constructing a hotel specially designed for conventions and balls. The Hotel Astor filled the entire block of Broadway and 44th. Under its mansard roof were multiple banquet halls throughout the lobby, mezzanine, and ninth floor, which hosted an assortment of private dining rooms.[6]

That same year, the George A. Fuller Construction Company bought a hotel called the Plaza on the corner of Central Park West and tore it down. The company hired the architect of the Waldorf-Astoria—and much of its middle-management staff—to build its new 21-story luxury hotel. Opened in 1907, *this* Plaza boasted 800 guest rooms, an oak-walled cafe, the Oak Room restaurant, a tearoom called the Palm Court, and a seemingly endless number of banquet and private event spaces. It required a full-time staff of 1,500 plus a commensurate number of extra seasonal workers.[7]

The Martinique, a French Renaissance-style building located in Herald Square, originally opened at the turn of the century. Taking advantage of its proximity to the new Pennsylvania Railroad station, the owners expanded the building by the length of Broadway between 32nd and 33rd streets, and it reopened in 1910. The New Martinique contained 600 guest rooms within its 17 stories. The large oak-walled dining room on the ground floor was adorned with portraits of French aristocrats. Two more dining rooms—one oak and the other a stone-walled tearoom—adjoined on the second floor. A spacious grill room filled the basement.[8] Rector's, soon to be renamed the Claridge, opened in 1911. Located across from the Astor, it offered 500 guest rooms, a restaurant, a cocktail bar, and full banquet services.[9] The Holland House, which preceded the Waldorf by one year, underwent extensive renovations in 1911 to keep up with the new class of hotels and in 1912 became a part of an East Coast chain of luxury hotels. A "New Hotel of the Highest Standing" located at Fifth Avenue and 30th Street, the new hotel had ten stories, 350 guest rooms, a 300-person capacity restaurant, and a cafe.[10] Emphasizing safety and durability over ostentatious opulence, the 20-story, 600-room Vanderbilt made its debut two weeks after New Year's Day 1912. Owned by a scion of the railroad empire that lent it its name, the hotel, located on Madison Avenue, touted a large marble-walled dining room, a buffet "Chinese Room," and an underground bar—also adorned with marble—called "the crypt."[11] The hotel building boom would reach a temporary climax that same year with the latest "tallest hotel" under construction at Herald Square. The

McAlpin would rise 25 stories with a capacity of 2,500 guests plus a convention hall, club room, and multiple restaurants. It would require a full-time staff of 1,500.[12]

Union organizers estimated that the hotel industry employed 30,000 waiters alone. The total industry workforce likely exceeded 100,000.[13]

Allied Crafts

The first recorded strike of New York hotel waiters took place a few years after the Civil War in June 1869. Three hundred and fifty workers at five midtown hotels, among them the Astor House and Fifth Avenue Hotel, went on strike for a $5-per-month wage increase and a reduction of hours. They called their union the Hotel Waiters Protective Association. This coincided with the rise of the National Labor Union, the first serious attempt at a federation that would tie together all the unions and labor parties around the country. Affiliated with the First International, and in correspondence with Karl Marx, it was spearheading the first Eight Hours movement, which would have appealed to the striking workers, who had been working 12-hour split shifts, which the *New York Times* haughtily noted was "less laborious than is often imagined." The strikers were reportedly "mostly Irish," and the hotels specifically advertised for "French, Irish and German" scabs.[14] The uprising was quickly defeated and the strikers were blacklisted. The NLU folded up shop a few years later.

By the turn of the 20th century, partly because of the service standards set by the Waldorf-Astoria, nearly three-quarters of New York's hotel and restaurant employees were immigrants. As successive waves of immigrants helped their fellow countrymen find employment, the workforce became "a honeycomb of ethnically based occupational enclaves."[15] Germans, Italians, and Frenchmen could be found in hotel kitchens, with the Italians specializing as bakers and the French handling desserts. In hotel dining rooms, Italians tended to bus tables while French waiters classed up the first-class banquet halls and restaurants. Jews predominated in kosher bakeries, delicatessens, and neighborhood restaurants that catered to the working class. The Irish were popular as bartenders. Black workers were rarely seen in the front of the house unless a hotel or restaurant served Black customers.

Out of this ethnic mix arose New York's first durable labor union of hotel and restaurant employees in 1886, a German Waiters Union affiliated with the Knights of Labor. Organizing under the banner, "An injury to one is the concern of all," the Knights were broadly inclusive of most workers—regardless of craft—except for corporate lawyers, bankers, professional gamblers, and liquor dealers.[16] That last prohibition was largely due to Knights leader Terence Powderly's teetotalism, and it made a union of restaurant workers a difficult fit for them.[17] In 1886, a new rival issued the demand for an eight-hour working day and led a series of general strikes for the cause. Powderly forbade the Knights to support or join the strikes, and workers' loyalties quickly shifted. This American Federation of Labor was an umbrella organization of craft unions with a strategy of defining, training, and vouching for the job skills of dues-paying members and striking employers who would not exclusively employ union members at the wage rates they demanded. It worked well for the most in-demand and highest-skilled workers in the economy—largely building trades workers and machinists. The AFL became the most durable labor federation in U.S. history, partly because its membership was made up of the most well-positioned workers in the economy who could not be easily locked out and replaced during periodic economic depressions. It did not work as well for workers who lacked irreplaceable skills.

Hotel workers attended the founding convention of the AFL even though they lacked a national union of their own. The AFL began directly chartering new union locals of waiters, cooks, and bartenders beginning with the Knights' former German Waiters Union which became the New York Waiters Union in 1887. Other charters included local bartenders unions throughout the city and a smattering of locals around the Midwest and as far west as Denver. Delegates, mostly from the east coast locals, convened in New York in 1891 to form the Waiters and Bartenders National Union. The AFL granted them jurisdiction over all waiters, bartenders, cooks, and workers in the "catering craft." In 1898, it changed its name to the Hotel and Restaurant Employees International Alliance and Bartenders International League, the grandiosity of which was aspirational.[18]

The New York Waiters Union became HRE Local 1. HRE's headquarters wound up in Cincinnati because that was where the union's General Secretary, Jere Sullivan, could secure rent-free office space in the local union. HRE claimed a wide jurisdiction of "allied crafts," but kept workers divided in locales by job types. Typical of the leaders of fledgling craft unions that lacked functional job control, Sullivan was a tin-pot dictator, happier running a chummy clubhouse than a fighting union. An inveterate racist, he denigrated New York's polyglot hotel workforce "as craven a bunch of scalawags as were ever induced or driven from their native slums" and essentially unorganizable.[19] He was intimidated by the grand scale of first-class hotels and the emergence of corporate chains. With their restaurants, banquet halls, bars, and lavish guest rooms serviced by waiters, waitresses, bussers, cooks, and bartenders plus the cleaning staff for the front and back of the house and all of the maintenance crafts like electricians and operating engineers, hotels were factories. What they produced was leisure for their clientele and varying degrees of misery for the "servants" in their employ, and HRE's lack of an organizing strategy mirrored other AFL craft unions' inability to grapple with the strategic considerations of mass production industries like steel and meatpacking. Nor did Sullivan have the ability. He did not like to travel far from his midwestern home or engage with workers who did not look or talk like him.

Bartenders, typically white English-speaking workers of Western European extraction, were in his wheelhouse. HRE was aided by craft solidarity. Local labor councils in cities around the country urged barmen to form and join HRE bartenders locals so they could get drunk in union shops. The largely ceremonial post of HRE president was customarily filled with men who were bartenders by trade, and Sullivan and his presidents busied themselves chartering the bulk of HRE's bartenders locals in the years between 1900 and 1904. By then, membership had expanded five-fold to 50,430—almost all of the growth coming from bartenders. Saloons lent themselves to top-down organizing. Many proprietors were convinced by HRE organizers that hanging a "Union Bar" sign in his establishment would encourage the steady flow of customers—good union men looking for good union beer. A dues-paying union bartender would have more control over his schedule and tips, while union officer positions provided ambitious bartenders with a pathway to political office. Precise union density figures are hard to reconstruct, but HRE successfully unionized the clear majority of the nation's bartenders.[20]

HRE largely ignored hotel workers in the "allied crafts" in this period of successful bartender organizing. Local 1 pleaded for assistance in 1901, claiming "opportunities to enlist some 30,000 waiters" into the union, but Sullivan turned them down.[21] The few union shops that existed for waiters were organized in a similar manner as the bartenders' locals. A "Union House" was a restaurant that signed an agreement with HRE to exclusively hire kitchen and dining room staff from the union hall at union wage rates and work rules. Where small restaurants and cafeterias in working-class neighborhoods hung a "Union House" sign, they were assured a steady clientele of hungry union members. This strategy was impossible in hotels and restaurants catering to the wealthy. Although HRE locals did go on strike to win union recognition and improve conditions, the craft exclusivity meant that only one classification of workers was walking out rather than entirely shutting down service. Cooks in New York had their own local union, the relatively tiny Local 719. Waitstaff were parceled out by jurisdiction among a handful of local unions that faded in and out of existence, including Waitresses Local 679 and Hotel Waiters Local 5. Waiters Local 1 was the most effective but only by being consciously smaller and more exclusive. They brought as many working-class eateries as possible under contract, won the highest wages possible, and then restricted their membership rolls to the greatest extent possible to guarantee their members steady work. Local 1 charged an astronomical $65 initiation fee, effectively keeping out new members and turning the local into a job trust.

Meanwhile, hotel workers needed a union. Like most workers of their time, they complained about long hours and low wages. They had more reason to complain about an onerous system of fines imposed by management to enforce an exacting standard of discipline. At the Belmont, waiters who made $25 a month could be fined two dollars for drinking leftover coffee, and any worker in the room who did not report him for it could lose a dollar. For smaller infractions like dropping a piece of silverware or talking too much to customers, a worker's paycheck could be docked twenty-five cents. The relatively new practice of tipping also served to enforce discipline. Soon it was used by management as an excuse to whittle real wages, and it left workers serving, as the common complaint went, "two bosses."[22] Exploitation began before workers even got hired, thanks to the "vampire system" of employment agencies that supplied extra or on-call waiters. By one worker's account from 1890, a day's wage of two dollars could cost a worker $1.50 in agency fees, and be whittled down further if the hotel headwaiter also demanded a kickback.[23]

Frustrations boiled over at the Waldorf-Astoria in 1899. A few weeks after George C. Boldt and Oscar Tschirky forced staff to shave their beards and mustaches, they posted a new weekly wage rate of $25 for waiters and $20 for bussers. It was less of a raise than the men expected for their service and sacrifice. They appointed a committee to address their complaints—particularly about the Waldorf's own system of fines which ate into their take-home pay—with Tschirky. "Very well then," he declared, "take off your aprons." Forty men did so, walked out, and were quickly replaced.[24] The Waldorf's swift retaliation had a chilling effect. Five years later, kitchen workers began agitating over similar issues. Cooks Local 719 managed to recruit 2,600 members through the efforts of its president Cesar Lesino. Most of them bolted within a year, frustrated by HRE's nativism and incessant focus on bartenders' issues, but continued to organize independently.[25] The stirrings of a new independent union prompted HRE's General Executive Board to fund an organizing grant for Hotel Waiters Local 5 in 1911. Joseph Elster, the business agent they hired, soon grew frustrated with the other New York locals' jurisdictional battles over dues and initiation fees.[26]

Untrained Troops

Elster and Lesino were not the only organizers frustrated by the elitism of the AFL's craft divisions, and their barriers to solidarity left many workers yearning for something closer to the spirit of the Knights of Labor's old slogan "an injury to one is the concern of all." Radicals of various stripes formed the Industrial Workers of the World in 1905. Aiming to organize workers into "one big union," regardless of craft, color, or skill, it also called for the "abolition of the wage system" and flatly declared, "The working class and the employing class have nothing in common."[27]

The Wobblies began agitating among New York's hotel workers almost immediately, sparking spontaneous strikes in some shops in 1905 and 1908 but leaving little trace of union activity in their wake.[28] The first serious organizing effort among New York's hotel workers was not led by the IWW but by HRE dissidents. German brothers Joseph and Paul Vehling began leafleting against the practice of tipping and the low wages, exploitative hiring, and unfair firings endemic in the hotel industry. Joseph Elster quit HRE Local 5 and led his last few dozen members into the Vehlings' movement. On October 29, 1911, Elster and the Vehlings staged a rally that ended in the formation of an independent union they called the International Hotel Workers Union. Joseph Vehling assumed the role of acting president. He named his brother Paul secretary; the meeting's chairman, Edward Blochinger, financial secretary; and Elster, whose "forceful, eloquent speech" had rallied the audience, business representative. The union's goal was to be broadly inclusive of "employees of all departments and of both sexes," not just the hotel and restaurant industry, but also railroad and steamship food service. The union made special appeals to clerical and housekeeping staff, although its first adherents were mostly waiters. It harbored ambitions to organize as far afield as New Orleans, Montreal, and San Francisco but struggled to raise enough resources to publish a second issue of its newspaper *International Hotel Work*.[29]

IHWU counted a few dozen members by May 1, 1912, when fifty members of the fledgling dual union marched in the annual International Workers' Day parade. Four days later, the tyrannical maître d'hôtel of the Belmont Hotel, Victor J. Pearl, began firing waiters who participated in the May Day parade—including Elster and Blochinger.[30] Angry co-workers contemplated a strike action. IHWU founder Joseph Vehling preferred legislation and litigation as union methods, and, as a result, he was pushed aside. The union voted on May 7 to strike during that evening's dinner rush. In addition to their demand to reinstate the fired workers, strikers demanded an end to disciplinary fines and an increase in the daily pay rate to $3.[31] One hundred waiters—four out of five on duty—walked out and set up an ersatz picket line to discourage other workers from taking their places. A hotel manager spotted Elster on the picket line and told a cop to confiscate his sign and arrest him. A night court magistrate discharged Elster with a slight reprimand.[32]

The pickets continued the next day. A few cooks joined the strike and management's attempts to procure replacement workers from the Knickerbocker and Waldorf-Astoria hotels largely failed when the workers encountered the union's picket line. By May 10, the Socialist Party was involved. The *New York Call* helped turn out 1,500 hotel workers to Bryant Hall, a shabby two-story building that abutted Bryant Park on 42nd Street. Under signs that read "Hotel Uniforms Are Spreading More Diseases Than House Flies" and "Cooks Are Dropping Dead From Overwork and Heat," Elster declared, "Speakers here have no right but to be anything but Socialists." The assembled workers voted to expand the strike beyond the Belmont and, after the meeting ended, more than 2,000 workers marched to the Belmont to circle the hotel with the largest picket line yet.[33]

The next night, the strike spread to the Astor and the Waldorf-Astoria, while Belmont management arranged to serve buffet dinners until the labor strife petered out. Elster organized a ridiculously militaristic strike during the oyster course. Responding to "Order No. 3," 600 workers serving 5,000 patrons across the dining rooms of the two hotels quit their posts, chanting the word "Oysters!" on their way out the door. After a few tense moments, management agreed to pay the workers $3 for the night if they finished serving the meal, and IHWU leaders directed the men to return to their duties. Elster was astonished that his plan succeeded. Trembling with emotion, the wannabe general told the press, "Some of our men were untrained troops, but, one and all, they showed the true courage which makes the real soldier."[34] In the days to come, the press would refer to diminutive Elster as the "'Little Napoleon' of the waiters' army."[35]

The following Monday, IHWU claimed to have expanded its membership to 7,000 waiters and cooks.[36] An evening meeting at the union's headquarters was an electric scene of workers across the industry sharing grievances, drawing up lists of demands, and plotting next steps. Workers at the Plaza, where Pearl had served as headwaiter before he moved to the Belmont, shared stories about his management philosophy "that a waiter should be a soldier and live up to the strictest rules" and how he bragged that "he does not even consider them as human beings." Waiters from the Knickerbocker and Waldorf-Astoria complained about how waiters were expected to pay bussers and other support workers out of their own wages and tips. Workers planned a general strike to demand "shorter hours, higher wages, a day off each week with pay, better sanitary working conditions, pay for overtime, better food, the elimination of fines and payment on a weekly basis."[37] Because it was banquet season and "many important dinners" were imperiled, the industry's Hotel Men's Association negotiated speedy settlements on behalf of the Gotham, Manhattan, and Waldorf-Astoria hotels. The day rate for an itinerant banquet waiter was temporarily increased to $3.[38] These first wins inspired still more strike action, as did management retaliation. Waiters at the Belmont staged another dinnertime walkout when Victor Pearl refused to

Strikers gather outside Bryant Hall. (New York Hotel & Gaming Trades Council, AFL-CIO.)

re-employ workers who led the first walkout on May 13.[39] The union threatened a citywide strike that it claimed would see 30,000 hotel workers walk out unless the Belmont fired Pearl and the industry abolished "Pearlism," their term for the disciplinary system based upon fines, by the end of the week.[40]

An uneasy truce followed as the union assessed the depth and breadth of its support and Financial Secretary Edward Blochinger struggled to process membership applications that flowed in. Chambermaids, bellhops, and even electricians were joining and attending IHWU meetings. An independent Chambermaids Union, which claimed 400 members, promised to join a citywide strike of hotel workers. But IHWU leaders hesitated to spread the strike, and still felt some loyalty to their craft and their chain of command in the hotels. Blochinger chaired a team that negotiated with Oscar of the Waldorf. They accepted Tschirky's flimsy excuse for why the Waldorf-Astoria provided strikebreakers to the Belmont and accepted a compromise of $2.50 when he walked back the previous week's deal for a $3 day. The IHWU decided to press its demands with the Hotel Men's Association, hoping that industry-wide standards that did not affect any one house's competitive edge might be more acceptable. Association representatives dismissed the union threat for its lack of support. The management group encouraged the Geneva Society, a professional association that enrolled many headwaiters and master chefs, to begin recruiting rank-and-file kitchen and dining room workers to set up a company union.[41]

On May 15, a man "in a shabby black suit" walked into the dining room of the Vanderbilt hotel at 7:15 and blew the familiar whistle causing 50 workers to walk out during dinner. The spreading labor unrest was still a novelty for the wealthy customers. "I know! I know!" exclaimed one socialite. "I was at the Belmont when they did it there. It is the strike." Management called the strike unwarranted and unprovoked.[42] Blochinger blamed management's abrupt termination of 15 busboys earlier in the day for the "nice and orderly" walkout. Joseph Elster was neither the day's spokesperson nor the evening's whistleblower because he had been arrested on the Belmont's picket line earlier that afternoon for arguing with a cop. Freed from night court after paying a two-dollar fine, Elster was cheered when he rejoined jubilant strikers at a bar around the corner from the Vanderbilt.[43] The workers were celebrating the news that Vanderbilt management had accepted most of their demands, including reinstatement and no blacklist for the strikers plus locker rooms, better food, the end of uniform laundry fees, and the prompt payment of weekly wages. In addition to the pending negotiations with the Hotel Association, Blochinger appealed to the State Labor Bureau for an independent investigation of working conditions in the hotels.[44] Offers of mediation poured in, including one from the millionaire socialist Rose Pastor Stokes, who was scheduled to address a union rally at the Amsterdam Opera House, a multipurpose entertainment venue in Hell's Kitchen, on Sunday the 19th.[45]

Just a Sign of What We Can Do

Rose Pastor Stokes fled anti-Jewish pogroms in the Russian Pale of Settlement to wind up a child laborer in a non-union cigar factory before her sideline gig as a women's advice columnist led to a full-time job in journalism. An heir to a vast mining and real estate fortune, J. Graham Phelps Stokes fell in love with the smart, attractive young woman as much as the symbolism of the union of upper-crust and working-class WASP and Jew. She shrewdly manipulated media interest in their marriage to keep her views regularly in the news. The couple's progressivism brought them to the Socialist Party. He was on its National Executive Committee, but she proved to be a more popular and compelling speaker. She became involved in the IWW and other labor struggles, particularly those involving women workers.[46] It was the independent Chambermaids Union that attracted her attention to the threat of a citywide hotel strike.[47]

At the Sunday rally Stokes read from the Belmont hotel's "book of fines" before a crowd of 2,000 IHWU members and sympathizers, decrying management's claim that they usually donate the fines to charity. "We ask them to do a grain of justice before they speak of charity," she shouted from the stage, "and the person who accepts a cent of money whipped out of underpaid and underfed waiters deserves to be shot." In a sign of the radicalism that would mark hotel workers unionism for decades, the "house went wild" when Mrs. Stokes mentioned socialism. She instructed workers to read *The New York Call* rather than the capitalist press to get news about their strike. Defending beat reporters, "fellow laborers in the field, underpaid as well," she presciently warned that "under the present capitalistic system they are working for papers that are friendly to you when they can afford to be."[48]

Surveillance convinced the Hotel Association that the IHWU had a limited following of no more than ten percent of the workforce. On May 22, they announced they would not meet with IHWU representatives after all, instead recognizing the Geneva Society as the legitimate voice of hotel waiters and cooks.[49] On Thursday night, over 3,000 members crowded Bryant Hall and voted to authorize a citywide strike if the hotel bosses didn't agree to arbitrate the union's demands, spreading the strike to the Belmont's kitchen staff that evening. Elster bragged it was "just a sign of what we can do."[50] The Association claimed to have 3,000 scabs lined up in preparation for a citywide hotel strike while the union claimed support pledged from "well organized" hotel workers as far afield as Chicago to deny the hotel owners the ability to import scabs. Each side accused the other of bluffing.[51] On Monday night, the union struck the Knickerbocker during dinner to send a message to Hotel Association chief James Regan, the hotel's proprietor.[52] When the Association met on Tuesday, Regan resigned his post "in a huff" when his peers rejected his proposal that each hotel deal with the IHWU's demands separately.[53] The Association promised the Geneva Society new wage minimums with a 20% wage increase, an end to the fine system, a half day off every week, and a full day off every other week. Geneva Society representatives declined to sign the agreement, knowing they did not command any serious loyalty among the strikers. The new terms were put into effect immediately at the Astor, Plaza, Vanderbilt, and Waldorf-Astoria.[54]

When Tuesday came and went without any *union* negotiations, the IHWU launched the long-threatened citywide strike of hotel and restaurant workers at dinnertime. The first night lacked military precision, but cops treated union pickets like an invading army just the same. Workers at the Holland House walked out, while those at the Belmont and Knickerbocker never walked in. The strikers paraded through the midtown hotel district to convince their comrades at other properties to join them. At the Algonquin and Manhattan hotels, they were repelled by waiting police firing warning shots into the air. At least nine strikers were arrested at police-instigated clashes, some on felony charges of "inciting a riot."

The next night, the strike spread to the Waldorf and Rector hotels. Before they struck, Oscar Tschirsky assembled his staff for a genteel captive audience before the evening dinner rush. He announced new wage increases and had the workers' pay envelopes ready. Tschirsky asked workers who intended to strike to do so at once, before the hotel's guests began arriving for dinner, and assured the workers that there would be no blacklisting or reprisals against any employee who joined the action. With that, 355 dining room employees—four-fifths of the workforce—walked out, and management calmly walked in 126 scabs that they had been hiding on the Waldorf's roof.

The Plaza's concessions convinced its waiters not to join the strike on Tuesday, but Plaza manager Fred Sterry made no similar promises about reprisals. On Thursday, May 30, he fired his entire waitstaff when some admitted that they belonged to the union. Sterry announced a bravado plan to supply his Hotel Men's associates with nearly 10,000 Black strikebreakers.[55] The Hotel Men fretted that this plan would require the availability of French interpreters to help read the menus, and it certainly would have required using valuable guest rooms to house the scabs.[56] Blochinger declared the IHWU ready and willing to enroll Black workers in the union's ranks, and he and Elster found allies in local Black clergy to educate the migrant workers about the strike and its causes. Some headwaiters quit when out-of-town Black waiters reported for duty, effectively joining the strike, and most hotel owners consigned the strikebreakers to back-of-the-house duties out of fear of offending racist clientele.[57]

Some employers found scabs who didn't require importation and housing. They recruited waiters from "popular eating houses." Used to being chummier with their diners, these scabs had to be admonished not to discuss the day's baseball game with customers. Elsewhere, Ivy League college students were happy to serve as strikebreakers for ideological reasons but less happy to do actual labor. One newspaper observed that "a freshman of an eastern university kept half a dozen patrons waiting while he drank a cocktail with an old friend who was dining at a nearby table."[58] Poor performance aside, college students, as Stephen H. Norwood has explained, were a common source of scab labor in an era when higher education was the exclusive preserve of the privileged.[59]

The workers at the Astor, Gotham, Imperial, Prince George, and St. Regis hotels joined the strike on May 30. At the Astor, scabs already in uniform were hiding in adjacent rooms. Customers applauded when they seamlessly replaced the striking waiters in the middle of dinner. By then, the total number of strikers was above 2,000, and membership applications continued to pour in. "If the employers are not sufficiently impressed by this," Edward

Blochinger threatened, "we are in a position to tie up the big systems of chain eating places such as Child's." The threat meant nothing to the hotel owners, as working-class cafeterias had no relation to their business; a sign that the excitement of the waiters' rebellion was overwhelming strategic considerations about how to win the strike.

The Amsterdam Opera House hosted another "monster mass meeting" on May 31.[60] Inside the hall were 3,000 workers; another 2,000 spilled out into the street. Five hundred cooks held a breakout meeting on another floor, as did small groups of workers who spoke no English. Rose Pastor Stokes again addressed the workers, urging them to hold out. "Why are they willing to grant every concession except union recognition?" she asked them. "They know that if you are not organized they can take away, later on, everything they grant you today." IWW leader "Big Bill" Haywood ridiculed the bosses and impressed upon the workers how powerful they were in unity. He told them he heard that "a man rich enough to buy half the hotels in New York went into a hotel and couldn't get ham and eggs. That man was Judge Gary," president of the U.S. Steel Corporation. "You are not only bigger than the Hotel Association, you are bigger than the steel trust," he told the laughing strikers.[61]

By the end of the week, 3,500 workers were on strike at 31 properties. A couple of hotels, Fifth Avenue and Carlton Terrace, had signed closed-shop agreements with the IHWU.[62] By June 2, the strike had reached at least 47 hotels and restaurants, and over 4,000 food service workers—including more cooks—were parading nightly through midtown.[63] Police continued to treat the mere act of picketing as criminal activity. At the Netherland and Savoy hotels, a swarm of cops descended upon a rally, fired warning shots, and corralled strikers who were charged with rioting.[64] An army of private detectives patrolled the Waldorf-Astoria to keep pickets at bay.[65]

Blochinger tried to get the other craft unions—electricians, engineers, firemen, and oilers whose work was crucial to maintaining the physical plant and daily operations of the hotels—to join the citywide strike. Some of the unions had contracts that contained "no strike" clauses. Since all of them were AFL craft unions that would be more likely to respect an AFL picket line, Blochinger also attempted to negotiate the independent IHWU's entry into HRE. However, organizers couldn't work out the financial terms. HRE's strike fund operated more like an insurance policy, or at least the international organizers treated it that way, calculating that the twenty-five-cent monthly per capita fee that IHWU members would pay to join HRE would cause the international union to pay seven dollars in strike support for every dollar it collected in dues. HRE Waiters Local 1, however, acted in solidarity with the striking waiters and cooks, securing floor privileges for IHWU representatives at a meeting of the Central Federated Union (the umbrella organization of AFL locals in New York City) to make an appeal for funds. Local 1 donated $15. Elster, who had his share of frustrations with HRE that preceded the strike, was openly courting the IWW, which explained Haywood's appearance.[66] In the end, neither the electricians nor the operating engineers could formally join the strike.[67] Here and there, the AFL's Firemen and Oilers union waged wildcat strikes in support of their catering employee comrades.[68]

The union's Monday offensive to expand the strike further was a bust. At most targeted establishments, lunch and dinner carried on without a hitch. Only 350 workers joined the strike on June 3. The culinary workers at the private Stock Exchange Luncheon Club walked out at lunchtime, joined by waiters at other Wall Street eateries, giving one *New York Call* reporter the pleasure of watching J. P. Morgan Jr. sitting in befuddlement at an empty table.[69] The union, however, showed the first public sign of a split in the ranks when the headwaiters in the Geneva Society proposed a compromise solution to the Hotel Association that they as individuals would (mostly) exclusively select waiters and cooks from the IHWU hiring hall, freeing the proprietors of any of the obligations of union recognition. A faction of the IHWU executive board proposed to end the strike on those terms, resulting in their expulsion from leadership by an angry membership, who also removed lightning rod Joseph Elster from duty as press spokesperson.[70]

As strikers who accepted the Geneva Society terms returned to work at the Netherland, Savoy, and Waldorf-Astoria hotels, IHWU finally succeeded in getting chambermaids to join the strike. The housekeeping staff at the Hotel Imperial walked out on June 4 and were greeted with rousing cheers when they arrived at strike headquarters.[71] While the women workers were certainly exploited by their employers and deserved to be organized, many of them had "live-in" terms of employment. Striking, for them, would entail walking out on their jobs *and* their homes. That was a huge ask of a segment of the workforce invited to join the movement as an afterthought. Outside of the Imperial, very few chambermaids joined the strike. As the second week of the citywide walkout dragged on, more strikers were returning to work under the new conditions. June was traditionally the end of banquet season. So the Hotel Men's Association was sure that having met the IHWU's material demands for the workers, the strike would soon fizzle out over the question of union recognition. Employers began taking a tougher position in the face of threatened walkouts. When a union organizer approached the manager of the Hotel St. Denis with proposed contract terms during lunch service, his only reply was, "My friend, blow your whistle."[72]

The Socialist Party tried to rally the workers to press on with the strike, arranging a rally at Carnegie Hall on June 5. The famed concert venue fit 3,500 strikers under its roof. Morris Hillquit joined Mrs. Stokes as a headlining speaker.[73] As the strike collapsed, Stokes—who lived on a private island on the Long Island Sound—set up an office in the IHWU headquarters on West 44th Street in order to set up a chambermaids division of the union. "Oh no; the strike isn't finished," she announced to the newspaper reporters gathered at her feet. "One or two waiters have gone back to work, but the men are standing solid. Why one man with a wife and children, who has been a waiter for thirty-five years is out."[74] Stokes was cagey about how much progress she was making because it was not likely much progress at all. Her organizing committee never grew beyond fifty women, and most of those were the Imperial strikers after she paid to have them register as guests of other hotels so they could organize the chambermaids on the property.[75] Hotel managers distributed pictures of Stokes to front desk clerks in case she attempted to check in and agitate the workers on duty.[76]

Inspired by Upton Sinclair's book, *The Jungle*, strikers began leaking stomach-turning details about sanitary conditions in the hotel kitchens. They told tales of reused food, rebottled glasses of wine, bloody fingers, and vermin infestations.[77] The entire front page of the June 12 *New York Call* was devoted to a muckraking expose of "Dirt and Reeking Insanitation" in the "Dark Underground Caverns Where Dainty Dishes Are Prepared."[78] Stokes began to encourage playful thoughts about sabotage, like replacing sugar with salt and water with vinegar.[79] Desperate strikers became more violent in their street demonstrations. One of the last major events of the banquet season was

Rose Pastor Stokes and Joseph Elster, at strike headquarters. (Library of Congress.)

a ballyhooed visit from three German naval ships, whose officers came ashore for meals. A small riot occurred outside the Waldorf-Astoria during dinner on June 10, resulting in 101 arrests when the waiters and cooks fought back against police violence.[80] Edward Blochinger protested to the mayor—who was hosting the German seamen—about the cops' rough treatment of the union pickets. Mayor William J. Gaynor responded by denouncing the IHWU leaders as "mean, low men" who disrespected his office by not providing loyal waiters for his event.[81] One hundred and fifty strikers descended upon Grand Central Station on June 13 to beat a trainload of scabs rumored to be imported from Boston. They also used cayenne pepper as an assault weapon. Seven men were arrested for the attack on scabs who ironically were being *exported to Boston* to break a totally unrelated strike.[82]

Through an intermediary, union leaders "were given to understand" that the Hotel Association would consider arbitration if the union would revise downward its original demands. Members spent the evening of June 14 at Bryant Hall debating minor concessions in their wage and hour demands. The Hotel Men indicated that they would concede almost every revised demand—except for formal union recognition. The members who crowded Bryant Hall on June 18 unanimously rejected the bosses' counteroffer.[83] Frustrations boiled over. Picketers smashed windows at the St. Regis during street fights with cops.[84] The Hotel Men were proven right that the end of the banquet season would also end the strike. Members crowded Bryant Hall on June 21 to vote on a motion to suspend the strike. Stokes argued in favor of ending the walkout while there was still time for the strikers to get their old jobs back. The motion failed, with 1,381 votes to continue the walkout and only 426 members voting to end the strike.[85] When the workers rejected Stokes' advice, she resigned from the union's executive board.[86] Desperate to look strong under the circumstances the union tried to spread the strike wherever it could, striking a hotel and a few restaurants in far-flung Coney Island.[87]

The union finally suspended the strike on June 25. Joseph Elster presided over the meeting at the Amsterdam Opera House. He convinced the majority that the strike committee had canvassed the hotels where the strike had been declared and confirmed that the Hotel Association's promised improvements were in effect.[88] As waiters and cooks scrambled to get their old jobs back, a Hotel Association spokesman made clear that while "many of the waiters will get back," there would be a blacklist for a "weeding of the more placid sheep from the violent goats."[89]

Better Men Have Been Electrocuted

"Big Bill" Haywood's appearance at the June rally was not a one-off, but the beginning of the IHWU's conversion to Wobbly principles and tactics.

In the fall, the union lowered its initiation fee to one dollar and its monthly dues to fifty cents. It reorganized as one big union of hotel workers, regardless of craft, race, gender, or nationality. It foreswore signing any collective bargaining agreement that included any timed "truce" or no-strike pledge.[90]

The hotels that conceded wage increases, a shorter workweek, and a reduction in disciplinary fines rescinded those concessions almost as quickly as they were granted—just as Rose Pastor Stokes had warned. While the hotels continued to pay the June wage increases, once banquet season started up again in the fall, they demanded longer hours and denied requests for days off, all while the Geneva Society conspired with the Hotel Men to deny reemployment to certain strike veterans. Joseph Elster publicly threatened to launch a new strike on Election Day, traditionally one of the busiest catering nights of the year. IHWU leaders realized that the biggest mistakes of the spring strike were timing it so closely to the end of banquet season and involving cooks and chambermaids so late in the struggle. This time, they declared, the cooks would walk out first so there would be no meals to serve when waiters blew their strike whistle. The union also had a special organizer for elevator operators—a job often performed by Black workers.[91] On October 23, they announced a November 1 deadline for a citywide walkout of all hotel workers if the Hotel Association did not recognize the union.[92] The following evening, 3,000 hotel workers jammed into Bryant Hall for a meeting to prepare for the strike. They coalesced around demands for "better food, semi-monthly payment of wages, abolition of fines, the six day week, the ten-hour day, and a minimum scale of wages."[93] Speeches extolling industrial unionism were made in French and Italian in addition to English.[94] The Hotel Association flatly refused to recognize the union. Charles Etzel, the IHWU's Secretary, walked back the November 1 strike date and warned "the strike of the hotel workers would come suddenly, without warning, at a busy time."[95]

Partly what delayed the New York hotel strike was that Etzel, Elster, and Blochinger had spent the intervening months traveling up and down the eastern seaboard to organize new locals of the fledgling union, hoping to spark a national, or at least regional, strike in the hotel industry. Brief strikes were organized in Buffalo, Boston, and Washington, DC, but it takes more than a few months to organize a proper international union and strike wave.[96] The delay frustrated New York's hotel workers, who loudly insisted that the local union drive not pass up the opportunity to impact the hotel and restaurant industries' biggest night of the year: New Year's Eve. The cooks, whose June wage increases had been paltry and who had no major gratuities at risk by skipping the big night, pressed for a strike vote, which took place between midnight and 3:00 AM on December 30. By the time most workers reported for duty on December 31, only one-third of the union's 12,000 members had cast ballots, and no strike call had been issued. Two hundred members met at Bryant Hall for breakfast to rally for the night to come. "Remember men, there are millions of dollars at stake tonight," one speaker cried out. "We don't need to use bombs or bricks to get our demands."[97] By the end of the night they did need bricks, at least at the Hotel Astor. Management beat and detained two outside agitators—a Wobbly organizer and an officer of the Machinists union—who blew the whistle that launched a job action. The Astor treated its own striking workers similarly and maintained a detention center in its basement. One escaped striker was chased in the streets by hired goons. When he reached the Belmont hotel's picket line, the goons faced off against brick-throwing strikers.[98] They chased them back to the Astor where a few windows were broken, and 19 unionists were arrested.[99]

Only four hotels—the Imperial, Hoffman House, Holland House, and Seville—saw total walkouts of the kitchen and dining room staff.[100] More cooks walked out on the first night. Many waiters stayed on the job to earn a least one more night of good tips before the anticipated privations of a long-term strike. The hotels didn't feel much economic pain, as New Year's Eve drinking and dancing continued through the night (if on emptier stomachs). Union spokespersons claimed that thirteen employers granted recognition before the walkout began. The IHWU executive board considered ending the strike following its first night of mixed results.[101] Instead, it dismissed Elster from his post as business agent and voted to ask the IWW's Arturo Giovannitti and Joseph Ettor to lead them.[102] Giovannitti was already in town, advising the cooks.[103] Ettor was in Lawrence, MA, where textile workers had just won the IWW's first major strike. The IWW dispatched Elizabeth Gurley Flynn to help. Flynn, who would ultimately become this second strike's lead organizer and the second woman to lead striking hotel workers, recalled that it was the Italians in the kitchens who wanted the help of IWW organizers. "They really wanted Ettor and Giovannitti," she self-effaced.[104]

This was not a "one day longer, one day stronger" strike; it was an intermittent strike that prized unpredictability. Sometimes union shop stewards would blow whistles in the middle of a meal, as the Belmont waiters had done the previous May. Other times, Wobbly organizers would engage in a bit of street theater. "Well-dressed sympathizers, as diners, would go into places not yet on strike and at an agreed moment blow a whistle which was a signal for all cooks and waiters to walk out," Flynn recalled years later, adding, "I was never in such a hectic strike."[105]

Two-thirds of the cooks at the Waldorf-Astoria walked out on January 2, inspiring the entire staff of cooks at the Belmont to strike the next day.[106] Waiters at the Endicott joined their cooks, who were already on strike, on January 3, and the union was touting 15 hotels and restaurants on its list of "Fair" shops that had agreed to the union's demands.[107] Flynn facilitated an all-night meeting of union members at Bryant Hall on January 7, in which their strike strategy was settled somewhat. Workers heard speeches in English, German, Greek, and Italian (the latter handled by Tresca and Giovannitti). "The question is are you waiters going to make this present strike more successful or are you going to allow the cooks to bear the burden alone?" The crowd—waiters and cooks, alike—roared in assent.[108]

The strike was formally on at just 17 hotels, but walkouts were happening across the culinary trades, with bakeries and private clubs pulled into the cooks' rebellion.[109] The tactic of having well-dressed union sympathizers pose as diners to call the strike was meant to address the waiters who hesitated to lose tips. Those who did not heed the whistle were not treated with kid gloves. Street fights broke out between waiters and cooks outside the Astor after dinner on January 8. When police arrived to beat up both parties, the strikers threw bricks through the hotel's windows.[110] Having learned hard lessons about police brutality in the spring strike, hotel workers in 1913 were quicker to fight back. Sabotage, too, was a much more discussed feature of this strike. Wobbly propaganda clearly had gotten the workers talking. One Socialist journal reported, "The French and German cooks and waiters declare that if they have to get jobs in non-union hotels they will burn the fried potatoes, boil eggs hard which were meant to be soft and spill bowls of gravy on the shirt fronts of well-dressed guests."[111] Striking cooks even resorted to stink bombs. Several cleared the dining room of the Hofbrau House by scattering asafetida, a spice common in Indian food that is used sparingly due to its powerful fetid odor.[112]

Joseph Ettor's delay in arriving in New York to lead the strike was a subject of breathless newspaper reporting.[113] Finally, on January 10, he addressed a mass rally of strikers at Bryant Hall. "Close all the doors of the big hotels," he rallied the workers. "And," he continued before an audience of thousands of strikers and dozens of reporters, "if you are compelled to go back under unsatisfactory conditions, go back with a determination to stick together and with your minds made up that it is the unsafest proposition in the world for the capitalist to eat food prepared by members of your union."[114] The speech brought a wave of negative publicity. The Hotel Men's Association called for Ettor's arrest.[115] One law enforcement official hissed, "Better men have been electrocuted than this evil, serpentine advisor." A day later, he was out of the city again. From Lawrence, Ettor tried to walk back his comments. "I did not make the remarks alleged," he protested. "Your cause is not to be won by any policy that endangers human life."[116] Since the workers' own talk of sabotage had focused more on shirking and recipe mix-ups, it's quite likely that Ettor did in fact call dining in non-union establishments the "unsafest proposition." But it's equally likely that he was riffing on the workers' playful fantasies of making food inedible by overcooking. Although some of the editorial condemnation of Ettor's comments recognized that he wasn't calling for poison, they were nevertheless offended by the idea of ruining the meals of patrons who didn't side with the workers' struggle. Newspapers vilified the strikers and especially the IWW leaders and cheered a speedy conclusion to the strike.

Despite the whirling controversy of Ettor's sabotage threat, Wobbly organizers managed to refocus the strikers. By January 13, Flynn became the de facto leader as Ettor was too much of a lightning rod to return to the scene. She brought order to what had been a series of spontaneous wildcat strikes, declaring the strike as formally on at 35 properties—now including the Martinique and Ansonia hotels. The Ansonia, located uptown on Broadway and 72nd, was owned by an eccentric member of the Stokes family; W. E. D. Stokes had vocally disparaged the strikers as "the most contemptible low-lived people in the world."[117] Flynn also pressed the strikers to make the abolition of tipping—clearly a source of divisiveness among the workers and a weakness of the walkout—a central demand of the strike, along with a $20 weekly wage, an end to the "vampire" hiring system, and an eight-hour day.[118] Two thousand workers held a marathon meeting on January 15 at Bryant Hall to unanimously endorse a general strike.[119] However, they did not set a date. IWW leaders led the strikers in a few days of puckish pranks, like the asafetida bombing, which were designed to raise the workers' spirits and build up their sense of power. On January 19, they held a rally outside (and occasionally within the lobby) of the Waldorf-Astoria where the lame-duck POTUS William Howard Taft was being feted. Flynn delivered a telegram to the President warning that the "conditions under which the food is prepared in the kitchens is filthy beyond description," and he advised Taft "to personally investigate the kitchens before dining." Earlier in the day, at a rally in Union Square, one IWW organizer joked about the stink bomb incident at the Hofbrau House and suggested that the wives and daughters of the strikers should make reservations at the dining rooms on the strike list, don their best evening wear, and bring pocketbooks full of asafetida.[120]

For a moment, it appeared that the union won a breakthrough victory at one of the larger employers, the Knickerbocker, when proprietor James Regan hastily agreed to the union's terms minutes before a threatened dinnertime walkout on January 22. It promised closed-shop union protections for over 500 workers and the possibility of Regan using his influence within the Hotel Association to negotiate a general settlement.[121] The pitfall of not signing contracts, however, was that once his immediate crisis was over, Regan was able to recruit scabs for the next day's shift. "I discharged 268 men early this morning," Regan declared in a statement for the Hotel Association, "because I did not care to let them run the Hotel Knickerbocker."[122]

The union finally launched the general strike after ballots were counted sometime after midnight on January 24. With no meals to disrupt, 2,000 strikers paraded through midtown and smashed hotel windows. Marching under a red flag, demonstrators threw bricks through almost every first-floor window at the Knickerbocker and broke a few more at the Belmont.[123] For all the broken glass, only 400 workers joined the general strike, which was a bust. The following night's midtown parade saw more flying bricks, at the Ritz-Carlton and Delmonico's. Police who dispersed the angry crowd were pelted with eggs and rotten vegetables.[124] Carlo Tresca was among the demonstrators arrested for disorderly conduct.[125]

By the end of the weekend, IWW organizers were encouraging the strikers to return to their jobs under the best conditions they could secure. "Of course I cannot speak officially," Flynn told assembled reporters on Sunday the 26th, "but I think the strike will be settled within 48 hours." She cast her eyes on the future. "The next time that a strike takes place the workers will be solidly united and their demands will be one."[126] The next day, she roused the strikers at a mass meeting at Bryant Hall with a more militant version of this advice. Workers were to return to work as shop committees with a type-written list of demands, which were mostly the terms of the Geneva Society "agreement" from the spring but began with the declaration that, "All workers who have been on strike shall be reinstated in their former positions." Formal union recognition was impossible, but Flynn's clever gambit was that by receiving a committee of returning strikers and their written "demands," workers would gain a de facto recognition of the spirit of a union. Two thousand workers marched out of Bryant Hall and up and down Broadway and Fifth Avenue before returning to their hotels as committees before the evening's dinner service. A handful of establishments accepted the returning workers. The larger hotels balked at taking back the goats *and* the sheep. Thus rejected, pissed-off demonstrators smashed windows at the Martinique, Imperial, and Waldorf-Astoria.[127]

On January 31, Flynn met with "several hundred disgruntled" hotel workers who were suffering under the blacklist. There was no shortage of bitter recriminations about lost wages. Flynn was honest about the ground that the movement had lost, but even her considerable organizing skills could not rally a bunch of men who had lost their jobs and convince them that they would win the next strike. The meeting ended, the IWW issued a statement that the strike was officially over, and the men who spilled out onto the street continued to argue with each other.[128]

It would take a few years before Elizabeth Gurley Flynn was proven right that there would be another general strike in the hotels. It would take yet another five years to absorb the lessons of the 1912–13 unrest to build a more durable organization. New York's culinary workers began 1913 with no shortage of organizational suitors. Ultimately, they would choose to blaze their own path.

2

Bolsheviki Methods
1913–1918

Four thousand hotel workers and their families paraded through midtown on Thanksgiving Day 1918. They were "almost entirely surrounded by policemen" prepared to violently disperse the crowd if they saw even one red flag as their route snaked past every hotel where they were on strike. Aghast at the revolution in Russia, Mayor John F. Hylan had banned public displays of socialistic banners, and the hotel workers' penchant for radicalism preceded themselves. The workers kept their red flags at home; some even carried small American flags to maintain the peace. They also carried signs that read, "Abolish the tipping system," and others castigated hotel owners' "patriotism" for their wartime profiteering.[1]

Though failures, the strikes of 1912–1913 had shown that hotel workers could be organized to take action against their employers. Both HRE and the IWW pursued these workers, attempting to form more stable local unions for them, but both federations had lost credibility with too many of the former strikers. However, observed Howard Kimeldorf, "the organizational logic of industrial syndicalism continued to influence the direction and content of American unionism." New York's hotel restaurant and club workers' "quest for a more organizationally sound expression of industrial syndicalism," he wrote, "would lead them from one union to another over the next three decades."[2] But, really, it was one long sustained effort that went by different names—sometimes through mergers, sometimes through rebranding. They always had a union, and over the course of the five years that followed the 1913 strike, it became more stable and durable.

Workers coalesced into a new-model independent union they called the International Federation of Workers in the Hotel and Restaurant Industry. Although its 1918 strike would once again fizzle out on New Year's Day, it still won the union a foothold in the industry. The workers never lost that foothold—regardless of mergers, splits, new affiliations, and raids—even when they did raise the red flag.

There Are No Factions

Three unions vied for the loyalty of New York's hotel workers immediately following the 1913 strike, but the frustrating experience of negotiating strike strategy, union dues, and craft rules left many skeptical of existing organizations.

The International Hotel Workers Union, which lost the leadership of the New Year's Day strike to the IWW, returned to the Vehlings' original vision with a focus on legislative lobbying. The union's signature initiative for the remainder of 1913 was Edward Blochinger's drive for a state law to abolish tipping.[3] Having had their first taste of direct action, as well as police repression, hotel workers had little interest in the law. The union's fortunes further plummeted after it passed a rule in November that barred dual membership in the IWW.[4] Lacking enough dues-payers, the IHWU suspended operations in 1914.[5]

After the IHWU unceremoniously dumped Joseph Elster following the New Year's Day walkout, his first act was to sue them for $67 in unpaid wages.[6] His encore was to publicly threaten to create a "new hotel workers union" affiliated with the AFL to interfere in the ongoing strike.[7] Whereas the mostly Italian cooks called in the IWW to lead the 1913 strike, Elster, whom they fired after the first night's walkout, had his base in the German waiters.[8] Within HRE, however, he was a polarizing figure. Waiters Local 1 welcomed him back into the union, and he became the Business Agent of HRE's new Cosmopolitan Hotel Waiters Local 94, which was chartered to compete with the independents. Elster managed to get it up to 49 members before he was denounced and expelled at HRE's international convention in June 1913 for having helped organize the "dual union" IHWU. Local 94 fell apart in April 1914 when its last—and, quite possibly, first—18 members stopped paying dues.[9]

Days after the 1913 strike ended, Carlo Tresca disrupted HRE's first recruitment meeting for Local 94, heckling the craft unionists in Italian, and led most of the workers out of the hall (helping to doom that effort).[10] The workers who followed him began agitating for a new industry-wide hotel strike before the next New Year's Eve celebrations.[11] But many hotel workers remained wary of the Wobblies, and 1914 came and went without any worker protest. The economy was mired in a recession that began in 1913, and the IWW refocused on its Unemployed Union of New York, led by Elizabeth Gurley Flynn, organizing rent strikes and demanding the government provide work or bread.[12] This was possibly the main contact that the IWW had with hotel workers as many waiters and cooks doubly suffered from layoffs and the post-strike blacklist. In March of 1915, the IWW finally chartered a new affiliate—Hotel, Restaurant, and Club Workers Industrial Union No. 110—with about 250 members. Again, they announced a plan to strike on New Year's Eve, agitating for an eight-hour day and an end to the "vampire" system of employment agencies. This time, they dismissed the waiters as an organizing base and focused on all help "below stairs." By that, they meant the workers who were least dependent on tips—the cooks and cleaners. The ethnic base of this new IWW drive was among the Polish, French, and Italians.[13] The Wobblies' strike never materialized.

Instead, HRE Local 1 launched a waiters' walkout on December 18. Claiming 8,000 workers, the strike call mostly applied to the "union house" restaurants where Local 1 exercised job control.[14] After a few days, they announced that 200 of the 300 affected restaurants capitulated to their demands for a 60-hour week, a ten percent wage increase, and recognition of the HRE as the exclusive collective bargaining representative of the waiters. These new terms applied to 4,000 workers.[15] Buoyed by this win, HRE threatened to extend the strike to the Broadway restaurants and hotels.[16] William Lehman, the head of Local 1, announced, "There are no factions which can spring up and oppose any action we may take. This is the first time in the history of the city that the waiters are united and ready to take united action on the demands."[17] Like the threatened IWW strike, this too failed to materialize.

Outside Unscrupulous Agitators

By 1916 a new group of rank-and-file leaders began regrouping as new independent unions. Some were veterans of the earlier strikes; others were relative newcomers to the city. John Assel was a German immigrant who joined HRE Local 1 in 1890 when it was still known as the German Waiters Union. He was a Socialist candidate for the Board of Aldermen in 1903. Perhaps soapboxing for socialism gave him confidence as a speaker and shop floor leader (or persuaded his coworkers to view him as a leader). Either way, he quickly connected with organizers when he became a waiter at the McAlpin.[18] Paul Coulcher spent his youth in Russia, before being exiled for his participation in the failed 1905 revolution. He studied in Zurich to become a teacher but wound up cleaning dishes at the Holland House. He was waiting tables when he joined the 1912 strike. He remained active in the attempts to build a waiters union that would endure beyond one strike.[19] Sam Kramberg was a banquet waiter in several of the city's private dining clubs. A Polish Jew, he moved to the U.S. in 1907 at the age of 20. He disdained the Socialist Party as insufficiently working class in character, viewing the workplace as the primary site of class struggle.[20] Cesar Lesino was a Paris-trained chef who had been President of HRE Cooks Local 719 before bolting with most of its members in 1904. He spent the next decade organizing a series of independent cooks unions.[21] Michael J. Obermeier left his native Germany as a footloose teenager, becoming a steward aboard steamships traveling to such exotic locales as Rio de Janeiro and Valparaiso. In England when the World War broke out, he was jailed as an enemy alien and only released on the condition that he take the first job available on a boat out of the country. He landed in New York where he was dependent on "vampire" employment agencies for seasonal work. By 1918, Obermeier was working as a waiter at the Vanderbilt, where he seethed at management's propensity to fire dozens of men a week on the slightest provocation.[22] Otto Wagner was a Bohemian Jew, an emigrant from the section of the Austro-Hungarian empire that would soon become Czechoslovakia. Fluent in German, he arrived in New York at the age of 24 and found work as a hotel busboy and waiter. He wanted to join a union but spent a decade being rebuffed by HRE because he lacked U.S. citizenship. Although he was active in Austria's Social Democratic Party, in the U.S., he "lost faith in political action" and became attracted to syndicalist thought and action.[23]

These workers recognized that all the workers—in the dining room and in the back of the house—dependent upon paychecks within the four walls of a hotel or restaurant needed to act in solidarity as one union. What they were still struggling with was how to practice solidarity across sub-industries that could vary wildly in scale and clientele, such as cafeterias serving up fast food, garment workers taking their lunch break, gilded hotels catering sumptuous banquets with caviar and oysters, and cigar-smoking millionaires. What would it mean for waiters and cooks to call a general strike when one business had no real impact on the other?

They experimented where they found unrest. In February 1917, a group of 125 workers calling themselves the "New York Club Employees Association" went on strike at the Bankers Club, housed within the Equitable Building skyscraper. The statement that accompanied their demand for a $48 a month wage declared that when the U.S. finally entered the war, "the banking, manufacturing and shipping interests of America will, to a great extent, depend upon the workingmen to sustain your now disputed rights to carry on your legitimate trade in all parts of the world without interference." But, it continued, how could a working man do so, "if he cannot buy sufficient food to nourish his body, and this we cannot do on our present wages."[24] Within a week, the strike had spread to six more private clubs near Wall Street.[25]

In August, Cesar Lesino called out 300 workers at the Horn & Hardart chain of midtown automats, on behalf of what he was calling "the Cooks Syndicate." The fast food of its time, automats were working-class cafeterias that dispensed hot food from vending machines. Because most of the workers were behind the scenes, newspapers took to calling it the "Strike Invisible."[26] Frank Hardart Jr. blamed the strike on "outside unscrupulous agitators," hired private detectives, and black-listed the strikers.[27] Just before December, cooks and dishwashers at a Brooklyn branch of the massive Childs cafeteria chain walked out in protest over a co-worker's unfair termination.[28] Within one week, that protest had evolved into a citywide walkout of as many as 1,200 workers across 47 locations. This group called themselves the "International Restaurant Employees Association," and they demanded an eight-hour day, a 25% wage increase, and better food.[29] The strike lasted for at least a month. The employer fought back with scabs, a blacklist, and court injunctions.[30]

HRE dispatched an international organizer to assist the Childs strikers who made the same mistake as previous organizers and tried to get the workers to join HRE's existing waiters and cooks locals as individuals instead of offering them a charter for their own union.[31] After the Childs strike failed, William Lehman petitioned the HRE Executive Board to fund an organizing drive in New York's "culinary trades." The Board authorized a small amount of money but declined to charter a new local for hotel workers. Later in the spring, a group of frustrated hotel workers petitioned the Executive Board to complain that Waiters Local 1 had no interest in recruiting hotel waiters, and requested assistance. Because Secretary-Treasurer Jere Sullivan directed the union's organizers, the Executive Board referred the matter to him and he mostly ignored it.[32]

Members of the fledgling union gather for their first outing and picnic in 1917. (New York Hotel and Gaming Trades Council, in possession of the union.)

Meanwhile in the hotels, whatever concessions the employers had granted during the season of unrest four years prior had been wiped away. Low wages made waiters even more dependent on tips, and employment agencies were once again extracting as much money as a waiter might earn in one month for the privilege of working for poverty wages.

The culinary workers in the private clubs, fast food cafeterias, and hotels coalesced as a new union they named the International Federation of Workers in the Hotel and Restaurant Industry. The IWW made a late play to reclaim leadership of New York's hotel workers, but the events of 1913 had discredited them in the eyes of the workers, and organizers beseeched them to stay away.[33] Perhaps in response, the new union attempted to establish additional locals along the East Coast. They temporarily hired Hubert Harrison, the Caribbean-born radical public intellectual who was a key figure in the emerging "Harlem Renaissance" movement, to travel to Atlantic City, Philadelphia, and Washington, DC—cities in which a higher proportion of kitchen workers were Black—to recruit new members.[34]

The New York City-based leadership reflected the continued ethnic divisions of food service work in the hotels. Otto Wagner was elected the IFWHR's secretary-treasurer, and Cesar Lesino became the General Organizer. They organized 15,000 members by 1918, which eclipsed the dues-paying base of any previous hotel workers union.[35] It gave the new union real organizing power in some of the largest hotels in the city and a credible strike threat across the industry. Members were eager to test their potential new power, and spontaneous job actions sprang up in all corners.

On May 24, cooks and waiters walked out in the middle of lunch at the Park Avenue Hotel. They demanded more money and an eight-hour day.[36] One week later, waiters walked out in the middle of a banquet at the Biltmore.[37] Cooks and waiters at the Claridge hotel struck and won an eight-hour day and a weekly wage increase of $3. No sooner had the Claridge settled than workers walked out at Healy's restaurant. Before June was through, the Ritz-Carlton and St. George hotels and the Produce Exchange Club all made settlements with the union after threatened or actual job actions. The strikes were becoming so unpredictable that the Hotel Men's Association threatened to lock out all the workers and close the city's dining rooms "indefinitely."[38] The newspapers sensationalized the menacing return of "IWW tactics" to the city's kitchens.[39]

Adding further noise to the situation was the United States' April 6 entry into the World War and its implementation of military conscription. U.S. Marshal Thomas D. McCarthy, a zealous warmonger who saw "unpatriotic and disloyal gatherings" everywhere that men weren't marching in uniform, led a raid of cops, secret service agents, and at least one restaurant manager on the IFWHR's union hall on May 29. They "slugged a number of union men," including Lesino, and arrested one who couldn't produce his military draft papers. William Karlin, a prominent Socialist politician, volunteered as the union's lawyer.[40] Striking hotel workers were also hassled by state law. New York had recently passed an "anti-loafing law," requiring that men of draft age who were not serving in the military be employed at least 36 hours a week in an "essential industry," or else they could be subject to arrest for vagrancy.[41] Following guidelines from the U.S. military's Crowder Order, state regulations deemed serving food in hotels and restaurants to be non-essential work.[42] *Refusing* to serve food during a strike definitely ran afoul of the law.

It Only Remains to Be Seen

Finally, in late August, cooks and waiters at the Knickerbocker hotel staged a one-day wildcat strike over the expense of laundering their uniforms.[43] With the exception of the Park Avenue hotel, where strikers were effectively replaced, the strikes were making material improvements for the workers, but the lack of coordination was becoming a liability. IFWHR leadership decided to take control, issue industry-wide demands, and organize a fall strike drive.

Union members decided to fight for $15 a week and a six-day workweek with 50 cents an hour overtime. The union launched the fall strike with no warning, as was becoming customary for hotel unionists. Just prior to the lunchtime rush on October 28, workers walked out at the Claridge, McAlpin, and Waldorf-Astoria hotels.[44] This time, waiters and cooks walked out in unity, along with a category of employees called "storeroom girls." These were female employees "who have charge of giving out and keeping account of all food supplies," but sometimes could refer to workers who "served" food to customers.[45]

The three hotels were targeted because they shared common owners and management.[46] In February 1918, Coleman T. DuPont, of the military-grade bomb manufacturer, bought the Waldorf-Astoria. He was already in partnership with an ambitious young hotelier named Lucius Boomer. DuPont owned the Claridge and McAlpin hotels, and Boomer managed them.[47] Boomer had apprenticed at the Plaza under Fred Sterry's tutelage. He was a strict disciplinarian with "a hell of a temper" whose "Boomer system of management" made the "Pearlism" of a few years earlier look quaint.[48] Boomer threatened that he would have the men drafted for essential war work if they didn't return to their posts.[49] Many of the strikers did "avail themselves of the opportunity to obtain remunerative employment during the strike," donating part of their pay to the union's strike fund while awaiting victory.[50]

Union members gathered at Bryant Hall throughout the evening of October 28 for a series of meetings to debate their next steps. Lurking in the crowd was an international organizer from HRE. Albert Martel had worked in the kitchen of the Waldorf-Astoria shortly after immigrating from France in 1898. He had his own strong ideas about how New York's hotel workers could successfully be organized, and his own frustrations with his union leadership's inability to grapple with the daunting challenge.[51] Conflating industrial unionism with HRE leaders' favorite new epithet, he reported to Jere Sullivan that "if anyone has any doubt as to what Bolsheviki methods are, he should have attended those meetings." He claimed that while some of the workers he talked to were "really disgusted with those methods," many more confirmed the rumors he had heard that the rank and file were "bitter against the American Federation of Labor, for no other reason than that our organization requires citizenship."[52]

On November 1, IFWHR leaders reported good progress in negotiations with the Hotel Men and predicted that strikers would return to work on Monday. As would become a pattern with the union's pronouncements, they were overstating their position. The Association, which was arranging for waiters to be replaced with female strikebreakers, announced their satisfaction with the new waitresses and refused to give in to the union's demands.[53] The strike rolled through Election Day, putting a damper on what was normally a lucrative night for banquet halls. A union spokesman bragged that the strike cost the employers $100,000 in revenue on that night alone. A few days later, the union could further brag that the inability to host high society parties celebrating the end of the World War cost the struck employers half a million dollars.[54] On November 9, the same day that the Armistice was announced, 500 workers at the Astor, Plaza, and Vanderbilt joined the ongoing strike.[55] It's not clear if the impending end of the war—and with it, the state's anti-loafing law—factored into the IFWHR's decision to step up pressure on the Hotel Men's Association. What almost certainly did factor in was a threatened strike by the Fireman and Oilers and the Operating Engineers unions that did not materialize.[56] The AFL craft unions, representing workers who maintained the heat and hot water in the hotels, had taken advantage of the moment and raised their own demands with the hotels, but apparently, they took a favorable settlement.

Four hours after the guns fell silent in Europe, the war in the hotels spread to two more properties: the St. Regis and the Knickerbocker. The scene of a wildcat strike in the summer, the Knickerbocker preemptively locked out its cooks, which caused the waiters and storeroom girls to walk out in solidarity. Management at the Biltmore and four related properties staved off the strike by entering negotiations with the IFWHR. That night, the union held a mass meeting where delegates from 100 hotels pledged to support the strikers.[57] Union members at shops that were not on strike pledged fifty cents a day to support their striking comrades.

The narrow targeting of the struck hotels, on the one hand, represented a huge advance in the hotel unionists' strategic thinking. For all the romance of a general strike, if all the employers in an industry feel the economic pain of a labor protest equally, they have less incentive to settle with the union. But an employer that is losing market share to his competitors because they remain open while he is closed due to a job action has greater motivation to negotiate. And the eight hotels that the union had singled out by November 11 were particularly strategic targets. As leaders in the industry, they could *only* lose market share to their smaller competitors. And they could better afford the financial demands of the strikers. The union presumably planned to turn around and force the smaller properties to accept the same terms once the DuPont hotels and the Plaza were again operating at full capacity and the strike threat was targeted at their more marginal enterprises.

On the other hand, it's entirely possible that the IFWHR simply struck where its support was strongest, hoping to rally workers at the smaller properties to join the strike later. The workers at these massive hotels were likelier to understand the vast sums of money that were at stake for their employers and how much damage a well-timed walk could do. It could also have been a measure of how the tyranny of the "Boomer system" and the arrogant management of hotels like the Plaza and the Belmont had driven workers to the brink. Union leadership was clearly concentrated in the nine hotels they were initially targeted.

There is evidence for both possibilities in the fact that IFWHR members voted down a motion to extend the strike to more properties on November 14, while voting to double the daily strike fund assessment on working union members. "The nine hotels are losing money every day now," Otto Wagner explained to the press. "It only remains to be seen how long they will care to continue the fight while other hotels which are giving good service by men waiters are making money and taking away their customers."[58]

Womanly Dignity

From the day the strike began, hotels began employing women as strikebreakers. Initially, the DuPont-Boomer hotels promoted "bookkeepers, telephone girls, house stenographers and office girls" already on payroll to the jobs—and the promise of lucrative tips—that had previously been closed off to them.[59] Soon, they began recruiting experienced waitresses from the shops where women had long found work in the trade.[60]

Roughly one-third of America's waitstaff were women at the turn of the 20th century. Waitresses tended to work in lower-paying jobs in cafeterias, lunchrooms, neighborhood cafes, and coffee shops.[61] In the highly gendered service sector, men had been seen as the ideal banquet waiters in fancy restaurants. Partly, this was because only men were assumed to possess the physical strength to carry a dozen full plates on a serving tray to each table. And this was partly because only men were assumed to be sophisticated enough to read the French, Spanish, or Italian items on a menu and provide the attention to detail that customers expected of a fine dining experience. At first, the hotels used the wartime anti-loafing law as an excuse. "We are not sorry they struck," Lucius Boomer declared. "The strike was needed to enable us to conform with the government's orders."[62] Pretty soon, hoteliers began to exoticize and eroticize the new waitresses. "They are attractive and move about their business with a womanly dignity which has won delighted comment from our patrons," gushed a manager at the Claridge. "Guests at the hotel seem to enjoy having a woman wait on them."[63] The McAlpin hired Chinese waitresses. "These girls lend an Oriental air," reported the *Evening World* newspaper, "and the management says they have proven themselves capable."[64]

As Dorothy Sue Cobble detailed in her history of twentieth-century waitress unionism, HRE made room for waitresses within its ranks since its founding. Although the union preferred to charter mixed or craft locals "regardless of race, color, sex or nationality," waitresses could petition for locals of their own if they chose. And many of them so chose, on the logic that only waitress locals would create the space for female leadership and a focus on women's issues. By 1918, the international union made a point of holding at least one seat on its General Executive Board for a waitress and kept a handful of waitresses on the staff of the organizing department.[65] New York's Waitresses Local 679 dissolved for lack of members shortly before the 1912 hotel strike. HRE in New York, writes Cobble, was "notorious for its underrepresentation of women," but responded to the wartime increase in female employment by opening a Waitresses division of Local 1 in 1919.[66] The IFWHR improved upon the mistakes of the independent unions that waged the 1912–13 strikes and made a point of organizing the women who traditionally worked in hotel dining rooms to walk out with their male counterparts. But these new waitresses—scabs for the moment—were new to the workplace and were recruited from corners of New York's service industry that no union had seriously tried to organize for a decade.

The strikers struggled to convince the women to respect their picket lines. When they could not, they tried to get them banned. The employers had a liability in a state law that prohibited women from serving alcoholic beverages in commercial establishments.[67] Boomer claimed that "hall boys," a sort of apprentice butler classification, were serving up the booze.[68] As the youth in the job title implies, many of these workers were themselves likely too young to legally imbibe. In addition to making "blue laws" complaints against the hotels, the union targeted employers for violations of protective legislation governing the length of women's workdays, and for health code violations related to the lack of separate dressing rooms for women.[69] But these laws had no effect on the hotels' staffing strategy. "Women are going to revolutionize the hotel business," crowed a Hotel Association representative. Strike or no strike, hotel managers let it be known that "although some men may be taken back whenever there is a position open, men and women applicants will be given equal consideration."[70]

Hostile to the Principle

Less than a week after the November 11 Armistice, a famous veteran returned home and offered to serve as a mediator to end the strike.[71] Fiorello La Guardia was a public interest lawyer whose track record of supporting labor struggles and appeals to ethnic Italians helped him beat Tammany Hall on their own turf in 1916, winning a seat in Congress. The progressive Republican voted for the war and promptly enlisted in the army's new aviation section, serving in Italy and rising to the rank of major. This macho act of patriotism earned him the endorsement of both the Democratic and Republican parties for his 1918 reelection.[72] He returned to New York a decorated military hero and wasted no time in trying to help settle the ongoing strike. The Hotel Men agreed to meet with the Congressman, but that was perfunctory. The employers issued a statement declaring that La Guardia "had presented nothing that would change their attitude." La Guardia reported that he found the Association's representatives "hostile to the principle of collective bargaining."[73]

On November 22, the Hotel Men's Association held a closed-door meeting ostensibly to discuss ending the strike. Since the dispute affected so few of the participants (only eight out of over a hundred members) the men instead discussed something that would affect everyone's business: the rapidly approaching ratification of the 18th Amendment, which would prohibit the sale of alcoholic beverages.[74]

Right before Thanksgiving, IFWHR members finally voted to authorize the strike committee to call an industry-wide strike "when necessary." The mass meeting was a logistical marvel, reminiscent of Elizabeth Gurley Flynn's management of the 1913 strike. Fifteen thousand members from 250 hotels and restaurants met in "relay" meetings all through the night. Because the Amsterdam Opera House had limited capacity, each "relay" was limited to 3,000 members.[75] The five-man strike committee announced a plan to extend the strike to 150 restaurants on Thanksgiving Day and planned a celebratory parade.[76] Getting approval for the parade required some delicate negotiations with the police. On November 18, New York Mayor John F. Hylan, in a sign of the antisocialist hysteria that was gripping elite society, ordered police to prevent the public display of red flags on city streets and to disperse any "unauthorized assemblages."[77] Perhaps because La Guardia had championed them, the union was permitted to conduct their parade with assurances that they would keep their flags at home. On Thanksgiving morning, 4,000 strikers and their families marched from Columbus Circle to the Amsterdam Opera House on W. 44th Street, snaking through the hotel district, under heavy police escort.[78] At the Opera House, Otto Wagner announced that the Society of Restaurateurs employers group agreed to wage increases and to enter collective bargaining. Therefore, the holiday strike was called off.[79]

Unfortunately, the "settlement" was a trick to get through Thanksgiving dinner. The next day, a spokesperson for the Restaurateurs denied making any wage settlement. They still met with union representatives the following week but came away from that meeting resolved to fight the union.[80] Several restaurants preemptively locked their waiters and cooks out. The Hotel Men's Association and the Society of Restaurateurs issued a joint statement that they would refuse to recognize the IFWHR and would support each other during the threatened industry-wide strike.[81] Ten restaurants, including George Rector's and Reisenweiber's, broke with the Restaurateurs almost immediately and settled with the union, extending union shop conditions to 3,000 workers.[82] By the end of the first week of December, 15 more restaurants had followed suit.[83]

Although the union's strike committee could call all its members out at any time, with history as their guide, hotel employers could safely assume that the industry-wide strike would not happen until New Year's Day. Union leaders maintained a small element of surprise by occasionally—and seemingly at random—spreading the strike to a new property here and there. Workers at the Hotel Endicott, Churchill's, and two other restaurants struck on December 3.[84] And those at the Belmont and the Prince George joined by mid-December.[85] The Hotel Martinique joined the list a few days before Christmas.[86]

Around this time, HRE President Ed Flore traveled to New York to meet with the strike leaders and explore how HRE could support their movement.[87] A bartender from Buffalo, Flore joined the union with political ambitions. At the union's 16th General Convention in 1911, he defeated the incumbent president, T. J. Miller, and immediately butted heads with Jere Sullivan. In its early years, by Sullivan's design, the secretary-treasurer was the "strong" position in the union. It was the only full-time salaried officer position and the staff reported to him, while the presidency was mostly ceremonial, with a small stipend and travel budget. But Flore was eager to do real work. New York City, with about 42,000 workers in HRE's claimed jurisdiction, was an attractive project, especially because of Sullivan's insistence that organizing was an impossibility.[88] Flore asked IFWHR leaders whether it was too late to undo the mistakes that led to New York's hotel workers organizing independently. It was. The craft divisions between waiters and cooks, craft rules of initiation fees and traveling cards, the blacklisting of Joseph Elster, the requirement that members become U.S. citizens, the anti-immigrant (and, particularly during the war years, anti-German) sentiment in the union's journal all bred resentments that would last for years.[89] Years later, when they were finally working together, Michael J. Obermeier recalled appreciating Flore's impulse towards solidarity and general honesty.[90] The President of the AFL, by contrast, did not impress the hotel strikers as nearly so honorable. As the threat of an industry-wide strike heated up, Samuel Gompers crossed a picket line to attend a society banquet at the Astor Hotel. Otto Wagner wrote letters of protest to the city's central labor union and the AFL's Executive Council.[91] Of course, since the IFWHR was not affiliated with the labor federation, the protest fell on deaf ears. In fact, in the increasingly twisted hostility to "dual unionism" that craft union leaders harbored, Gompers likely believed he was duty-bound to ignore a picket line of a union that "competed" with an "official" union in the field. When Flore informed Gompers that HRE was trying to affiliate the IFWHR, Gompers gave Flore a statement that he did his best to respect the picket line by staying in his room while the banquet was served and only emerged to make his speech at the end of the evening.[92]

As New Year's Eve approached, the *New York Call* threw the "largest Christmas party in New York city" for the wives and children of the strikers on December 23. The newspaper collected financial contributions from "thousands of union men and women in all trades," which paid for the toys and candy that Santa Claus distributed at the Amsterdam Opera House festivities.[93] While the children played, the men prepared to ballot on the long-anticipated general strike. In the end, there was no element of surprise when the union announced on Christmas Day that it would extend the strike to all hotels and Broadway restaurants that had not agreed to the union's terms before dinner on New Year's Eve.[94]

It was a fizzle. Only "3000 or so" workers out of the union's claimed membership of 15,000, were reported as out on strike.[95] Otto Wagner kept up a brave front for the press, calling the strike "the most complete tie-up ever seen in New York"[96] and announcing his confidence that the Hotel Association would soon enter negotiations with the union. "How does Mr. Wagner get that way?" scoffed a spokesman for the Hotel Association. "The strike was lost last night if it wasn't before, and he and all the strikers know it."[97] Actually, it would take another month for Wagner and the IFWHR to admit it was over. Although the holdout hotels resolutely refused to meet any of the union's demands, many of the Broadway restaurants did improve their pay. By February 5, the picket lines were suspended, and strikers began returning to their jobs.[98]

The Soul of the Revolution

Hotel workers were not alone in wanting to raise the red flag of revolution in 1918. Many workers drew inspiration from the Russian Revolution of the year before, and a tight labor market vastly increased union militancy. The hotel strike was just one of many that rocked New York in 1918. Garment workers, harbor workers, building trades workers, newspaper pressmen, and more fought their employers in industry-wide strikes at the same time as the IFWHR. Nationwide, 1919 would see one of the largest strike waves in U.S. history. One in five workers—about four million—were to go on strike that year. Three hundred and fifty thousand of those strikers walked out of the steel mills on William Z. Foster's signal in September.[99]

Born in 1881 to a working-class Irish Catholic family, and one of only a handful of his mother's 23 children to survive into adulthood, Foster's experience of "death at my feet" continued as a globe-trotting itinerant worker. In his memoir, he soberly recounted watching a shipmate get washed overboard during a storm and listening to a fellow hobo's life story while the man bled out after being run over by a train, as well as his own disgusting experiences with lice and tuberculosis—experiences that shaped a native-born American who was truly impatient for a workers' revolution.[100]

Foster gravitated towards the IWW, gaining attention as a writer and organizer, and was assigned to represent the Wobblies overseas in 1910 where the French trade union federation, Confédération générale du travail unitaire (CGT), made the greatest impression on him. The CGT was several years into a massive strike wave, one which made heavy use of sabotage and demonstrated, in Foster's words, "utter contempt for capitalist life and property."[101] They were practicing a form of syndicalism—a radical unionism that sought to replace capitalism with democratic workers' control through a general strike—that the IWW preached. Foster, according to biographer Edward P. Johanningsmeier, was "struck by the fact that within the CGT, the syndicalist leadership was a militant minority that was able to dominate a trade union movement very similar, in its decentralized structure and cautious, craft-conscious membership, to the American Federation of Labor."[102]

Upon returning to the United States, he campaigned to convert the IWW to a campaign of "boring from within" the AFL.[103] Radicals disparaged him as "E.Z. Foster" for abandoning the "hard work" of building up the IWW. Rejected, Foster established a series of his own propaganda leagues throughout the 1910s. With names like the Syndicalist Militant Minority League and the Syndicalist League of North America, they never commanded the loyalty of more than 2,000 radical workers around the country.[104]

By 1916, Foster cooked up a plan to organize the Chicago meatpackers that were the subject of Upton Sinclair's *The Jungle*. Thirteen craft unions claimed the right to a segment of workers at Swift, Armour, and their competitors. Instead of forming a new start-up union like the IWW or IFWHR, Foster's plan was to deal in every union that had a craft claim to the industry into the organizing campaign, but they had to affiliate with a new umbrella union—the Stockyards Labor Council—that would be the union of record. The craft unions would get their members and their dues, but the workers got one big union for the industry.

The plan won funding and support from the AFL. Samuel Gompers was personally invested in it. After Foster organized a credible strike threat, Gompers appealed to Woodrow Wilson's National War Labor Board for mediation, resulting in employer recognition, union work rules, the eight-hour day, overtime pay, and wage increases across the board. Taking credit for these gains, organizers convinced over 62,000 workers to join the union by the end of the war.[105] The Stockyards Labor Council was an unparalleled success and a new model of trade union organization. Foster could have used his new base as a springboard to higher office within the AFL. Instead, he set his sights on an even more ambitious organizing target.

Beginning in 1917, Foster and his organizers recruited over 100,000 workers to join the twenty-four unions of the National Committee for Organizing the Iron and Steel Workers. Unlike the stockyards campaign, the timing was not on his side. President Wilson made federal support for union rights contingent on a strike ban in essential industries, insisting that 1919 was still a time of war. Gompers held the steel workers back from launching the strike, even while the steel corporations ignored federal mediation and refused to bargain with the unions. When Foster finally launched the steel strike over Gompers' objection, it coincided with a postwar depression that would have idled the factories anyway.[106] The Great Steel Strike was lost, and steelworkers would have to wait another 20 years to finally win a union.

The 1919 strike wave coincided with the birth of a new Communist Party. Inspired by the Russian revolution, activists who looked for guidance from the Communist International, or "Comintern," adapted the Bolshevik decision-making model of "democratic centralism"—which held that after a robust internal debate, once the party votes on a policy or course of action, no member may publicly deviate from the party line—and attempted to stake out the most "left-wing" political positions.

Russian leader Vladimir Lenin found much to criticize. "These people want to *invent* something quite out of the ordinary, and, in their effort to be clever, make themselves ridiculous," he complained. In 1920, he published a pamphlet directed to his international audience, titled *"Left-Wing" Communism: An Infantile Disorder*. For as dogmatic as Lenin could be, *"Left-Wing" Communism* displayed extraordinary strategic flexibility and pragmatism. Lenin's advice to Communists was essentially to go where the workers were. On the question of "reactionary" labor unions, Lenin wrote, "There can be no doubt that people like Gompers are very grateful to 'Left' revolutionaries who ... like some of the revolutionaries in the American Industrial Workers of the World, advocate leaving the reactionary trade unions and refusing to work in them."[107]

There it was! William Z. Foster's "boring from within" labor strategy, given pride of place in the leader of the Russian Revolution's explicit directions to Communists the world over! Foster was validated. It confirmed for him that his own instincts were correct while also convincing him of the wisdom of world Communist leadership. When the Comintern moved to organize a new global federation of revolutionary labor unions, Foster traveled to Russia in 1921 for the inaugural convention of the Red International of Labor Unions (also known as the "Profintern"). Writing to his American audience from the convention, Foster observed, "Once in awhile, one has an experience that can never be forgotten as long as life lasts ... It seemed as though I saw the soul of the revolution."[108] He returned with the news that his new Trade Union Education League was the exclusive American affiliate to the Profintern.[109]

The red flag-waving leaders of New York's hotel workers union preceded Foster in joining the Communist movement. Their embrace of independent unionism would put them on a collision course with the Party's new trade union leader. How they navigated their disagreements would profoundly influence both the union and the Party for the next three decades.

3

Practical Trade Union Tactics
1919–1924

Michael J. Obermeier entered the Plaza Hotel on May 21, 1923, as lunch was being served. The previous Friday, he served management a union demand that the kitchen staff's pay be raised by $2 to $3, and he was promised a response by 1:00 PM on Monday. When they had none for him, he called the cooks—all 85 of them—out on strike. "Had there been a grievance," Plaza management complained in a press statement, "their complaints would have been entertained." Management called the walkout "unjust," warning that the union planned to extend the strike to other prominent hotels in the city.[1] They did not. The days of trying to spark spontaneous industry-wide strikes were over. The union would spend the 1920s improving working conditions by singling out individual employers who bucked the union pay rates.

In this, they were advised by William Z. Foster, the Communist Party's preeminent labor expert. Foster would also try to redirect the union's organizational form and its independence—efforts that were less successful and that clearly rankled some activists. Nevertheless, union leaders would continue with Foster on their own journey from syndicalism to Communism. James R. Barrett has shown that Foster's biography demonstrates "the continuity between American communism and earlier forms of radicalism." However, despite "deep roots in the American labor movement, Foster nevertheless symbolized the triumph of dogmatism on the American left."[2] That role is exemplified in New York hotels, as he would remain a profound influence until the 1950s.

The union did change its form in these years. With a merger between IFWHR and an independent bakers union, it became the Amalgamated Food Workers, with a focus on culinary employees in the hotels. The AFW was one of the most substantial independent unions of its era and represented a continuing maturation of industrial unionism. Like their Wobbly forefathers, they eschewed written contracts and no-strike agreements but their emphasis on *targeted* quickie strikes to enforce closed-shop union wages and rules won them a degree of organizational stability that eluded their predecessors.

As Far as Possible, Act as One Shop Unit

Although the 1918 strike did not result in formal union recognition, the IFWHR did emerge with a rudimentary form of representation in about 30 shops where the workers stayed organized.[3] Managers in the kitchens and dining rooms would pay the wage rate that the union demanded, take recommendations to hire union members, and adjust grievances with shop floor delegates. Union members had collectively taxed themselves $89,622.39 to support the 14-week strike, and the IFWHR entered the new year with a tidy nest egg. The leadership launched a new subscription drive in the spring to raise funds to buy a new union headquarters.[4] By October 1919, the IFWHR had stabilized its membership at around 15,000 dues-payers and held a large meeting of "all crafts" that elected an executive board that made no craft distinctions between either job categories or the employers' role in the hotel industry.[5] The experience of the previous years had convinced Otto Wagner that he was "temperamentally unfit for practical leadership."[6] John Assel took over as General Secretary.[7]

The union's attempt to organize outside the culinary departments was thwarted by a company union. Like the Geneva Society, the Greeters' Association included managers but also claimed to represent clerks and housekeepers. At a large meeting dominated by the managers, "the radical element" arguing for a union to demand higher wages was bullied and outvoted on a resolution that in lieu of higher wages, the Association should work to increase the "prestige" of the Greeters with semi-monthly dinners and entertainment at the hotels.[8]

Partly in response to this frustrating development, IFWHR unionists began to think of themselves as food workers. They pursued an "amalgamation" with a like-minded independent union, the Journeymen Bakers' and Confectioners' International Union of America, as "the first step of bringing all the workers in the Food industry into one organization."[9] The bakers had been a handful of dissident New York locals of an AFL craft union that were suspended when they tried to organize without regard to craft lines. After seven years of independence, the union had more than doubled its membership.[10] By the time of the merger, the bakers had around 5,000 members spread across 750 closed union shops. In addition to its financial stability, the union shared with the IFWHR a polyglot ethnic and immigrant makeup, as well as cutting-edge leftwing political tendencies. After a few weeks of negotiations, the two unions held a joint convention for six days beginning on

May 24, 1920. The delegates, described as "a mixture of self-made practical idealists, convinced industrial unionists, political and non-political actionist and, here and there, scattered over the Convention Hall a small number of critically mooded intellectuals," formed the new International Workers in the Amalgamated Food Industries.[11] They soon shortened the name to the Amalgamated Food Workers.

The new union's constitution spoke of "sharply antagonistic" class interests, eschewed political action, and declared, "It is impossible to accomplish anything worth while by following the old system of craft or trade unionism." The bakers preferred to call their subdivisions "locals," while the hotel and catering workers called theirs "branches." Similarly to the IWW, the top officers of the union and its subdivisions were secretary-treasurers and general organizers—but never presidents.

No less than eight constitutional subsections were devoted to the rules for calling strikes and boycotts, the gist of which was: "In all such cases the workers shall, as far as possible, act as one shop unit." The dues (not to exceed $1.50 a month) and initiation fees (not to exceed $5) were not cheap, but also not prohibitive. They, along with a Strike Fund composed of voluntary assessments, were designed to fund an effective fighting organization. The AFW enforced closed shop standards but refused to sign contracts with a "time limit" on new job actions, and forbade officers from conducting any meeting behind closed doors with a boss. At least one additional worker had to be present for any meeting with management. In practice, this meant compelling a hotel to only hire from the union's hiring hall, and to pay the union wage rates. With no signed contract the union could and did engage in quickie strikes when an employer tried to chisel at the union wage rate but was also vulnerable to getting locked out and replaced by scabs. At non-union hotels, the standard practice was to make workers sign one-month employment contracts with a commitment to provide at least eight days' notice before a resignation or else to forfeit wages owed. The employer was, of course, free to terminate employment at any time. These "yellow dog" contracts were used as the basis of employers' frequently successful attempts to get court injunctions against picket lines for interfering with their property rights. The AFW constitution forbade any member from signing such a contract with an employer.

Germans and Italians still predominated the ethnic makeup of the union. The union's newspaper, *The Free Voice of the Amalgamated Food Workers*, was published in English, German, and Italian, and campaign literature was also published in French, Greek, Polish, Russian, Spanish, and Yiddish. The AFW's constitution specified that "the English language shall be used in all official business," likely an effort to facilitate agreement and find common ground.[12]

Each of the AFW's predecessor unions had considered itself an "international" union to rival the AFL's HRE, but they had little organizing success outside of Manhattan. The AFW, on the other hand, had over a dozen locals throughout the tri-state area, as far south as Philadelphia and as far west as Chicago and Cleveland. For this reason, the union separated its national office from the three-story building on West 51st Street that the hotel workers had secured prior to the merger.[13] AFW General Secretary August Burkhardt ran that office downtown in Union Square, and he kept his focus mostly on bakers' issues and competing with AFL craft unions in any sector of the food service industry in any part of the country where craft union divisions let workers down.[14]

Burkhardt had been the Journeymen Bakers' Secretary-Treasurer since 1913 and continued in that role for the newly merged AFW. He'd worked as a baker since emigrating to the United States from Germany as a 14-year-old in 1886.[15] The New York Hotel Workers Branch, which was what remained of the IFWHR, united around Michael J. Obermeier as their Secretary-Treasurer. Other prominent names in the Amalgamated Food Workers never worked in a hotel. The union's attorney, William Karlin, was frequently a keynote

The Renovated Home of the Hotel and Restaurant Workers Branch
133 West 51st Street, New York. N. Y.

AFW Hotel Branch Headquarters. (*Free Voice of the Amalgamated Food Workers*, Volume 8, Issue 6 [June 1, 1927].)

speaker at the union's mass meetings. Karlin had served a term in the New York State Assembly before earning fresh fame as the attorney who (along with future Supreme Court Justice Charles Evan Hughes) led the legal battle to seat five democratically elected Socialist Assemblymen in the New York State legislature during the postwar "Red Scare." Another frequently lauded speaker at the union's mass meetings was Ludwig Lore, who addressed the crowds in German. Born Arthur Ludwig Heilborn in a Jewish community on the mutable border between Germany and Poland, he came to America in 1904 at the age of 29.[16] A Social Democrat in Germany, he became a Wobbly and an activist within the Socialist Party's leftwing in America. A writer and editor for the *New Yorker Volkszeitung*—a large-circulation, German-language daily newspaper with socialist sympathies—he helped Leon Trotsky find work during the Russian revolutionary's brief stint as a New Yorker. At one dinner party in his Brooklyn home in 1916, Lore hosted Trotsky and another emigre who would become a leader of the worldwide Communist movement, Nikolai Bukharin. The Americans who attended represented, in retrospect, the roots of American communism.[17]

Amalgamated

The new union's use of the word "amalgamated" was a signal of both its political philosophy and its ambitions. "Since the phenomenal success of the Amalgamated Clothing Workers, it has become the fashion to use this word when radicals found or reorganize independent unions," David J. Saposs observed in a 1926 book surveying the decade's *Left Wing Unionism*. A field researcher and instructor at Brookwood Labor College, Saposs wrote of the AFW, "Its leaders demonstrate a fundamental knowledge of practical trade union tactics." Instead of waiting for a spontaneous general strike, he explained, "they deliberately concentrate on individual establishments." He continued, "By striking at strategic times they generally secure concessions at least and are gradually winning a foothold." Saposs noted the AFW's place within a wider trend of "former immigrant adherents" of the IWW to eschew the phrase industrial unionism in favor of "amalgamation," and concluded, "It is now one of the independent unions that are definitely communistic."[18] To some, an "amalgamated" union suggested a middle path between craft unionism as practiced by the AFL and the kind of independent—and revolutionary—form of industrial unionism as practiced by the IWW.[19] To others, to be an "Amalgamated" union signaled independence from AFL leadership and the embrace of radical politics.

Left trade unionists of the 1920s saw in the Amalgamated Clothing Workers not just a new model for how to run a union, but also a new hope for an alternative to the American Federation of Labor. Through effective strikes, the ACW negotiated citywide industrial agreements that all employers and subcontractors eventually signed. This effectively took wages and working conditions out of competition and helped stabilize a highly competitive industry. During the terms of an agreement, the union and its industry partner evolved a court of labor relations jurisprudence with a tripartite panel of judges. Grievances that could not be settled on the shop floor would wind up before one representative of the ACW and one representative of the employers who were joined by an "impartial chairman" who served as a mediator.

It was a premiere example of the ACW's approach to what was called the "new unionism." Healthcare and life insurance cooperatives would follow. The ACW also started its own bank so that workers could have access to free financial services like checking and savings accounts and unsecured loans that other corporate banks placed out of reach of working-class customers. In fact, the first mortgage that the Amalgamated Bank ever issued allowed the Amalgamated Food Workers' NY Hotel Branch to purchase and renovate its West 51st Street property in 1927.[20] The ACW would again be a model for the advent of industry-wide bargaining in the hotel industry in the 1930s.

Other independent unions formed around this time adopted similar names. Examples include the Amalgamated Metal Workers, which was also founded in 1919 "by a radical group which seceded from the International Association of Machinists"; the Amalgamated Tobacco Workers, which broke away from Gompers' own home base; the Cigar Makers International Union in 1920; and A. J. Muste's Amalgamated Textile Workers.[21] It is also noteworthy, although coincidental, that the largest unions involved in William Z. Foster's famous organizing drives also had "amalgamated" in their names. The Amalgamated Meat Cutters and the Amalgamated Association of Iron and Steel Workers claimed the widest jurisdictions in the multi-union stockyards and steel organizing drives and would have been full-fledged industrial unions if the craft unions had not insisted on the right to represent their handfuls of workers. Perhaps that is why for some conservative union leaders "amalgamated" became a scare word synonymous with the TUEL's policy of "boring from within" the established craft unions of the AFL.[22]

Trade Union Education

The early activists who set about forging American communism struggled to agree on anything. Two different factions had marched out of the Socialist Party's 1919 national convention in Chicago; each formed a new and rival organization. One, the first to stake out the name Communist Party of America, had its base in the Russian and Slavic foreign language affiliates. The other, the Communist Labor Party, had more of a bohemian and intellectual character. The CLP's early social network could be traced to the meetings that Lore hosted at his Brooklyn home in 1916 with Leon Trotsky, and its

Toiler newspaper gave favorable coverage to the independent "amalgamated" unions.[23] Sam Kramberg and Michael J. Obermeier were at least two of New York City's hotel worker leaders who joined the CLP in 1919.[24]

The Communist International, in Moscow, continued to insist upon one unified Communist party per country. While the underground Communist factions fought for control, there was a struggle to create a "legal" expression of Communism. For this, they founded the Workers Party of America at a convention in New York City in December of 1921.[25] AFW activists were founding members of the Workers Party and the union's *Free Voice* newspaper greeted the new party warmly, if warily. A January 1 editorial vaguely alluded to prior "wicked and foolish attacks" on the union (likely over disagreements on the appropriate role of radicals within the official trade unions of the AFL). Still, the *Free Voice* expressed optimism that, "The Workers' Party is to be the leader of the struggle of the revolutionary workers on the political field against the master class, while the revolutionary industrial union movement will lead the struggle on the economic field."[26]

The Amalgamated unionists were eagerly repeating an old political formula just as the Communists were instituting a new party line. A decade earlier, the "political action" faction spent the early years of the Industrial Workers of the World trying to align the Wobblies with the Socialist Party. The effort ended acrimoniously over strategic disagreements about dual unionism and sabotage. The Russian Revolution inspired the "former immigrant adherents" of the IWW in the AFW to look eagerly to a party for leadership, while they hurriedly organized a new federation of radical independent unions. Two weeks after the Workers Party was founded, AFW delegates joined with representatives of the Amalgamated Metal Workers, Amalgamated Textile Workers, and seven other independent unions to form a new labor federation. The New York unionists had been operating an independent central labor body, the United Labor Council of New York, since 1920.[27] By the end of 1921, it claimed an affiliated membership of 30,000 and plans for new sister councils in Chicago and Detroit. The "Convention of Labor Bodies," which took place at the AFW's Hotel Branch headquarters in New York, concluded with a resolution to affiliate with the Profintern.[28]

The fledgling national federation, the United Labor Council of America (also called the Labor Unity League), particularly saluted the Profintern's "program of One Union in One Industry."[29] Of course, they imagined themselves as the one true union in their respective industries. The report that the AFW's delegate to the Red International of Labor Unions' first congress brought back was a rude awakening. The Profintern condemned "dual unionism." Over "Big Bill" Haywood's vociferous objections, Wobbly delegates were ordered to convert what remained of the IWW into a propaganda organization that would operate within the craft unions of the AFL to win them over to the industrial form of organizing. Ultimately, they refused to do so.

Independent unions, like the AFW and its allies in the Labor Unity League, were ordered to liquidate and join the AFL craft unions as communist cells. William Z. Foster's Trade Union Education League, which became the official U.S. affiliate of the Profintern, continued to press the point with the AFW.

At its August 1922 convention, TUEL made the "Food Trades" one of its 13 "industrial sections," as it continued to insist that the AFW dissolve and the hotel workers join the AFL's Hotel & Restaurant Employees while the bakers rejoin the craft union that had kicked them out. Clearly smarting at being judged in absentia from a Chicago conference room, the *Free Voice* editorialized that the TUEL "has been kind enough to decide for us, the Amalgamated Food Workers, what to do, how to act, what steps to take in the future in order to keep step with the 'progressive' program laid out by the league."[30] The paper also repeatedly criticized the "boring from within" strategy, noting instances when leftwing activists were expelled from AFL unions and amalgamated union structures like the Stockyards Labor Council were torn apart by craft unionists. August Burkhardt pointedly directed the AFW's "international" resources to organize in Chicago's meatpacking industry when union-busting employers began to pit the crafts within the Stockyards Labor Council against each other. The AFW's Chicago campaign was its largest effort outside of the New York region as it tried and ultimately failed to rally the workers around a purer industrial union.

By the end of the year, an English-language summary of the Moscow convention was finally published. Alongside the "boring from within" directives was a little bit of wiggle room for other independent unions like the AFW. Those were encouraged to "co-ordinate their activities, and come to an understanding with those labor councils which officially belong to the American Federation of Labor, but agree with our tactics."[31] Still, the AFW could reasonably complain about "contradictions" and "confusion." At the second Profintern Congress, in November of 1922, TUEL delegate Jack Johnstone condemned the AFW in shockingly specific terms: "We fight the I.W.W. because it conducts a reactionary policy, hostile to Soviet Russia. We fight against the independent Metal Workers and Food Workers, because they represent only a small part of the workers and have no right to independent existence."[32]

To redirect some of the amalgamated activists' efforts, Foster convened a meeting of TUEL's Food Trades section in New York City shortly thereafter. Resigned to the existence of some independent unions that were shut out of the AFL by xenophobia and antidemocratic chicanery, he nevertheless thundered against the formation of alternative central labor bodies of independent unions like the United Labor Council of New York. In reference to that meeting, the AFW's *Free Voice* newspaper commented that "the number of fanatic and confused confusionists is on the increase."[33] Foster, in the TUEL's *Labor Herald*, reported that a "splendid spirit prevailed."[34]

In January of 1923, the TUEL formed a new "General Committee for the Amalgamation of all the Unions in the Food Industry" that conceded that the AFW was an equally legitimate union to its AFL rivals. Amalgamation now meant an effort "to consolidate and rejuvenate" the AFL's hotel and restaurant, bakers, brewers, and butchers unions along with the independent AFW. "Before long," this aimed-for amalgamation would be a "definite factor in the general food industry." This new line only papered over the continuing programmatic disagreement between radicals who wanted to forge an independent union in the food industry that would outcompete the AFL craft unions and the Communists who wanted to contest for power and influence within the established labor federation.

While the AFW's Hotel Branch respected HRE Local 1's jurisdiction in the "union houses" where it effectively controlled the work, and Local 1 in turn recognized the independents as the city's actual hotel waiters union, the bakers were not ready to make peace with the AFL. The bakers section aimed to drive the bakers craft union from which they had disaffiliated out of New York City entirely and continued to organize in AFL shops, forcing Foster to negotiate and enforce "no raid" agreements.

In April 1923, the TUEL published its definitive policy on independent unions. It continued to denounce dual unionism and directed leftwing militants who found themselves expelled from their official AFL unions (as the AFW's bakers section had) to resist forming new unions and instead "fight their way back again into their old organizations." Where a rivalry between a radical independent union and an official AFL trade union existed (as it did in at least two sections of the food industry that the AFW laid claim to), the TUEL directed a two-pronged course of action. In the situations where leftwing militants were basically isolated, "weak in numbers and influence," they were still commanded to dissolve and rejoin their old AFL craft unions. But for unions like the AFW that were "strong numerically and actually function as mass organizations the League shall do its utmost to upbuild and maintain them." Still, such unions that were exempted from the "boring from within" edict were nevertheless directed to respect the claimed jurisdiction of AFL craft unions and to take pains to avoid "raiding" them, and to continue to strive for the eventual amalgamation of all of the craft and independent unions within their industry "into one industrial body."[35]

The TUEL's 1923 policy on independent unions also sought to redirect the energies of the "industrial unity" activists who had spent the previous years building up alternative city central labor bodies back into the project of amalgamation and boring from within. The new policy proposed regional "councils of action" (eventually called "Red International Committees") that would serve as "periodic meetings between official representatives of the Trade Union Education League, and of such unions, A.F. of L. or Independent, as are now or later become affiliated to the R.I.L.U." To avoid charges of dual unionism, the new policy insisted that these regional meetings "not accept formal affiliations, issue charters, or accept per capita tax." It continued, "They shall not take on the character of a separate labor movement."[36]

The Labor Unity Council of America, as well as its NYC central body, faded from historical record almost as quickly as it appeared. At the TUEL's second convention, the League's Eastern District organizer, Joseph Manley (Foster's son-in-law) reported slow progress (and his own "sorely tried" patience) in convincing the various amalgamated activists to abandon their plans for a new, pure independent labor federation in favor of an "R.I.C." of local unions.[37]

The Old Militant Spirit

By February of 1923, Michael J. Obermeier and the NY Hotel Branch's leadership team felt that they had assembled enough of an activist cadre in the hotels (and saved enough money in the bank) to launch a new membership drive.[38] They waived initiation and reinstatement fees for members who paid up for two months in advance. One thousand new members joined in the first weeks of the campaign.[39] "The old militant spirit of 1918, that splendid spirit of organization, of protest and revolt is getting hold again of the slaves in the big kitchens and high-class dining rooms," the *Free Voice* trumpeted.[40] By the middle of May, organizers bragged about "1500 new converts to the cause of organized labor" and claimed that many shops were "100 per cent organized."[41]

During the labor shortages of the war years and the 1918 strike, the Hotel Men's Association briefly operated a free employment bureau for staff recruitment, but by 1921 the "vampire system" had returned. The AFW countered this with their own union-run "free employment hall," which "100 per cent" union shops were expected to rely upon for furnishing kitchen and dining room workers.

Animating the organizing drive were demands for a straight eight-hour day for kitchen staff and a nine-hour day within a 24-hour period for dining room workers with extra pay for overtime. They also demanded weekly payment of wages, sanitary working conditions, separate dressing rooms, and the abolishment of the disciplinary fine system—one of their longtime demands. For wages, they demanded a $3 day for dining room staff and a $25 week for kitchen workers.[42]

Despite a decade of union agitation, work hours remained long. A ten-hour or longer workday was not unusual. Worse, culinary employees often worked in split shifts with unpaid breaks in between peak service times of anywhere from an hour and a half to three hours. Waitresses had even less time to themselves—and less money to show for it—due to the widespread practice of "living in" work requirements. Touted as a fringe benefit, room and board (and the promise of generous tips) was more often used as an excuse for low wages. "All too often," according to Dorothy Sue Cobble, "waitresses were stuck with minimal wages, a stingy clientele, and substantial employer deductions for a room and meals."[43]

For housekeeping staff, living in was often less of a "perk" than a requirement. In 1922 the Consumer's League of New York published an investigation of women's working conditions in hotels. Their report, "Behind the Scenes in a Hotel," revealed that the average of $11 a week most housekeepers earned in wages was eaten up by deductions for room and board.[44] As a radical union, the AFW considered hotel housekeepers a part of the food industry workforce they were seeking to organize in 1923. But women were clearly an afterthought in the union's campaign. Nearly a quarter of all kitchen, dining room, and pantry staff were women, and when accounting for the housekeeping departments, women comprised 40% of hotel workers. Yet the union made no specific wage demand for housekeepers and featured no waitresses on its organizing team or in its mass meetings.

The most prominent woman featured in the campaign was Elizabeth Gurley Flynn, leader of the 1913 strike. Flynn was dedicating most of her time to legal defense for Red Scare political prisoners. A founding member of the American Civil Liberties Union, she later described this period of her activism as a "united front," as she continued to work with comrades both new and old, but she wouldn't actually become a Communist until the official "Popular Front" period of the 1930s. "I was still an IWW in my convictions and hesitated to join a political party, although the Russian Revolution and association with the suffragists and the Communists were modifying my views considerably," she later wrote of this time.[45] Arturo Giovannitti, another Wobbly hero of 1913, also spoke at one of the union's mass rallies in June.[46] As did William Z. Foster, who addressed an overflow crowd at the Hotel Branch's headquarters on May 10. According to the *Free Voice*, he warned against "premature action" and counseled that if the union would "organize the hotel and restaurant workers thoroughly a strike would not be necessary."[47]

Two weeks later, during the lunchtime rush on May 21, Obermeier pulled the Plaza Hotel's kitchen staff out on strike after negotiations for the $25 week broke down over the weekend.[48] The union's June 1 newspaper issued a front page bold-faced "WARNING" to out-of-town "cooks, waiters, waitresses and all other hotel and restaurant workers" to "STAY AWAY FROM NEW YORK!" Dissatisfied by low wages, the union warned potential scabs that "workers are like a seething volcano" and that an "ERUPTION MAY OCCUR AT ANY MOMENT."[49] This propaganda was meant to warn other employers. The AFW by mid-decade saw more value in targeting specific employers at times of peak business demands to wrest greater wage and hour concessions than in industry-wide strikes. "The men of the Plaza Hotel are still out and small individual strikes are a daily occurrence," the *Free Voice* reported in June, although by one account, management conceded most of the union's demands within four days.[50]

The AFW's practice of not signing collective bargaining agreements gave them the freedom to engage in spontaneous job actions, but it also made them vulnerable to lockouts that came with little advance warning. The union's newspaper was peppered with stories about brief and unsuccessful lockouts, such as a two-day lockout at the Strand-Roof restaurant in October of 1923, which organizers called "a 100 per cent victory for the branch."[51] The biggest conflict of this type was when the Salvin & Thompson chain of ten "high class" restaurants (which included the Moulin Rouge, Palais Royal, and 400 Club) ended six years of union recognition with an abrupt lockout in March 1924.[52] The union predicted a quick victory, citing its "rigid" picket lines, the support of the HRE Waiters Local 1, and the "absolutely inefficient" quality of the "few scabs the bosses were able to secure." The dispute ultimately lasted over six weeks and resulted in the closure of the businesses. When the Salvin & Thompson chain obtained a court-ordered injunction to break up the union's picket lines, union leaders saw their only opportunity to eke out a victory as a pyrrhic one. They informed the U.S. District Attorney that their former employer had been serving alcohol, and the restaurants were promptly shut down.[53]

The Salvin & Thompson restaurants were hardly the only otherwise legitimate restaurants to serve alcohol on the sly during the Prohibition era. Such establishments that doubled as speakeasies depended upon their workers' discretion, as the workers depended on their paychecks. As we shall see, this practice made HRE vulnerable to organized crime, but, as the AFW showed the hotel and restaurant industry, it also made the speakeasies vulnerable to locked out workers with nothing left to lose.

Mostly overlooked by historians, the Amalgamated Food Workers was one of the most successful independent unions of the 1920s and a rare example of effective union representation in the service sector prior to the New Deal. It was also one of the Workers (Communist) Party's major projects in the labor movement and a major zone of influence in its first decade. Together they forged an American expression of Communism rooted in IWW-style syndicalism in the early part of the decade. Approaching the 1930s, the twists and turns in the Communist Party line, driven by factionalism in Russia and Stalin's inexorable rise, would further change New York's hotel workers unions.

4

Strange as It May Seem
1925–1929

Sam Kramberg and Michael J. Obermeier spent most of May 1929 expecting to get arrested at any moment. As the leaders of a strike and boycott campaign against garment district cafeterias that featured frequent acts of violence and sabotage, they were defying a strict injunction to cease picketing, handbilling, or even talking to workers or customers anywhere near a targeted cafeteria chain. They had already been fined, but, as hundreds of activists were jailed during the course of the strike, they preferred arrest to paying the fine. "Each of the defendants contemptuously and willfully advised and counseled disobedience to the injunction," fumed the judge who ordered their arrest. The picketing continued, countered Obermeier, "because the strikers refuse to be driven back to 12-hour open-shop slavery and miserable wages by either wholesale arrests and police brutality or by the injunction."[1]

Their actions—the decision to organize workers outside of the hotels, to invite violence and sabotage, and to flout the injunction—were guided by the Comintern's so-called "Third Period" policies, which predicted an imminent capitalist crisis and called for heightened conflict, not just with bosses but with erstwhile allies on the broad political left. These policies served Joseph Stalin's factional interests within the Soviet Union. When transposed to America, Harvey Klehr has concluded, they "served to isolate American Communists, destroy a promising alliance with segments of the non-Communist left, and lead the Party into some futile rhetorical episodes."[2] Although these changes spurred the union to organize in new sectors of the food industry and brought more women into the ranks of labor, the AFW would end the decade on the verge of a consequential split.

The AFW had already split once in the middle of the decade when one of their comrades, Ludwig Lore, was attacked on Comintern orders as a proxy for Leon Trotsky. In Theodore Draper's seminal narrative, the "Loreism" episode was a key stage in Russifying the faction fights within the U.S. section of the Comintern. Still, it mattered only to Party insiders like William Z. Foster, who was previously associated with Lore and "fled from him as a political leper."[3] But one of the projects that Foster and Lore worked on together was the Amalgamated Food Workers, and the unfair treatment of Lore roiled the union. It caused a breakaway faction to find a new home within the AFL's Hotel and Restaurant Employees, who would be at odds with the AFW in the 1929 strike.

By the end of the decade, the loyal Party cadre—men like Foster, Kramberg, and Obermeier—learned how to toe the Comintern line (and maybe even influence it or figure out how to maneuver with a degree of autonomy within it). But the ranks of disillusioned ex-Communists and jilted allies also swelled, and the grudges they nursed would be long and deep.

"Loreism"

If AFW leaders struggled with the Party line on "boring from within" the AFL, they would learn to follow the sudden and bewildering changes in the Workers (Communist) Party's strategy in the 1920s or leave the Party, the union, or both. Motivating those tactical contortions was a leadership struggle at the highest levels of the revolutionary Russian government. Vladimir Lenin was gravely wounded in an assassination attempt in the summer of 1918, and health problems would increasingly sideline him for much of his remaining years until he died at the relatively young age of 53 in January 1924. Russian leadership, in the form of the executive committee of the Communist Party, or Politburo, was already paranoid about how revolutions fail. Operating in the name of a dictatorship of a proletariat that was largely destroyed by the recent civil war, they feared Russia's peasant majority as unpredictable and disloyal and saw every advanced capitalist nation as an avowed enemy. They turned on the head of the Red Army, whose brusque and imperious manner left him with few friends in leadership. Leon Trotsky was censured by the Politburo and forced to give up his military post. A year later, he was kicked off the Politburo. In 1927, he was expelled from the party and forced into exile, but in 1925, few outside the highest decision-makers in Moscow knew about the attack on Trotsky, and Comintern leaders wanted to keep it that way.

Thus, Ludwig Lore's friendship with Trotsky was a liability. During the U.S. Party's debate on what to do in the 1924 presidential election (which ultimately saw William Z. Foster's talents wasted on a Workers Party ticket), Lore questioned Comintern guidance in a way that, combined with his friendship with Trotsky, put him firmly in factional crosshairs. He was expelled from the party in 1925, and "Loreism" became one of the American party's first coded heresies. "We were pretty mean and heartless about Lore," Benjamin Gitlow later confessed. Foster's 1924 running mate, Gitlow became one of the Communist Party's most prominent early defectors by decade's end. "But at the time we did not even question the ethics of hounding an innocent scapegoat at the behest of the Comintern leaders," he wrote of the "Loreism" controversy in 1939.[4]

The "Loreism" innuendo split the ranks of the AFW, with some determined to reduce the influence of the Party on the union and others, led by Paul Coulcher, resolved to leave and form a new union. The attacks on comrades with whom he had worked in insurrections and strikes left him grumbling that the AFW was altogether too "interested in isms," just as HRE assigned a new organizer to New York.[5]

Heading In the Right Direction

For a craft union that claimed a wide jurisdiction of hotel and restaurant workers—waiters, waitresses, "countermen," bussers, "pantry girls" and assistants in the dining rooms, cooks up and down the line in the kitchen, bartenders, and "the allied trades" (the catch-all)—the AFL's Hotel and Restaurant Employees were, at heart, a bartenders union.

If, as the old joke goes, work is the curse of the drinking class, then Prohibition was the curse of working-class bartenders, who lost their livelihoods and union protections. From a high of 65,938 members in 1917, HRE had hemorrhaged over a third of its membership—largely the bartenders—within eight years. By 1925, total membership stood below 40,000.[6] New York's Waiters Local 1 was largely unaffected, as the kosher restaurants and cafeterias that it represented were not as dependent upon booze for their bottom line.

Hotel Waiters Local 5 was revived in the same 1919 reorganization that saw Local 1 open up a waitress division. Long a champion of Joseph Elster, Local 1's William Lehman successfully fought to end the apostate organizer's blacklist in the HRE.[7] In addition, Lehman again challenged the HRE General Executive Board to organize New York City. He insisted it could be done with a large influx of organizers, but they needed to speak Italian, Polish, and French. The GEB funded a few organizers in the city for a while but also dismissed the city as the "Tower of Babel."[8] Elster made limited progress and many of the members he signed up were put on trial by Local 1 to recover fines and unpaid dues to prevent them from transferring into Lehman's hiring hall.[9] Frustrated by these actions, the tempestuous Joseph Elster launched an opposition movement against him. Lehman won the "hotly contested" leadership election, and Joseph Elster was kicked out of the union again.[10] Lehman was rewarded with a vice president slot on the HRE GEB, the first national representative to hail from the industry's biggest market.

That so few of New York's hospitality workers belonged to HRE remained a sore spot among activists in other parts of the country. "New York strange as it may seem *has no union*," reported San Francisco leader Hugo Ernst. "They have a 'job trust' which they call Waiters Union Local 1." The future HRE president made a tour of HRE locals around the country in 1923, and Jere Sullivan felt obliged to publish his "Very Interesting Survey and Report" in the union journal, *Mixer & Server*.

As a political refugee from Austria-Hungary, Ernst bussed tables at Brooklyn's St. George Hotel but left before the 1912 strike. The official history of HRE, published in the mid-1950s, would describe the San Francisco waiter as a "dandy" and a "lifelong bachelor" who "loved travel" as well as a cosmopolitan intellectual who gravitated towards socialism and industrial unionism.[11] With hindsight, he was clearly an outsider who embraced other outsiders and would go on to become an important ally to the radical New Yorkers.

While visiting, Ernst met with a committee from the AFW. In his report, he heaped praise on the union that HRE organizers cursed as a "dual organization." Ernst recognized the AFW as the city's *de facto* hotel workers union. He reported his varying degrees of astonishment at how the union was "able to control the larger hotels" with "no signed agreements of any kind." He was equally impressed with the union maintaining its own hall and with the AFW's prosecution of the Plaza hotel strike, which occurred during his visit and which he deemed a success. Ernst was surprised to learn about the previous efforts by Ed Flore and others to affiliate the AFW and its predecessors and lamented that those efforts "fell flat," largely due to HRE's missteps.[12]

His criticisms roiled the leaders of the New York locals and remained a controversial topic at HRE's 1923 convention. A resolution to launch a nationwide organizing campaign at corporate hotel chains like Statler withered under skeptical interrogation from Secretary-Treasurer Sullivan and failed to win majority support.[13]

Finally, in September of 1925, HRE found a field marshal to scale the "Tower of Babel." Actually, he had been on staff all along. Albert Martel, who had briefly worked in the kitchen of the Waldorf-Astoria as a new French immigrant nearly three decades prior, was fluent in English and French and could also compose organizing leaflets in German.[14] Martel was the HRE organizer who skulked around the union's 1918 strike headquarters, sneering about "Bolsheviki methods." He was itching to compete with the dual organization, convinced that a more conservative approach would appeal to the workers *and* management. Jere Sullivan assigned Martel to organize kitchen staff, across the high-end hotels and the working class cafeterias, into Mixed Local 219 and Cooks Local 719. Martel planned to work through the culinary societies that occasionally doubled as company unions—the Geneva

Society and Vatel Club—to organize the cooks through the encouragement of the Gardes Manger and Chefs du Cuisine and attempt to win a system of arbitration with the Hotel Association.[15]

He spent his months in the city in and out of hotel kitchens. When Paul Coulcher's frustrations with AFW's "isms" came to a head, Martel was not hard to find. HRE needed a new local for hotel workers.[16] A founding convention was hastily organized in December 1925. William Lehman chaired the meeting and Ed Flore presided over the installation of officers. Paul Coulcher was elected its first president and another AFW secessionist, Otto Rezac, its secretary.[17] "There are good reasons to believe," Martel bragged, that Hotel Captains and Waiters Local 16 "will soon be a banner local in a short time." Rather than amalgamate with the cooks, it was HRE's intention to run simultaneous organizing campaigns with the cooks.[18]

The *Free Voice* howled in protest that the nucleus of the new local was "a bunch of ex-officials, disappointed aspirants and disgruntled members" of the AFW. "The organization of which they have been members for so many years all at once became too 'bolshevik' for them."[19] HRE put Coulcher on the temporary payroll as a special local organizer and rented an office six blocks away from the AFW, on West 47th Street.[20] Starting with 87 charter members, Coulcher recruited over 300 members by the summer of 1926. The AFW responded by stepping up membership drives in the spring and fall. In addition to waiving initiation fees, chastened organizers downplayed all "isms" except for industrial unionism.[21] It worked. The AFW recovered some former members and gained new recruits. Local 16's membership declined to about 200 hardcore supporters and remained a small operation for the rest of the decade.

Martel and Lehman mostly left Coulcher to organize the hotel waiters by himself. Their organizing was more focused on chefs at hotels and high-end restaurants as well as cooks and servers at delis, cafeterias, automats, and other fast food restaurants. In February 1926, they chartered Cooks and Pastry Chefs Local 24 and Delicatessen Countermen and Cafeteria Employees Local 302. The charter members of Local 302 were also AFW secessionists; in this case, led by a man named Abe Borson.[22] This latest defection inspired the AFW to also launch an organizing drive in fast food. What distinguishes a cafeteria from a restaurant is the lack of waiters and table service. There were cooks, of course, "countermen" to dish out the food on a buffet line, and some cleaning staff to clear the tables. But all (with the possible exception of the cooks) were viewed by employers as low-skilled and utterly replaceable. The wages were low and the hours long. After three years of effort, Local 302 never managed to attract more than 143 members at any given time.

Martel was obsessed with Local 24 and made substantial progress for a year. By the end of 1926, the local had over 500 members. Most of his organizing was focused on convincing the head chefs, through their societies, to hire union men from Local 24. Men who needed the encouragement of their supervisors to join a union were unlikely to have been members of the AFW. So, unlike the Local 16 effort, HRE's cooks' campaign was less of a raid and more of an attempt to foster a competing model of labor-management partnership, one aimed at a scope of representation limited to bargaining with the societies over their hiring hall rules and working out a system of dispute resolution with the Hotel Association. The acting chef of the Waldorf-Astoria endorsed Martel's efforts, saying that the AFW had made "many very bad mistakes" and that many cooks "will play the waiting game, but as soon as they see that you intend to do business and are heading in the right direction, you will get them in bunches."[23] What they got instead was a strong signal from management that they intended to do business as usual. Whatever form the Hotel Men's anti-union campaign took, the result was that Local 24 lost over 200 members in March 1927 and had less than 100 members by May.[24] Local 24 was hemorrhaging so many members that Martel was desperately recruiting in the McAlpin—an AFW stronghold—which he acknowledged would be difficult. As they had in 1918, the workers read him the riot act about HRE's citizenship requirement.[25] Martel was reassigned to the West Coast in May, and Local 24 completely collapsed by the end of the year.[26]

The disappointing results of the New York City culinary organizing drive was a source of contention at HRE's 1927 convention, with most of the blame pinned on Local 1's stubborn resistance to expanding its membership rolls and the usual jurisdictional squabbling. Neither Local 16 nor 302 could afford to send delegates to the 1927 convention in Portland, but Local 16 managed to circulate a letter among the delegates complaining about the end of its organizing subsidy. Jere Sullivan ridiculed Local 16 for wanting a handout and threatened to withdraw all of the New York locals' charters to start fresh with clean jurisdiction and no outstanding fines among the unorganized workers.[27] That was a bluff, but delegates did vote to amend the constitution to wrest control of the organizing staff from the union's geriatric secretary-treasurer and place them under the supervision of President Flore.[28]

Automats

HRE's chartering of Local 16 instigated controversy, and possibly a bit of soul-searching, within the AFW. The "bunch of Benedict Arnolds" who were charter members of the AFW's new craft union competitor turned the Workers (Communist) Party into a lightning rod within the Amalgamated.[29] The union held its contentious third convention the weekend of December 12–13, 1925. The voting power of the Hotel Branch was diluted by giving the smaller Butcher's Section an equal number of seats on the Executive Board.

"Within the ranks of the organization were, and still are, to be found pure and simple Trade-Unionists, Anarchists, Syndicalists, Communists, and Socialists of varied shades, all convinced of the advantages of industrial unionism over the old form of craft and trade divisions," the *Free Voice* explained. "But, if we are not mistaken, the last convention has found the way; it has laid the basis from which to proceed with the real work."[30]

The advent of HRE Local 302 forced the AFW to seriously pursue the growing cafeteria and automat industry as an area for potential organizing. AFW organizers had carried on occasional agitation among cafeteria workers for years, but within weeks of the of Local 302's formation, the AFW found a group of interested "old-timers in the business" and formed a "Provisional Committee" for a new branch of the union. The AFW's organizing call exhorted workers, "Are you ready to stand up as MEN, and refuse to be miserable slaves?"[31] While the Provisional Committee was likely all men, the broader cafeteria workforce had a substantial number of women workers. Whether that line was a temporary oversight or a case of the experienced AFW leaders allowing their newest rank-and-file organizers to speak in their own (sexist) voice, women quickly found the cafeteria union. "The men and women employed in the many 'Automats' in New York are also awakening, the *Free Voice* reported two weeks after the launch of the drive.[32]

Women were prominent at the first mass meeting of cafeteria workers one month into the drive. "Some of those well-organized trades are now starting a nation-wide movement for the 40-hour work-week," organizer Rebecca Grecht challenged her audience, "while you, in the cafeteria and lunchroom business are still working 12 and 14 hours the day." Following her speech, membership cards were distributed, and the *Free Voice* reported "a veritable rush to fill them out" and take advantage of a promotional $1 dues rate for the first month.[33] In July, the AFW chartered its Cafeteria and Lunch Counter Workers Branch.[34] Before the summer was over, the new branch had successfully prosecuted its first strike over its wage and hour demands, against a coffee shop located four blocks away from the union's 51st Street office. Following that, news about cafeteria workers organizing made infrequent appearances in the *Free Voice*.

HRE and the AFW sparred for the next few years. In one embarrassing episode, in the fall of 1927, HRE raided the AFW for the union shop rights of a new co-op cafeteria. The restaurant, located on the ground floor of a Union Square building that also served as the home of the Russian-language *Novy Mir* and the Yiddish *Freiheit* labor newspapers, was to be operated on "strictly co-operative lines." Shares could be purchased for $5, which promised a 6 percent interest rate, voting membership, and access to the cafeteria service, which promised, "pure food, quick service and comfort," according to the *Free Voice's* glowing coverage, which also noted, "All employees, from the chef to the busboy and porter, will be organized workers and members of the Amalgamated Food Workers."[35] However, when the restaurant opened at the end of September, the AFW found its members locked out and members of Local 16 serving the food, with cooks from Local 719 in the back of the house. Apparently, the shareholders of the co-op, the good Socialists that they were—or, as the *Free Voice* put it, "being convinced advocates of the liquidation policy as applied toward the independent unions"—had voted to ensure that their co-operative would be an AFL union house.[36]

The "liquidation policy" could also be called "boring from within," which was still the Party line and official policy of the TUEL. Communist activists in the culinary trades who were not employed by hotels or other parts of the industry in which the AFW was the main union were still expected to join their appropriate AFL craft union to contest for power and win their unions to the industrial form of organizing and other radical causes. The AFW spent 1928 trying to foster a better working relationship with the HRE locals in the city where their comrades had established factions. This happily coincided with a directive that came out of the AFW's third convention to work towards industrial unity across union lines (and with Comintern directions to divide and conquer within the AFL). Cooks Local 719 had a cell of TUEL activists, led by Robert Long. Communists in Locals 1, 302, and 719 agitated within HRE's New York Local Joint Executive Board (LJEB) for a joint cooks and waiters organizing campaign in the fast food restaurants of the garment district.[37] Paul Coulcher still hated his ex-comrades, but Julius Knispel, who transferred in from Portland, had no baggage with the Communists and credulously dealt with the AFW.[38]

Locals 16 and 719 joined the AFW-organized Culinary Trades Conference. Their common cause was that old enemy of hotel and restaurant workers, the private employment agencies that charged unemployed workers a fee for the opportunity to be on call for a job.

The campaign included a rare appeal to the state. Long, of Local 719, joined August Burkhardt and three members of the AFW Hotel Branch and gave testimony at a State Industrial Survey Commission investigation.[39]

Failing to find a sympathetic ear at the state commission, the Culinary Trades Conference organized an open meeting in December 1928, with Sam Kramberg chairing and Local 16's Knispel joining Local 719's Long. They called for activists to collect written statements from workers who had been financial victims of private employment agencies and to inundate the state License Bureau with thousands of new complaints.

Emanuel Kovaleski, a Vice-President of HRE and the New York State AFL, led the pressure campaign to drive out the Communists and "dual unionists."[40] By the end of the year, Long was expelled from HRE, and promptly marched 200 members of Local 719 directly into the ranks of the AFW. A small faction of leftists in Local 302 were also expelled.[41]

Vicious Cycle

Such punishments as Robert Long and his comrades received for attempting to join and contest for leadership within AFL craft unions were hardly unusual. As the 1920s drew to a close, the Party line of encouraging reds to work within, or at least closely with, established craft unions was facing a crescendo of criticism from rival leftist factions, dissatisfied rank-and-file workers, and its Comintern benefactors. TUEL activists found that even as they took pains to swear loyalty to an AFL union, where they ran against incumbent leadership, they were still charged with dual unionism and often expelled. Profintern leader Solomon Losovsky objected that this left Communists with *no* union. He cabled to William Z. Foster, "THE QUESTION OF SETTING UP AN INDEPENDENT UNION MUST BE RAISED, otherwise you will never escape from this vicious cycle."

This sudden shift away from "boring from within" and back towards revolutionary "dual unionism" could be explained, in part, by events taking place half a world away. As Joseph Stalin consolidated his leadership of the Comintern, he declared the start of a "Third Period" of revolutionary activity in 1928. This kicked off a brief era of extreme sectarianism as Communists around the world broke apart coalitions, split unions, and attacked liberals and social democrats not merely as insufficiently radical but as "social fascists." Operating within, and working in coalition with, conservative craft unions did not fit the "Third Period" framework.

Not that the change in direction from Moscow was simply a matter of foreign control over the U.S. movement. As Edward P. Johanningsmeier has shown, American activists who disagreed with Foster's dogged "boring from within" had pleaded their case at Profintern conferences and in private audiences with Russian leaders. And exiled in Moscow was an American who had long been at odds with Foster: former Wobbly leader William D. "Big Bill" Haywood. Although he was ill-suited for Marxist-Leninist doctrine, the respected union organizer was given a fair hearing on how best to organize American workers. He spent the 1920s chafing against Foster's dismissal of his IWW and making the case for the need for independent union organizing in the basic industries. Haywood argued that AFL craft unions were very good at representing their members in bargaining and grievances, publishing journals, and paying out sick and death benefits. Craft unions, he explained, were simply too bogged down by this bureaucratic—though necessary—day-to-day activity to take up the tremendous challenge of organizing large mass production factories. "The remedy," he wrote "is not the TUEL confining itself to the AFL." What, he pleaded, "becomes of the revolutionary slogan 'To the masses?'" Haywood won the day but missed the actual moment of his biggest Moscow triumph. He suffered a stroke on the eve of the Profintern conference that would formalize the strategic shift towards building new revolutionary industrial unions and passed away in May of 1928.

Knowing that a change in Party line was coming, and perhaps not knowing exactly what it entailed, Communist activists made a play to assume leadership of the entire AFW. They won two bakers locals to their side, and in April of 1928, they unsuccessfully ran Carl Gerpig of Bakers Local 164 against August Burkhardt for general secretary. The following February, Michael J. Obermeier ran for the same office in a bitterly contested election. The Communists accused the AFW's stalwart leader of "Loreism," of bureaucratic fumbling of organizing opportunities, of craft union sympathies, and of undemocratic machine politics. Again, Burkhardt prevailed. Never more than since their initial merger did the Amalgamated seem like two unions sharing a name in a marriage of mutual convenience.

Agitators of the Worst Type

While Obermeier challenged August Burkhardt for AFW leadership, Sam Kramberg was elected Secretary of the Amalgamated's Hotel Workers Branch. He had also become a full-time paid functionary of the Party.[42] In March 1929, he published an "account of the existing situation in the food industry and of ourselves" in order to "try to learn and correct our mistakes." It wasn't an *obviously* factional document, but it was preparing for a new stage of activity. He highlighted improved conditions that the AFW had won in its union shops. These included the eight-hour day and six-day workweek, overtime pay, just cause dismissals, and better food and sanitary conditions. In terms of "outstanding mistakes," he listed a vague "lack of experience and leadership in trade unionism," a lack of training for shop chairmen and other worksite representatives, and a lack of trade union education and class consciousness for the general membership. His most telling criticism was as follows: "We paid too much attention to the silver and gold braid aristocracy of the so-called Broadway waiters and insufficient attention to the kitchen workers who are the bulk of the proletarian base of our industry."[43]

Two weeks later, on March 17, Kramberg and Obermeier announced a renewed cafeteria workers organizing drive, focused on the working class eateries in the garment district.[44] The nascent Needle Trades Workers Industrial Union had been prosecuting a strike against employers that recognized the ILGWU as their workers' bargaining agent since early February.[45] The Party aimed to create an insurrectionary climate through coordinated industry-wide strikes in a working class neighborhood that had long been a stronghold of their rival Socialists. On April 3, AFW members voted to authorize a strike at 125 restaurants employing 3,000 workers, located between 25th and 39th Streets and between 6th and 9th Avenues.[46] Five hundred workers walked out the next day; thirteen were arrested for picket line violence and disorderly conduct.[47] Both numbers would rise.

The union's strike demands included the eight-hour day, six-day workweek, and hiring through the union's hiring hall. They demanded a minimum wage that varied from $50 a week for cooks to $25 for "vegetable men" and $44 for bussers and dishwashers.[48] "A strike for union conditions has become a dire necessity," Sam Kramberg declared as the union's official spokesperson. "The fact that these workers have never been organized, that the open shop has been universal, that there has always been an army of unemployed always at the call of the employers anxious to work for whatever they could get until they could find jobs in other industries, have produced the worst conditions of any industry."[49] HRE's dormant Local 302 of Countermen and Cafeteria Employees saw its own opportunity to present itself as a more reasonable alternative. Cafeterias that signed closed-shop agreements with Local 302 made small improvements in wages, but, more importantly for the bosses, they could go to court to enjoin the AFW from picketing their establishments.

By April 5, the number of workers on strike had risen to 1,900, and the cops' daily haul of arrested picketers was 80, including 15 "women and girls."[50] Owners complained that AFW pickets would enter targeted cafeterias during the lunchtime rush pretending to be paying customers only to vandalize the establishment if the workers on duty didn't heed the call to walk out.[51] True or not, the NYPD called up its reserves to disperse a crowd of 2,000 demonstrators at 35th and 7th on April 11. One striker was beaten badly enough by the police to be brought to Bellevue Hospital. Twelve more, including eight women, were arrested.[52] Cafeteria owners seized upon this press narrative to go to state court, seeking a broad injunction against the AFW's pickets. The picket line violence merely added color to their pleadings. Their main argument was that the scabs were working under a collective bargaining agreement with HRE Local 302. The Amalgamated's picket lines, which beseeched all workers to refuse to work at the struck establishments, interfered with the owners' right to contract, they argued. The owners had found a sweetheart union and were using hastily negotiated contracts to lock AFW strikers out!

In public statements, the Restaurant Owners Association continually tried to hide behind the respectability of "official" Local 302, and painted the independent AFW as "floating agitators of the worst type, who are unable to make headway in the regular union ranks."[53] A press release dismissed the AFW as a "Left wing band," responsible for "gang violence" on the picket lines. It claimed, "The association has been unable to discover the slightest signs of labor difficulty among the regular union employes."[54] Throughout the legal proceedings, the owners would argue that the independent AFW were not a "legitimate" union as it lacked an AFL affiliation, leaving it with no standing in a court of law. The AFW's lawyer countered that "the union had been in existence since 1912 and that it owned a building worth $150,000."[55]

The Communist Party, which dropped its dual identity as the Workers Party, was a much more visible supporter of the strike, which its opponents pounced on as another sign of the AFW's illegitimacy. The CP endorsed the strike and joined picket lines and rallies under its own banner.[56] The AFW strikers received "revolutionary greetings" from the Soviet Catering Workers Union as the *New York Times* noted the number of strikers arrested that day.[57] The Restaurant Owners Association used *The Daily Worker*'s supportive coverage to disparage strikers in court and argued for continued and extended injunctions against union pickets.[58]

Kramberg and Obermeier were charged with contempt when picket lines continued. Kramberg gamely pleaded in the press that "it was not within the union's power to stop the picketing." The workers, he argued, were determined to strike and, anyway, the judge had not enjoined *peaceful* picketing. "We shall keep on with peaceful picketing until we have won this strike, as we are confident of doing," Kramberg insisted.[59] Police began arresting individual picketers for violating the injunction, slowly at first. One hundred and five strikers were arrested and charged with contempt on April 19.[60] Within two days, fully one-quarter of the workers out on strike had been arrested.[61] Before the end of May, 1,324 picketers were arrested out of 2,000 strike supporters.[62] Initially intended to serve as a warning, somewhere along the way, mass arrests became the order of the day, and the picket lines ceased being peaceful.

One rally turned into a "riot" that took over 100 cops to disperse. One officer was brought to Bellevue with his left thumb "nearly bitten off."[63] In another demonstration, "crowds of sympathizers" that swelled to 500 activists swarmed a police officer attempting to arrest a "woman picket who became noisy" and could only be dispersed at gunpoint after two detectives had been "bitten in the hand."[64] Adding to the violence was the return of sabotage to the union's arsenal of protest tactics. A stampede of 200 customers was provoked at one cafeteria when "workers broke capsules emitting evil-smelling liquid" during the lunchtime rush.[65] Stink bombs were a routine occurrence during the strike, with the *Times* reporting four stink bomb attacks on April 20.[66] The union expanded the strike east of 6th Avenue by having activists pose as lunchtime customers in three different cafeterias, before announcing, "This place is on strike," overturning tables and smashing plates and glasses.[67]

On May 8, New York State Supreme Court Justice Henry L. Sherman, who had issued the earlier injunction, ordered a new injunction directly against Obermeier and Kramberg that even the *New York Times* called "drastic." It prohibited strikers from congregating anywhere near the affected restaurants, talking to patrons, or distributing leaflets. A separate motion to punish the strike leaders for violating the previous injunctions was heard the next morning.[68] They were fined $250 each on May 18, with the employers vowing to return to court to apply for greater punishments, including jail sentences for their continued defiance.[69] "We will not pay the fines imposed upon us," they declared in a press statement. "Like the hundreds of strikers who have gone to jail for sentences ranging from 2 days to 6 months, we will likewise go to jail as a protest against the vicious injunction which robs the strikers of all their rights to organize and strike for shorter hours and higher wages."[70]

They were arrested on June 3 and spent five days in jail until union lawyers could secure a stay, pending appeal.[71] A criminal court judge freed dozens of strikers who were sentenced to 60-day jail terms for failing to pay $100 fines, saying the police had no authority to make arrests for violations of a civil court injunction. But by then, the strike was winding down. The *Free Voice* counted a total of 115 strikers who previously reported to the workhouse for a total sentence of 1,275 days of hard labor ("2 for 6 months, 15 for 30 days, 7 for 15 days, 16 for 10 days, and 45 for 2 days"). "No cafeteria striker can harbor any illusions about 'democracy and Justice' after seven weeks of co-operation between bosses, police, gangsters, courts and Tammany Hall," it concluded.[72]

By July, the strike was over. In its typical fashion, the *Free Voice* claimed victory.[73] And indeed, individual shops had recognized the AFW and settled with the union's shop terms throughout the strike, while others that continued to hide behind Local 302's "Union House" sign nevertheless improved wages and hours in order to hold on to their employees.[74] The AFW castigated William Lehman and Ed Flore (along with the AFL's new president William Green) as "corrupt bureaucrats [who] have once again exposed themselves before all workers as traitors."[75] Clearly, Stalin's "Third Period" was already changing the way that the Communist Party activists within the AFW related to AFL craft unions, and the TUEL cadre within the Amalgamated were preparing for what came next. Specifically, William Z. Foster was organizing a founding convention of a new Trade Union Unity League (TUUL) of new dual unions.

Michael J. Obermeier and Sam Kramberg were two of the more prominent signers of the convention call. The obvious irony is that the two men and their comrades began the decade building just such a federation, the Labor Unity League, and resisting the soon-to-be-defunct TUEL's directions to disband it and "bore from within" the AFL craft unions. Now, as the decade ended, they were being directed to rule or potentially ruin what they had managed to build up in food workers unity and trade union solidarity.

A Matter of the Past

The Communists blamed William Lehman for HRE's petty scabbing during the cafeteria strike and accused him of graft. In July, those who were "boring from within" Local 1 organized a special membership meeting that ejected him from office and suspended him from membership.[76] HRE immediately placed Local 1 under trusteeship. Lehman was reinstated, and several Communist members were expelled. At HRE's 25th General Convention in August, a floor debate erupted over the section of President Flore's report that called for expelling the union membership ban on Communists. Hugo Ernst spoke forcefully against the proposal. "I deny anyone, be it the American Federation of Labor, our own international or the courts of the country the right to punish anyone for his beliefs." Other delegates spoke against a Communist ban on civil liberties grounds and trade union organizing principles. But most delegates had no experience with the Communist Party, which, for most of its first decade, was largely confined to New York and Chicago. Those delegates had plenty of complaints about "strong arm squads," about attempts to manipulate debates and divide and secede locals.

Revealingly, however, the complaints often amounted to how difficult it was for leaders to maintain order and their own leadership positions with Communists in membership. "The only trouble in our organizations today is caused by the Communists," Abe Borson, of Local 302, complained. A delegate from Lehman's faction in Local 1 dismissed the whole matter: "I believe the report came into this organization a little too late. If it had come into the convention in 1919 I would agree with the President and the committee. The Communist Party of America is a matter of the past and not of the future." The convention declined to pass a ban on Communists in the union, allowing the matter to still have some future left to it.[77]

The same convention body belatedly removed the word "Bartenders" from its name, becoming the Hotel and Restaurant Employees and Beverage Dispensers International Alliance, and renamed *Mixer & Server*, its longtime monthly magazine, *Catering Industry Employee*. The name change may have scrubbed the suggestion of an illegal activity from the union's name. However, with its New York City locals who were bereft of membership dues and political influence and with local leaders nursing grudges and dashed ambitions and already dabbling in petty corruption, the union would soon be ensnared in a web of organized crime and an inevitable conflict with the city's independent food workers unions.

The disunity of 1929 would be intensified over the next few years, largely by and in response to the Communist Party line.

5

Political Sentimental Giddiness
1929–1934

The year 1934 was a season of strikes, and members of the Amalgamated Food Workers spent the evening of January 24 voting for a general strike, the first in New York hotels since 1918. President Roosevelt's first New Deal promised industry labor standards and a right to organize. Lucius Boomer responded by organizing a company union, the Geneva Society by another name, and began firing workers who remained loyal to the AFW, sparking a walkout at the Waldorf-Astoria. Under pressure from their rivals, the new Trotskyist leadership of the union needed to expand the strike. AFW Hotel Branch Secretary B. J. Field pounded his fists and pressed his remaining members "to decide whether you are going to back up the men in the Waldorf, prepare for future recognition of our demands and improve our living conditions, or whether we are going to back down and admit that our Union means nothing to us."

HRE Local 16 Secretary Paul Coulcher denounced the strike at a press conference. "The Amalgamated does not control a single restaurant or night club in New York City, and has no influence on Broadway," he lied. "We are not cooperating with the Amalgamated in any way." His lawyers even filed an injunction to prevent the AFW from picketing any HRE "union houses."[1]

The Food Workers Industrial Union (FWIU), formed by Michael J. Obermeier in 1931, also voted for a general strike and pressed for unity. "The rank and file waiters in the three unions have no differences," declared FWIU Local 119 Secretary William Albertson. "They want a united militant leadership for struggle to win better conditions."[2]

That there were three separate unions for hotel workers was the fault of the Communist Party, its doctrinal zigs and zags driving one group of dissidents into HRE before driving its own cadre of activists into a new union affiliated with the Trade Union Unity League. The TUUL has been maligned by many historians as a sectarian boondoggle that isolated Communists from the mainstream labor movement. "Very nearly stillborn by its second anniversary," Harvey Klehr declares, "the TUUL was a ghostly presence in most industries, where its organizers demonstrated an eerie talent for losing what strikes they did succeed in calling."[3] Other scholars have taken a fresh look. Philip S. Foner documented that the TUUL pursued a wider variety of strategies than mere "dual unionism," and Ahmed White has shown that TUUL activists who remained as salts in the steel industry were particularly reliable union organizers during drawn-out campaigns for union recognition. Victor G. Devinatz has argued that the better measure of the TUUL's legacy was in the hundreds of thousands of workers who followed its leaders out on strike at a time when few unions were striking and that by practicing "a far-sighted industrial unionism that was meant to appeal to workers not traditionally represented by labor organizations, such as agricultural, African American, women and young workers" it planted the seeds for the 1934 strike wave.[4]

What New York's hotel workers' history shows is that the competition between unions led to rising demands and increased militancy. This frustrated the employers' and federal government's attempts to enforce labor peace in 1934. Haggling over "Blue Eagle" hotel labor codes had the effect of raising workers' expectations, exasperating union competition, and encouraging the hotels to create company unions.

In the years since their 1929 split, the FWIU followed Moscow's trade union policy and focused on basic industry and lower-skilled workers—particularly women and Black people—and on forcing confrontations and strikes wherever possible. The AFW developed a healthy ecosystem of the anti-Stalinist left, as the Socialist Party and Communist breakaway groups gave advice and aid to preserve and rebuild a strong independent union in the food service industry, but rebuilding was difficult in the face of FWIU interference and massive layoffs due to The Great Depression.

Adding more noise to the New York hotel labor scene, an organized crime syndicate captured two moribund locals of the AFL's Hotel and Restaurant Employees union, which turned a sweetheart union into a protection racket that viewed the independent unions as a threat. The result was an industry-wide strike—the last one before the advent of collective bargaining. Although the 1934 strike was not a success, it would lay the groundwork for the ultimate triumph of a unified hotel workers union by the decade's end.

Trade Union Unity

Sam Kramberg and Michael J. Obermeier had already signed on to the "Call for Trade Union Unity Convention" before launching the 1929 cafeteria strike.[5] Scheduled for June 1, the convention was postponed by the Profintern to give William Z. Foster enough time to travel back and forth to Moscow for consultation.[6] The postponement freed Kramberg and Obermeier to submit to arrests for their strike-related injunction violations on June 3.[7]

They were almost certainly among the thirteen AFW members who joined 690 committed activists who attended the rescheduled founding convention of the Trade Union Unity League in October.[8] Obermeier was elected to the League's ten-member National Executive Board.[9] Workers in Chicago formed a Food Workers Industrial League—not a "union," at least not yet—on September 24 based in the city's hotels, stockyards, and meatpacking houses, with plans to expand into other midwestern cities.[10] Whether this was the TUUL biding for time until the AFW became affiliated or applying pressure on the Amalgamated to merge is also unclear, but the determination that there would be a broadly defined industrial union for food workers within the TUUL was clear.

Anticipating controversy at the upcoming AFW convention, August Burkhardt devoted generous amounts of space in every issue of the *Free Voice*, beginning in October, to "Convention Discussions" from all factions. Obermeier took the lead for the TUUL faction. In the divisive style that Communists in this period employed in debates, he attacked Burkhardt's leadership (though not by name) and the bakers locals for maintaining a "craft consciousness," and settling agreements with employers that—while not written contracts—nevertheless guaranteed employers periods of labor peace. He railed against them for making no effort to organize the thousands of workers at the city's National Biscuit Company factory and blamed leadership for the AFW's declining membership of just 6,000. "No longer is it a question of industrial unionism against craft unionism," he wrote," but of bosses' unionism against revolutionary labor unionism."[11]

Members opposed to TUUL affiliation clearly saw it as an attempted Communist Party takeover of the AFW (at a time when at most only ten percent of AFW members were affiliated with the Party).[12] Joseph Henkel of Bakers Local 3 warned of "Too Much Political Sentimental Giddiness." Clearly frustrated, he declared, "Once and for all the union shall not be used as a cat's paw." The actual resolution that the Hotel and Cafeteria Workers Branch submitted was not designed to pass on the convention floor, but instead to alienate and denounce the opposition and cleave off some of their members in the inevitable split. One "whereas" accused Local 3 of "class collaboration" and of competing with the AFL bakers "as to which can outdo the other in selling-out union standards in small shops;" another "whereas" denounced the "Muste-Lore group, which has a few generals without an army;" and the resolved section authorized the TUUL to rewrite the union's constitution.[13]

After the convention, Kramberg led efforts to disaffiliate the Hotel and Cafeteria Branch from the AFW. The now-Food and Packing House Workers

Industrial League operating out of Chicago took the lead on publishing a newspaper, *Food Worker*, and chartering new locals in the rest of the country. It wasn't until October 30, 1931, that the League met in New York City and formally created the FWIU, with Obermeier as its first National Secretary.[14] The new union was fairly centralized, with a 24-member national committee that met regularly between annual national conventions but still left room for differentiation based on the market or the sub-industry.[15] For instance, in Detroit, Sausage Distributors Local 122 was separated from United Sausage Workers Union Local 120. The Packinghouse Workers Industrial Union functioned as a national affiliate of the FWIU. There were FWIU locals in Boston, Chicago, Detroit, Los Angeles, Newark, Pittsburgh, San Francisco, St. Louis, and the Twin Cities.[16] There were thirteen separate locals in New York City—mostly matching the AFW's focus on bakers, butchers, and hotel and cafeteria workers—some with an esoteric focus, like Pretzel Bakers Local 137.

The AFW secessionists formed the two biggest locals. Cafeteria Workers became Local 110, led by Kramberg, with Harry Reich as full-time organizer. Hotel and Restaurant Workers became Local 119 with William Albertson as secretary. Local 119 operated as a minority union competing directly with the AFW for membership dues and shop floor leadership. It probably commanded the loyalty of no more than a quarter of all organized hotel workers. The secessionists walked out of the AFW with the deed to the old headquarters on 51st Street. The building, so long the pride of the Amalgamated and Exhibit A of the union's legitimacy, was sold to free up financial resources for new organizing.[17] The FWIU focused more of its attention on workers whose physicality put the "industrial" in industrial unionism. The factory workers of the National Biscuit Company were a constant organizing target.[18] And in 1932, the FWIU led a strike at the Bronx fish market, organizing workers who were the closest thing to longshoremen in food work.[19]

TUUL unions were directed to seek out women and Black workers and to be more explicitly anti-racist. One result of this orientation was a strike in the laundry department of the Commodore Hotel in March of 1933. Hotel management had cut the women's wages and sped up their working conditions so that, they complained, they were doing six days' work in four days for $5 instead of the $12 they had been earning.[20] The two-week defensive action was the first recorded strike that originated in a housekeeping department and was a win for the workers.

Wage and hour cuts were quite common. The country was already in a severe economic downturn when the AFW prosecuted its cafeteria strike in the spring of 1929. After the stock market crashed in October, it was widely recognized that global capitalism was facing its greatest economic crisis in modern times. In the United States, the Great Depression brought half of all industrial production to a halt and threw millions of workers into unemployment.[21] The FWIU, like all CP-aligned front groups, was directed to organize demonstrations of unemployed workers, including marches on the nation's capital. It might have accounted for most of the union's organizing activity in 1932.

In League

Four TUUL affiliates preceded its founding convention in 1929: the National Miners Union, National Textile Workers Union, Needle Trades Workers Industrial Union, and Auto Workers Union. The FWIU joined a Steel and Metal Workers Industrial Union, Marine Transport Workers Industrial Union, Cannery & Agricultural Workers Industrial Union, Shoe and Leather Workers Industrial Union, Tobacco Workers Industrial Union, Lumber Workers Industrial Union, and Furniture Workers Industrial Union as the TUUL's new national industrial unions. Though their names implied a great geographic reach into masses of industrial workers, their actual size was exceedingly small. The TUUL unions, collectively, never had more than 50,000 members around the country and even that was concentrated in targeted locations and industries.[22]

Under direction from the Profintern, the TUUL unions focused on workers—Black, female, immigrant, and southern—who were excluded from AFL craft unions. They focused on the mass production and extractive industries that were essential to American and global capitalism and where craft unionism had no toehold and limited appeal. Potential membership numbers possibly explain why New York's hotel and cafeteria workers were directed to break from their own independent union and merge into this doubly dual union. Still, by 1932, the FWIU only managed to amass 4,000 members, accounting for a little less than ten percent of the TUUL's nationwide membership.[23]

Whereas the TUEL mostly encouraged its activists to organize where they were, but in areas of the economy where AFL craft unions already existed, the TUUL directed cadre to relocate to areas where essential organizing targets existed and to join the rank and file in those unorganized industries. This is how New York's hotel workers gained their future leader, Jay Rubin. Born Julius Rabinovitch in Grodno, Poland, on March 14, 1904, Rubin came to the United States in 1922.[24] A member of the Jewish Labor Bund in his homeland, he joined the Communist Party's Young Workers League, learned the craft of upholstery, and became a minor official in the tiny AFL Upholsterers union.[25] Rubin exemplified "Big Bill" Haywood's critique that Foster's "boring from within" could confine able leftwing activists within craft union bureaucracy. As soon as the TUUL was created, Rubin decamped to New Jersey, where he spent a year supporting NTWU strikes in Paterson and Passaic.[26] By early 1931, he was organizing with the Food Workers and rapidly rising within the ranks.

In August 1932, Obermeier left New York to represent the U.S. at the Comintern's 12th Plenum in Moscow. He stayed for a year to study at the Lenin Institute.[27] After the purges and defections of leaders and their followers who were sympathetic to Trotsky, Bukharin, or at least critical of Stalin, Obermeier was especially valuable as a loyal adherent to the Moscow line. Not only was he a member since 1919, but he had worked to make the TUUL and the "Third Period" party line shift as successful as it could have been under the circumstances. It is not surprising that he would be elevated within Comintern leadership at this time. Jay Rubin's presence in New York helped, as Rubin assumed the duties of national secretary of the FWIU—and its de facto leader—while Obermeier took on more international duties.[28] A decade later, the trip would prove a liability for Obermeier, as he had not applied to become a naturalized citizen during all the years he lived in the U.S.

Another personnel change affected the TUUL. While campaigning for his third presidential run in 1932, William Z. Foster suffered a heart attack but continued to push himself at an incredible pace. "I had hardly ever known that I had a heart," Foster wrote in his most personal memoir, *Pages From a Worker's Life*. "I urgently needed rest, but how could I get it?"[29] Foster had also experienced an undiagnosed stroke and multiple bouts of tuberculosis, as well as several police beatings over the years (which were harder to ignore). Added to this, the stress of constantly defending his position within the Party and the reversal of his labor policy made his physical breakdown very likely a nervous breakdown as well.[30] Foster simply referred to his compound illness as a "smashup."[31] He spent a year in the Soviet Union, receiving the best medical care of his life, but he faced a long period of recuperation when he returned to the United States and was basically sidelined until 1937.[32] Jack Stachel directed the TUUL in Foster's absence. Foster's former assistant, Earl Browder, had better anticipated the changing Moscow line over dual unionism. It was Browder who first declared that the TUEL needed to be reorganized and proposed the name, Trade Union Unity League.[33] His maneuvers put him in the perfect position to become the CP's general secretary during Foster's long convalescence.[34]

All Those Who Are Loyal and Want to Stay

The AFW tried to move on quickly after the split. They tacked two extra days onto their December 1929 convention to reorganize. The Hotel, Restaurant and Cafeteria Workers Branch elected a new General Secretary and found a new headquarters just north of Union Square.[35] A few months later, the AFW had to reorganize again as the new leadership of the Hotel Branch was withholding per capita fees from the Amalgamated and scheming to affiliate with the FWIU.[36] "All those who are loyal and want to stay" were directed to the AFW's headquarters a few blocks south of Union Square to start all over again.[37] John Assel resumed leadership of the Hotel Workers Branch.[38]

The AFW loyalists relished the opportunity to finally explicitly name and blame "the destructive forces that have been at work for a long time in the Amalgamated Food Workers' Union, hindering all progress and constructive activity." Many of those who remained in the AFW were ex-CP members at this point, while others had always maintained a critical distance from the Party. "The ranks of 'Great' who 'have been' in the Communist Party are growing apace," the *Free Voice* editorialized.

The Hotel Branch eventually established a new headquarters in Times Square.[39] Although it appears that most of the shops remained loyal to the AFW, the Hotel Branch had difficulty maintaining a stable leadership. Practically every year saw the election of a new secretary. Dues-paying membership declined as well, due to widespread layoffs in the hotels. The hotel industry spent the years leading up to the stock market crash encouraging speculative investment in properties old and new. Older properties, like the grand 42nd Street hotels Belmont, Knickerbocker, and Manhattan were converted to office buildings.[40] Others were torn down only to be rebuilt to massive new heights, like the Savoy which reopened as the 29-story Savoy-Plaza, taking up the entire city block at Fifth Avenue and 58th Street. Eighty-four new hotels debuted between 1927 and 1933, expanding the industry's stock of guest rooms by a staggering 66%.[41] Most of this construction was financed through Wall Street bonds that simply could not be repaid at the depths of the Great Depression. Many hotels were in foreclosure proceedings, which pressured the employers to cut back on the cost of labor.[42]

On March 21, 1931, the AFW celebrated its tenth anniversary with a ball that maxed out the capacity of Irving Plaza. The ball offered hot food, baked goods, no booze (except possibly on the sly), a live orchestra, a souvenir journal, and a lapel pin. Ludwig Lore gave an address that was met with "great applause," and guests stayed on the dance floor until the ballroom's management insisted upon closing at 2:00 AM.[43] Even though its leaders considered their union to have been in continual existence since 1912, it had been ten years since the Journeyman Bakers merged with the hotel workers union and began using the Amalgamated name. In any event, they clearly needed an excuse to celebrate their continued survival.

With the TUUL cadre gone, the AFW gained many allies in the anti-Stalinist left. Lovestoneite Communist Opposition led the early fight against the TUUL splitters.[44] The "Muste-Lore group" that the Communists denounced was the Conference for Progressive Labor Action (CPLA). Its leader, A. J. Muste, founded Brookwood Labor College in the 1920s. It served as an opposite pole of labor radicalism within the AFL to the TUEL; a space where activists could study and critically reevaluate trade union strategies without directives from abroad. Moving from education to action, Muste and his comrades founded the CPLA one month before the TUUL convention, staking claim to the political space that the TUEL had ceded as the organized left-wing pressure bloc within the AFL unions for industrial unionism and militant action.[45]

The AFW frequently turned to Muste's group for advice and resources. An ex-Communist who found influence in the post-split AFW was James P. Cannon, who would soon (albeit, briefly) merge his forces with Muste. After Foster, Cannon was perhaps the most credible worker organizer of the CP's first decade. His focus in the 1920s had been on winning freedom for labor's political prisoners. He was expelled in 1928 for smuggling Trotsky's criticism of Stalin's Comintern program out of Russia.[46] Unlike Ludwig Lore, who was merely guilty of friendship with Trotsky, Cannon was a Trotskyist. His organizations (the Communist League of America, now; the Socialist Workers Party, later) were the American affiliates of Trotsky's attempts to create a new Fourth International. Cannon's group had spent its first years engaging in propaganda aimed at picking up as many defectors from the CP as possible. By 1933, they decided to engage in mass work in the trade unions and noticed their modest membership base in what was left of the AFW. Cannon assigned B. J. Field, a young intellectual, to work with the union. Field was a new recruit to Trotskyism, but he was fluent in French, which would give Cannon's group an "in" with the French waiters and cooks who remained natural shop floor leaders. They took an immediate liking to the "brilliant" young man and his Trotskyist comrades. When elections were held for secretary of the Hotel Branch at the end of the year, the Frenchmen nominated Field to the post.[47]

It's not surprising that the activists who remained loyal to a union with a lineal connection to the revolutionary IWW would seek advice and inspiration from a bunch of revolutionary socialists who rejected the Moscow line. But the AFW's political ecumenism extended to the social democratic left and the electoral arena. Although there were far too many anarchists in its ranks for the union to make an endorsement, the *Free Voice* wrote favorably about Norman Thomas' 1932 Socialist Party run for president.

Like the FWIU, the AFW advocated for unemployment insurance and organized jobless demonstrations.[48] The FWIU also goaded the AFW to give more of an organizing priority to factory workers.[49] Its Bakery Workers' Factory Branch staged a strike of macaroni workers at 37 plants for a few days in

December of 1931, winning shorter hours and a two cents per pound increase in the workers' piece rate.[50]

The FWIU continued to manipulate the AFW, now through proposals for "united front" activity. In one instance, Jay Rubin proposed a common program to fight back against wage cuts in the bakery industry in April of 1932. While mulling the proposal, the FWIU organized a United Front Conference where, AFW leaders complained, FWIU supporters then "tried to force their views and proposals on the others who participated." Nevertheless, a membership meeting of all AFW bakery locals held one week later voted to formalize the united front.[51] The *Free Voice* carped that Rubin's entreaty was "a left-handed admission that the tactics of the C.P. were wrong before in trying to get the workers to give up their organization." So, it concluded, "the name has been changed and the T.U.U.L. under the name of 'United Front Committee' is to repeat the old mistakes under new names." The Amalgamated could see their Communist menace coming from a mile away but were unprepared for it.

Treated as Slaves

By 1932, the problem of judicial injunctions against union organizing activity was so obvious that Congress passed the Norris–La Guardia Act. It declared federal policy to encourage the "full freedom of association, self-organization, and designation of representatives … free from the interference, restraint, or coercion of employers."[52] More practically, it outlawed "yellow dog" contracts and forbade federal courts from issuing injunctions that restrained workers' strike and picket line activity. The Republican president signed it into law in 1932. It fit Hoover's voluntarist approach to economic matters as it essentially directed an arm of the government to stay out of private affairs between workers and their employers in industrial disputes.

Hoover and the Republicans were turned out of office in a wave election that November. Although the new administration was determined to direct major functions of the economy, the federal judiciary was not. The signature labor policy of Roosevelt's "first" New Deal was the National Industrial Recovery Act. The president's main goal with the Act was to exempt companies that cooperated with its National Recovery Administration (NRA) from antitrust laws so that entire industries could collude on pricing, production, and markets.[53] Its aim was to stop the race to the bottom that was dragging the Great Depression economy further down. But the law also tried to stop the race to the bottom on wages and working conditions by adopting labor standards for each industry's "Blue Eagle" codes. Its Section 7a guaranteed the right to organize unions, although it was silent on what repercussions would occur if employers refused to recognize those unions or actively fought them.

Strong unions, like the Amalgamated Clothing Workers and the United Mine Workers, expanded their reach within their respective industries by a combination of raising workers' expectations about the new industrial order and bluffing about the importance of section 7a.[54] Weaker unions, like those in the hotel industry, were left to grapple with concentrated corporate power and collusion in a rapidly changing situation.

HRE found a bottom below their 1925 post-Prohibition nadir of 40,000 members. The international union could count no more than 24,500 members by 1933. It was so cash-strapped that it had only one full-time organizer left on staff and had to postpone its 1931 biennial convention for an entire year. Where it had collective bargaining agreements, it was caught in an endless cycle of concessionary demands and employer lockouts.[55] When the NRA began considering its hotel and restaurant codes, HRE's leadership—Edward Flore, Robert Hesketh, and Hugo Ernst—basically moved to Washington, DC. They found themselves outgunned by industry representatives. (FDR generally endorsed shorter hours and a minimum wage of up to $15 a week, the wage standard that New York's hotel workers had been fighting for since 1918!) However, "service trades" like the hospitality industries enjoyed a special exemption under the law. Hotel owners insisted upon longer hours (up to 70 a week) and lower wages (as low as $8 a week), given the "fringe" benefits of tips, free meals, and forced lodging that they insisted their employees continue to "enjoy."[56]

Unloved in its time and largely unremembered today, the NRA dithered on the question of the proper role of unions in society. This stemmed partly from its greater statutory priority to prop up capitalism by encouraging corporate collusion and partly from the patrician background and outlook of many of the Agency's board members and staffers who saw their role in class warfare as one of helping poor workers *as individuals* rather than strengthening the institutional power of unions to achieve a degree of industrial democracy. Mostly, it was hampered by employers' stubborn refusal to recognize unions as bargaining partners or even as the legitimate representatives of their employees.

The NRA's labor rulemaking was a tripartite structure of one representative each: the employers, the workers, and an "impartial" representative of the public. Roosevelt created a National Labor Board, and a structure of regional labor boards to investigate and mediate labor disputes under the NRA, but it could not compel settlements or union recognition.[57] Since employee representation was mandatory, many employers decided to represent their workers through company unions.

In the late summer of 1933, the unions in the hotel industry held a conference to try to hammer out a common program with the assistance of A. J. Muste, who was able to get representatives of HRE, AFW, and FWIU all in the same room for two days.[58] They agreed to push for a $20, 40-hour week, but they participated in the NRA code hearings separately.[59] William Albertson represented the FWIU at two days of hearings in late September, pressing for the recognition of independent shop committees of workers, the unfettered right to strike, a 40-hour week with no split shifts, and unemployment insurance for laid-off and reduced-hour workers.[60]

The first hotel industry codes were approved over labor's objections in December of 1933. Flore denounced it in the press, complaining that hospitality workers were "treated as slaves," and threatening "wave of strikes" (that he could not possibly deliver on).[61] Frances Perkins, the Secretary of Labor, set the codes aside because the proposed 10-hour day ran afoul of many states' protective laws for women workers. The NRA's central administrator Hugh Johnson and his staff intervened further to have the codes improved slightly. Women's hours were reduced to eight; men's to nine, and wages rose to $12 for a six-day workweek. Where a collective bargaining agreement provided for higher wages, it would remain in force.

The Dutchman

Another major federal policy change would impact New York's hotel workers. The 21st Amendment, repealing Prohibition, was ratified in late 1933. If some of HRE's locals were already made complicit by their members tending bars on the sly and working in speakeasies, the end of that racket made them more attractive as a target to the racket men.

"I'm coming from the Dutchman," Jules Martin announced after entering Local 1's union hall in March 1933. Martin ran the Metropolitan Cafeteria & Restaurant Owners Association for the "Dutch Schultz" gang and insisted that Benny Gottesman, Local 1's Secretary, suspend a strike he was conducting against an uptown eatery. "Jimmy Hines is behind this move," he declared, throwing down the business card of the Tammany Hall district leader. "Here's his card. Call him up. Call the police if you want to." When Gottesman protested, Martin stuck a gun hidden in his coat pocket into the union man's ribs and threatened, "Either you take that picket line off or I'll walk you out."[62] Abe Borson, leader of HRE's New York Local Joint Executive Board (LJEB), had accompanied Martin and implored Gottesman to temporarily suspend the picket line, which he reluctantly did.

"The Dutchman" was the alias of Arthur Flegenheimer, also known as "Dutch Schultz." His associates borrowed the nickname from a burlesque comedian because of what the newspapers called his "reputation for wittiness," and they thought it was particularly cold to deliver threats by introducing themselves as representing "the Dutchman."[63] The Dutchman's business was bootlegging. He was "the Beer Baron of the Bronx" until the end of Prohibition, which inspired him to expand his racket.

Around the time that Dutch Schultz was diversifying his portfolio, he would have noticed the rough-and-tumble nature of union recognition fights in the restaurant industry. The AFW's 1929 strike revived HRE's Cafeteria Workers Local 302, which swooped in to sign sweetheart union contracts with employers who resisted the radical independent union. It had 32 cafeterias under contract by October 1929.[64] In May 1930, the HRE General Executive Board rewarded Local 302's "good" organizing with a grant to the LJEB for a temporary local organizer, and assigned an HRE staffer to New York.[65] The organizers followed HRE's traditional top-down model of approaching owners and managers with a copy of the union contract and a "Union House" sign and promising a steady supply of workers and customers to any shop that signed with the union. Despite the economic depression, their reports showed a surprising uptick in activity, with regular picket lines against employers who refused union recognition.[66] Hotel Waiters and Captains Local 16 reported four new houses under contract in February 1931.[67] In April, the international organizer, John McDeavitt, reported four more union houses and one picket line for Local 16 and four of each for Local 302. He also reported that one anti-union employer swore out "John Doe" warrants for disorderly conduct to have cops arrest pickets, but the Tammany judge surprisingly threw them out and released the men.[68] His June report included more injunctions being litigated in court and more new shops (five for Local 302; two for Local 16), new dues revenue, and new business agents on payroll. More disturbingly, he reported that one of those business agents, Siegfried Frohman of Local 16, was punched in the jaw on an uptown picket

Union House Sign from HRE, circa 1930s. (Photo by Kate Ostler, from the author's personal collection.)

line by an irate proprietor and that Local 16's offices were burglarized and its correspondence and records rifled through.[69]

In retrospect, the events of 1931 were Dutch Schultz's charm offensive. He had methods to compel cafe and restaurant owners to recognize a union, sign a contract, and hire union waiters and countermen at union wages. He also presented a very real threat of violent reprisals for union leaders who didn't cooperate with him. Most importantly, he offered access to the halls of power, through Tammany Hall. In an era when judges routinely issued injunctions to shut down labor strikes and cops would violently break up picket lines, having the government on its side could remove a significant obstacle to a union's organizing success. Tammany Hall's roots went all the way back to Aaron Burr's cultivation of a mass voter base of poor and working New Yorkers to defeat Alexander Hamilton's Federalists. Over the century that followed, the Democratic machine was no stranger to corruption, but its grip on power had begun to slip. Previously dependent on ethnic Irish voters in Manhattan, the city's increasing ethnic diversity and its physical expansion across the five boroughs meant that Tammany needed new allies. Rackets offered new sources of campaign donations and access to new Jewish and Italian voters.[70]

Dutch Schultz wanted control of HRE's central body, the LJEB, to manipulate the money flowing through working-class cafeterias and delis, upscale Broadway restaurants, and possibly even hotel banquet rooms. Its secretary-treasurer, Abe Borson, was an anti-Communist who quit the AFW in 1925 to run the pure and simple Local 302. He spent two years negotiating the

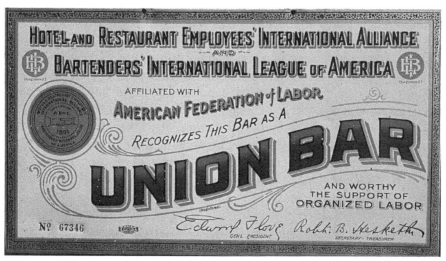

Union Bar Sign from HRE, circa 1930s. (Photo by Kate Ostler, from the author's personal collection.)

Schultz gang's shakedown demands for a cut of his new membership dues revenue while trying to run an honest union. Borson seemingly resisted a formal entanglement with the Dutch Schultz racket. Nevertheless, by the end of the year, Local 302 ordered a hundred "Union House" signs from HRE, exclaiming "Watch us grow!" and HRE staffer McDeavitt got himself reassigned to Canada.[71]

Paul Coulcher was the first to lead a couple hundred members out of the AFW—and into HRE—in disgust over the Communists' Aesopian turn against Leon Trotsky, Ludwig Lore, and various "isms" in 1925. He had drifted out of union leadership but was an enthusiastic participant in the 1931 organizing drive. Coulcher jumped on the opportunity to "make himself a power in the union by taking over and organizing the large Broadway restaurants."[72] Two friends who joined him in rotating executive duties for the tiny Local 16, Aladar Retek and Charles B. Baum, also happened to wait tables at Max Rosen's, a midtown restaurant owned by Dutch Schultz lieutenant Jules Martin.

The four men cooked up the idea to organize the bosses into an employers association. The Metropolitan Restaurant & Cafeteria Owners Association would collect a $250 initiation fee and $5 weekly membership dues from employers who submitted to the Schultz gang's strong-arm tactics and signed a union contract (and the Schultz gang would skim heavily from both the Association's and the unions' treasury). Union organizers would ask for meetings with restaurant owners, show them the master collective bargaining agreement, wage rates, and "union house" sign, and promise labor peace and a steady stream of pro-union working-class customers if they recognized the union. The Dutch Schultz gang, via the Owners Association, would bring political pressure through Tammany Hall and stink bombs and other strong-arm measures to pressure management to recognize the union. The HRE union wage scale was significantly higher than the $15 a week that the AFW had been fighting to win and maintain since 1918, and represented a 50% increase for most non-union restaurants. For a different fee—as high as $17,000—the Schultz men promised to make union picket lines and organizers go away with no contract.[73] Sometimes, these were genuine organizing campaigns in which organizers had a group of workers who wanted the protections and wage increases that come with an enforceable collective bargaining agreement. Other times, Jules Martin might approach a business where HRE lacked any organizing prospects with assurances that he could keep their business union-free.

They moved Local 16's headquarters to a larger building on W. 46th Street, near Martin's restaurant, and ran their racket behind the scenes for over a year before they felt the need to lock down their control of the union. The small regular membership must have been leery because Martin had three of his goons to supervise the December 1932 election that made Baum president,

Coulcher secretary, and Retek business agent.[74] The Schultz gang used Local 16 and the LJEB as a base to expand their reach within the HRE craft locals. Coulcher tried to convince Local 1's leaders of "the value of gangster connections" in building up a union.[75] When that failed, Jules Martin, accompanied by Abe Borson, paid his menacing visit to Benny Gottesman. Amazingly, Gottesman and Local 1 held strong for an entire year of underworld pressure tactics to join the racket. Around the same time, in March 1933, Borson introduced Local 302 leaders to Dutch Schultz emissaries. "We came to take over the union," they declared, "and if you stand in our way imagine how you will look without ears." One business agent, Irving Epstein, fled to California in a panic. A month later, on May 12, Borson telegrammed, "Temporary settlement financially," and urged Epstein to come back. "We've settled with those hoodlums for $2,500," he explained upon Epstein's return.[76] Borson agreed to pay the racket men a percentage of the new dues revenue the local gained from shops that signed legitimate union contracts after the gang's rough tactics brought them to settle.

While trying to run a legitimate union within the wider racket, the leaders of Local 302 appealed to their international union and city labor council to help keep the underworld out of the union's internal affairs. HRE President Edward Flore reportedly dismissed the seriousness of the gangsters' violent threats and told them it was a local matter and to talk to Joseph P. Ryan, the president of the New York Central Trades & Labor Council. Ryan claimed there was little he could do and advised Borson to take the matter to the District Attorney. This meeting with Ryan, who was mired in his own underworld connections through his work in the longshoremen's union, may have doomed Borson. Dutch Schultz's men descended upon Local 302's headquarters within days of the meeting, immediately threatening the lives of anyone who followed Ryan's advice: "If anyone goes to the District Attorney's office or the police station, we'll know before he walks out. He won't walk very far."[77] A few months later, seven members of Local 302 were nevertheless brave enough to testify before a Manhattan grand jury about the protection racket and their leaders' complicity in it. While the witnesses were in protective custody, police raided Local 302's headquarters on October 29, 1933, and arrested Borson, the local's president Max Pincus, and its secretary, John J. Williams, along with six other men.[78]

Next came a demonstration of the "value of gangster connections" that Paul Coulcher had extolled. Flegenheimer had been paying Tammany Hall $1,000 a week since 1932 so his Harlem bookmakers and numbers runners could operate relatively unmolested by local law enforcement.[79] As soon as Borson, Pincus, and Williams were released on bail, Martin arranged a private meeting for them at the Centre Arms hotel with Tammany leader Jimmy Hines. Hines promised the men that he would take care of them.

"Possibly we can avoid any trial at all," he said, explaining that there could be no trial until after Election Day, as the District Attorney was on the ballot. The incumbent was retiring and Tammany's candidate was William C. Dodge. "We can then get the case dismissed," he assured them, making sure to add, "You boys do the best you can to elect Dodge."[80]

A few days after the election, on the evening of November 12, 1933, Abe Borson was pulled off a picket line by men posing as detectives. He and another picket, George Johnson, were taken for a ride in a dark blue sedan to the countryside north of the city. Just before midnight, when the car slowed to navigate a tight turn, Johnson opened a door and jumped out of the moving vehicle, making a daring escape. When the abductors stopped the car to shoot at Johnson as he sprinted to the nearby woods, Borson got out and ran in the other direction. He was shot in the back and left to die.[81]

Although they interpreted the assassination as "a message from the Dutchman," the New York locals claimed that Borson's killers were hired by the owners of the Times Square cafeteria that he was picketing. HRE's leaders credulously accepted their account and hailed Borson as a martyr in the pages of *Catering Industry Employee*.[82] There may have been a good deal of truth in the story. If Borson had real—not paper—members at the cafeteria striking for a wage increase, then he might have felt that he couldn't take down the picket line just because the shop's owners paid a higher fee to the Metropolitan Restaurant & Cafeteria Owners Association for strike protection. Not only was Borson not adhering to Flegenheimer's expectations of appropriate union activity within the racket, but there was also the possibility that his arrest provided him an opportunity to cooperate with the District Attorney. Within weeks of Borson's murder, Dodge's Court of Special Sessions grand jury dropped the case for lack of evidence.[83]

This Is No Private Fight

Section 7a of the National Industrial Recovery Act and the rhetorical promises of the early New Deal had raised the expectations of masses of workers while the lack of policy follow-through and legal enforcement frustrated them, resulting in 1934's strike wave. Nearly a million and a half workers participated in over 1,800 strikes that year, including general citywide strikes in San Francisco and Minneapolis.[84]

New York's hotel workers led the way when the Waldorf-Astoria hotel fired Andre Fournigault, an AFW shop floor leader. Although this was not the same building where Oscar Tschirky hid hundreds of scabs on the roof in 1912 (as that older location was razed to make way for the new Empire State Building), Oscar still worked at the Waldorf and was still conducting captive audience meetings. On January 19, he called one to force his kitchen staff into a company union called the Federation of Hotel Guilds, which was an umbrella of the fraternal organizations, like the Geneva Society, that the Hotel Association had last tried to employ as a company union during the 1912 hotel strike.[85] Fournigault's termination four days later was meant to serve as a lesson to employees who would not comply.

The new Secretary of the AFW's Hotel and Restaurant Workers Branch, B. J. Field, had just been elected on December 9 and was untested in a union-busting fight like this.[86] The Hotel Association began pressing a company union drive in several hotels when the NRA codes were announced. The Park Central hotel similarly fired an AFW shop leader three weeks earlier, and Field urged against a hasty job action.[87] The AFW formally rejected the unity entreaties that the FWIU had been making since the NRA hearings on the day of the Waldorf action.[88] The FWIU sensed an opportunity to undermine the AFW and stake a new claim for militant leadership in the hotels. When B. J. Field could not negotiate Fournigault's reinstatement, 600 workers in the kitchen and dining room walked out at dinnertime on January 23.[89]

The AFW threatened to expand the strike to every hotel where it retained leadership. Paul Coulcher of HRE Local 16 denounced his former comrades in the AFW on behalf—or so he claimed—of all the city's AFL craft locals. "We are not cooperating with the Amalgamated in any form," he declared in a press statement in which he threatened the AFW with an injunction if it spread the strike to any shops where any HRE local had signed agreements.[90] The FWIU immediately leafleted throughout the hotels, calling for a general strike.[91] On the evening of January 24, 3,000 hotel workers met at the AFW's Times Square strike headquarters and overwhelmingly voted to expand the strike. Four hundred of them marched to Park Avenue and 49th Street and descended on the Waldorf's underground parking garage to harass high-class customers and low-class scabs.[92] The following night at Bryant Hall, 1,000 hotel workers met under the FWIU's banner and also voted for a general strike, electing a committee to negotiate a "united front" program with the AFW. The AFW rejected the outreach.[93]

As the parties prepared for industrial warfare, President Roosevelt's hand-picked chairman of the NRA's Industrial Advisory Board, fellow silver spoon Pierre DuPont, confidently predicted that the new tripartite industrial order would put an end to labor strikes. Speaking at an American Arbitration Association luncheon at the Hotel Astor (one of his family's corporate properties) he declared that if only labor and management would embrace FDR's new industrial order and "learned to settle their grievances in the proper way, and not by strikes and refusing to abide by their codes, there would cease to be these talks about hardships."[94] After the AAA and NRA men cleared out, the Hotel Association threw themselves a seven-course dinner that included six kinds of champagne and 3,000 Cape Cod oysters. Former police commissioner Edward P. Mulrooney, who served as chairman of the state's post-Prohibition Alcoholic Beverage Control Board at the time, joked that he was blushing because of the "intoxication that comes of hearing people talk about me," rather than the crate loads of bubbly. A New Jersey politico made light of the threatened strike, claiming that he had traveled to the gala with a corned beef sandwich in his pocket just in case the waiters and cooks walked out in the middle of the banquet.[95] (One hundred workers did, in fact, walk out during dinner the following night.[96])

While the AFW prepared to launch a citywide strike, HRE Local 16 filed for an injunction in state court on January 26th, and the Federation of Hotel Guilds publicly bristled against its characterization as a company union and threatened to do the same.[97] This injunction is exactly what the Norris–La Guardia Act meant to ban, but the law only applied to federal courts. The New York state legislature was still debating its own "baby Norris–La Guardia" to similarly restrict state court judges.[98] The 1934 hotel strike would be a prime example of the need for the state law that was passed in 1935.

Dining room staff at the Lincoln and New Weston jumped the gun and walked out before dinner on January 26. The following morning, B. J. Field announced a successful start to the strike at the Breevort, Breslin, Essex House, Lombardy, Sherry-Netherland, St. Moritz, and the Plaza. By the end of the day, the union counted a total of twenty-five hotels on strike.[99] Almost every hotel claimed to be fully operational in the face of the strike. The Hotel Association bragged that only 1,000 workers in total were participating and that most of their positions had been filled by scabs. "The number is hard to say," Field bluffed to the *New York Times*. "Better do your own guessing. Thirty thousand are involved."[100] Challenged on his picket numbers, Field announced the AFW would hold a mass meeting to demonstrate the size of its support. Three more hotels, the Biltmore, Greystone, and Pennsylvania, joined the strike on January 28.[101] The union began pulling out workers at freestanding restaurants to pad its numbers, claiming the strike now affected forty-one "hotels, restaurants and clubs."

At a newly struck Longchamps restaurant on Broadway, a street fight erupted as police beat two AFW pickets.[102] Field blamed the violence on FWIU "gorillas" (he possibly meant "guerillas") who began chanting "down with the government" and "down with La Guardia."[103] The FWIU convinced the workers at the New Yorker and Park Central hotels to join the ongoing strike. The Park Central workers began the strike demoralized after Field's inaction when management fired *their* shop floor leader. A week into the strike, they switched loyalties to the TUUL union.[104] The *Daily Worker* had a striker wearing an AFW picket sign shake hands with a picket wearing an FWIU sign for a photograph outside the hotel, as a bit of propaganda for the Food Workers' continued jockeying for "unity."[105]

The waiters and kitchen staff at the Algonquin Hotel joined the strike just before dinner on January 29. A group of customers calling themselves writers served the meal (or possibly didn't; the entire story might be made up).[106] These writers were not the famous ones who gathered for a daily lunch of barbed witticisms at the hotel during the 1920s. The "Algonquin Round Table" had mostly broken up by 1929, although their slow migration to Hollywood was only recognized in retrospect.[107] The writers who planted the story of their "lark" in order to get their names in the press took the liberty of including the names of people who hadn't visited the hotel in years. So, in addition to being scabs and liars, the writers who participated in the stunt were hacks who were coasting on the fame of their more successful peers. Incensed by the implication of their reputations in such tawdry scabbing, three of the original wits of the "vicious circle," Robert Benchley, Dorothy Parker, and Alexander Woollcott participated in a brief "consumers' strike" at the Waldorf-Astoria a week later. Organized by *Common Sense* editor Alfred M. Bingham, dozens of literati made dinner reservations in the hotel's Empire Room. When the orchestra took a break at 8:00 PM, they stood on their chairs and made noise about the ongoing strike. "The manager of this hotel caused the strike by repeatedly firing union men," shouted Selden Rodman. "We are leaving this hotel immediately as a protest of the outrageous conduct of the Waldorf management." At this point, hotel detectives and scabs began to beat the men involved in the action. Mrs. Parker is reported to have yelled, "This is no private fight. Let's all get in," as she joined the melee.[108]

The Waldorf was either the biggest base of union support or the highest-profile villain in the strike, as it was the scene of not just the most colorful protests but also those with the highest turnout. On January 30, an estimated 2,500 activists protested outside of the hotel during a gala celebration for President Roosevelt's 52nd birthday. It was one of many galas around the country, and FDR was not in the house. The AFW could not count more than 3,200 hotel workers as active participants in the citywide strike.[109] B. J. Field decided to cut his losses and appeal to the NRA's Regional Labor Board to help mediate a face-saving way out of the conflict. The RLB's "acting chairman," Mrs. Eleanor M. Herrick, seemingly unsure of her statutory duty, merely declared that she was "watching the situation closely."[110]

A Grievously Exploited Group

On January 31, the AFW held the mass meeting that B. J. Field had promised to demonstrate the size and scope of the strike's support. Six thousand strikers and their supporters filled the exhibition hall at the Madison Square Garden indoor arena on 49th Street. Speakers included A. J. Muste and James P. Cannon, as well as Heywood Broun of *The Nation,* and a "telegram of support" from Norman Thomas was read.[111] The FWIU held a separate rally at Bryant Hall that mustered 600 strikers before they converged on MSG.[112] They were able to lure a combined force of 4,000 workers after the rally to march through Times Square and hold mini rallies in front of 50 separate hotel properties.[113]

At the same time, Herrick agreed to engage the NRA in a fact-finding report about the cause and extent of the strike and to engage the parties in mediation.[114] Seeing the strike's failure to shut down the hotels, Field was just trying to get strikers their jobs back. The FWIU again saw an opportunity to undermine B. J. Field's leadership by criticizing his approach to the government mediators.[115] The FWIU blasted him for proposing no wage increases nor reduction of hours and for not putting the proposed settlement

Scenes from the 1934 strike. (New York Hotel and Gaming Trades Council, in possession of the union.)

in front of any committee of strikers or shop delegates before "secretly" sending it to the NRA.[116] Trotskyist leader James P. Cannon, in his *Militant* newspaper, charged the *Daily Worker* with promoting lies and published the AFW's proposed wage scale. Yet he editorialized that any form of union recognition should be prioritized over wage gains. "The fight for better conditions, higher wages and a shorter working day is inconceivable without union organization and direction," he wrote. The recognition he proposed, naturally, was that of the AFW as the exclusive representative of the hotel workers.[117]

The Communists relished the opportunity to pin any blame for "mismanagement" of the strike on "renegade" Trotskyists and blasted Field for taking Cannon's advice.[118] Cannon, meanwhile, was chafing at the fact

Scenes from the 1934 strike. (New York Hotel and Gaming Trades Council, in possession of the union.)

that his former protege had *stopped* taking his advice, which was to quit wasting his time with the NRA and to organize more militant job actions.[119] The strike became a battle to lead New York's organized hotel workers, a proxy war among the various left factions, and a direct action plebiscite on the New Deal approach to the labor question. Benjamin Gitlow, temporarily associated with Cannon's group, addressed an audience of 600 AFW members at their headquarters a few days before the Madison Square Garden rally. "I am a Communist," Gitlow declared, "but, I warn you don't affiliate with any Communist organization. This is an industrial organization, and that is a political organization." Gitlow also put a surprising—and to his FWIU rivals, a damning—amount of confidence in the unreliable NRA. "You have been recognized by the NRA as a union, and that means, if you stick, for the first time the food workers will have a strong, well-organized, recognized union."[120] Norman Thomas, who supported the AFW but saw the New Deal as a poor substitute for the Socialist Party's platform reacted to the news that Herrick would mediate the strike dubiously: "Will the N.R.A. be a straightjacket for workers or will it help get them on their feet?"[121] Thomas organized his own committee of inquiry to work publicly and in parallel with the NRA. Members of his committee included *Nation* publisher Oswald Garrison Villard, the *Jewish Daily Forward's* B. C. Vladek, ACLU attorney Morris Ernst, and others in the Socialist Party's orbit.[122]

Herrick scheduled the hearing for Monday, February 5, and asked Field to submit a list of demands and a report of the strike. The AFW report claimed that 100 hotels were affected and that 10,000 workers had participated. It also complained that the New Deal jobless program, the Civil Works Authority, was supplying the struck hotels with replacement workers. The Hotel Association claimed that as far as they were concerned the strike was over and the hotels had returned to business as usual.[123] Both sides were lying, as *the Militant* had surveyed dozens of hotel dining rooms and found that while they were all open, menus were limited if they could offer any choice at all.[124] Herrick publicly expressed sympathy for the plight of the workers: "There is no question but that hotel workers generally have been a grievously exploited group." Yet he had less use for the AFW and doubted Field's numbers.[125] "The regional board cannot be expected to pull the chestnuts out of the fire for either employers or employes [sic]," Herrick haughtily chastised Field. "This may be taken as a general statement of policy." She upbraided Field for launching the strike before taking the matter of Fournigault's termination to the labor board, scolded him to stop spreading the strike to new hotel properties, and made clear that the NRA would not compel the employers to recognize any union.[126]

The FWIU howled about the misplaced faith in the NRA that the AFW leadership and allies had employed as a strategy. "The N.R.A. will do nothing for the strike unless they are forced to act by militant mass pressure of the strikers," William Albertson declared.[127] At the same time, HRE Local 16 won the first of its injunctions against the AFW. This had the immediate effect of provoking several violent incidents at union demonstrations. At the Casino de Paree restaurant, glass bottles rained down upon the heads of picketing strikers, and, in a melee outside the Waldorf, one demonstrator bit a cop's thumb. The injunction also caused Herrick to question the legitimacy of the AFW, and she accused Field of waging the strike as a jurisdictional dispute.[128] While Field tried to comply with Herrick's hectoring that the union should run fewer and more orderly picket lines, the FWIU tried to increase both the number and the militancy of the pickets at the hotels where they were gaining leadership. Workers from Park Central marched nearly a mile from 56th Street and Seventh Avenue to 34th and Eighth—protesting struck restaurants along the way—to join their comrades at the New Yorker. Six hundred strong, they proceeded to menace the nearby Hotel Pennsylvania.[129] At one of the AFW's routine rallies outside the Waldorf-Astoria, dozens of windows were pierced by slingshot projectiles.[130]

Beyond slingshots, the Communists did occasionally focus their obnoxiousness on more deserving targets. The *Daily Worker* launched a campaign to expose and harass agencies that were providing scabs to the hotels. This included taking up B. J. Field's charge that the Civil Works Administration was steering unemployed workers to fill the strikers' vacancies.[131] (Indeed the government relief agency had tried to supply the strikers themselves to the struck hotels when they sought unemployment assistance and denied them any further federal assistance when they refused.[132]) It also included publishing the names of private employment agencies it confirmed to be supplying scabs to the struck hotels, along with their managers' names and contact info. One called the paper's city editor, Si Gerson, to beg him to stop publishing his company's name and was rewarded with a front-page story about the call.[133]

The AFW and its allies in polite society were able to similarly target and leverage hotel banquet customers. On February 6, a luncheon to celebrate the settlement of a labor code in the women's hat industry had to be relocated from the Waldorf-Astoria. The NRA's Regional Labor Board begged the AFW to suspend its picket line for a night so that First Lady Eleanor Roosevelt could attend. B. J. Field actually agreed to the request, provided Waldorf management also agreed to meet with the union for settlement negotiations. Waldorf management refused to even acknowledge that there *was* a strike and lost the event.[134] Secretary of the Interior Harold Ickes similarly had to relocate a speaking engagement from the Astor due to the ongoing strike. AFL president William Green, whose predecessor Samuel Gompers had crossed independent picket lines in 1918, had a Non-Sectarian Anti-Nazi League dinner in his honor relocated from the Roosevelt Hotel a few days later.[135] The union maintained a whitelist of hotels where there was no outstanding labor dispute and boycotters were encouraged to take their business instead. It was a short list: just the McAlpin, Ritz-Carlton, and Governor Clinton.[136] The Hotel Association threatened breach of contract lawsuits against organizations that respected the union picket lines. If such a practice were continued, the hotel bosses complained, "It would mean that if a labor organization for any cause decides to picket a hotel, even though there be no justification for a strike, such a hotel would be discriminated against by the withdrawal of patronage of official or semi-official character."[137] One semi-official character who did *not* respect the picket line was the NRA's General Counsel, Donald Richberg, who spoke at an event at the Astor. Taking neutrality to a ridiculous conclusion, Richberg stated, "I don't know the facts of this strike situation and so naturally I wouldn't want to express an opinion."[138]

With the NRA showing such indifference to their interests, the AFW asked Mayor Fiorello La Guardia to appoint an arbitrator to help settle the strike.[139] As a congressman, La Guardia tried to mediate a settlement to the last hotel industry strike in 1918. Ever a friend of labor, his greatest accomplishment in Washington was the landmark 1932 anti-injunction law that bore his name. The Republican reformer won his new office just three months earlier and only after a corruption scandal devastated the Democrats' Tammany Hall political machine. The best settlement that the NRA could work out did "not imply any recognition by the [Hotel Association] of the Amalgamated as spokesman for the hotel workers in this city," insisted Eleanor Herrick. On this point, the hotel men had been "perfectly clear."[140] The hotels refused to not only recognize the Amalgamated as the workers' exclusive representative but also to let go of their scabs to make room for the returning strikers. On February 10, the mayor threatened to let health inspectors loose on hotels that disrespected their workers' rights.[141]

After a week of RLB conferences, the Hotel Association offered to rehire any strikers who reapplied for their jobs as individuals if the strike was put to an immediate end. The Association also vaguely committed to "correcting whatever abuses in working conditions that may be established as fact" by the labor board. "It simply provides that the strike be called off without further ado," B. J. Field scoffed at the proposal. "It is ridiculous on the face of it."[142] At their nightly parade through the theater district—now down to just 300 strikers—AFW booed at the hotels and jeered the Hotel Association's obstinate position.[143]

Throughout the NRA negotiations, Field refused to meet with Cannon's Communist League, and he was communicating less and less with his own executive board and strike committee. With the FWIU gaining members and influence, Cannon worried that Trotskyists would get a bad reputation for not knowing how to run effective strikes and that his Stalinist rivals would take advantage. "We had the name of leading the strike but not the influence to shape its policy, thanks to the treachery of Field," he explained years later.

The Trotskyists put Field on trial in absentia and expelled him from the League.[144] *The Militant* began to join the *Daily Worker* in denouncing Field's strike leadership.[145]

On February 15, Field forced a vote on the best deal he was going to get from the Hotel Association and the NRA. Fifty vociferous FWIU partisans objected to ending the strike out of a membership vote of 2,000.[146] "The only thing to do," Field argued, "is to go back and get your jobs."[147] Eleanor Herrick had compelled the hotels to terminate their scabs to make room for the returning strikers. The employer group still hedged and insisted that the workers return as individuals, and even then, would only guarantee their return "so far as conditions permit."[148]

The FWIU, which had been assailing the NRA's "secret individual conferences," now decisively reclaimed leadership of the hotel workers union movement.[149] The Food Workers made sure that every group of strikers returned to their hotels with a shop committee of recognized rank-and-file leaders to ensure that no activist was discriminated against. Hotel management across the board refused to deal with union committees and declared the peace settlement broken. Hoping to scapegoat official union leadership, Herrick's lieutenant, attorney Benjamin Golden, charged that B. J. Field had "twisted to further your own ends the offer for settlement of the hotel men." But it was the FWIU that maintained picket lines, and their hard core of 250 supporters paraded through the theater district, breaking hotel windows on the evening of the 16th.[150] Herrick understood that a minority faction of hotel workers was pressing the strike, but she still held Field and the AFW accountable for living up their side to the rapidly disintegrating deal.[151] The next day, nine shop committees marched into their hotels ready and willing to work the day's shift, and all were rebuffed. Herrick washed her hands of the dispute and Field again appealed to Mayor La Guardia.[152]

Though they were manipulating the situation, the FWIU leadership was choosing an appropriate hill to die on should it come to that. Shop committees were a union standard that the workers had won and kept in effect since 1918. Eschewing collective bargaining agreements, shop committees were the minimum standard of union recognition throughout the 1920s. Surrendering them, as Field had seemingly done, would effectively roll over in the face of union-busting. The FWIU continued to lead whatever workers they could muster in picketing the next week. They called for a united front and a joint strike committee and propagandized with letters to AFW leadership announcing a plan to "beat the blacklist." At AFW membership meetings, rank-and-filers began to demand votes on FWIU proposals which Field rejected as "not on the agenda."[153]

Finally, the mayor publicly intervened, calling on both parties to abide by the NRA settlement. In a neat move, he chalked the dispute up to a "misunderstanding" about whether picket lines should be removed before or after "the strikers' committees were to have been received by the hotels."[154] Even though recognition of union committees was not a part of the NRA settlement, La Guardia was insisting on it as a part of the peace deal. B. J. Field again called off the picket lines with the expectation that the hotels would now receive the union committees (the FWIU and their followers in the AFW rank and file continued picketing).[155] The Hotel Association's response was to mail La Guardia a copy of the signed settlement agreement made before the NRA. The arrogance of management's response infuriated the intemperate mayor, who threatened to unleash the full force of city health inspectors on hotels that did not comply with his interpretation of the settlement. "If they cannot understand the spirit of cooperation in which the Mayor approaches them to settle this very vexing disturbance," La Guardia said of the hotel managers, "then they must assume full responsibility."[156]

On February 21, city health inspectors descended upon a half dozen of the largest hotels, for a "crackdown" on any violations of the sanitary code. Dinner service at the Park Central and Hotel Astor was disrupted while hundreds of scab employees lined up for a humiliating medical exam, and 70 summonses were issued for employees who lacked proper work permits from the city's health department. The "raid" on the St. Regis began at 4:00 PM and lasted 20 hours.[157] After two days the city had issued over 600 complaints.[158] The mayor played it up in the press, calling the report he received from the city's Health Commissioner "astounding, startling, shocking and revolting."[159]

Paul Coulcher, of HRE Local 16, had the gall to protest the Mayor's support of the AFW's "small minority group." In a telegram that he shared with the press, he demanded that the mayor make clear to the public that "legitimate organized labor" was not supporting the strike.[160] Two days later, his union and its racket employer association won an injunction against the AFW at the chain of four Longchamps restaurants.[161] Hotel Association representatives rushed to City Hall to smooth things over with La Guardia.[162]

Meanwhile, B. J. Field jumped at the request by the junior senator from New York, Robert F. Wagner, to travel to D.C. to brief him on employer misconduct during the strike.[163] Senator Wagner was drafting a new federal bill to introduce an enforcement mechanism for when employers refused to respect their workers' Section 7a right to organize. While Field was away, the Hotel Men made a point of visiting La Guardia at City Hall, proverbial hat in hand. Frank A. K. Boland, of the Hotel Association, and Lucius Boomer of the Waldorf, committed to complying with the NRA agreement a bit more speedily this time (particularly on the matter of rehiring strikers), but there would be no formal union recognition.[164] The press were treating La Guardia's "crackdown" as a shockingly indecorous overreach. The *New York Times* editorialized that he should have deferred to Mrs. Herrick, whom it felt was better acquainted "with all the facts."[165] Faced with the limits of his authority in the labor dispute, La Guardia "washed his hands" of it, declaring that the NRA would oversee the final details of the settlement.[166] "The strike was resolved until the Mayor butted in," Boland complained at the court hearing in which the 600 health department cases were adjourned.[167]

Finally, on February 28, Field returned to the NRA's office to meet with Hotel Association representatives and accept the same deal as had been offered two weeks prior. There would be no recognition of union committees, and strikers would get their jobs back "as conditions permit." Mrs. Herrick would appoint a five-member public committee to hear complaints from workers about the implementation.[168] True to form, Field appended to the announcement of the strike's end that "the question of wages, hours and conditions are to be arbitrated two weeks after the men are back to work." Bluffing about the scope of the five-member board's authority, he added, "We are informed that the Hotel Men's Association has agreed to these terms." Hotel Association representatives roared that they had agreed to no such thing. Ben Golden, the NRA representative, chided Field for "deliberately seeking to mislead his own membership and the public," and Field quickly walked back his claims.[169]

Amalgamated—First—Last—and Always!

The final NRA-brokered agreement with the Hotel Association was not ratified by any union's members, but the strike was over. Even the FWIU suspended picketing, and its members and their sympathetic allies in the AFW returned to work. The *Daily Worker* blasted Field, Cannon, and Gitlow for "betraying" the workers during the course of the failed strike.[170] In its own post-mortem on the strike, the *Free Voice* acknowledged that Field's "sudden and unjustified declaration" that the strike was over had damaged the union's cause.[171] The strike was formally voted to an end at a March 19 membership meeting, where Field was dismissed and new elections were scheduled.[172] On April 6, the Hotel and Restaurant Workers Branch elected Sal Gentile as its new secretary.[173] An old-timer in the union, he had been censured in the 1930 aftermath of the split for whatever role he played as he had remained close to Sam Kramberg and Michael J. Obermeier.[174] Gentile's election was celebrated in the pages of *Food Worker* as a signal that the AFW was ready to work more closely with the FWIU.[175]

Three weeks later, members of the two unions met at Irving Plaza and made plans "to bring final merger in the food industry."[176] In the May issue of *Food Worker*, the union issued a statement proposing a merger for the members of the FWIU, AFW, and other independent unions "into one mighty mass Union of food workers throughout the United States." It laid out a specific plan for a joint planning committee, composed of an equal number of FWIU and AFW representatives. The committee would negotiate with the various locals, draft a new constitution, and investigate the actual dues-paying membership numbers of the two unions to determine a fair allotment for a unity convention. The statement pointedly announced that the FWIU was against affiliating with the AFL.[177]

Although the Amalgamated's Hotel and Restaurant Branch as well as its key Bakers Local 1 supported this plan, there were still hard feelings that the merger—like the 1929 split that preceded it—was being directed by Comintern politics.[178] As locals negotiated the merger, an unsigned editorial in the June 1934 issue of the *Free Voice* complained about a process that had bypassed the AFW's executive board and was announced as a *fait accompli* in the Communist press. "The Amalgamated will not refuse to negotiate," it insisted. "As in the past there will be organizations," it still warned, "because they insist on domination at all costs, [which] will inject fraternal discord into the struggle of the workers for better conditions."[179]

The sentiment that the AFW had to merge with another union was widely shared, but members were torn between the FWIU and finally making peace with the AFL unions. The AFW's new general secretary, John Wawrika, who replaced the ailing August Burkhardt in July, hailed from Bakers Local 1, which was on record as supporting unity.[180] Wawrika insisted that the FWIU merge back into the AFW, declaring in his first editorial, "Amalgamated— First—Last—and Always!"[181] In a remarkable debate between the *Free Voice* and *Food Worker*, Jay Rubin accused Wawrika of walking back the commitments he had previously made and of surrendering to the more conservative bakers element in the AFW, which, to forestall the possibility of being forced into a Communist-led union began "reaffiliation" negotiations with the AFL's Bakery & Confectionery Workers International Union, the very union that they had seceded from 21 years earlier.[182] Wawrika shot back a defense of the bakers' organizing record and accused Rubin of reneging on a commitment to disaffiliate from the TUUL.[183]

In October, Jay Rubin declared, "We are sincere in our efforts to merge all independent unions into one Union," and proposed—suddenly—that that union be the AFL's Hotel & Restaurant Employees.[184] While this ploy to hold on to the bakers might have seemed an inexplicable about-face and a violation of the Comintern's Third Period line, it was in line with an evolving Party line. In fact, while the published correspondence debate between Wawrika and Rubin was going on, Rubin was in Moscow on a Party assignment as "technical campaign manager."[185] The Seventh World Congress of the Comintern would, in 1935, call for a Popular Front of unions and political parties (Communist and non-Communist) against the rising global threat of fascism.[186] This accelerated a process that was happening organically in the U.S. labor movement. Throughout the NRA era, and particularly during 1934, TUUL affiliates were engaged by necessity in united front work with AFL and other independent unions in organizing around industry codes, and the 1934 strike wave revived many AFL unions. Many TUUL unions dissolved themselves so that Communist activists could return to boring from within the AFL. By December, the Comintern and the CP Central Committee called on the remaining TUUL affiliates to join their AFL counterparts under any conditions.[187] The conditions for New York's hotel and restaurant industry were terrible. The HRE locals were controlled by racketeers. Part of the calculation must have been that, between them, the AFW and FWIU had the membership numbers to drive the racketeers out of HRE if it came to that. In any event, the TUUL's demise removed the most vexing issue that was preventing actual unity. Sal Gentile brought the membership of the AFW's Hotel & Restaurant Branch into the FWIU in January 1935.[188] This wasn't so much a merger as an abandonment of the AFW, which suspended the branch for failure to pay dues and quietly dropped its name from the union directory.[189]

The Amalgamated Food Workers, which began life fourteen years earlier as a merger of the independent bakers with the hotel and restaurant workers, was now dissolving along similar lines and winding their way back into the AFL. The rump of the AFW rapidly concluded re-affiliation negotiations with the AFL's Bakery & Confectionery Workers International Union, winning the ability to come in as industrial locals. Local 3 voted to join the B&C in January of 1935, and by March, the rest of the locals had either re-affiliated or merged to add 3,000 members to the AFL's ranks.[190] The AFW held its last General Executive Board meeting on March 26, 1935, mostly to deal with matters of dues stamps and transfer cards for their re-affiliation with the B&C union. They resolved to print one last issue of the *Free Voice* in April. That issue celebrated the union's decades of struggle, eulogized departed comrades, and looked forward to a brighter future. John Wawrika closed the issue out, writing: "With the spirit that lies in the words 'Workers of the World, Unite!' once more we look forward—united—to a better, a brighter future, for sunshine and happiness for the working class."[191]

New York's hotel workers, long divided by competing organizations and still longer skeptical about the merits of the AFL's "official" Hotel Employees union, were changed by the experience of the 1934 strike. They saw the limits of organizing the culinary crafts alone and of dividing their efforts across organizational lines. Through the trial by fire, trusted leaders emerged at the top, and the hard work of coalition building held out the promise of unity of purpose. The employers learned as well that federal and local political authorities would not tolerate obstinate anti-unionism much longer. The experience of negotiating competing union claims made the prospect of dealing with just one responsible union more attractive. HRE leaders watching from afar surely saw the potential gains to be won if only they could make an accommodation with New York's radical hotel worker leaders.

6

An Industry Has Been Freed
1934–1938

Over 700 celebrants representing 20 AFL unions filled Irving Plaza to salute Jay Rubin on October 13, 1936. The Food Workers Industrial Union was busily liquidating itself, and its general secretary was now a member of HRE Local 302 and secretary of a "National Unity Committee of Food Unions" successfully leading an organizing drive in the city's cafeteria chains. HRE Locals 16 and 302 as well as the International Brotherhood of Electrical Workers Local 3 were enthusiastic participants in the "united front" effort, looking forward to a new state labor law to push for collective bargaining in the hotel industry.

"I am glad to see that this is truly a banquet for the American Federation of Labor," toasted Local 16 leader Paul Coulcher. "The sooner we have unity in the ranks of the food workers, so much sooner will their miserable conditions be improved." Even he, a committed anti-Communist under a cloud of suspicion for gangster connections, was compelled to embrace this moment of unity.

The occasion for the celebration was Rubin's brief respite from union work to recuperate from an unspecified "health" condition.[1] A likelier explanation is that Rubin was returning to Moscow for counsel before he officially became leader of a significant fraction of the AFL.[2]

In *Reds or Rackets?* Howard Kimeldorf explored why dockworkers in the same craft wound up with radical leadership on the West Coast and corruption in the East.[3] In the case of New York's HRE locals, the choice between Reds and rackets was more explicit, both before the start of the criminal conspiracy and when Thomas E. Dewey prosecuted Coulcher and the gang.

As Mary M. Stolberg explained in *Fighting Organized Crime*, Dewey's goal as special prosecutor was to connect the rackets to Tammany Hall. In pioneering racketeering litigation, he allowed the actual violent gangsters to escape justice while some leaders of Locals 16 and 302—more victims than perpetrators—were caught in Dewey's wide net to prove guilt by association. Since his political goal was to win higher office, he strived in public statements to praise and contrast the leadership of the FWIU unionists then negotiating a merger.

The Dewey trial, the messy 1934 strike, a new pro-union mayor, and state labor law all contributed to the FWIU being welcomed, albeit warily, into HRE. The "united front" strategy that the FWIU pursued in 1933–1934 evolved into the "Popular Front" that would see the CP enjoy great success and mainstream acceptance as part of the Congress of Industrial Organizations' alliance with New Deal Democrats. Although HRE embraced industrial unionism in these years, it did not join the breakaway CIO. New York's hotel workers became a rare instance of a Communist-led union in the more conservative AFL.

Finally, in a turn of events that would have been unthinkable at the start of the decade, by 1938 the unified union would have a neutrality agreement with the Hotel Association and a framework for organizing New York's hotels into one big union.

A Determined Campaign

Ed Flore was beaming as he addressed HRE's 27th international convention in August 1934, assembled in Minneapolis weeks after the celebrated citywide general strike. "I may be optimistic," he declared, "but I expect to report at the next convention that we have the largest membership in our history."[4] The NRA codes had been good for HRE. As uneven as the bargaining power was when the codes were initially set, the fact that HRE could claim to represent hotel and restaurant workers fighting to win lower hours and higher wages gave workers across the country reasons to join. Membership stood at 50,000, nearly double its 1932 nadir. As toothless as the Section 7a "right to organize" was, it was still enough to inspire workers to challenge the bosses. Under Hugo Ernst's leadership, San Francisco locals joined the general strike that started on the docks, shutting down nearly 2,000 restaurants, intentionally leaving just 19 cafeterias open for working-class business. In Los Angeles, seven HRE craft unions copied San Francisco's Local Joint Executive Board model and launched an amalgamated industry-wide organizing campaign. The previous convention had declared HRE for the industrial model of organizing, either in one big local or as an amalgamated joint board. Los Angeles was putting it into practice.

With high hopes, HRE encouraged "spring membership drives," by giving locals a tax holiday on per capita fees if they increased membership by 25 percent.[5] Optimism was surely tempered by the embarrassing state of

HRE'S New York locals, which were either craft exclusionist or dominated by gangsters. The problem wasn't confined to New York. In Chicago, which had already seen one local president shot dead in a 1922 gang war, the remnants of Al Capone's syndicate dominated Bartenders Local 278.[6] The underworld sought more power in the international union. Paul Coulcher attempted to run fellow racketeer John J. Williams for vice president against incumbent William Lehman at the 1934 convention. He was thwarted by Flore's quick parliamentary maneuvering. Chicago's George B. McLane, however, couldn't be beaten. He joined HRE's General Executive Board (GEB) as a vice president.[7]

Despite that alarming development, the convention approved a resolution sponsored by Local 1 calling on the GEB "to initiate a determined campaign to eradicate every sign of racketeering, corruption and gangsterism" throughout the union.[8] The GEB saw plenty of signs during its pre-convention meetings. Coulcher demanded time on the agenda to argue that Local 16 should "include all workers coming under the jurisdiction of this International Union" in Manhattan, the Bronx, Staten Island, and Long Island. He vehemently denied charges that he supplied scabs in the hotel strike earlier that year and that his union was "controlled by racketeers in any way, shape or manner," an "unwarranted" rumor he blamed on the Communists.

The GEB rejected what they suspected was a Dutch Schultz grab for more turf. At the same time, a desperate delegation from Local 302 appealed for the international union to bifurcate the local into an "A" branch, composed of delicatessen workers (whose shops mostly fell outside the bounds of the racket), and a "B" branch of cafeteria workers (which was controlled by the racketeers).[9] Board members expressed befuddlement about why the matter was before them—the internal structure of 302 was entirely a local matter—and kicked the issue to President Flore, who coached the local's leaders through a gentle disentanglement.

Local 302's secretary-treasurer embraced the idea for Branch "A." Max Pincus had been implicated in the 1933 dragnet that also ensnared Abe Borson. Like Borson, Pincus seemed a reluctant participant in the racket. A Socialist, he'd bounced between HRE's old Hotel Waiters Local 5 and a smaller independent waiters union in the Jewish Lower East Side that eventually merged with Local 1. He and Sam Kramberg knew each other and could frankly discuss conditions in the industry and in each other's unions.[10] The idea of creating a new auxiliary within Local 302 coincided with Jay Rubin's merger entreaties. Rubin proposed a joint organizing drive with Local 16, Local 302, and locals of the Teamsters and the Bakery & Confectionary unions.[11] The targeted cafeterias were affiliated with the United Restaurant Owners Association (not to be confused with the Dutch

Schultz's Metropolitan Restaurant & Cafeteria Owners Association), which had a sweeping injunction against the FWIU. The practical purpose of the "united front" was to allow FWIU organizers to conduct legal picket lines under AFL banners, to which Pincus readily agreed.

The union coalition launched an industry-wide strike on October 18, 1934. Although the Depression economy meant that the cafeterias could easily find scabs, the participation of the other AFL unions—the Teamsters, in particular—meant that they lacked fresh meat, vegetables, and bread. After about ten days, the Owners cut a quick deal on behalf of multiple cafeterias with an HRE vice president who was serving as acting president while Flore was overseas on union business. John J. Kearny shook hands on the deal, which offered modest wage gains, and ordered the locals to withdraw the picket lines.[12] Local 302 had already rejected its terms during an NRA conference in August, frustrating both Elinore Herrick and Mayor La Guardia.[13]

The strike continued as FWIU leadership agitated for higher raises. Kearny, "quick to wrath," suspended Local 302, pending a reorganization under new officers when Pincus sided with the FWIU.[14] Flore returned to New York to face an angry delegation. Rubin passionately argued that a better deal was possible. Pincus threatened court action to get his charter restored. William Lehman threatened to turn his own charter in and take Local 1 independent if Local 302 was not restored.[15]

Flore ruled that Kearny exceeded his authority and restored Local 302 and its officers to good standing.[16] He promised to do what he could to rescind Kearny's tentative agreement with the bosses and tacitly approved of Rubin leading the "united front" negotiations. Shortly thereafter, the strike ended with a major breakthrough. Chains employing nearly 1,200 workers across 20 stores, including the Tip Toe Inn and Sherman cafeterias, signed a closed-shop agreement formally recognizing the unions, establishing a grievance procedure, and raising wages by a dollar across the board—all improvements over Kearny's deal.[17] Rubin, along with Coulcher for Local 16 and Williams for 302, signed the contract on behalf of the FWIU. Under the jurisdictional agreement laid out at the onset of the campaign, the FWIU gained 900 members while the AFL locals split 290.[18]

HRE was gaining members regardless of its conduct during the joint organizing drive. Early in 1935, Local 302 agreed to Sam Kramberg's proposal to form a joint organizing committee with FWIU Local 110. While they negotiated a potential recognition agreement with the Silvers chain and made fast organizing progress at three more chains, the two locals also began merger negotiations.[19] Local 16 refused to enter into any discussions with the FWIU's hotel workers Local 119. Jay Rubin decided to go over their heads and propose a national merger agreement to HRE President Ed Flore.

In Good Faith

Flore surely received Rubin's merger proposal in March 1935 with great interest. The FWIU, now with 14,000 members mostly centered in New York and Chicago, could rout the racketeers and improve HRE's organizing potential.[20] Flore responded, "We are approaching these negotiations with an open mind, hopeful of their success."[21] Slow to launch the racketeering investigation that the Minneapolis convention ordered, he now faced the choice of Reds or rackets.

Communist strategy was in transition. In July 1935, the Comintern's Seventh Congress would launch the Popular Front policy that directed them to ally with liberal and social democratic political parties and trade unions in opposition to the global fascist threat.[22] Just as the 1929 cafeteria strike had anticipated a coming change in Comintern policy towards "Third Period" sectarianism, so too did the FWIU's "united front" organizing presage the new Party line. The structure of the NRA's labor codes forced AFL and independent unions to coordinate bargaining demands and allowed the tiny TUUL unions to exercise an outsized influence in strike policy. The fact that so many AFL unions went on strike in 1934 convinced Communists that the AFL could, after all, be a vehicle for organizing masses of workers.

Flore similarly began 1935 in an evolution of thought. His long-standing position was that members of any dual union should join HRE as individuals. A few months earlier, HRE chartered a new local that already had 500 members. Flore assigned Miguel Garriga, a new Spanish-speaking HRE international staffer, to organize cooks through various culinary associations like the Geneva Society and Vatel Club—exactly the strategy behind Albert Martel's ill-fated 1925 effort. The difference in 1935 was that the ongoing Depression made the societies want to cooperate to stabilize wages, and Garriga had already pulled off a similar feat in Chicago.[23] Flore initially directed Garriga to keep his efforts secret for fear that the Communists would enter or disrupt Cooks Local 89. Then, he assigned Garriga, along with Lehman and a vice president from upstate New York named Emmanuel Koveleski, to explore a potential merger. The FWIU merger committee—consisting of Rubin, Obermeier, Kramberg, and Albertson—met with the HRE team in April.

The two sides had a lot of history with each other—not all of it good. Lehman, long-time secretary-treasurer of Local 1 had a solidaristic relationship with Kramberg and Obermeier for much of the 1920s. Local 1 respected AFW picket lines, and the independent union, in turn, stayed out of Local 1's "union house" jurisdictions. But during the Party's Third Period, the Communists turned on Lehman. The *Daily Worker* hurled accusations of "graft" and "racketeering" against Lehman, and Communist entryists disrupted Local 1 and briefly ousted him from office before they were banned.[24] The hostility inspired Flore to press for an anti-Communist constitutional amendment at the union's 1929 convention. Vice Presidents Kovaleski and Kearny supported him, while Hugo Ernst led the successful floor fight against a membership ban, possibly to leave open the possibility of an eventual merger with the independent unionists in New York.[25]

Rubin and Garriga, who lacked that baggage, likely helped the parties keep their focus on the future. Finding the independent unionists serious about joining and growing the AFL, the HRE reps invited Rubin to meet the GEB in Cleveland on May 15. On that day, Coulcher, with Pincus and Local 16 Labor Chief Harry Koenig in tow, vociferously opposed the merger after previously feigning support. Flore was blindsided and the best he could manage out of the meeting was a commitment to continue studying the matter.[26]

Twelve days later, the "right to organize" that had so improved HRE's fortunes came to a sudden end when the Supreme Court overturned the National Industrial Recovery Act. The federal system of labor boards shut down immediately. The legislation that Sen. Robert Wagner was drafting to strengthen that right to organize quickly became the FDR administration's new approach to labor law. Wagner's bill would codify a number of "unfair labor practices" that employers routinely committed, like running a company union and discriminating against union activists, and would create a new agency to adjudicate worker complaints. This National Labor Relations Board could also certify the existence of a legitimate union and direct an employer to bargain with it "in good faith," with the refusal to do so itself being a violation of the Act. Conscious of a conservative Supreme Court majority that was inclined to overturn any New Deal legislation that interfered with private property and business interests, Wagner explicitly pegged his bill's constitutionality to Congress' authority to regulate interstate commerce. Roosevelt signed the National Labor Relations Act into law on July 5, 1935.

AFL unions took the opportunity to put hundreds of organizers into the field. Nine AFL leaders, led by John L. Lewis, formed a Committee for Industrial Organization (CIO) in November 1935 to act as an organized bloc within the Federation to fight for industrial unionism in the steel, auto, and rubber industries. For a frustrating year, craft union conservatives refused to budge on the jurisdictional question and accused the CIO leaders of "dual unionism." All the while, the NLRB certified industrial bargaining units and directed employers to deal with CIO affiliates on behalf of all workers regardless of craft. After the Supreme Court ruled the Wagner Act constitutional in April 1937, the CIO leaders became convinced of the necessity of a decisive split in order to fully endorse and work on behalf of President Roosevelt's reelection, and they reconstituted the CIO as the Congress of Industrial Organizations, a rival federation. HRE did not join.

Although the NLRA did not apply to hotels and restaurants at first, HRE leaders were hopeful that states might create "baby" Wagner Acts for workers under their jurisdiction, as many had with the Norris–La Guardia anti-injunction law. The strong possibility of a pro-union labor law would factor in every action taken by unions, employers, and public figures in New York's hotel industry over the next two years.

The Most Critical Times

The GEB report that Flore commissioned as a backstop against Coulcher's formal opposition to the merger gave him enough of what he needed. It favored unity but insisted that FWIU members enter the union as individuals. It left the decision to accept them up to the locals.[27] Coulcher balked at welcoming his ex-comrades into Local 16 while Pincus was already negotiating with Kramberg.

On September 10, 1935, a coalition of twenty-five AFL unions held a rally to kick off the organizing drive they declared would finally bring collective bargaining "on an industrial 'united front' basis" to the hotels. Two thousand workers attended. The ambitious project, dubbed the "United Amusement, Hotel and Restaurant Unions," included crafts as diverse as electricians and operating engineers, the musicians union, and several of the HRE craft locals, including—whether Coulcher liked it or not—Local 16. FWIU organizers worked with Garriga on turnout and recruitment, in the hope that an influx of new members would force Coulcher's hand on the merger question. The rally's speakers reflected the emerging Popular Front coalition. George Meany, president of the NYS Federation of Labor, spoke, as did city labor council president John P. Ryan, who delivered remarks for an absent Mayor La Guardia, and AFL President William Green addressed the crowd via telephone. Sen. Robert Wagner spoke about his federal law and the need for more reforms. Rep. Vito Marcantonio, who held La Guardia's old seat in Congress, gave a "fiery speech" denouncing the Supreme Court and calling for a total rewrite of the U.S. Constitution.[28]

On November 27, 1935, HRE Local 302 and FWIU Local 110 approved the merger at a joint membership meeting. Pincus remained the local's president, while Kramberg became secretary-treasurer.[29] Prior to the merger, in September, Harry Reich reported over 500 new members organized in the joint campaign. Some members came from independent cafeterias that voluntarily recognized the union, sometimes after a brief strike. Others were joining from chain systems like Horn & Hardart and Childs in anticipation of union elections.[30] These workers were transferred to Miguel Garriga's Cooks Local 89. Across the river in Newark, FWIU Local 133 merged into HRE Local 410, with the local FWIU leader David Herman becoming secretary-treasurer (within a year HRE hired him as an organizer).[31]

Under rank-and-file pressure, HRE Local 16 finally merged with FWIU Local 119 in December 1935. *Food Worker*, which was serving as both a campaign newsletter and as a scold against "ex-members of our union who deserted our union in the most critical times" such as the unnamed Paul Coulcher, who "are now taking the lead in the fight against unification and the establishment of one union," ceased publication.[32] Taking a victory lap, the paper serialized Michael J. Obermeier's history of the independent hotel workers unions from 1912 to 1936, but it had not yet run the final installment when publication suddenly ended in January 1936.[33] The union had more future than past.

Such Nonsense

Meanwhile, Dutch Schultz's future was all used up. In the spring of 1935, a "runaway grand jury" seized headlines by exceeding its charge to independently issue subpoenas targeting alleged racketeers and their connections to Tammany Hall. The "Fusion" coalition of liberal Republicans and reform Democrats who elected La Guardia mayor used this to embarrass District Attorney William C. Dodge and Governor Herbert Lehman, both "regular" Democrats who needed some distance from the machine, and pressured them to appoint a special prosecutor. They selected Thomas E. Dewey, a federal prosecutor with experience investigating organized crime, and gave him wide leeway to hire his own investigators and attorneys.[34]

As an assistant district attorney with a budget that dwarfed Dodge's and the power to empanel "extraordinary sessions" grand juries, Dewey's top priority was Arthur "Dutch Schultz" Flegenheimer. In the U.S. Attorney's Office, Dewey twice prosecuted Flegenheimer on tax evasion charges similar to the ones that put Al Capone in jail. One ended in a mistrial; the second in acquittal. Dewey was pursuing state charges when Flegenheimer was murdered in an orgy of violence that wiped out the leadership of his gang in October 1935. Deprived of the opportunity to nail J. Edgar Hoover's "Public Enemy Number One," Dewey instead elevated Charles "Lucky" Luciano as a threat to public welfare.[35]

Dewey spent the months of Luciano's trial leaking details to the press about his other investigations, and Flore could not ignore evidence that Coulcher and Pincus were implicated. He asked Emmanuel Koveleski to make some "discreet inquiries" of his old friend. No sooner than he had written, Pincus showed up in Koveleski's Rochester office. "Jealousy, nothing else," Pincus complained of the allegations. "You can be sure of one thing: there is nothing in my life now or in the past that I am ashamed of, and I don't like to have letters written to me about such nonsense." The trip to Rochester was easily a six-hour drive from the Bronx, leaving his friend and union brother deeply skeptical of Pincus' professed innocence.[36]

Rochester was also the planned location for HRE's 28th international convention in August 1936. Convening at a location that same six-hour drive from where Dewey was investigating its NYC locals wasn't ideal, but they had chosen it two years earlier as a courtesy to Koveleski. The convention celebrated Flore's "silver jubilee" as president and the union's new membership milestone of 82,000.[37] Resolutions reflected the populism of the times and the new influx of progressives. It banned all membership restrictions based on race or national origin. It pledged money to fight Franco's fascists in Spain. One of the largest affiliates of the AFL, it passed a resolution drafted by David Herman condemning efforts to expel the CIO unions that still belonged to what remained for the moment the one true "house of labor." Flore reported a union treasury overflowing with funds (nearly $200,000!) ready to be spent on new organizing campaigns.[38]

Officer elections were held on the convention's fourth day. George B. McLane was reelected Seventh vice president, without opposition. Leaders from Locals 16 and 302 had been touting Max Pincus in the months leading up to the convention and nominated him to run against William Lehman for Second vice president. On the strength of Local 302's growth, and his purported ability to foster unity, Pincus beat Lehman by a margin of two to one.[39] The convention adjourned for dinner and was scheduled to return for an evening session after delegates went out on the town.

Harry Koenig, Local 16's labor chief and Coulcher's lieutenant on the labor side of the cafe racket, dined with a handful of delegates and their spouses—none of whom knew their host very well. Upon exiting the restaurant, they were greeted by a hail of bullets from a drive-by shooting, which struck two of the other delegates and a passerby while mortally wounding Koenig. Flore interrupted the evening session's proceedings to break the disquieting news that three delegates had been shot. He adjourned the convention for the night with a plea for those who were able to report to the hospital to donate blood.[40]

The violent incident was sensationalized in the press. Dewey's investigators rushed to the scene, hinting that Koenig had been cooperating in their probe.[41] The event cast a pall over the convention. What should have been a shining moment of one of the largest and most progressive industrial unions in the AFL was marred by the election and reelection of two vice presidents with suspected ties to organized crime and a local union leader murdered by gangsters. To clean up the union, the honest trade unionists in HRE would need help from outsiders, not just the leftwing activists who were busily expanding the union's ranks.

A Liberal and Sympathetic Attitude

The HRE unionists celebrated Jay Rubin at Irving Plaza on October 13, 1936, looking forward to unity and new organizing drives. Exactly one week later, on October 20, the locals in the LJEB planned to hold a dinner in Max Pincus' honor to celebrate his elevation to international vice president, but Thomas Dewey secured a secret indictment for 14 alleged members of the cafeteria union racket that day. Pincus, Coulcher, and others spent the night in the Tombs instead.[42] While the identities of many of the conspirators were obvious, who was truly running the racket and responsible for the violence of maintaining the conspiracy was not. Dewey, as would become his modus operandi, faked it until he could make it. He blamed the initial organization of the racket on four dead men. Arthur Flegenheimer was murdered and what remained of his known lieutenants were similarly wiped out the previous October.[43] Jules Martin, who had been Flegenheimer's main contact with the unions (and his violent enforcer), was found in a ditch in upstate New York in March 1935.[44] Abe Borson, the LJEB president who tried to maintain an independent union within the wider conspiracy, was "taken for a ride" in 1933.[45] Lastly, there was Harry Koenig, who was whacked at the Rochester convention. Dewey claimed the racket was taken over by four unnamed individuals. Nine men were arrested following the indictment.[46] Paul Coulcher and Max Pincus were the most prominent union officials named. Four others—Charles B. Baum, Irving Epstein, Aladar Retek, and John J. Williams—held a variety of staff positions in the locals and alternated in officer and delegate positions in the LJEB. Three more men, including two attorneys from the Metropolitan Cafeteria & Restaurant Owners Association, were included in the dragnet: Abraham Cohen, Phillip Grossel, and Harry A. Vogelstein.

Dewey held the press rapt as he announced new names and warrants in an expanding probe of (unrelated) labor rackets in the garment and bakery industries. It was a combination of vamping for time, baffling his audience with bullshit, and genuinely following leads. A day after the first arrests in the cafeteria case, extradition warrants were issued for the Schultz gang's bag man, Louis Beitcher, and its reputed new kingpin, Sam Krantz, both of whom had fled the state before the NYPD could catch them.[47] The next day, at a bail hearing, Dewey implied that the indicted conspirators had ordered all of the murders.[48] Coulcher and Cohen were pinned as the ringleaders. Four men remained fugitives, including the actual gangsters who were likely the violent enforcers if not the true ringleaders.[49] Sam Krantz was never captured. His "No. 2 man," Louis Beitcher, was arrested in Connecticut and extradited on December 11.[50]

With his waning power, Paul Coulcher made sure that Local 16 responded to the charges with a press release announcing a unanimous executive board vote "to stand solidly behind" him on October 26.[51] Four days later, a regular membership meeting got out of their control. The new members voted to suspend the entire executive board. David Siegal, a long-time dissident in the local, was elected president and Obermeier became secretary with Miguel Garriga supervising on HRE's behalf. The members empaneled their own nine-man grand jury to investigate any member implicated in the Dewey racket case on violations of union principles.[52] Local 302 took similar measures, except that Max Pincus voluntarily stepped down. William Mesevich, an old-time AFW member and early joiner of Local 302 who resisted the lure of the Schultz racket, was elected president and Sam Kramberg became secretary.

Pincus continued to attend union meetings. Colleagues observed that he was "increasingly despondent" and nervous as the January trial loomed. They last saw him at a general union meeting on December 28 that stretched past midnight with all the activities and reports of the organizing drive that Kramberg was successfully prosecuting. Pincus returned to his Bronx apartment and spent a few hours smoking and pacing nervously before joining his wife in bed. Sometime after 7:00 a.m., he arose from bed without waking her. He sat outside a fifth-floor windowsill for several moments, his bare feet dangling over the street below, before he jumped to his death.[53]

The nine remaining defendants went on trial on January 18, 1937.[54] On the first day of jury selection, Dewey arranged for Louis Beitcher, the only actual gangster in the case, to dramatically plead guilty after agreeing to testify against the union and restaurant men in exchange for a lighter sentence.[55] Beitcher was poised to get a slap on the wrist by pinning the blame entirely on the trade unionists whose real responsibility for the racket—particularly for its violent enforcement—remains unclear to this day while gang boss Sam Krantz remained at liberty. Louis B. Waldman, an attorney for one of the defendants and a prominent Socialist, argued that the conspiracy prosecution was an attempt to undermine organized labor at a time when workers in the hospitality industry were demanding and winning better conditions. The defense placed the blame on the restaurant industry, which was notorious for long hours and low pay and, said Waldman, "small side rackets by which the overworked and impoverished waiter was still further imposed upon." It was the restaurant owners, defense attorneys pointed out, that had welcomed the bootleggers into their operations during Prohibition, leaving the unions subject to prey when the criminals needed a new racket.

Dewey delineated who was responsible for the racket on a four-foot-by-five-foot chart laying out the names, responsibilities, and roles of the members of the racket—the kind of chart that has since become a staple of courtrooms and television detective shows—with the name of the deceased (but still notorious) Arthur "Dutch Schultz" Flegenheimer at the top. According to Dewey's team, there were three distinct teams in the racket operation. The first was the strong-arm crew, which was responsible for the violence as well as stink bombs and vandalism committed against restaurant owners and union activists who refused to cooperate. This, according to prosecutors, was Flegenheimer and Martin until their deaths, then Krantz and Beitcher—none of whom were on trial. The second team was the union men "who called strikes and made outrageous demands on owners." Owners were allegedly compelled to pay anywhere from $2,000 to $17,000 to make the labor dispute go away, depending on whether there would be a signed collective bargaining agreement or any wage gains for the workers in the shop. Five of the defendants, led by Coulcher, were accused of running the union part of the racket. The third team was the bogus owners association, which charged a $250 initiation fee and $5 weekly tribute to the restaurants it shook down for "labor peace." Two lawyers and the nominal head of the association were charged for this part of the conspiracy.[56]

Benny Gottesman, the Local 1 officer who resisted gang orders even as Jules Martin pointed a gun at him, emerged as the hero. Gottesman's testimony also provided Dewey with his political reform goal of connecting the racketeers to Tammany Hall. Gottesman testified that Jules Martin bragged about how the gang advanced Paul Coulcher's career through its connections to Tammany's boss.[57]

On the stand, Beitcher implicated most of the defendants. He claimed that he initially met Martin and Krantz at the Tammany Hall clubhouse when Pincus recommended him for the $60-a-week job as the racket's money collector and that Coulcher vied for leadership of the gang after Martin's murder. The "solidly built man with curly hair and a non-committal face" claimed that he was nowhere near the actual decision-making and engaged in no acts of violence, going about the job of collecting shake-down money with an apologetic air: "I'm sorry, but you gotta come across with $5,000." "You're a contemptible liar," shouted Aladar Retek, briefly interrupting Beitcher, "I can't stand this lying." Beitcher's testimony could only add $100,000 to the $400,000 Dewey could account for—far short of the $2 million his team had sensationally charged in the indictment.[58] Before the prosecution rested, it asked the judge to dismiss twenty of the original forty-nine counts.[59]

Seeing where this was going, Waldman managed to get his only client, Charles B. Baum, severed from the trial. As Baum was the only union officer that Beitcher could not connect to the racket, Dewey agreed to end his ordeal with a mistrial due to his advanced age and "illness." Waldman and Baum exited the court to a "chorus of objections" from the remainder of the defendants.[60]

The union men's defense portrayed them as victims of a violent takeover, whose pleas for help were dismissed by union leaders. On the stand, Irving Epstein described Jules Martin's offer that he couldn't refuse: "If you stand in our way, imagine how you will look without ears."[61] The new President of Local 302, William Mesevich, defended Epstein, telling of an April 1933 executive board meeting that broke into bouts of weeping at the realization that the gang would wreck the union if it couldn't take it over. He described a futile trip to Buffalo that Pincus, Borson, Epstein, and he had made to appeal to Edward Flore for help: "Mr. Flore told us our problem was a local matter and he thought we were men enough to take care of our own troubles." Flore's advice led to them reporting the gangsters to the district attorney. Epstein noted that the trip to Buffalo was soon followed by Borson's murder.[62]

Dewey's team protested that Borson's murder had nothing to do with the case, lest the defendants garner sympathy from the jury as gang victims. They claimed that Borson was murdered months before the Times Square Cafe that he was picketing paid its protection money and that three men unconnected to Dutch Schultz were currently sitting in Sing Sing for the crime. The curious fact of the matter is that a disturbed young man from a wealthy Boston family, Charles E. Folsom Jr., confessed one year after the murder, telling a fantastical story of a botched interrogation he organized as an unsolicited audition for the Burns Detective Agency. Folsom got 20 years, while two other men involved in the abduction and slaying received much lighter sentences. As convenient as the convictions were to both Dutch Schultz and Thomas Dewey, even if true, it still painted a picture of an industry in which unionists had reason to fear for their lives.[63]

It took the jury four hours to convict the seven extant defendants on every remaining count of extortion, attempted extortion, and conspiracy. As the foreman repeated the word "guilty" 182 times, the convicted men began to break down. "I'm not guilty," John J. Williams shouted at the judge. "I want to go back to the Tombs." Aladar Retek protested, "I'm not a gunman, not a murderer." Dewey boasted to the press that he considered the convictions a present for his 35th birthday, which fell the day before, and further, "An industry has been freed from the extortions and domination of these criminals masquerading as labor leaders, association officials and lawyers."[64] They were sentenced on April 7. Paul Coulcher got fifteen to twenty years; Irving Epstein, ten to fifteen; Aladar Retek and John J. Williams each received terms of seven and a half to fifteen years. Abraham Cohen and Philip Grossel of the Metropolitan Restaurant Association each got ten to fifteen years, and "Dutch Schultz' policy lawyer," Harry Vogelstein, got five to ten. "In no sense were you victims," the judge scolded the convicts for attempting to wrap themselves "in the mantle of labor" at a time when the state's laws were "adopting a liberal and sympathetic attitude toward organized labor."[65]

Dewey would prosecute Hines by the end of the year, but his cockiness and prosecutorial sloppiness made him suffer one mistrial before finally convicting the disgraced machine boss in 1939. Coulcher, Retek, and Williams cooperated with Dewey's investigation, finally coming clean about how money passed between Flegenheimer, the owners association, lawyers, and Tammany politicians. Prosecutors kept Coulcher in a different jailhouse from the rest of the men, who feared and loathed him and reported that it was he who paid off Harry Koenig's killers at Flegenheimer's request.[66]

Dewey, on his way to the Governor's Mansion, won the office of district attorney in November, on La Guardia's reelection ticket. Both Republicans enjoyed multiple union endorsements—AFL and CIO—and the crucial cross-endorsement of the American Labor Party. On the eve of the election, Dewey continued to trot out Benny Gottesman as an example of the kind of honest trade union leader his investigations had freed from racketeering. He called the ALP endorsement one of the "happiest moments" of his life, after "false friends of labor" had charged him with anti-unionism during the racketeering trials. And he took as much credit as he could for Local 16's near-tripling of its membership from 6,500 at the time of the March convictions of Coulcher and his associates to 15,000 dues-paying members on the first Tuesday in November.[67] Unmentioned was the new leadership that the HRE union had gained even before the convictions. William Albertson, on behalf of Local 16, announced to the press on April 16 that Coulcher, Retek, and Baum had been impeached and expelled by a membership vote and that the union was now clean.[68] In a telling indication of what honest trade unionists thought was the actual misconduct of the union men trapped in the racket, they also suspended a business agent named Leo Stenzler for permitting strikes to be declared and settled without input from the workers or any attempt to improve working conditions.[69] Meanwhile, Jay Rubin and Miguel Garriga spent these months working out and driving an elaborate organizing plan.[70]

There Is No Quarrel

As anticipated, the New York state legislature passed a "little Wagner act" for workplaces left out of the NLRB's definition of interstate commerce on May 14, 1937. The Doyle-Neustein law replicated all the vague unfair labor practices, union certification procedures, and bargaining obligations that were the federal law's main features.[71] Gov. Lehman appointed to the three-person State Labor Relations Board a Catholic priest, John P. Boland; a former state conservation commissioner, John D. Moore; and a lawyer who had worked for the NRA's labor board, Paul M. Herzog.[72]

Now that there was a process to compel hotel and restaurant employers to bargain collectively, there needed to be a structure for Hotel and Restaurant Employees. There were eleven HRE locals in the New York LJEB (not counting Brooklyn and Queens). There were three waiter and waitress locals, two bartender locals, a bartender *and* restaurant employee local, a delicatessen counterman *and* cafeteria worker local, a cooks local, a railroad dining car employee local, and a soda dispenser union. With high hopes for a coordinated organizing drive in the hospitality industry, they adopted the San Francisco model of putting much of the decision-making power in the LJEB that brought them together as an amalgamated form of industrial unionism.

They held a kick-off rally for the organizing drive at the Palm Garden, a two-story dance hall in midtown, on April 1, 1937. Over 1,000 workers turned out to hear Al Grubb, president of Detroit's HRE Local 207, speak about his union's recent sit-down strikes. Obermeier laid out a plan of organization and Garriga pledged the international union's full support for a determined drive.[73] In June, Garriga and Rubin presented the ambitious organizing plan they'd drafted to the HRE GEB on behalf of the LJEB. It called for organizing not only all hotel workers from wall to wall, but also the culinary workers in the large cafeteria chains, the Broadway restaurants, and the private dining clubs and to restore bartenders' union density to pre-Prohibition levels. In all, they estimated 100,000 potential members.[74]

To fund the campaign, they asked the GEB for a $25,000 match to the money the locals would raise through a 25-cent monthly per capita assessment. The Board readily agreed to the funding formula, which would pay for up to fifty full-time organizers. The hiring and other financial expenditures would be run through a Hotel, Restaurant and Cafeteria Employees' Organizing Committee of which Garriga would be executive director and Rubin, general director. Decision-making was rounded out by a board of directors, each with a specific charge: Obermeier for hotels, LJEB President Al Kronen for bartenders, Sal Gentile and Harry Reich for restaurants, and Arthur Bary for cafeterias.[75]

A rotating cadre of part-time organizers from all the locals filled many of the staff lines. The full-time staff hired by the Organizing Committee were almost exclusively members of the Communist Party. Charles Martin, a veteran of the independent unions, first worked at the McAlpin in 1922 and continued to work as a cook for hotels and private dining clubs in the years that followed. In 1934, he brought the workers of the Downtown Athletic Club out in the industry-wide strike and lost his job when the picket lines were suspended.[76] Antonio Lopez was a 28-year-old chef who was born in Puerto Rico.[77] As a Spanish-speaking organizer from a rapidly growing demographic in hotel employment, Lopez was an essential addition to the team. Black workers were also largely employed in "back of the house" jobs. Charles A. Collins, a community activist in Harlem, was hired to focus on this group. Recommended by upper Party leadership, the 31-year-old native of the British West Indies and City College graduate with good connections to the *Amsterdam News* conducted as much of his organizing in the Black neighborhoods of upper Manhattan as he did in the hotels.[78]

The largest demographic that would require special attention was women. Waitresses were briefly employed in hotel banquet halls during the 1918 strike, but women workers abounded in the back of the house. Women staffed the laundry, housekeeping, spa and pool, and front desk departments. They also performed other clerical duties and worked as telephone operators and hat check girls. Ironically, for a union movement that saw its first two industry-wide strikes led by prominent woman organizers—Rose Pastor Stokes in 1912 and Elizabeth Gurley Flynn in 1913—the succession of independent unions that formed in their wake were almost entirely led by men and maintained a membership base in the traditionally male occupations in the dining rooms and kitchens. Hiring skilled, experienced women organizers was key. As Jenny Carson has documented in *A Matter of Moral Justice*, Helen Blanchard was an organizer for the Women's Trade Union League. Earlier in 1937, Blanchard successfully aided the mostly Black workers in the subcontracted industrial laundries to win a collective bargaining framework and union recognition with the Amalgamated Clothing Workers. Some hotels shopped out their laundry; others ran massive facilities in the bowels of their towers. These Black women, who did not have as long a history of union struggle as the workers in the dining rooms and kitchens, would be essential to organizing wall-to-wall in the hotels.[79] Gertrude Lane was a 28-year-old graduate of Hunter College. Born Gertrude Levine, she became active in a revolutionary street theater group while in school. In 1932, she joined the TUUL's Office Workers Union. Adopting the Party name Lane, she stood out as an effective builder of shop organizing committees at Macy's and Gimbel's and was elected by the union's board to be a full-time organizer, where she led a sit-down strike at Klein's department store.[80] She would prove to be one of the union's most talented and dedicated organizers.

Two other young Communists were hired for their energetic commitment and loyalty to the Party. Don Tillman was a 25-year-old alum of Columbia University.[81] Martin Cody, 26, was a native-born New Yorker who served in the military prior to the stock market crash and likely got involved through the Party's organizing among the unemployed.[82] Other young Communists took jobs as elevator operators, bellhops, housemen, and doormen in order to salt the front service and back of the house departments that were not traditional bases of union support in the hotels.

Organizers made heavy use of literature. An "Organization Drive Committee of 100" published a one-sheet newsletter called (in a nod to 1918) *The Hotel Worker*. "We will organize along industrial lines," it promised. "There is no quarrel between two kinds of unions. Ours are the only unions in the field. We can be an example of a unified solidified union." It blasted "bloodsucker" employment agencies and issued an initial set of demands on the hotel industry: a "general wage increase for everybody in the hotel" with a standard minimum wage, an eight-hour day with no split shifts, an end to making employees pay for their uniforms and laundry, "good food" in the employees' cafeterias, no firing "without reason," no fines, fingerprinting, or intimidation, and finally, recognition of the union as the collective bargaining agent. On the back page was a tear-off "pledge card" to join the organizing drive.[83]

The Organizing Committee's main flyer for all the crafts in the citywide drive promised independence, explicitly linking the 1937 organizing drive with 1776 and 1861, when "American labor rallied around the victorious banner of Lincoln, threw off the yoke of slavery, and declared all men free and equal." In the cafeteria drive, where the union was conducting representation elections through the SLRB at individual shops, flyers emphasized the protections of the law: the SLRB vote was a secret ballot, no one could legally be fired for voting for the union, and employer intimidation was illegal. Flyers addressed to hotel employees agitated around rising prices of food and stagnating wages. One flyer directed to hotel bartenders and "bar boys" printed a minimum wage and other demands for 8-hour days, vacations and paid legal holidays, reading like a promise or guarantee. Flyers also responded to boss campaign talking points. At the New Yorker and Pennsylvania hotels, flyers warned of attempts "being made to hinder your own organization campaign for higher wages and better conditions." Each listed hotels in other cities owned or managed by their chain system that had successfully organized and won better pay (Detroit's Book Cadillac and Chicago's Congress—among others—in the case of the New Yorker; Statler hotels in five cities in the case of the Pennsylvania). A postcard to employees at the Roosevelt explained that its Welfare Association, which offered low-interest loans and discounts on food and medical services, could not perform as a union to raise pay and win job security. One of the most verbose pamphlets took five pages to rebut a captive audience meeting that Lucius Boomer staged at the Waldorf-Astoria, in which he claimed that the union was misleading workers by claiming to speak for them before an SLRB certification election was conducted and portrayed the union as outside agitators. "The workers decide," the pamphlet replied, "the union, in cooperation with them, carries out action."[84]

The union printed calling cards—the kind of polite society nicety that a visitor might leave with a hotel guest in lieu of a formal visit—listing the names and telephone numbers of the organizers assigned for each hotel. They also widely distributed stickers, each calling out a different craft of workers—countermen, waitresses, bartenders, and maids—all highlighting the union campaign office at 711 8th Avenue as "The Place To Be." At the campaign office, there were nightly meetings; sometimes for workers at a specific hotel, other times so that workers of a specific craft could meet with their peers from across the city to discuss their specific issues and propose bargaining demands. The office was staffed throughout the day as well so that workers who heeded a sticker or a card could join the union and be recruited to further tasks like getting co-workers to join or attend a meeting. By summer, the union was developing a representational structure with organized departments within hotels electing delegates to the citywide Organizing Committee, where decisions about bargaining demands were debated and voted on.

The Organizing Committee's first real test of the SLRB was at the massive Childs Restaurant chain, which had refused to recognize Local 302 at any of its 52 locations for at least three years. The union won a union certification election 2,181 to 493.[85] After a strike authorization vote, the chain settled with the union three weeks later. Workers won their long-sought $15 a week, plus three free meals a day, no more out-of-pocket expenses for uniforms, and one week of paid vacation a year.[86] Shortly thereafter, the union won voluntary recognition at 97 cafeterias organized under a legitimate employers association. The "blanket agreement" they negotiated brought another 4,000 members into Local 302 which could now boast a dues-paying membership of 10,000.[87] The notable exception to the cafeteria workers' forward march was the Horn & Hardart automat chain, which hired a detective agency, conducted coercive captive audience meetings, and flooded the SLRB voter list with hundreds of newly hired part-time workers, causing Local 302 to lose its representation election despite having a majority of Horn & Hardart employees in membership.[88] A five-month-long strike ended without union recognition.[89]

Signing the first contract with the Childs Restaurant chain. From left: George D. Stromeyer, Thomas E. Dewey, Jay Rubin, Miguel Garriga. (New York Hotel and Gaming Trades Council. Located in Hotel Employees and Restaurant Employees International Union, Local 6 Photographs PHOTOS.098, Box 2, Folder 12; Tamiment Library and Robert F. Wagner Labor Archive, New York University.)

In preparation for the long-awaited hotel drive, the Organizing Committee's Hotel Division cemented an alliance with the International Brotherhood of Electrical Workers Local 3 and Locals 94 and 94A of the International Union of Operating Engineers. This was a slimmed-down, more practical version of the "United Amusement, Hotel and Restaurant Unions" that was announced to great fanfare two years earlier. These maintenance locals literally kept the lights on and the water hot in the hotels. Their participation in any strike called by the kitchen and dining room staff would more effectively shut a hotel down. Harry Van Arsdale Jr., Business Manager of Local 3, was the most enthusiastic of the craft union leaders to support the hotel effort. Under his leadership, the electricians' union already represented a mix of industrial bargaining units in addition to its traditional base in the skilled trades. Although he had a reputation as a labor movement conservative, Van Arsdale was open-minded enough to join an American trade union delegation to the Soviet Union, touring factories and construction sites and joining Joseph Stalin on the reviewing stand for that year's May Day parade.[90]

By autumn, the Organizing Committee was conducting mass general membership meetings at the Manhattan Opera House, a 3,100-seat capacity theater on West 34th Street. They would hold one meeting at 2:30 PM, before the night shift, and another at 9:00 PM for day shift workers, so that members could hear progress reports and vote on issue demands. Thomas Dewey was touted as a guest speaker at a round of meetings on October 14.[91] Four days later, on October 18, 1937, the members voted to approve union representatives reaching out to the Hotel Association to begin negotiations over union recognition. The management group agreed to meet three days later.[92]

Members Only

As soon as HRE joined forces with the maintenance crafts, a new craft union tried to carve out a racket in the city's hotels. The Building Service Employees International Union, an AFL union representing building janitors, elevator operators, and doormen, saw the apparent inevitability of collective bargaining in hotels as an opportunity to expand its jurisdiction.

Its president, an ex-con and a "fixer" on the edges of legitimate labor relations named George Scalise, got his first job in the union in 1932, thanks in part to connections to Arthur Flegenheimer and the Chicago mob. Through a familiar mix of semi-legitimate employer associations, strong-arm tactics, and kickback schemes, Scalise and his allies built up a substantial operation in an alphabet soup of BSEIU locals numbered 32 in New York. On the strength of his membership gains, he was appointed by the union's executive board to fill the vacant BSEIU presidency in 1937.[93]

James J. Bambrick assumed control of BSEIU's New York Joint Board. Another dubious character, he helped nearly 14,000 residential apartment building janitors and doormen gain union representation in Local 32-B.[94] In February 1936, while the HRE unions were busy with mergers and legal defense, Bambrick threatened a strike of elevator operators, on behalf of Local 32-C, at 210 hotels.[95] In October of 1937, with the SLRB gearing up its machinery to certify unions and order collective bargaining, and with HRE organizers all over the city, Bambrick swooped in and signed a "members only" collective bargaining agreement with the St. George Hotel. The beneficiary, Local 32-A, claimed jurisdiction of "bell boys and swimming pool attendants" among others. The deal called for a 48-hour workweek with time-and-a-half for overtime pay, seniority, arbitration of grievances, a no-strike clause, and some other "improved working conditions." The employer defended the quick deal it had cut with a union that few if any of the affected employees had ever interacted with by claiming it was exactly what U.S. Steel had done with the Steel Workers Organizing Committee when the NLRA was declared constitutional.[96] The key difference was that U.S. Steel settled with the only union that had organizers in the field, to avoid a repeat of bruising fights like the 1919 steel strike, with the understanding that the Steelworkers would then focus on organizing its smaller competitors to take the wage and hour gains out of competition. The St. George, on the other hand, was interjecting a new sweetheart union into the hotel industry after the workers had finally unified and driven out the crooks.

Around this time, Scalise sent a professional killer from Chicago to menace Bambrick if he wouldn't find a way to pay tribute from the local unions' treasury. Bambrick embezzled $10,000 from Local 32-B and sent it to Scalise, who found a way to kick back $2,500 to Bambrick, embroiling him in the racket.[97] None of this was publicly known at the time, but Rubin and Obermeier would have known that BSEIU was connected to the underworld gangsters they had just helped flush out of the HRE as they were contemplating working out a jurisdictional agreement with Local 32-A.

Ed Flore wanted to fight for HRE's jurisdiction as BSEIU locals in Chicago and Seattle had also recently organized hotels. AFL President William Green's initial ruling that gave BSEIU the right to organize "those employed in apartment houses and apartment hotels particularly where no restaurant employee, cook or waiter is employed," Flore felt, gave BSEIU far too much leeway. "If it is a declaration of war, let us have it and we will see who knows the hotel business best, a hotel worker or a building service man!"[98] HRE insisted the AFL Executive Council issue a definitive ruling. In September 1937, the Council unanimously ruled in HRE's favor. BSEIU had no jurisdiction in hotels, regardless of whether there was food and beverage service. HRE had the exclusive right to represent all hotel workers.[99]

If Local 32-A did not comply with the AFL's jurisdictional lines (and they did not seem so inclined), the punishment could eventually be BSEIU getting kicked out of the AFL. But enforcing jurisdiction could be a very long process, and independence would remove any kind of labor movement accountability for Local 32-A's officers. The prospect of ongoing jurisdictional raiding threatened the labor peace that the hotel union coalition could offer for the terms of recognition by the Hotel Association. On October 15, Rubin, Obermeier, Reich, and Garriga weighed their options and decided to seek a deal with Local 32-A. Over Garriga's objections, they asked the NY State Federation of Labor to call a conference between the locals to mediate and for William Green to again convene the international unions.[100]

A 100% Union City

The conference between Hotel Association representatives and Jay Rubin's craft union coalition was held on October 21, 1937. At the time, the Association had 160 member hotels, employing about 75,000 workers.[101] The hotel managers were noncommittal but agreed to look at a draft agreement. The unions engaged their members seriously, with department committees and surveys. On November 23, they wrote up a proposed contract calling for the union shop, seniority, a 40-hour week with time and a half for overtime, paid vacations, and a wage scale. They sent it off to the Hotel Association's bargaining committee, which spent the rest of the year mulling union recognition.[102]

There are a few reasons why the Hotel Association would consider voluntarily recognizing a collective bargaining agent after refusing to agree to any form of union recognition to end the industry-wide strike three years prior. First, this wasn't the old Hotel Men's Association that fought the union in earlier decades. The name change was not a nod to gender equality; it was an acknowledgement that the Association was no longer dominated by the egos and interests of individual owners and managers. The 1920s building boom and depressed economic conditions of the 1930s forced many of the hotels into foreclosure, where they were purchased by banks. The Bowery Savings Bank alone owned four hotels and the Emigrant National Savings Bank had three. Other institutional investors like life insurance companies and even an endowed retirement home for sailors on Staten Island called Snug Harbor bought these hotels in a fire sale.[103] They wanted a reliable long-term return on their investments—no more, no less.

The hotel industry had been rocked by citywide strikes in 1912 and 1913, and again in 1918. The 1934 strike was financially damaging enough that it probably pushed several marginal hotel corporations into foreclosure. With no labor peace, union leaders could and would launch more strikes and the

Hotel Association knew it. Besides that, the 1934 strike season evolved into a wave of sit-down strikes. Nearly 400,000 workers went on strike in 1937, many of them sit-down strikes.[104] The hotel industry was no exception. In Detroit, the sit-down strikes that began in the auto industry spread to the Statler Hotel and others, also resulting in union recognition agreements. Cleveland hotels came within 16 hours of a citywide strike in May before giving in and recognizing HRE.[105]

Another factor was the newly reelected mayor. La Guardia spent his first term using the powers of his office to drag recalcitrant employers into bargaining and mediation. Increasingly since his first failed attempt with the hotel industry, these efforts were ending with union recognition and signed collective bargaining agreements. It was an essential part of the mayor's self-identity and his promise to voters. "I am criticized by cheap politicians," he boasted, "because they say I favor labor. I do."[106] The previous June, on the eve of his reelection campaign, the mayor pledged to do everything within his power to make New York "a 100 per cent union city."[107] This pledge did not extend to his own employees in the city's workforce, but La Guardia used his platform to advance the cause of union recognition in the private sector. There was also the city's $26.7 million investment in the coming World's Fair, which promised to bring millions of tourists to New York and revive the economic fortunes of the city's tourism and hospitality industries.[108] New York's hotel workers unions had a proud tradition of launching strikes during New Year's Eve celebrations and Thanksgiving luncheons. Did anyone doubt that they would disrupt the World's Fair if there wasn't a union recognition agreement in place?

La Guardia inserted City Council President Newbold Morris as a mediator into the negotiations, along with the SLRB's Father Boland. A majority of Hotel Association managers were convinced, as many bosses in hypercompetitive industries had been before them, that if they had to deal with a union, they preferred to deal with just one union and just one uniform set of wage rates and work rules, seeing an opportunity to bring order out of chaos and to stop competing in a race to the bottom over wages and working conditions that drove their workers into periodic episodes of insurrection. However, there was dissension in the ranks. As many as 18 hotels had either recognized BSEIU Local 32-A, had a 32-A bargaining unit certified by the SLRB, or were considering signing an agreement modeled on the St. George contract. And some hotels, particularly the older boutique hotels that remained privately owned, fretted that they wouldn't be able to afford a uniform wage scale that large hotels could while some egotistical hotel men bristled at the thought of sharing power with their workers.[109] Lucius Boomer, a one-time head of the Hotel Association, resigned in protest over the decision to meet with the unions.[110]

The Hotel Association's Labor Committee retained an attorney, David Drechsler, who represented employers in the men's garment industry for many years under the terms of peace that had been worked out with the ACW two decades prior. They intended to copy its system of impartial arbitration and industry-wide labor standards. On the union side, Jay Rubin was convincing his union partners to embrace another decades-old labor representation formula, that of William Z. Foster's multi-union councils of the stockyards and steel organizing drives.[111] The parties received reassurances from Boland that the SLRB would certify Rubin's labor council as the sole bargaining representative for eligible employees at any hotel where the council could establish majority support.

As the Hotel Association was preparing to come to an agreement with the unions, HRE had one more bit of organizational restructuring. Even with the racketeers gone, Local 16 was saddled with Paul Coulcher's bad debts and investments. Its Executive Board remained riven by arguments over who resisted—and who abetted—the racketeers during the Dutch Schultz years, and there was a sizable faction who distrusted or despised the Communists.[112] When the local union elections delivered a split decision for an Albertson/Obermeier slate, Rubin and Obermeier appealed to Ed Flore for a fresh start. On February 4, 1938, HRE chartered a local with jurisdiction over all hotel and club workers in New York City, with the exception of mechanical and maintenance trades.[113] As a demonstration of how important the new local was to HRE, it was assigned the lowest local number available and became Hotel & Club Employees Union, Local 6. Miguel Garriga became its president, while Michael J. Obermeier assumed the office of secretary-treasurer.

Four weeks later, on March 23, 1938, the unions met with the Hotel Association and signed a framework for union recognition. Essentially a neutrality agreement, it committed the Hotel Association to negotiate an industry-wide collective bargaining agreement on behalf of any affiliated hotel whose labor council the SLRB certified as the exclusive bargaining agent. They called the document they signed the "Status Quo Agreement."[114]

7

Status Quo
1938–1939

Martin Cody, an organizer for Local 6, crossed the street from Penn Station and into the lobby of the Governor Clinton on March 20, 1939. Dinner was being served, guests were checking in, and a fashion show was underway upstairs. Cody was distributing stacks of flyers to the hotel staff; that was their signal. Workers at the 1,200-room hotel voted for union representation via a card check election eight months prior, and the Hotel Association signed the Industry Wide Agreement (IWA) in January. That obligated the Governor Clinton to also sign, but management at the hotel, which was in financial receivership, claimed they were unable to enter into any contractual agreement regarding wages without bond holder's approval.

The workers began distributing Cody's flyers, which apologized for the inconvenience of the surprise work stoppage, calling it a "last resort" that was "necessary to protect our legal right to enjoy collective bargaining" and blamed management's "continued stubborn refusal" to sign the contract. The elevator operators parked the eight guest elevators on random floors and then sat down. One small group of uniformed hotel workers began a picket line outside the property while another group distributed the flyers in the bar and grill to patrons who sat before half-served dinners and empty glasses and in the lobby to 300 guests who were stranded with their luggage. The remainder of the night crew of bellhops, doormen, waiters, waitresses, and cooks descended to the locker rooms in the basement and waited for news about whether they were returning to work that night. After a half hour, police removed the elevator operators to the picket lines outside the hotel, and by the end of the night, the bosses managed to get at least three of the elevator cars operating with white collar workers.[1] Management and the union spent the next day arguing about who was responsible to get back to the bargaining table and about the effectiveness of the strike, which would last a year and a half and end with a return to "Status Quo."

It was a long road to the Governor Clinton picket lines. First, the union had to negotiate a real collective bargaining agreement *and* be certified as the collective bargaining agent for workers in as many of the hundreds of hotels affiliated with the Hotel Association as possible.

Sectoral bargaining is rare in the U.S. There are not many histories that delve into the painstaking work of creating, expanding, and enforcing a multi-employer, industry-wide collective bargaining agreement. Many treat examples as if they came together all at once. Actually, a large number of hotels opposed the framework and seceded from the Association. Many more refused to ratify the agreement despite union certifications and bargaining orders and had to be dragged to the table by job actions and boycotts. The Governor Clinton, a particularly egregious example, would not sign the IWA until 1950.

Nevertheless, for something called "Status Quo," the March 23, 1938 agreement kick-started a revolution in New York's hotel industry. It neutralized the Hotel Association as a would-be union-buster. It brought the state in as an actively pro-collective bargaining mediator. It enabled the union to score immediate wins for workers while it was asking them to join and vote for it. Within a year, it would lead to substantial pay raises, begin a stable system of union recognition and dispute resolution, and make the hotel workers unions some of the fastest growing in New York and within the AFL.

Union organizers had to adapt to the conciliatory framework of the IWA, to the limits of labor law enforcement, and to uneven union support across corporate properties and hotel departments. Still, by the end of 1939, they would permanently surpass every previous effort to organize hotel workers, achieving a stable dues-paying membership base of 25,000 with the protections of a union contract.

Any Grievances That May Arise

"A step characterized as assuring peace in the hotel industry of the city was taken yesterday," *The New York Times* cover story reported.[2] "Status Quo" was not a collective bargaining agreement. It was a shared statement of principles of what collective bargaining would look like in the hotel industry. There were three of them.

First, there would be one contract to apply wages and work rules equally across the industry and take them out of competition. The Hotel Association would stay out of the unions' way while they organized individual hotels. The Hotel Association would negotiate an industry-wide collective bargaining agreement with the unions, but only for affiliated hotels and only those where the majority of workers wanted a union.[3]

Second, it would "establish machinery for the settlement by conciliation and arbitration of any grievances that may arise." Importing a core concept from the garment industry, the parties agreed to name a "person who will assume the office of Impartial Chairman in the industry."[4] This person would be the tie-breaking vote if management and labor could not agree on a final settlement of a grievance or negotiation. The federal government experimented with a coerced form of tripartite conciliation during the early days of the New Deal. The NRA process led directly to the bruising hotel strike of 1934. Why would Rubin and Obermeier agree to such a framework four years later? The answer lies in their effective strike threat. If the history of union organizing in New York's hotels—stretching back to 1912—involved wage and hour demands that the employers summarily rejected before the workers ultimately went on strike, why not build in a step where a mutually chosen neutral third party could maybe talk some sense into the hotel managers? The union could still go on strike if it got outvoted two-to-one.

Finally, there would be just one union. The Hotel Association was not going to deal with competing claims and balkanized bargaining units if it could help it. The hotel men left it to Rubin's labor council to work out which union got what members and whose bargaining interests would be prioritized when the Association finally sat down with union representatives to hammer out a collective bargaining agreement. As a result, the unions spent the months that bookended the March 23 agreement bargaining more with each other than the bosses.

A few days after HRE Local 6 was chartered, Rubin got his union partners in the electricians and operating engineers unions to sign off on a new umbrella organization that would serve as the collective bargaining agent for all unionized hotel workers, and, thus, supersede their representational authority. The proposed New York Hotel Trades Council was modeled on William Z. Foster's 1916 Stockyards Labor Council, probably designed in consultation with him, as he was beginning to engage in more union work following the long recuperation from his 1932 "smash-up." Another maintenance craft union, Firemen and Oilers Local 56, soon joined. These workers tended to the massive boiler rooms in hotel basements, and their participation in any job action would literally throw cold water on any attempt by hotels to maintain operations without them during a job action.

BSEIU's claimed jurisdiction in the hotels remained a thornier problem for NYHTC. A few weeks before "Status Quo" was inked, Rubin and Garriga's Hotel, Restaurant and Cafeteria Workers Organizing Committee signed a closed shop agreement with a Greenwich Village apartment hotel called One Fifth Avenue. The one-year contract provided for raises of between 5 percent to 20 percent, a 48-hour week with no split shifts, paid vacations, and free uniform laundering.[5] One Fifth Avenue was not affiliated with the

Hotel Association and was exactly the kind of residential hotel lacking food and beverage that Local 32-A considered its turf. Signing the contract—which, without fanfare, was HRE's first collective bargaining agreement with a New York City hotel—was a way of demonstrating that not only could Rubin and company out-organize 32-A on its own turf, but they could negotiate better contracts too.

In February, the AFL Executive Council revisited the ongoing jurisdictional dispute. Still mostly siding with HRE, AFL leaders granted that BSEIU was the legitimate union for elevator operators, subcontracted window washers and exterminators, and gave it a wide latitude in "apartment hotels" that lacked food and beverage service.[6] Neither would give BSEIU many members. Thoroughly shut out of the potentially lucrative "Status Quo" framework, Scalise permitted Local 32-A president Herbert V. Kallman to participate in mediation that George Meany and Father Boland arranged between his union and Local 6. Assured of control over contract negotiations with the Hotel Association and with the Council's power to collect (and withhold) dues serving as a potential check on any wayward affiliate, Rubin not only welcomed 32-A into NYHTC but granted it further jurisdictional concessions. Local 6 ceded the doormen, bell staff, bathroom janitors, and lobby cleaners in addition to the elevator operators, window cleaners, and exterminators that the BSEIU tended to represent in other cities. Beyond that, Local 6 agreed that 32-A could organize the apartment hotels that were not affiliated with the Hotel Association.[7]

Representatives of its first five locals met on April 26, 1938, to formally constitute NYHTC, with plans to affiliate additional AFL unions. Rubin remained president and IBEW Local 3's Peter A. Moroney became the new secretary-treasurer. Although Local 6 was within its rights to claim jurisdiction over all workers that the other four locals did not, the Trades Council directed its affiliated locals to turn over dues and authorization cards from painters and upholsterers.[8] Rubin had been vice president of Upholsterers Local 76 in the 1920s. It's possible he still had comrades there, a membership card, or possibly just a respect for the craft. New York's District 9 Painters were one of the exceedingly rare *other* AFL unions with a substantial base of members in the Communist Party under the leadership of Louis Weinstock. In fact, Weinstock and Rubin had worked together for years within the CP's New York labor committees.[9] But the period of 1938 to 1940 was a brief interregnum that saw Weinstock turned out of office by conservatives in the union.[10] NYHTC preserved a space for them—and other "miscellaneous" crafts like telephone switchboard operators that may yet be claimed by their appropriate AFL craft unions—as directly affiliated members of the Council until after the IWA was settled and further craft jurisdictions could be negotiated.[11]

Immediate Concentration

The NYHTC Executive Board voted to focus "immediate concentration" on the Astor, New Yorker, Pennsylvania, and Waldorf-Astoria hotels for SLRB certification.[12] The Astor and Waldorf were older hotels with significant banquet operations where food workers unions had long had members. The New Yorker was owned by Ralph Hintz's National Hotel Management Company, located on the North-West corner across from Penn Station. Due east of the Pennsylvania Railroad hub, on 7th Avenue, the Hotel Pennsylvania was managed by the Statler corporate chain. Since they were targeted because their respective ownership groups were expanding into new operations, getting their New York flagships under contract would provide useful leverage for winning other new shops. In each case, a Local 6 organizer took the lead, supported by organizers from Locals 3 and 32-A.

That the Hotel Association began bargaining a full-fledged collective bargaining agreement with NYHTC even before the union was certified as bargaining agent at any hotels would seem an enormous boon to organizers, who could portray the union as fighting to win improvements on the job that workers could assist by joining and voting for the union. It was better, the Hotel Association agreed, to allow union grievances over unfair terminations be heard through the "conciliation process" outlined in "Status Quo," with Father Boland or other SLRB representatives temporarily serving as the Impartial Chairman, seemingly removing the threat of termination and blacklisting for union activity that had plagued organizing efforts for decades.

However, while the Hotel Association agreed to be neutral, individual hotel managers still campaigned against unionization. Lucius Boomer held captive audience meetings warning his employees that benefits and work rules at the Waldorf could get worse with bargaining, while he introduced new benefits and social activities. Management at the Roosevelt turned its Employees Welfare Association into a company union, in which management selected employee representatives for "bargaining sessions." The union took measures to get the Association's articles of incorporation rejected by the state and filed an Unfair Labor Practice against the hotel.[13] Ethically dubious groups purporting to be CIO unions also leafletted hotel workers, sowing confusion. A Hotel & Restaurant Workers Industrial Union Local 356 urged workers to "Follow the Lead of John L. Lewis" and a Building Service & Maintenance Local 225 (of a supposed United Building Workers Organizing Committee) advertised itself as "an honest upright organization like the C.I.O." Neither group had anything to do with the CIO (except perhaps having their charter applications rejected), as the rival labor federation respected HRE's industrial jurisdiction, and neither group made much progress.[14]

Beyond that noise, touting the union as the recognized representative of hotel employees whose gains would be passed on to workers who voted for it caused many workers to wait and see precisely what was in the contract before signing a union card. On June 23, the union finally pulled the trigger on its first SLRB certification petitions. They filed to represent workers at seven hotels, making NYHTC the legal bargaining representative for 2,774 workers.[15] In a press statement touting the "outstanding achievement," Obermeier claimed the union won the certifications by a high of 78.9 percent to a low of 53.3 percent.

In a closer look, only the Pennsylvania was on the initial list of organizing priorities. They had to tinker with the voter list to eke out a win. The SLRB counted 594 union cards against a list of 1,114 employees on payroll. The 53.3 percent "yes" vote was achieved by getting the SLRB to strike 224 additional employees (mostly white-collar clerical or supervisory) out of the bargaining unit. The historic McAlpin hotel, long an AFW stronghold, produced a more solid majority. Sixty percent of the 702 workers on the approved voter list signed union cards, with just 116 employees excluded from the bargaining unit. At the Park Central, where the union got management to back off an announced five percent wage cut the month before by convincing the Hotel Association that it was improper under "Status Quo," they won with 56 percent. The SLRB matched 292 union cards against a list of 521 bargaining unit members, after excluding 135 employees at the 1,600-guest room midtown hotel. At the 26-story New Hotel Victoria, 130 cards were counted against a list of 243 workers for a 53 percent win. And "definite majorities were established" at the uptown Park Crescent, the downtown Brittany and the Kimberly (a boutique hotel on the East Side).[16]

Local 6 filed more certification petitions at private dining clubs, which would bargain separate contracts with just that local. It won certification elections at about a dozen clubs, including the Harvard Club, the Princeton Club, the University Club, and the Racquet and Tennis Club.[17] Each club employed between 100 and 250 kitchen and dining room workers in addition to dozens of seasonal banquet waiters. Kallman of 32-A groused that Local 6 was collecting more initiation fees and dues, and, because it produced more leaflets and its organizers served as campaign leads, hotel workers identified with Local 6 more than NYHTC. He demanded the Council get a separate headquarters, clerical staff, and bank accounts. He and Obermeier feuded over the direction of the organizers and the issuance of leaflets targeted to front service employees.

Kallman kvetched about the momentum of the card drive. Organizers collected 484 signed authorization cards during the third week of May and 407 the following week. By the third week of June, they were down to only

120 new cards and 125 the next week. The drive had stagnated and Kallman worried "that it was common knowledge to the Hotel Association."[18]

The union wouldn't file another certification petition at any hotels for an entire month. In late July, the SLRB conducted three more card checks: at the Governor Clinton, Lincoln, and White hotels.[19] Whatever hotel owners thought about the union's organizing progress, several more hotels voluntarily recognized the union, forgoing an SLRB card check. On July 24, Rubin and McDonald issued a statement to announce the Hotel Trades Council to the world and the steady organizing progress that had made it the bargaining agent for workers at 40 hotels. Among the large hotels that voluntarily recognized the union, according to the statement, were the Breslin, Edison, Times Square, and St. George (which was transferring its previous recognition of 32-A to the Trades Council).[20] Heading into August, NYHTC was the bargaining agent for nearly 12,000 workers.[21]

Overwhelming Sentiment

During the campaign, the New York locals sent 95 delegates—a larger number than had ever represented the city—to San Francisco for HRE's 29th convention, opening on August 15, 1938. Credentials reflected the dynamic changes in the locals. Rubin attended as a Local 302 delegate. Garriga, still its president for the moment, led Local 89's delegation. Young Local 6 raised funds with a "Midnight Sail and Dance" on a Hudson River showboat to send a small, diverse delegation.[22] Aside from Obermeier, it sent Gertrude Lane and Scotty Eckford, night shop chairman at the Hotel Cameron and president of the local's Negro Council.[23] Fewer than one in five delegates were women, with many locals sending none.[24] While Black delegates were not *uncommon*, they faced discrimination. One of the hotels that served as a convention headquarters, the Whitcomb, refused to host Black guests, causing a frenzied search for alternate accommodations for them and the white delegates who checked out in solidarity.[25]

The New Yorkers brought resolutions that contributed to the progressive tenor of the convention. William Mesevich and Sam Kramberg sought to ban "Union House" signs at properties with craft-exclusive bargaining units, to end all vestiges of racial exclusivity in craft locals and pushed for a nationwide organizing committee to take on the hotel chains. William Albertson and Miguel Garriga introduced several resolutions on the Spanish Civil War (a matter close to the Spanish-born Garriga's heart).[26]

They joined Ed Flore in opposing efforts to affiliate with the CIO. Although there was strong membership sentiment to do so, if HRE joined the CIO, the AFL would certainly have chartered a new hotel union to compete with it, while the CIO respected its jurisdiction as an industrial union. Instead "the fastest growing organization" in the AFL called for labor movement reunification.[27]

Recognizing his role in New York's success, Ed Flore tapped Miguel Garriga to run on his leadership slate. The convention scrapped its ranked seniority system of vice presidents with no specified duties, replacing it with eight geographic districts, in which each vice president would receive a handsome salary for full-time oversight of the locals within his district. New York, New Jersey, Pennsylvania, and Maryland became the Second District, and Garriga would be its vice president.

First, he had to win the election, which due to its circumstances made the atmosphere in the convention hall "extremely intense." Encouraged (reportedly at gunpoint) by Frank Nitti, George B. McLane, the international vice president from Chicago, was running for president against Flore. Worse, Flore's secretary-treasurer, Robert B. Hesketh, whose office was based out of Chicago, was running on McLane's slate.

Hesketh paid fawning attention to Local 278's membership gains and McLane's bargaining prowess in *Catering Industry Employee* for years and began publishing monthly advertisements for "union-made" whiskey and free Wurlitzer-Simplex jukeboxes for union bars.[28] The union bug on a bottle of booze was a perfect cover for the Chicago Outfit's racket, and nickels and dimes in jukeboxes left no paper trail, making them efficient money launderers.[29] It was plain that Hesketh had been dealt in on a nice side income from McLane's connections. Nitti told McLane that he only needed him to serve a single term, which he felt would be long enough to "parcel out different parts of the country."[30]

The large influx of new members in New York would again be essential to preventing racketeers from dominating the union. McLane understood this and traveled in advance of the convention to ask Rubin, Obermeier, and Garriga for their support. Styling himself as an opposition reformer, the most he could say in his favor was that Flore "had no guts." They were not impressed. "Your platform, then, is to revitalize the International?" Rubin archly inquired. "That's it," McLane replied. "And I think I'm the man to do it." McLane arrived in San Francisco with no illusions that he would pick up any votes in New York and instead spent the convention red-baiting Flore for his association with the Communists.[31]

San Francisco was Hugo Ernst's home base, and California comprised 27 percent of delegates. Together, with the New York locals, who had 15 percent of the voting strength in the hall, they were the backbone of Flore's "Progressive" caucus. McLane's support came from bartenders and smaller locals in the Midwest that needed his group's financial assistance for travel. His campaign arrived ten days early and hosted an open bar in a suite at one of the designated official hotels. Unfortunately for him, that hotel was the Whitcomb, and the anti-segregation boycott cost him much of his planned boozy electioneering. McLane's other ploy was a series of parliamentary maneuvers to delay the officer elections until the last day of the convention. Elections were traditionally held the night before the last day, and if the McLane group could drag out the proceedings, then delegates whose expenses they weren't paying would have to leave, improving the electoral math. When this failed, they resorted to straight-up thuggery. Miguel Garriga was "brutally" beaten by unidentified hoodlums during the Tuesday lunch break while he was touring the city with his wife and six-year-old child.[32]

The violence backfired. Delegates passed a resolution denouncing gang violence and rained a chorus of boos and shouts of "racketeer" on Chicago delegates who spoke in favor of McLane's candidacy. On the day of the election, Ernst arranged for plain-clothes cops to frisk delegates before they entered the hall. The cops hauled off "some twenty-six revolvers and an assortment of knives and blackjacks."[33] Flore won his dramatic reelection by a two-to-one margin on Thursday night, and the convention adjourned for the day.

Nominations were opened for secretary-treasurer as the first order of business the next morning. Flore planned to run Hugo Ernst against Hesketh, as punishment for breaking ranks, but "eighty per cent of the convention delegates rose to their feet and applauded," Hesketh's official minutes recorded, "for several minutes, demonstrating that the splendid work done by him was appreciated." Ernst declined the nomination to avoid an unsavory episode. "I think Bob now realizes that the overwhelming sentiment of the convention is with the leadership of President Flore," he said, endorsing "closer cooperation between Hesketh and Flore, so that our organization will grow."[34] As it happened, Hesketh "fell ill" immediately after the convention and never returned to his duties. An embarrassed and broken man, he died a year later, whereupon Ernst was selected by the GEB to replace him.[35] Other candidates on McLane's slate watched the results of the Presidential contest and declined to suffer a similar drubbing, including Albert Kronen of Bronx Bartenders Local 29 who was running against Garriga on an anti-Communist platform. George McLane, however, chose to run for reelection, but Flore retained no residue of sympathy for the ethically compromised union official. Ed Miller, a young leader from Kansas City, handily defeated McLane to become the vice president of the Fifth District.[36]

The criminal element was removed from national leadership, but it would take a few more years for the Chicago locals to get cleaned up. In fact, McLane was reelected with great fanfare to the presidency of the Chicago Hotel Trades and Crafts Council, the NYHTC-inspired umbrella organization of AFL unions that bargained (separately) with Windy City hotels.[37] It wasn't until 1940 that he was suspended from Local 278, and that was less of a fall-out from his corruption than it was a power struggle with the local's president.[38] In 1943, McLane gave a grand jury testimony in a racket case, but balked at testifying in open court, and the case collapsed.[39] Chicago would remain mired in sketchy business for years to come.

Meet the Challenge

By October 1938, the union had been bargaining with the Hotel Association for seven months. The basic framework—recognition, grievance procedure, vacation pay, and other benefits—had tentative agreements. Early sticking points—the closed shop, the right to hire and fire, and a wage structure that was agreeable to all the hotels—remained on the table.[40] By the end of the month, the Hotel Association submitted a draft agreement to union negotiators who testily rejected it for going backwards on points that had already been conceded. In particular, the understanding that the Hotel Association could sign the contract on behalf of SLRB-certified affiliated hotels was gone.[41] This would put the onus on the union to make recalcitrant hotels sign the agreement. Taken together, the outstanding issues pointed to serious divisions within the Hotel Association—between the large hotels and the smaller ones, and between the institutional investors and the old-school Hotel Men—that put an industry-wide framework in peril.

NYHTC assembled 2,500 delegates on November 1 for a negotiations update. Rubin focused on wages, which workers cared about more than the legal minutia. The union's public demand was "an immediate general increase of 15 percent for all hotel workers." The Association's offer, Rubin revealed, was a ten percent increase that wouldn't even kick in until April 1. The delegate assembly voted for a November 15 deadline to cut off negotiations unless a deal was reached and authorized NYHTC to enter negotiations with individual hotels if talks with the Hotel Association broke down.[42] The pace of negotiations picked up with many sessions going past midnight, and enough progress was being made that the Council agreed to work through the November 15 deadline.

On November 26, the union again rejected the Association's latest counteroffer, saying it failed "completely to cover points agreed upon." By telegram and in the *New York Times,* the union announced plans to raise a $200,000 defense fund.[43] As a show of strength, the union staged a brief work stoppage at the McAlpin hotel, closing the restaurant and bar and stopping the elevators for the lunch hour. Rubin, who was in bargaining at the time, coyly claimed that the "spontaneous protest" was initiated by impatient shop delegates. Bargaining continued until 5:00 PM that day, and the parties announced that they would resume at one o'clock the following afternoon, hopeful to end the day with an agreement.⁴⁴ For a group of workers who spent the quarter century since 1912 following radical union leaders out on violent and disruptive strikes over unilateral wage and hour demands pressed upon obstinate economic royalists, labor peace arrived in a surprisingly conciliatory manner. Following the McAlpin job action, Father Boland attempted to find common ground between the parties' last, best offers to each other and drew up a tentative agreement.

On December 21, the Hotel Association's board of governors met to consider the document. In a sign of the difficult road ahead, only eight of the 15 voting hotel managers approved the Industry Wide Agreement. Two abstained, and the rest voted against the agreement, which passed narrowly. On December 27, the Hotel Association's full membership met in a "stormy" five-and-a-half-hour session at Carnegie Hall to ratify the tentative agreement. It was approved, but several members marched out of the room, announcing that they would not be bound by the actions of the remaining Hotel Association members.⁴⁵ The renegade hotels, said to number as many as 60, formed a rival Hotel League. Led by the Algonquin's Frank Case, their primary objection was the Industry Wide Agreement's union shop clause, compelling represented employees to join the union. Although the group was primarily composed of residential and boutique hotels, its members included large luxury hotels like the Plaza, Ritz-Carlton, St. Regis, and Savoy-Plaza.⁴⁶

NYHTC leaders viewed Boland's compromise more favorably, as it promised to institutionalize union recognition in the industry and put the union on a solid footing for more organizing wins and future contract gains. Two days after the hotel managers met, nearly 2,000 union members filled the Manhattan Center to unanimously ratify the "historic" agreement and to "meet the challenge" of employers that threatened to resist signing on to the CBA with "any action necessary, including that of striking."⁴⁷

The contract was signed and dated January 18, 1939. Wage increases were made retroactive to December 15. Each bargaining unit member would receive a wage increase of at least $1.00 a week, depending on where they fit on the new wage scale, with another $1.00 raise scheduled for July 15, 1939. Since many hotels lacked any wage standards, some workers would see substantial raises as wages equalized across the industry. The skilled maintenance crafts had the highest minimum salaries: $40 a week for the operating engineers, $30 for the electricians, $18 for telephone switchboard operators, and $17 for elevator operators.⁴⁸ The kitchen and dining room workers—the backbone of the union for decades—came out ahead, too. White jacket cooks got $24 a week, banquet bartenders got $30, waiters got $9 plus tips, and waitresses received a prorated wage of $7.50 for their shorter workweek. Chambermaids, relative newcomers to unionization, won a substantial wage of $14.50. The bellman, deemed to be a "tip classification" received only $4—which would remain a sticking point with BSEIU.[49]

The contract had an expiration date of January 31, 1942, but permitted a wage reopener on October 1, 1940. Workers also won an annual week of paid vacation after one year of service, an uncommon benefit in 1939. Uniforms would be provided and laundered by the employers, and the agreement placed upper limits on the amount of money they could charge for meals. The contract included the union shop provision that the dissenting hotel managers found so offensive. Not only did it provide for payroll deduction of dues and require newly hired employees to join the union within 15 days or face termination, but it also called for the termination of any member suspended or expelled from the union.

The IWA settled on the Hotel Association's nominee, Edward P. Mulrooney, as Impartial Chairman. Rubin convinced his board that the employers' trust in the former police commissioner and State Liquor Authority chairman and his healthy pension were assets. The union still insisted that labor and management jointly fund a generous salary to compensate him for his duties as a neutral party.

The union made several concessions in the agreement, some with tradeoffs. The hours of work remained long. For waiters and busboys, it was a 54-hour week. For all other men, it was 48. Women would see their hours shortened by the state's minimum wage law. But, for all, overtime would be paid at time and half. It allowed the employers who currently practiced the "custom" of "maintaining long and short watches and split shifts in certain categories of employees" to continue to do so, but it restricted any extension of the practice and put proposed changes squarely under the authority of the Impartial Chairman. Also under the purview of the Impartial Chairman were Article 28 "Exceptional Cases" in which individual hotels could claim that an "unusual hardship" prevented them from paying a contractual wage increase. They would have to open their books to scrutiny from the Impartial Chairman as well as the union, and the union had to consent to any wage modification.

The Hotel Association insisted upon broad latitude in its right to manage and make staffing decisions based on economic conditions as its price for agreeing to a union shop and payroll deductions for union dues. The Amalgamated Food Workers spent a decade and a half trying to enforce "closed shop" union standards in which hotels had to accept members dispatched from its hiring hall as employees. No more. Hotel management retained the exclusive right to hire and fire through Article 14(a) of the IWA. Although management's right was not "subject to contest or review," the union did retain the right to "confer" with an employer on behalf of any laid off or discharged employee.[50] The IWA failed to slay the "vampire" employment agency system. Management explicitly retained the right to hire "from whatever source it finds desirable," although it agreed to form a labor-management committee to study "the advantage of a joint employment agency."

Paradoxically, the IWA committed the union to herding hotels into the framework, if not the Hotel Association itself. It forbade the union from signing any other collective bargaining agreement with a hotel that offered better terms than the IWA, or a different expiration date, and required NYHTC to make any nonmember of the Hotel Association submit to the same grievance and arbitration procedure as the IWA and to pay its proportional share for funding the Office of the Impartial Chairman.[51]

The slim agreement, 31 clauses in total, was, like most first union contracts, a foundation to build upon through future rounds of bargaining and judicious use of labor-management conferences and the grievance process. The speed and ease with which NYHTC members ratified the agreement underscore how much of a win it was for the workers. Now the challenge would be to get the owners and managers who signed paychecks to sign the contract and implement its terms.

Continued Stubborn Refusal

On January 26, 1939, nine of the hotels most committed to the new era of labor peace met to sign the IWA, bringing the benefits of the contract to over 4,700 workers. The largest of these was the Pennsylvania, with over 1,000 bargaining unit members. The McAlpin and Park Central, among the first certified bargaining units, like the Pennsylvania, joined it. The Taft, owned and operated by the Bing & Bing chain, voluntarily signed on behalf of 850 employees. The Vanderbilt, in operation since 1912, was owned by the New York Life insurance company also signed the IWA as an act of voluntary recognition. Four smaller residential hotels also signed. Among them, the Brittany and Park Crescent were the first bargaining units certified in June 1938, and the Cameron, which was in foreclosure, had voluntarily recognized the union the previous spring.[52]

Six more hotels, all of which had voluntarily recognized the union, signed in February. Another Bing & Bing property, the Alden apartment hotel on the Upper West Side was one. Two other midtown hotels, the Woodstock and Piccadilly, were part of separate small chain management systems. One, the Capitol, was owned by a bank. March saw nine hotels sign the IWA through voluntary recognition, including the New Yorker and the massive full-service hotels of the New York Central group. Owned by the railroad company of the same name and all adjacent to Grand Central Terminal, the three hotels—the Biltmore, Commodore, and Roosevelt—collectively employed over 2,700 workers.

That deal was nearly sabotaged by George Scalise. Scalise never liked the "Status Quo" framework, which offered fewer opportunities to shake down individual employers. He also opposed Mulrooney's selection as Impartial Chairman, preferring an executive from the Governor Clinton, with whom he believed he could cut better deals, and he believed Local 32-A could win better wages and hours by going its own way. He saw NYHTC's slow progress in signing hotels up as an opportunity to strike alternate deals. Knowing this, when Rubin arranged the meeting with the railroad men on March 26, he only gave Scalise 15 minutes' notice to participate. Scalise attended the meeting unprepared to properly sabotage it and spent two weeks brooding over Rubin's ploy.[53]

Despite the progress in voluntary recognitions, there remained over 40 Hotel Association affiliates with SLRB-certified bargaining units that refused to sign the IWA. The union got more aggressive with the holdouts. On March 3, Scotty Eckford walked through the Algonquin's dining room at lunchtime, passing out fliers to guests about the labor dispute he was about to begin. The kitchen and dining room staff walked out, canceling lunch, and stayed out until 8:30 PM. The Algonquin was leading the breakaway Hotel League group that refused to sign the IWA, and the union wasn't even the certified bargaining agent yet. The brief strike was to protest at least one retaliatory termination of a union activist. It ended when Frank Case agreed to submit the case to arbitration and appeared to agree to a card check at the SLRB.[54]

That same night, Martin Cody led food and beverage workers at the Buckingham, "an apartment hotel of distinction" owned by "the Taylor interests," in a brief strike to protest the termination of a bartender. The strike ended with the worker restored to his position and management agreeing to card check.[55] On March 4, workers staged a surprise strike during dinner at the Lincoln, leaving 200 guests unserved at tables in its famed Blue Room nightclub. Workers took the elevators out of service, leaving guests stranded across its 29 floors. The strikers staged a noisy sit-in in the hotel's basement for a few hours, until police ordered them to vacate the premises. They repaired across the street to the union's headquarters at 44th and 8th while Obermeier negotiated a settlement. The job action was not an attempt to fully shut down the full-service hotel. Notably, it started at 6:30 PM, when most of the housekeeping and laundry employees had clocked out for the day. Another hotel with common ownership, the Edison on 47th Street, took no part in the protest. The nighttime strike was settled before the AM shift began. Mrs. Maria Kramer, the owner of the properties, agreed to submit the dispute to Impartial Chairman Mulrooney—the first dispute submitted to his office—resulting in her signing the IWA for both the Lincoln and Edison on March 10.[56]

The speedy success of the Lincoln job action tempted the union to try it again—to much diminished returns—at the Governor Clinton two weeks later. On the second day, the union claimed that 400 out of 425 bargaining unit members remained on strike. In "continued stubborn refusal," management claimed that only 75 employees did not report for duty and that it felt no rush to resume bargaining "because service is normal." It was not. The hotel could only offer coffee service in the morning, had to close its coffee shop in the afternoon to open its bar, and couldn't staff any of its restaurants. However, what strength the union could muster in the culinary departments was not matched by housekeeping and other essential hotel services.[57] The hotel remained operational for guests, and by the end of the week, scabs were recruited to get the restaurant and bar back to full service. NYHTC filed an unfair labor practice charge against Governor Clinton management for their refusal to bargain, began paying strike benefits of 35 cents a day (plus a lump sum of $7 for strikers with families or $5 for single workers), and dug in for a long-term fight.[58]

Direct Encroachment

As quickly as the IWA was settled, NYHTC began parceling out jurisdiction for miscellaneous crafts of hotel workers. There were hundreds of job titles, some held by a handful of workers on whose behalf the hotels were deducting and remitting union dues to NYHTC. Swimming pool lifeguards and "locker men," for example, went to Local 32-A, while Turkish Bath attendants were directly affiliated with the Trades Council in case there was an AFL craft union that came along to claim them. Other job titles were combined, or split across multiple departments, requiring jurisdictional settlements. Incinerator operators who worked in the engineering department went to Firemen and Oilers Local 56, while those who incinerated trash went to 32-A. Housemen (a Local 6 job title) who also washed windows (a Local 32-A job) went to 32-A. Many compromises of this sort went to BSEIU's benefit, as it was easier to placate George Scalise over a handful of dues-payers than get into a turf war over thousands more.

IBEW decided that telephone operators, who patched electrical cables into a switchboard, were electrical workers. IBEW president Daniel W. Tracy, chafing against Harry Van Arsdale's progressive proclivities and fearing his ambition, issued a charter for a new local—one of eight that he issued in a one-year timespan—meant to chip away at his rival's membership base. NYHTC duly recognized IBEW Local 1005B as the representative of the largely female workforce.[59] Mary T. Regan, a switchboard operator at the Park Central, became the new local's president and the only woman to lead a NYHTC affiliate.[60] While NYHTC waited to affiliate the Painters and the

Upholsterers, word got out among AFL unions that there was an opportunity to claim already-organized members in the hotel industry.

One of the first unions to come calling was Laundry Workers International Union Local 280, which sent a sternly-worded demand to affiliate, accusing the Council of "direct encroachment" on their jurisdiction."[61] This AFL craft unit utterly botched the organizing opportunity of a 1933 strike wave sparked by a "united front" action of the TUUL in coalition with the Women's Trade Union League in New York's industrial laundries, and getting dealt in on the hotel industry's jurisdiction was its last, best hope for becoming an effective union.[62] The Trades Council Executive Board gave representatives of the AFL craft union a polite hearing, but ultimately turned them down.[63]

NYHTC asked the Building Trades Council to facilitate efforts to bring other mechanical crafts into NYHTC. The Building Trades could be important political allies, but many of the crafts still had not changed their constitutions to permit membership in industrial bargaining units. The Plumbers, in particular, still required all members to go through an apprenticeship to be members in good standing, and hotels hired plumbers with little regard to formal training or union membership. Whether that was an issue with the Painters, or whether its leaders were uncomfortable with the unique structure of the Council or that the union was more focused on organizing subcontractors that the hotels occasionally hired, the relationship between NYHTC and DC 9 deteriorated badly by the fall. Beginning in September 1939, DC 9 put jurisdictional picket lines outside of several hotels, including the Pennsylvania and Taft. Some 400 painters and wallpaper hangers were employed in hotel maintenance departments covered by the IWA, waiting for DC 9 to claim them. Now it was demanding the right to collect dues from workers that it had done nothing to organize and was disrupting the labor peace that was essential to the framework of the IWA. David Drechsler and Edward Mulrooney, on behalf of "the Hotel Industry," wired a protest to Mayor La Guardia imploring him to "USE YOUR HIGH OFFICE TO PREVENT DEMORALIZATION OF AN INDUSTRY THAT HAS SOUGHT TO COOPERATE AND COOPERATE WITH LABOR." Rubin explained the controversy to the IBPAT international president, seeking a resolution, and diplomatically suggested that "if the District Council wanted to act to establish decent conditions in hotels that purpose would be served far better if picket lines were aimed at some of the open-shop hotels."[64] The picket lines came down but the tensions remained for a year until Louis Weinstock's slate was returned to office in the summer of 1941. The once and again secretary-treasurer of DC 9 got a charter for a new local of hotel maintenance painters, which was finally welcomed into NYHTC. The organized painters were transferred into the new local, and by October, Weinstock was sending organizers into the field to participate in the hotel organizing. Painters Local 1422 became the seventh NYHTC affiliate.[65]

Question or Controversy

The St. Regis voluntarily recognized the union and signed the IWA on April 6, 1939. Owner Vincent Astor wanted the status of being the first luxury hotel to recognize the union.[66] With 600 new members, NYHTC numbered well over 10,000 members at 26 signatory hotels. With the Governor Clinton strike dragging on, the union found different ways to protest recalcitrant employers who still refused to sign the IWA. Beginning April 14, organizers began conducting routine picket lines outside of Emigrant Industrial Savings Bank locations. The bank owned three uptown residential hotels with certified NYHTC bargaining units: the Alamac, Kimberly, and Sulgrave. Generally, while union pickets might ask guests at a transient hotel to check in someplace else, organizers were deferential and even apologetic towards permanent residents of apartment hotels for the noise and inconvenience of picket lines and work stoppages. The bank branches made sense for targeting the owners' bottom line without antagonizing the hotel residents. Still, it took Emigrant two months of picketing to sign the IWA for its properties.[67]

While hotels with year-old SLRB certifications resisted signing the contract, union organizers won a score of new certifications. With the IWA settled, organizers could campaign on the material improvements that workers would gain. "We at the Hotel New Yorker," one leaflet went, "beginning next week, will enjoy our second pay raise under the contract since it went into effect in our hotel." The leaflet cajoled workers at the Belmont-Plaza hotel across the street, "Start having wage increases and other benefits you have long wanted to obtain. Organize!"[68] In April alone, twelve new hotels became union shops, and five more followed in May. Each of these were card check certifications and resulted in the employers promptly signing the IWA. SLRB rules allowed for secret ballot elections where a "question or controversy concerning representation" existed. As a matter of law, the "mere allegation" of a controversy was sufficient to force an election.[69] Essentially, then, every NYHTC certification had been a form of voluntary recognition until management at the Essex House demanded an election to prove that its employees wanted the union. The union won the May 8 election 266 to 17, and management signed the IWA one month later.[70] The St. Moritz *was* a matter of controversy. The owner of the luxury hotel, S. Gregory Taylor, had previously indicated to Jay Rubin that he would join the January 26 signing of the IWA by the first union hotels and then got squirrely. Along with his brother Charles and their financial backers, the Taylors had interests in half a dozen hotels, including the Buckingham.[71] None had signed the IWA, and Taylor decided to keep it that way. With the Essex House election win under its belt, the union filed cards at the SLRB for the St. Moritz. The August 16 election was the first loss for the union. Of the 429 ballots cast, 282 were against unionization.[72]

As the July 15 wage increase kicked in, 50 hotels, employing over 12,000 workers, were under contract.[73] The union went on a new offensive against the stubborn holdouts. On August 6, NYHTC accused 40 hotels of bad faith bargaining for their refusal to sign and publicly threatened to file unfair labor practice charges with the SLRB.[74] Organizers also began staging daily picket lines outside of the Algonquin.[75] Despite the Norris–La Guardia Act and state law protecting the right to picket, police limited union picket lines to four people at a time. Still, every few days, the union would try to form a mass picket line of 50 or so members, effectively blocking all the doors at its West 44th Street frontage, before being dispersed. The Hotel League's Frank Case returned from his summer home on Long Island to engage in some damage control, insisting that his employees were not on strike and that he wasn't opposed to collective bargaining. He even hired someone to picket the union pickets! It was a short-lived stunt. Organizers mobilized a flying squad of 200 union members to surround Case's picket until police dispersed both sides.[76]

The union attempted to form an Algonquin Guests' Committee to get some of the hotel's more famous residents to put pressure on Case, but it turned out that their likeliest supporters had relocated. The writer Alexander Woollcott fondly recalled his participation in the brief "consumer's strike" at the Waldorf-Astoria in 1934, but he had moved to Vermont. Still, he called Frank Case and provided statements of endorsement for the union's leaflets. So, too, did Orson Welles. The actor and director of the Mercury Theater wrote back from Hollywood on RKO Pictures letterhead, "I am sorry that my film work here will prevent me serving on the Algonquin's guest committee, but I wish you well."[77]

The Algonquin and the union had held a conference at the SLRB following the one-day strike back in April and although NYHTC could prove majority support, Case refused to accept a card check certification. In September, the union finally filed for an election, scoring a narrow 43–39 win on September 27. Legally compelled to bargain with union representatives, Case ran out of excuses for resisting the IWA. He signed on October 2, as did another leader of the Hotel League, an uptown apartment hotel called the Whitehall.[78] The Hotel League was dissolved and the breakaway hotels returned to the Hotel Association (if they ever even left) and the "Status Quo" and IWA framework was restored to most of the hotel industry.[79] An SLRB certification for the union at an employer affiliated with the Hotel Association—which was once again most of them—should have meant quick acceptance at the IWA, but there were still some hotels that would drag it out for years.

Hundreds of Grievances

The new dues revenue coming in from signatory hotels meant that the union could transfer organizers off the Hotel, Restaurant and Cafeteria

Workers Organizing Committee's payroll and onto Local 6's. By summer, the technical, representational, and organizing staff numbered 45, with a payroll of approximately $1,400.00 a week.[80] One of the union's "new" hires was John Assel, who helped found the Amalgamated Food Workers and served as the general secretary to one of its predecessors. He was brought in to lend gravitas to trainings and new member orientations, and he served as "officer of the day" to minister to members who walked into the union office with questions or complaints.[81] Local 6 business agents, whose job was to adjust grievances with management, were directed to spend only one day a week in the office. They were expected to spend at least five days in the hotels, meeting with members and making sure the contract was being followed. Business agents would face election on the Garriga/Obermeier Administration slate in December. Organizers, who were tasked with winning SLRB elections at non-union hotels, were appointed positions—some employed by NYHTC. In all cases, including the technical and administrative staff, if they weren't CP members when they were hired, they would be pressured to join shortly thereafter. NYHTC had its own staff. The more conservative affiliates, particularly the IBEW locals, would not have appreciated an ideological litmus test; the staff's political affiliation was more of a "don't ask/don't tell" situation.

Grievances, both those formally filed with the Impartial Chairman and those that were informally settled by a business agent or rank-and-file shop delegate, were essential for turning hotels into true union shops. There was no training for department managers on the terms of the contract, and most were conducting business as usual until challenged. Even something as significant as the July 15 wage increase could not be taken for granted. Many hotels continued to hire new employees at the old base rate. The union filed grievances with the Impartial Chairman's office contending that the across-the-board wage increases raised the base rate. Laundering uniforms and paying overtime wages similarly had to be enforced through grievances and conferences.

Most employers had a practice of providing employees meals at break times and deducting the cost of those meals from their paychecks. Many employers, however, simply treated the wages minus meal deductions as the regular rate of pay regardless of whether they actually ate the food. The union adjusted early grievances against the practice where members raised the issue. Later, as members took their new contractual vacations, the union found the widespread practice of employers deducting the cost of meals from vacation checks, which Obermeier used as an issue to rile members up and show that the union was methodically taking on every chiseling practice that hotels had been getting away with. The union also took on hotels that did not offer their employees a "suitable" place in which to take their meals, convincing individual hotels to convert rooms into proper employee cafeterias instead of expecting workers to eat on their feet or in stairwells.[82]

Although section 14(a) of the IWA gave the union little formal recourse in the case of employee terminations, business agents defended members who were fired and tried to convince department managers to convert some terminations into warnings. In October 1939 alone, union representatives successfully got five terminations reversed at three hotels.

In the banquet departments, where union activists had contested job security, tips, and arbitrary work rules since 1912, the union formed shop committees to establish house rules for each shop. In conferences with management, they created or revised "steady lists" of captains and waiters who were guaranteed year-round jobs. The workers were selected by seniority and satisfactory performance, and the list was limited to the number of workers that the hotels needed even on a slow day. The committees tried to get hotels to hire extra waiters through the union during the busy season. Shop committees also worked out formulas for pooling tips, which by then, were collected by management as a percentage of receipts from a particular event. The rules varied significantly from shop to shop, with captains sometimes earning a larger percentage than waiters, and maître d'hôtels and other managers sometimes getting dealt in.[83]

In housekeeping departments, the union pressed to reduce the quota of rooms that a worker had to clean to constitute a working day. Overtime grievances helped convince management to hire more cleaners to spread the work around.

Grievances that could not be settled with hotel management were brought before the Impartial Chairman. The Office of the Impartial Chairman would evolve over the years to become a kind of labor court, where dozens—sometimes hundreds—of cases were tried and decisions would set a precedent for the rest. But in its early years, Mulrooney was a mediator, helping labor and management see both the weaknesses and strengths in their arguments and bringing them towards an amicable settlement. Most sessions were essentially negotiations, with Mulrooney acting as umpire. Every grievance regarding the base rate of pay, for instance, was settled in favor of the union (because Mulrooney strongly signaled his inclination to agree with the union's position). Only nine cases required formal decisions imposed on the parties in 1939. Four of them were filed by employers requesting Article 28 relief from the July 1 wage increase. Two of those were rejected outright. In the case of the Mayflower, a new management company had just assumed operations when the contract took effect. Mulrooney ordered the hotel to pay half of the wage increase right away and gave them two months' leeway to pay the rest. In the case of the Whitehall, Mulrooney ordered the hotel to pay half the increase right away but gave them four months to make up the rest.⁸⁴ Thirteen more hotels would appeal for relief over the next two years, accounting for nearly half of the formal orders issued by Mulrooney. All but twelve were rejected outright, and only one achieved a minor delay in paying the contractual wage increases.

The other largest grouping of cases—three in 1939, seven in 1940—were ones where the union alleged that workers were fired for union activity. Most terminations were reversed at the hotel level, but in deference to management's right to hire and fire, when cases came before Mulrooney for a formal decision, he usually sided with management in ways that would be unthinkable in a more mature collective bargaining relationship. In fact, the very first Impartial Chairman decision featured a delegate in the laundry department of the Park Central who was fired for getting into an argument with the hotel paymaster over the correct amount of dues to deduct from members' paychecks. In the heat of the moment, the delegate, Benito Huamani, dismissively told the manager that he didn't "believe anything" he had to say. Mulrooney ruled that it wasn't Huamani's union activity that was objectionable, but his insubordination, calling his behavior "disrespectful and contumacious." If management's justification for the termination seemed reasonable to the Impartial Chairman, he sided with management, no matter how much of an activist the fired worker was. It wasn't until Mulrooney was presented with an egregious case of management firing a delegate in the act of—and *admittedly because* of—her actions enforcing the contract that he ordered a terminated activist to be reinstated, and that didn't happen until January 1941. In that case, housekeeping delegate Esther Weilburg, *also* of the Park Central, was organizing her coworkers to clean no more than 18 rooms a day. The daily quota was not uniform, with maids cleaning anywhere between 17 and 21 rooms each day. That already unreasonable workload became impossible when the state's new minimum wage law compelled management to reduce women workers' daily hours from eight to seven, which management did without reducing the room quota. Weilburg was interrogated by management. She stated her position that she was conducting a valid job action to comply with the law and the IWA and was summarily terminated for insubordination. Here, finally, Mulrooney found "ample evidence" that the delegate's union activity was "distasteful to management" and the true cause of her termination, which he reversed.⁸⁵

After a year's experience of adjusting grievances, Michael J. Obermeier reported to a general membership meeting that nine out of ten disputes were settled before getting submitted to the Impartial Chairman. Gertrude Lane, who as general organizer directed the business agents, reported that "hundreds of grievances," basically most except for terminations and disputes over vacations and employee meals, were settled by rank-and-file delegates and shop committees.⁸⁶

The Strength and Power of Our Organized Ranks

In October, the union scored 100 percent election wins at the Mayflower and Brewster hotels, a 97 percent win at the Oliver Cromwell, 93 percent at the Regent, and a 76 percent margin of victory at the Adams. Despite overwhelming worker support for union representation, elections were becoming the norm.

Yet, one October election was anything but normal. The members-only agreement that the St. George hotel signed with Local 32-A finally expired. Rubin and Scalise worked out a deal with property manager Bing and Bing to bring the union house under the IWA, but an independent union intervened. "The Hotel and Residence Club Industrial Workers Union of Brooklyn, Local 28" initially claimed to be "affiliated with the CIO (application pending)," but later emphasized its independence. Behind the effort was Paul Zack, a former BSEIU organizer. After he was fired, he applied to work for NYHTC. Rejected, he decided to exploit workers' complaints about their experience in Local 32-A. If he could win and bargain a contract, collecting dues from 700 bargaining unit members would set him up with a well-paying job as union president.[87] Zack garnered 256 votes to NYHTC's 202 in the October 20 election. Forty workers voted against unionization, and 15 ballots were challenged or voided. The SLRB determined the results to be inconclusive, as Local 28 failed to win a majority of ballots cast. NYHTC appealed for a run-off election between the top two vote-getters; that is to rerun an election between NYHTC and Local 28 *without* a "no union" option on the ballot. The March 1940 rerun (covered later) got even more complicated.

Moving forward, the union continued to file for certification at hotels where it had a showing of majority support, hoping for voluntary recognition. When employers raised a "question or controversy" (as they usually did), organizers assessed their support before issuing a recommendation to the NYHTC Executive Board about whether to move forward with an election. Likely, they weighed how many bargaining unit voters were dues-paying members or activists and how many had merely signed a card expressing interest in belonging to the union. In November, NYHTC leadership voted to withdraw petitions at five hotels and move forward at three. Only one resulted in certification before the year's end. The Gramercy Park Hotel, a luxury residential hotel that offered guests a skeleton key to the legendarily exclusive private park, agreed to a card check on December 5. Management was navigating foreclosure proceedings and didn't need an additional headache.[88]

As 1939 came to a close, the union threw a Christmas party for the Governor Clinton strikers and their families. Members from across the city pitched in to make it special for the kids, with presents, ice cream and cake, and entertainment that included a magician and a Punch and Judy show. The union had paid out over $49,000 in strike benefits to the members by then, and the strike and picket lines would continue through the winter.[89]

The union maintained an active caseload of Unfair Labor Practice (ULP) charges against employers who refused to sign the IWA. It filed twelve cases in December alone, including most prominently the large luxury hotel Savoy-Plaza, where worker-led marches on the boss inspired management to offer Christmas bonuses to turn down the heat (resulting in a new ULP). Even at this early stage of robust mediation by the SLRB, the ULP was slow and frustrating and usually a last resort. The union was running informational picket lines at the Buckingham, Hampshire House, and Raleigh hotels and was running a boycott campaign against the Astor's banquet operations.

In his end-of-year message to members, Rubin highlighted the latest employer to sign the IWA, a residential hotel on Central Park West that was owned by City Bank Farmers Trust called the Mayflower. Workers voted 100% for unionization three months prior. "In a number of other hotels signed contracts will be won shortly if through the strength and power of our organized ranks we make it clear to the employer that the workers are determined to get for themselves the protection of the union agreement," he wrote encouragingly.

At least 63 hotels had signed on to the IWA by the end of the year, and union membership stood at 25,000.[90] It was one of the fastest growing AFL affiliates in the city. It was a power broker within Mayor La Guardia's governing coalition, and Local 6 was a vitally important base of power within HRE. This would make the political affiliation of its leaders a flashpoint of controversy as the country braced for geopolitical realignments and a seemingly inevitable Second World War.

8

Only the Question of Final Alliances Remains
1939–1941

Miguel Garriga led a 31-member delegation to Cincinnati for the Hotel & Restaurant Employees' international union convention in April 1941. It was the union's "Golden Jubilee" and no local had grown faster or larger than Local 6. It should have been a moment of triumph. Instead, Garriga's reelection for Second District vice president was facing a challenge from his own secretary-treasurer, Michael J. Obermeier.

Among the architects of the union's biggest success story, Harry Reich of Local 89 urged delegates who were confused by this disunity "not to be misled by any rumors or slanders that may be circulated from whatever source they may come from, and if we do, I am sure we will leave this convention at the end of its sessions inspired ourselves, strong and powerful, so we can go out and come to the next convention with a powerful International Union and defeat those who seek to destroy us." It was a subtle allusion to the fact that HRE's success in New York was the result of a brokered coalition between the Communists and the AFL trade unionists, one that could be broken. Reading Reich's statement as a secession threat, a riled Garriga, snapped back: "There is only one question I want to ask, and I don't know whether it can be answered, had our International Union not appropriated $35,000 for the organization of the workers in the city of New York in 1937 would these elements have remained loyal to the American Federation of Labor?"[1]

The issue roiling the union was Communists' opposition to the war in Europe, in the interests of the Soviet Union. Maurice Isserman's *Which Side Were You On?* depicts the period between the start of the war and U.S. entry as years of isolation and peril for Party activists. Though most members "felt this was a testing period in which they would have to prove their mettle," he writes, "For liberals and independent radicals who had allied themselves with the Communists in the Popular Front, no similar satisfactions were available. Many felt a sense of personal betrayal."[2]

To HRE leadership the abrupt shift of their erstwhile allies—one day anti-fascist, the next anti-interventionist—made them seem as never before so alien. What began as a marriage of convenience to organize New York blossomed into Popular Front comradeship and became once again a tenuous and occasionally acrimonious amalgamation.

Non-Aggression

Ludwig Lore had been hounded out of his post as editor of *Volkszeitung* and driven to the edge of suicide by his Communist adversaries. By the mid-1930s he found a new career as a foreign affairs correspondent for the *New York Post*. A 1938 dispatch concluded, "European nations expect war in 1940; only the question of the final alliances remains to be settled."[3] Josef Stalin arrived at a similar conclusion, paranoid that the likeliest alliance was the great capitalist and fascist powers aligned against the Soviet Union. Stalin's emissaries attempted to reach accords with England and France but found them indifferent to Soviet concerns about Hitler invading neighboring Baltic states as a springboard to Soviet invasion. In the summer of 1939, Germany and the Soviet Union began secret negotiations and swiftly concluded a "Treaty of Non-Aggression" on August 23. Aside from a guarantee that neither party would attack the other or join any alliance with a country that declared war on the other, it bought Stalin time to build up Soviet military capabilities and a security sphere on its borders.[4] It gave Hitler the ability to invade Poland without facing any serious military opposition, which he did on the first of September. Britain and France declared war on Germany a few days later, and the second World War began with the USSR unaligned and invading the eastern portion of Poland.

The announcement of the pact caught the Communist Party of the United States flat-footed. Earlier in the summer, Earl Browder scoffed at rumors of such a deal. "There is as much of a chance," the CP leader declared, "as of Earl Browder being elected President of the Chamber of Commerce."[5] Now, the long-threatened war against fascism had begun and the Communists proclaimed, "The Yanks Aren't Coming." Popular Front organizations saw mass defections and liberal allies denounced Communists for being so obviously in the service of the Soviet Union and for violating the anti-fascist principles of the Popular Front.[6] "No American trade union dare assume the risks imminent with people holding these views in official position," editorialized HRE's magazine, *Catering Industry Employee*.[7]

Miguel Garriga took those words to heart. Garriga was a quintessential Popular Front-era fellow traveler. He served on the boards of front groups like American League for Peace & Democracy and the Friends of the Abraham Lincoln Brigade. He helped organize the 1938 May Day parade. His speeches were given pride-of-place coverage in the *Daily Worker*.[8] His break with the CP was utter, and his working relationship with his erstwhile comrades progressively deteriorated in the months before Pearl Harbor.

The first casualty of this new disunity was the LJEB, where some leaders like David Siegal and William Mesevich nursed anti-Communist grudges dating back to the old Amalgamated days. They began the year with plans to forge the LJEB into one big union of culinary workers by consolidating the number of craft locals; publishing a newspaper; and coordinating bargaining, strikes, and organizing. They ended the year mired in jurisdictional squabbling and factional intrigue. The World's Fair produced a constant tug of war over whose members got particular jobs at its concessionaires, and Local 6's wall-to-wall jurisdiction in hotels frustrated the other locals. In those days, union members got their life insurance, death burial benefits, and sometimes even their medical benefits through their local union membership. A waiter who took a job in a hotel stood to lose accrued benefits. Local 6 tried to work out cases with individual members, allowing their dues to be remitted to Local 1 or 16, but systematically, the leadership of the waiters locals were locked out of using their hiring halls for hotel jobs (some of which they used to control). When the Broadway-Central, a 70-year-old Greenwich Village hotel, signed the IWA in December 1940, Local 1 picketed, claiming that the hotel's banquet operations used to have a closed-shop agreement with them and that the hotel's restaurant jobs should be theirs. President Flore temporarily awarded Local 1 the jurisdiction just to bring the embarrassing spectacle to an end.[9]

The simmering dispute led to a reshuffling of officers in the LJEB. Miguel Garriga was "forced to relinquish" his staff job as executive manager "because of the pressure of his duties as international vice-president and as president of Local 6."[10] In June 1940, a Mesevich-endorsed and anti-Communist candidate for President of Local 302 prevailed over Kramberg's running mate.[11] Local 16 President David Siegal pushed William Albertson off his "Non-Political Controlled Union" administration ticket.[12] In turn, an anti-Communist was squeezed out of the LJEB presidency and replaced by Sam Kramberg.[13]

It was not merely their anti-war stance that made HRE's Communists a lightning rod. Many in the labor movement had severe misgivings about entering another world war. Even the American Federation of Labor was resolved in 1940 to "a firm determination to avoid involvement in European conflicts or in European wars."[14] The issue was how quickly American Communists shifted from anti-fascism to non-aggression, how obviously it was in the service of a foreign government, and how the Party line would repeatedly change in defense of the Soviet Union.

Local 6 mostly limited its anti-war work to agitating against profiteering defense contractors and tax unfairness in the pages of the *Hotel and Club Voice*, a new weekly newspaper it began publishing in June 1940.[15] The *Voice* quoted—at length—William Green's statement of opposition to the Burke-Wadsworth military conscription bill. The AFL president called for "voluntary action before compulsion," an "absolute guarantee" that draftees would only be employed in homeland defense—not in a "foreign war"—and pressed for job protections for workers who would be conscripted.[16] "Peace-time conscription will destroy civil liberties, will be used as a club over labor's head, will be 'Hitler's easiest Victory,' in the judgment of millions of members of organized labor throughout the United States," the *Voice* warned after FDR signed the act into law in September 1940.[17] By the time the draft was passed, the AFL had come to view it as a necessary act for "the assurance of peace," but continued to criticize the lack of legal force given to seniority and other job protections of men who would be pulled out of good union jobs for compulsory military service.[18]

Although published by Local 6, the newspaper was widely distributed within the hotels and was, in effect, one of the primary communications that NYHTC members received from *any* union. The Council, itself, however, avoided taking any position on the war (at least until Germany invaded the Soviet Union). As president of a multi-union coalition that included more conservative mechanical trades locals, Rubin couldn't toe the Party line and hold the Council together. He quietly resigned from Party membership, relegating himself to fellow traveler status.[19] Scores of union leaders did the same in these years. These Party "influentials" were still seen as comrades, as they continued to allow the Party to recruit members and fundraise within their unions and to push the Party line in their newspapers, meetings, and demonstrations while keeping themselves just far enough above the fray to maintain credibility and working relationships with more moderate allies. It was only years later that this organizational distance between the Party and its labor influentials would manifest as a "growing doubt about the wisdom of the Party's leadership."[20]

Fight and Play Together

Agitating to stay out of the world war was a sideline to the union's primary tasks, which were to improve working conditions, increase member involvement, and turn the union into a vital community—especially for those members who were new to the labor movement. Women were a particular concern. They comprised perhaps half the NYHTC membership. Few had prior activist experience, and many became union members through the deceptively easy manner of neutrality card checks. Local 6 formed a women's committee, which was a safe meeting space for women to ask questions, learn about the contract, and express opinions without feeling intimidated by men. The women's committee sponsored an annual scholarship for members to attend the Hudson Shore Labor School, a six-week residential program affiliated with Bryn Mawr. Charlotte Ferris, a waitress at the St. George, was the first to attend. Her diary of the experience for the union newspaper turned into a regular feature, "Listen, Sister!," a breezy social column peppered with pot shots at hotel bosses. Local 6 frequently turned entire issues of the *Voice* over to the women's committee, who used it to give members visibility and confidence and open up space for women in other industries to write about their labor struggles.[21]

One of the major projects of the women's committee was organizing around the Hotel Minimum Wage Board, which could set statewide wage and hour standards for hotel workers. The tripartite board, consisting of representatives for workers, businesses, and the public, conducted hearings around the state to offer a recommendation to the Department of Labor's Industrial Commissioner, who usually accepted a board's recommendation, particularly if it was unanimous. Drafted in excessive fear of the conservative Supreme Court, the 1937 state law only directly applied to women and children. Its coverage was further limited to industries that were not already covered by the federal minimum wage law, which continued the narrow definition of interstate commerce that was written into the Wagner Act.[22]

Helen Blanchard was appointed one of the three labor representatives on the Board, which began meeting in May 1940. Although its proposed minimums—26 cents with deductions for meals, aiming for a weekly paycheck of $10—were lower than the IWA standards, Local 6 mobilized dozens of members to testify at the public hearings. "Although this is a step forward it certainly is not adequate," declared housekeeper Esther Weilburg, who told the Board that she earned $13.50. "We do 22 rooms a day and 12 baths. We dust, scrub closets, wash fingerprints, etc . . . If any one of you would watch the girls as they go home you would see how tired they look and how rough their hands are and how their legs are swollen with varicose veins." The new minimum wage went into effect in November. Although the Local 6 women's participation in the process was and continued to be both solidaristic and aspirational, the minimums still put a floor underneath the IWA, providing a stronger argument for the October wage reopener, and put the union in the enviable position of scoring a real win for unorganized hotel workers.[23]

The union didn't limit itself to fixing problems on the job. Local 6 established a Welfare Department. Under the direction of Charlotte Stern, it encouraged members to walk into the union office with all manner of problems in their home life. Housing was a common issue, with some members needing advice for handling disputes with public housing authorities and private landlords and others needing help securing mortgages. Laid-off members needed help applying for unemployment. Foreign-born members were offered assistance in securing citizenship. The Welfare Department mostly gave advice and made authoritative-sounding phone calls on members' behalf, but occasionally offered financial assistance.[24]

The union sponsored a slew of recreational activities. "Fight and Play Together," the *Voice* editorialized when announcing its growing program of sports leagues, theater groups, dancing classes, summer camp options and even a stamp collectors club. "As hotel and club workers come together to throw their united strength in the scales for economic justice, they learn that they have other interests in common."[25] Reviving an old AFW tradition, the union hosted a large annual ball. The "First Annual Frolic" preceded the IWA's settlement in November 1938. Over 5,000 members and guests (including Hugo Ernst, who traveled in for the event) packed the Manhattan Center for the second annual ball. A slightly smaller crowd of 3,000 attended the following year, probably because the union used the ball as a fundraiser to purchase the building it had been using as a headquarters.[26]

The Local 6 Dramatic Group gave members opportunities to write, direct, and act in short plays and skits about working life. Its first play, a one-act called "Union Label," won first prize in a Trade Union Drama Tournament in December 1940 and toured around union halls and other venues.[27] Sports programs enrolled hundreds of members in weekly activities, starting with baseball. The 1940 season saw the Hotel Wellington's "55th St. aggregation of Satchel Paiges" top the team from the Hotel New Yorker in a three-game playoff to claim the championship.[28] Workers at dozens of hotels and clubs formed teams to join the league. The Sports and Culture Committee, with a designated staff liaison organized tournaments in bowling, basketball, handball, tennis, and ping pong. Bowling, like baseball, stuck around to be long-standing parts of the life of the union.[29] Even chess tournaments were organized when business agents Martin Cody and Richard Sirch opened up their "favorite relaxation" to challengers.[30] Some of the sports were organized under the aegis of the Trade Union Athletic Association, which affiliated 61 AFL, CIO, and independent unions in the New York area. In addition to its recreational activities, the Association was a tool for the CP to campaign against segregation in professional sports.[31]

Another organized group sport, one more typically associated with union activity, was volunteering for "flying squad" picket lines to protest the many hotels that continued to refuse signing the IWA.[32] Taking a page from the industry-wide strikes of long ago, the union's informational picket lines routinely snaked through midtown visiting one unfair hotel after another, as on

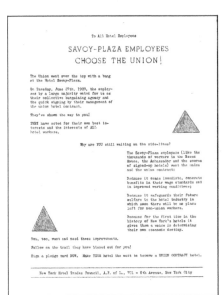

A collection of organizing leaflets emphasizing gains made in the Industry Wide Agreement. (New York Hotel and Gaming Trades Council. Located in Hotel Employees and Restaurant Employees International Union, Local 6 WAG.148, Box 15, Folder 2; Tamiment Library and Robert F. Wagner Labor Archive, New York University.)

June 4, when demonstrators at the Ambassador marched up Fifth Avenue and through the lobby of the Gotham before continuing to the Savoy-Plaza to do the same. Although the pickets were peaceful and orderly and the anti-injunction law protected their activity, the anti-union habits of beat cops died hard. Eleven pickets were arrested for "disorderly conduct" outside the Savoy-Plaza, including Scotty Eckford and Antonio Lopez (who was punched in the face and given a black eye and bruised jaw). The magistrate regarded the charge as so trivial he immediately released them from custody.[33]

One of the largest holdouts was the Hotel Astor, whose General Manager, Robert K. Christenberry, was on the Hotel Association negotiating committee that settled the IWA that he now refused to sign. The Astor had a busy banquet operation that was easily disrupted by boycott campaigners. No sooner was an event booked on the calendar than organizers reached out to the sponsoring organization to convince them to switch venues. In retaliation, the hotel fired 13 waiters and one captain in the dining room and "voluntarily" gave bartenders a $2.50 raise, provoking unfair labor practice charges in July.[34] The bitterest holdout, the Governor Clinton hotel, successfully staved off the IWA on April 8, 1940, when the year-long strike came to an ignominious end. The settlement, brokered by Mulrooney, La Guardia, and the SLRB included an agreement to rehire the strikers and to revert to the Status Quo Agreement.[35]

The Governor Clinton defeat did not cause the union to abandon strikes, but simply to be more judicious about calling them. On May 23, 1940, the union called a strike at the Bolivar, a 15-story residential hotel on Central Park West. The union had won an April 4 SLRB election, and management fired a handful of union activists. One hundred percent of the workers joined the strike, which lasted five days, until management signed the IWA.[36] Twelve hotels in total signed the IWA in 1940, adding another 1,000 members to NYHTC rolls.

In September 1940, the Council voted to reopen the IWA at the end of its first year. They proposed a ten percent across-the-board wage increase, a 40-hour workweek for mechanical maintenance and engineering workers (44 hours for everyone else), a second week of annual paid vacation, an explicit prohibition on charging employees for meals while they were on vacation (an easy and well-telegraphed-in-advance win), a stronger commitment to hire new employees through a union- or jointly-operated hiring hall, and a somewhat cheeky proposal that if hotel workers were caught up in the peacetime draft, employers would pay the difference between their military pay and what they would have earned as union members. Bargaining broke down in late January 1941, and the dispute was submitted to the Impartial Chairman.[37]

Un-American Activities

Other hearings would concern Rubin and Obermeier, perhaps without their knowledge. The CP's break with the New Deal coalition accelerated an ongoing process of investigation and legal regulation of Communist organizations, activists, and allies that would vex them in the short run, but ensnare them in a fight for their political lives in the long-term.

Anti-Communist union leaders, clustered chiefly—although not universally—within the AFL, were by 1938 frustrated by the closer relationship between the Roosevelt administration's National Labor Relations Board and the CIO, which they saw as infested with Communists. As Jennifer Luff detailed in *Commonsense Anticommunism*, to undermine their CIO rivals, the AFL turned to red-baiting and a conservative Democratic congressman from Texas who hated both Communists and the New Deal and was happy to connect the two in the public's mind.

That August, Rep. Martin Dies had the first witnesses sworn in before his new Special Committee on Un-American Activities. One of the first witnesses to volunteer testimony to the committee was Minnesota AFL leader John P. Frey, who complained of "Moscow's instructions to 'bore from within' the American labor movement" and named 280 organizers on the payroll of the CIO that he swore were Communists.[38] "CHARGES LEWIS AND CIO RULED BY COMMUNISTS," blared one sensationalized headline.[39]

Feeling fully legitimized at that point by its role in the CIO and the New Deal coalition, the *Daily Worker* brushed off Frey's testimony and the entire Dies Committee inquiry. "Wherever there are workers, there are Communists because the Communists themselves are workers." The August 16, 1938, editorial went out of its way to mention HRE as a "small part of a long list of A.F. of L. unions" that proudly had Communists in its ranks.[40]

The Nazi-Soviet Non-Aggression Pact gave the House Un-American Activities Committee a new focus in probing precisely how much of the Party's work was directed from Moscow in the Soviet Union's interests, and many more witnesses ready to name names. Earl Browder appeared before HUAC on September 7, 1939. He attested to the Party's wholly homegrown nature, and breezily answered affirmatively to the question, "Mr. Browder, have you ever traveled under a false passport?"[41] The frank admission resulted in a four-year prison sentence for passport fraud.[42]

Benjamin Gitlow, now an anti-Communist, testified two days later. After a few hours of questions about CIO leaders and staff, Dies inquired, "Now, to what extent has the Communist Party penetrated the A.F. of L.?" The committee only had one name, the Painters' Louis Weinstock. Gitlow offered up Rubin and Obermeier. He identified Rubin ("I'm not sure of his first name; I think it is Jay Rubin") as a district organizer and executive board member of the CP. He was under the mistaken impression that the two were still in Local 16 and that they had taken control by making common cause with gangsters (he didn't even name the correct gang, confusing the Irish "Legs" Diamond with the Jewish "Dutch Schultz!"), but there was enough truth in what he put on the Congressional record.[43]

Later, Joseph Zack, who organized the old Labor Unity League before William Z. Foster's "boring from within" directives made him shut it down, confirmed an inquiry about Obermeier's Party involvement. Maurice Malkin, a union activist who had signed the 1929 "Call for Trade Union Unity Convention" along with Obermeier and Kramberg and helped them build the FWIU, also identified Obermeier as an NYHTC leader and Comintern representative.[44]

By fall 1940, President Roosevelt was embracing the anti-Communist agenda of the more conservative congressional Democrats. In October 1940, he signed into law the Voorhis Act, which required "foreign controlled" political organizations to register with the federal government and to submit answers to 225 questions covering the names of members, donors, and sponsors as well as submit all published pamphlets and periodicals.[45] Denouncing the law, the CP made a show of formally disaffiliating from the Comintern in November in order to escape the new law's scrutiny.[46]

FDR also urged a law to prevent "Fifth Columnists" from becoming citizens. Congress passed the Smith Act, which made it a federal crime to "knowingly or willfully advocate, abet, advise, or teach the duty, necessity, desirability, or propriety of overthrowing or destroying any government in the United States by force or violence," or to belong to an organization that did. This included publishing, public speaking, and organizing. The Act further required foreign nationals to be fingerprinted and to sign an affidavit regarding the date and place of entry to the United States, the intended length of stay, the activities he or she expected to be engaged in, his or her criminal record (if any), and other information that the Immigration and Naturalization Service might request.

Although the Smith Act did not explicitly mention the CP, it was widely considered a Communist containment law, drafted in response to the government's inability to deport CIO longshore leader Harry Bridges.

In response to the Bridges deportation case, and anticipating a change in immigration law that would make membership grounds for deportation, the Party changed its constitution in 1939 to bar non-citizens. Michael J. Obermeier formally resigned from the Party around this time, although he remained a faithful fellow traveler. The Nationality Act of 1940 added to the Smith Act's "at any time" affidavit regarding membership in a revolutionary anti-government organization.[47] Rubin became a naturalized citizen in 1929—just outside the bounds of the Nationality Act's ten-year window—while

Obermeier, for whatever reason, waited until after Harry Bridges' difficulties to apply for citizenship in 1939. Both men's decisions would be fateful.

A Criminal of the Vilest Type

A twist of fate would provide Rubin and Obermeier another opportunity to remove a criminal element that preyed on unionized service workers. In January 1940, nationally syndicated columnist Westbrook Pegler published an open letter to William Green. "I am going to tell you today that the head of one of your big international unions was sentenced to Atlanta penitentiary for four years and six months for white slavery," he wrote of George Scalise, whom he called "a criminal of the vilest type that it is possible to imagine and a member of an old mob in Brooklyn."[48]

Paul Zack pounced on the allegations, as well as the CP controversies, in the scheduled March 1 run-off election against NYHTC at the St. George. "If you want a union not exploited by racketeers or utilized for the politics of a foreign power (Communist Party) vote for Local 28," read one leaflet. Another portrayed a many-tentacled "parasite" labeled "Scalise and Stalin" crushing the "Hotel Industry." Zack's dirty campaign resulted in a messy election. He garnered 297 votes to NYHTC's 234, with 64 challenged ballots remaining sealed.[49] NYHTC blocked certification of the results, and demanded that the challenged ballots be counted (which, if all were valid and cast for NYHTC, would give the union a one-vote victory over the Zack outfit).[50] Clearer than the results of the election was the conclusion that Scalise was an albatross.

Pegler's accusations also attracted Thomas Dewey's attention. The District Attorney was running for the GOP presidential nomination. Investigating Scalise offered another opportunity to burnish his reputation as a racket-buster and labor reformer while making headlines around the country.[51] Dewey had Scalise arrested at 3:00 AM on April 21 so that reporters had the colorful detail of the union head spending a night in the Tombs in his white silk pajamas. He was charged with running a $100,000 extortion racket. Campaigning in San Francisco, Dewey spoke by phone with the *New York Times*, predicting investigators would find a total of "about $1,000,000" extorted from hotels and janitorial firms.[52] Like his exaggerations in the earlier HRE racket case, this figure would eventually be quietly dropped, as would the entire extortion angle. Dewey's initial investigation aimed to find a novel way of prosecuting company unions from which the Wagner Act had withdrawn all legal protections. He abandoned the strategy because of the uncomfortable questions it raised about employer motivations. Who, exactly, was extorting whom when residential hotels cut deals with Scalise's 32-A in order to keep the more militant NYHTC out? Ultimately, Dewey prosecuted Scalise for embezzling $60,000 from his union.[53]

Indicted on April 26, he pleaded not guilty, and tendered his resignation "in justice to the international union," vowing, "my job is to be vindicated." The BSEIU executive board had already suspended him from office; its international convention was scheduled to open on May 6 in Atlantic City to pick his successor.[54]

On May 2, NYHTC took the extraordinary step of arranging a soft trusteeship of Local 32-A. Rubin excluded BSEIU officials from a special meeting in which the union decided to hold the local's dues money in escrow. The following week, one thousand members—half of 32-A's membership in NYHTC—attended marathon meetings organized by the Council at the Hotel Edison. It was the first membership meeting that any union leader had called for the front service workers in two years.[55] NYHTC secretary-treasurer, John J. Sullivan, joined Rubin in addressing the workers.[56] Hailing from IBEW, Sullivan's participation made this more a matter of cleaning up corruption within the AFL than a jurisdictional turf battle between HRE and BSEIU.

Because NYHTC—and not its affiliated locals—was the exclusive bargaining representative in the IWA, it was to the Council exclusively that hotels sent workers' payroll dues deductions. After taking its cut of per capita fees and expenses, NYHTC remitted the appropriate dues to the locals.[57] But now it deprived Local 32-A of its revenue because of its undemocratic and unrepresentative leadership. NYHTC's new Hotel Front Service Employees Union petitioned the BSEIU for a clean charter from the international union.

Local 32-A sued both NYHTC and the Hotel Association to block these moves.[58] Its president, James A. Seamon, and secretary-treasurer, Hy Eisenberg, charged that the new breakaway union was a Communist front.[59] It was. Because the Hotel, Restaurant and Cafeteria Workers Organizing Committee had salted jobs like bellman and doorman with CP activists when the hotel drive was originally started, a cadre of activists was well-positioned to take over the new local. NYHTC held elections to pick five rank-and-file members to serve as business agents while the Front Service local awaited its charter, and five Communists prevailed.

Drama followed at BSEIU's Atlantic City convention. Some of it was manufactured by a showboating Dewey who personally interrupted the proceedings to place four delegates, including acting President William McFetridge, under "technical arrest." Dewey complained that they were not doing enough to cooperate with the grand jury. The New York D.A. had no authority to arrest men from Illinois in the state of New Jersey, but Dewey still got his headlines.[60] Despite that, the convention elected McFetridge, who "had never been accused of any impropriety" to a term of his own as president and passed some modest reforms. Officer expense accounts were limited and subject to greater scrutiny, the international was given greater authority to investigate local union finances, and conventions were mandated to be held on a biennial basis. James J. Bambrick, more concerned with optics than substance, proposed a different local union numbering scheme in New York because "the number 32 creates confusion in the public mind."[61]

Scalise's trial revealed embarrassing details of how he ran his New York locals as sweetheart unions, offering organizers and lawyers a percentage commission for members they could enroll. One organizer received a charter to organize a Chinese Waiters Union in order to undercut an HRE organizing drive. He confessed to not caring at all about the workers' long hours and low pay but salivated at the 12,000 workers in the industry.[62] The paper trail that the prosecution reconstructed showed incredibly sloppy methods of embezzlement, abetted by a near-total lack of union democracy. A typical example involved Local 32-A, with a 1937 memo requesting a wire transfer of $2,500 from the union's secretary-treasurer. Scalise's only documentation of how he used the money was a $1,500 payment to the hotel local, while officers of 32-A swore they had never received more than $300.[63] On September 14, 1940, the jury convicted him of one count of embezzlement and four counts of forgery but deadlocked on five counts of grand larceny.[64]

It was political housekeeping time for BSEIU. Hoping for a deal that would allow them to run some kind of union, Seamon and Eisenberg wrote to McFetridge and graciously acceded to the demand for a new charter for workers "in the hotels having restaurants" but still insisted that they "retain jurisdiction of building service employees in this city working in rooming houses, residence clubs and hotels not having restaurants."[65] On October 10, McFetridge placed ten NYC locals under trusteeship but "expressed confidence in the principal officers" of Local 32-B and left them out of the purge. BSEIU finally granted the Hotel Front Service Employees Union a new charter as Local 144 in January of 1941.[66] John Goodman became secretary-treasurer. The new local's jurisdiction was limited to exactly what Seamon and Eisenberg were willing to concede: the hotels with restaurants that were the responsibility of the Hotel Trades Council to organize and represent. Local 32-A would continue to be a headache for BSEIU's leadership for a few more years.

These Are Not Normal Times

There was also drama at HRE's 1941 convention, which was pushed back a year to celebrate the union's golden anniversary, allowing the seething resentment between the CP and its detractors an extra year to fester.[67] "In normal times it would have been easy and delightful to dwell upon ... the proud achievements recorded through a half century of life," Flore lamented. "But these are not normal times. Today, as we observe this great milestone anniversary, our nation stands on the verge of either possible or probable participation in the greatest human struggle of all time. In every sense except armed fighting, we are in that conflict now."[68]

The Communists began the convention whipping votes for Jay Rubin to challenge Garriga, and when their headcount pointed towards a lopsided rout against him, they substituted Obermeier as the sacrificial lamb.[69] Left delegates attempted to amend the constitution so that each district vice president would "be elected from and by each of the eleven districts." Proportionally, the left was stronger in the Second District than it was when spread across the entire international union (although there were pockets of left support on the West Coast), but the move was handily defeated.[70]

Local 1 brought several anti-Communist resolutions to the convention. Local 16's David Siegal joined them in calling for an investigation into Communist activities.[71] None of these made it out of committee as Flore and Ernst tried to maintain some degree of unity. Partisan antagonists made heavy use of points of personal privilege to offer cryptic speeches to explain the sudden schism between the New York unionists to bewildered delegates. "When the name of this International Union was being dragged in the mud," Local 89's Harry Reich spoke of the Dutch Schultz scandal: "When the membership had lost complete confidence five or six years ago, we kept aloft the banners of the International Union and brought from chaos, from confusion the International membership in District No. 2."[72]

One constitutional amendment that did pass clarified the General President's authority to impose trusteeships upon affiliated locals. Throughout HRE's difficulties with criminal infiltration, the only constitutional remedy available was the suspension of a local charter. The union lifted the charters of its locals in New York and Chicago in the 1920s for their involvement in speakeasy operations only to watch the locals that replaced them become ensnared in protection rackets after the repeal of Prohibition. Ed Flore did not suspend the charters of Local 16 and 302 partly in fear that Dutch Schultz would continue to run them as independent unions with even less accountability. The General President was authorized—subject to the approval of the GEB—to suspend local officers found to be "dishonest, or grossly incompetent, or that the organization is not being conducted for the best interests of the Local and International" and replace them with a trustee "empowered to take full charge of the affairs."[73] The trusteeship article would loom over them like Chekov's gun through long years of factional discord.

The big showdown between Obermeier and Garriga was a fizzle. Garriga handily won reelection as HRE Vice President, with 1,712 votes to Obermeier's 384. The delegation of Local 6, with the obvious exception of Miguel Garriga, voted for Obermeier and were joined by the other Communist-led New York locals, but, even within just the Second District, Obermeier won less than a quarter of those votes.[74] Regardless of the method of election, the incumbent Vice Presidents were President Flore's HRE leadership slate. Flore was not about to abandon one of his vice presidents, particularly one who had been instrumental in so much of the union's growth. And no local leader who nursed ambitions for higher office or desired financial and organizing support for local campaigns dared buck the leadership at election time. David Herman, for instance, was still on staff as an international organizer and made sure to be outside the hall when his name came up during the roll call vote (although the rest of his Newark delegation felt free to vote for Obermeier).

Whether the purpose of challenging Garriga was to demonstrate that the Communists could not be taken for granted or to underline Harry Reich's bluff about departing for the CIO, all it demonstrated conclusively was that Miguel Garriga would not be the president of Local 6 much longer.

Experienced in the Way the Union Operates

As the world war worsened, the cold war within the labor movement thawed. After Paris fell on June 14, 1940, the AFL abandoned its isolationism and came out strongly for "rapid development of the nation's national defense," pledging "active and cooperative support with industry and with every appropriate governmental agency having to do with production and construction of material for national defense."[75] When Germany invaded the Soviet Union one year later, the CP just as swiftly returned to its Popular Front-era anti-fascism and stopped referring to the war as an imperialist contest. The *Hotel and Club Voice* gave extensive coverage of the AFL's "100% for Defense" campaign to buy defense bonds and proudly published the AFL's statement calling for "All-out" aid to the Soviets to "fight the Nazi war machine" on its front page.[76] HRE's *Catering Industry Employee*, for its part, declared, "We welcome the help that Soviet Russia's forced entrance into the war is giving our democracies and hope our people give freely and liberally of their resources to help the British-Russian alliance for the crushing of Hitler and Hitlerism."[77]

Despite the more congenial political atmosphere, the Communist leadership in Local 6 still moved to consolidate their power by planning a constitutional convention in November. The bylaws needed significant revisions to meet the needs of a local union that had grown to 15,000 members in the three years since they were written. The amendments that the convention approved balanced craft and shop floor representation with democratic centralism. The highest decision-making body in the union, between conventions, remained the Shop Delegates Council. "Each established and recognized unit" of a hotel or club elected a representative to confer with department managers and adjust grievances. Most other unions refer to this role as a shop steward, but since "steward" was a dining room job classification, the term "delegate" was used instead and had the double meaning of being a delegate to quarterly meetings of the SDC. It was a large body, well over 200 members, and it would grow as the union did. It debated and voted on matters such as bargaining priorities and political endorsements. It was more of a sounding board than a rubber stamp, and, crucially, one of its exclusive powers was to nominate candidates for the general officers. Although the President and other officers were elected by a secret ballot vote of the full membership, this ensured that only insiders were on the ballot. A smaller executive board met at least monthly to direct the activities of the union. It was composed of the board members of the union's seven craft-based departments: Banquet, Bartenders, Clubs, Dining Room, Housekeeping, Kitchen, and Miscellaneous.[78]

The convention decided that there should be one business agent per 1,000 members and debated a requirement that members serve at least one year on either the SDC or EB before they could even be nominated. "Our growth has put a tremendous responsibility upon us and our business agents should be experienced in the way the union operates," Obermeier explained of the proposal. "A year's prior training on the Shop Delegates Council is little enough to ask of prospective business agents." The convention delegates approved the extra requirements. They also approved a general statement that the local's president should be a full-time organizer. It was a clear statement that Miguel Garriga, whose responsibilities as HRE Second District vice president took up the majority of his time and effort, could not run for president again. It was not presented as a rebuke but rather as reflecting the growing union's needs.

By the time the SDC convened its nominations meeting in January 1942, they magnanimously nominated Garriga for one of the two vice president slots—unopposed. Helen Blanchard was nominated for the other slot.[79] Obermeier was, naturally, the full-time organizer who became president. The Party fraction wanted to move Gertrude Lane up to secretary-treasurer, but Ed Flore and Miguel Garriga were strongly opposed because she was so clearly associated with the CP.[80] It's also possible that they were reacting to the worst kept secret in the union: that she was quietly in a slightly scandalous romantic relationship with Jay Rubin. It started sometime in 1938, when she was on the staff of the Hotel, Restaurant and Cafeteria Organizing Committee and he was her supervisor. At the time, Rubin was married to and living with another woman, Mollie Rubin, and their three-year-old son, Donald.[81] In April 1939, Lane gave birth to a daughter whom she named Audrey Janice Rubin, and soon afterward, Rubin leased a second unit on the same floor of the West Side apartment building where he lived with his first family.[82] Like many Communists, Jay Rubin did not involve the state in his love life so there are no marriage records, but by 1941, Rubin and Lane were in a common-law marriage.

In any event, Flore and Garriga found Martin Cody to be a more acceptable candidate for secretary-treasurer. He was also a Communist, but he kept a lower profile at the international convention and within the LJEB, and, perhaps more importantly, he was not particularly close to Jay Rubin. Cody did not run unopposed. William Raymond, a bar department delegate at the Savoy-Plaza who would become a perennial opposition candidate, garnered 39% of the vote in the February 4 election.[83]

The Results of These Conferences

The Impartial Chairman hearings over the October 1940 wage reopener dragged on in 1941. Edward Mulrooney was loath to impose a wage order on the Hotel Association, lest it taint his reputation for impartiality. With only six months remaining before the expiration of the IWA, the parties were convinced to reenter direct negotiations and on June 27, 1941, they signed a new three-year agreement. The Hotel Association gave in to "an approximately 10% general wage increase," with a guarantee that no one would receive less than a $2 per week wage increase. This was made more palatable for the hotel owners by splitting the increase across two years. Half the wage increase would be paid upon ratification and the other half on June 1, 1942. As with the first IWA, there was provision for a wage reopener in the second year of the contract. The agreement made clear that newly hired employees would be paid the new effective base wage and that meals would not be deducted from vacation pay. It also added language guaranteeing "better and more adequate meals."[84]

Most of the IWA signatories signed the new agreement within two months, enjoying the guarantee of the agreement's no-strike clause until the summer of 1944. The union seized the moment to launch a new drive on open shop hotels. "Special concentrated efforts" were planned at the Astor, Sherry-Netherland, Plaza, and Waldorf-Astoria.[85] In its drive, union organizers had workers form organizing committees and also elect members to delegate and departmental representative positions as existed in the union houses under contract. As the Status Quo Agreement binding employers affiliated with the Hotel Association to sign on to the IWA was still in effect, organizers could campaign around wage and hour improvements that were all but guaranteed should a majority of workers join and vote for the union. With the drive declared and the expansion of union activity obvious, some employers voluntarily began bargaining with Jay Rubin.[86]

The first major hotel to sign after the IWA settlement was the St. George on July 3, bringing another 700 members into the union. After counting the challenged ballots, the SLRB ultimately certified NYHTC as the winner of the January election. Workers at the Savoy-Plaza, incensed at missing out on two wage increases even though the union had been their certified bargaining agent since the summer of 1939, formed a new organizing committee and began holding lunchtime rallies outside the hotel in August.

When negotiations stalled, twenty members conducted a march on the boss, cornering the general manager outside his office and demanding that the hotel simply sign the IWA, which its board of directors agreed to do two weeks later.[87] The union gained another 700 members and the bragging rights of winning the substantial back pay of the two raises in the IWA from a high-class holdout. "Pledge cards went like hot cakes in unorganized hotels, with workers signing them because they realized that their employers' failure to sign a contract deprived them of wage increases which they greatly need just now because of the steadily rising cost of living," the *Voice* reported.[88]

At the Hotel Victoria, one of the first to be certified by card check in 1938, workers also formed an organizing committee to finally win the benefits of the IWA. By the end of August, they voted to authorize "whatever steps are necessary to bring about the signing of a contract," which were basically a new unfair labor practice charge and a strike authorization vote. The organizing committee marched on the boss the first week of September. He was conveniently "not in the building," but headwaiter Felix Mormstein spent the following week running captive audience meetings. In them, he doubted that the union had a majority and told workers to come directly to him if they wanted raises and insulted one union delegate: "You have no right to belong to the union. You are a shoemaker. You are not a waiter." To smack down management's "question or controversy," the union turned to the SLRB to conduct a new election on September 19, which it won decisively: 122–46. Management finally signed the IWA one week later. Three days after the Victoria vote, workers at the Cornish Arms, a residential hotel in Chelsea owned and managed by the Knott hotels chain, voted nearly unanimously for union representation. Management signed the IWA one month later, adding another 74 members.[89]

"This is to advise that I am conferring with Mr. Jay Rubin, President of the Hotel Trades Council, who has made representation that the Hotel Trades Council should be the collective bargaining agent of Hotel Astor," Robert K. Christenberry haughtily announced in early October. "You will be advised of the results of these conferences."[90] The union had been running an effective boycott campaign against the Astor's banquet operations for over a year, and workers were restless that unionized hotels had gotten three wage increases in two years while the Astor had frozen the already low wages of its employees. After two weeks of conferences, Christenberry publicly committed to abide by the IWA and to accept the results of an SLRB card check, which took place on December 3.[91]

At the Plaza, which continued to have a strong base of dues-paying union members as it had for decades, union organizers and shop delegates could confer with management and adjust grievances, as when Antonio Lopez was able to reverse a decision to lay off cooks by proposing an alternative schedule rotation. The union used small victories like this to inspire workers to press on for the full protections of the IWA.[92] The contract settlement at the Savoy-Plaza, under common ownership and across the street from the Plaza, also helped to spur the workers on. Management tried to forestall the organizing drive's progress by granting across-the-board wage increases in October. If management was trying to send a message that workers didn't need a union to get more money, they inexplicably bungled that message by failing to match the union's weekly pay standards. A dishwasher's pay, the union propagandized, only increased to $12.15 a week—well below the IWA base rate of $15.[93] The union opened a special campaign office on Eighth Avenue just south of Columbus Circle, in space lent to them by Cooks Local 89. Workers were invited to walk in to join or get information, and regular meetings were scheduled. The campaign office was also employed to aid in organizing the other large luxury hotels clustered around Central Park South, particularly the Pierre, Sherry-Netherland, and St. Moritz.[94]

By November, union organizers were ready to file for an election. Plaza Management stipulated a consent election for 812 employees. It would be the largest union election held in the hotel industry by that point. It was an iconic hotel, an industry leader, and its various owners had been resisting union recognition for three decades. Union supporters won a smashing victory of 563 votes for the union to 206 against on December 5, 1941. Workers who gathered at the employee entrance on 58th Street to hear the results that Friday night began chanting, "Now for a contract!"[95]

Sunday brought news of the sneak attack on a U.S. military installation in the territory of Hawaii by the Japanese empire. A cascade of declarations of war put the United States in the middle of World War II.

The war would be the dominant factor in daily economic life for the next four years and would shape the labor relations paradigm for decades to come. The tensions over the Communist Party's influence on New York's hotel workers unions would be put aside for the duration of the war as all factions united to win the war effort. But, like the back-and-forth experiences of the Party line on dual unionism before it, the sudden shifts in union policy around war resistance and military preparedness—so clearly directed by the Communist Party and obviously in the service of Soviet interests—built a resentment and mistrust that threatened the long-term viability of the partnership between the Communists and HRE's mainstream.

9

We Cook, Serve, Work for Victory
1941–1945

"The hotel worker was so long neglected and abused in the days before the union came into the field," Jay Rubin declared in September 1944, "that it becomes a striking fact that hotel operators are now to assume some of the social responsibility they owe their workers." The dramatic revolution he was celebrating, an "industry-wide social security plan" covering life, sickness, accident, and hospitality insurance—administered by the union but fully funded by the employers—came about in a quite undramatic fashion.[1]

An inflation-fighting National War Labor Board restricted union-negotiated wage increases but exempted fringe benefits. NYHTC made insurance benefits its centerpiece demand in that year's IWA wage reopener. Placed before the "3-Man" Commission—union representative Rubin, management representative Fred O. Cosgrove of the Knott hotel chain, and Impartial Chairman Edward P. Mulrooney—the social security plan was ordered and approved by the NWLB within weeks.

In his seminal *Labor's War at Home*, Nelson Lichtenstein explained the NWLB as a key process "in which business and labor firmly established the industry-wide collective bargaining that would prove routine throughout most of the postwar era."[2] His was a study of CIO unions in which "industry-wide" meant pattern bargaining with massive national corporations. The New York hotel industry was a rare example of a multi-employer collective bargaining agreement subject to wartime federal regulation. Elsewhere, in his biography of Autoworkers leader Walter Reuther, Lichtenstein explains that many CIO leaders "proved notably unenthusiastic about exploiting" the NWLB's "Little Steel" formula to win employer-sponsored insurance, preferring to fight for a national health plan through an expansion of the Social Security Act, a social democratic impulse endorsed by CIO Communists.[3] It's interesting then that AFL Communists, in NYHTC leadership, joined the many AFL unions that won employer-sponsored benefits during the war and created a miniature system of socialized medicine for the hotel industry.

Compared with the controversy and strife that preceded American entry into the war, and that which would follow the war's end, the war years stand out as a period of relative political peace within HRE. Former allies forged new partnerships, particularly in support of the war effort—on the home front, in combat, and in foreign service. Leadership elections were largely uncontested, and organizing drives were well-funded and coordinated between the international union, LJEB, and its locals. Rubin and Michael J. Obermeier even found time to document and celebrate their union's history. However, the emerging diplomatic tensions between the erstwhile Allied powers—portending the Cold War—would soon be felt within the union.

Support and Loyalty

The Allied war effort facilitated a unity of purpose that had been lacking in HRE. Sixty-five LJEB leaders assembled a few days after Pearl Harbor to plan the hospitality industry's war support work. They were convened by Miguel Garriga, who was tapped by the AFL's Central Trades and Labor Council to lead it.[4] In February, Garriga ceremonially installed the newly elected Local 6 leaders. The acrimony of the past year was quietly disremembered. He expressed personal pride in the successful unionization of the industry and his hope to remain a member of Local 6 "for a good many years to come." Turning to President Obermeier, he declared, "As far as my support and loyalty are concerned, I don't have to emphasize that you have them."[5]

The *esprit de corps* extended to management. On December 18, Jay Rubin and Hotel Association executives met with Treasury Department officials to plan a war bonds drive.[6] Shop delegates pledged to raise $500,000—half from workers' payroll deductions and half from management contributions—at its January 1942 meeting.[7] The LJEB pledged $1.25 million in a separate drive. By the end of January, twelve Manhattan locals had raised a million dollars in war bonds.[8] By summer, Obermeier was leading a blood drive, seeking a pint from every member.[9]

War activities, however, did not distract from organizing opportunities. The union won one more SLRB election before 1941 ended. Workers at the Hotel Chelsea, the famous residential haunt of artists and bohemians, voted for NYHTC on December 16, rejecting a raiding CIO union by a vote of 33–17.[10] In early January, the 700-room Hotel Empire finally returned to the bargaining table—over two years after the union was certified by the SLRB—when 100 workers staged a nine-hour strike.[11] It would be one of the last official wartime jobs actions.

NYHTC entered 1942 with 83 hotels under contract, representing 13,500 members. Some of the largest hotels, however, remained non-union. These bastions of the industry like the Plaza—recently certified as a union bargaining unit but not yet under contract—and the Waldorf-Astoria were scenes of long years of struggle for the city's hotel workers unions. "As long as there remains even a small section of the industry that is on an open-shop basis, some bosses will take full advantage," Jay Rubin argued as he pressed the Council to wage a renewed organizing drive.[12] The union opened a new field office around the corner from the Waldorf and relaunched its membership drive in January with high hopes of bringing the hotel's 1,500 workers under the terms of the IWA before the end of the year.[13]

And After

As the factional strife within HRE was pushed aside, the Communist Party's pariah status during the Soviet-Nazi non-aggression pact was similarly papered over now that the Soviets were a U.S. ally. This helped make the CP's sometimes-awkward association with the Soviet Union—to the extent of appearing to do its bidding in U.S. domestic politics—generally more palatable.

Nearly 15,000 Communists signed up for military duty, although military brass looked warily upon "potentially subversive personnel" and held many back from active fighting until the demands of the planned D-Day invasion made them less picky about who was going to charge at German guns.[14] Over 1,100 members of Local 6 similarly volunteered in that first year, including business agents Leo McCarthy, Glen Stocks, and Don Tillman and *Hotel Voice* editor Jerry Fling. Stocks was awarded a Silver Star after being wounded on a North African battlefield.[15] Important next-generation union leaders also volunteered. David Herman left HRE staff to become NYHTC's administrative director.[16] John Steuben, a veteran steelworkers organizer and author of a book and several pamphlets, was hired by Hotel Front Service Local 144 to be its education director, at the direction of Party leaders who wanted someone with gravitas and ideological grounding to direct its hotel fraction since Obermeier and Rubin were no longer formally members.[17] Both men volunteered within months of being hired in 1943.[18]

Obermeier volunteered for the Office of Strategic Services (OSS), the predecessor of today's Central Intelligence Agency, after the agency asked the Party to vet activists who spoke multiple languages, had foreign contacts, and knew how to cross international borders undetected.[19] He provided intelligence gathered from European comrades, and recorded German-language radio speeches that praised "the degree of freedom accorded a German in the United States [that] was unknown anywhere in the world." These were broadcast by the Office of Naval Intelligence to German fighters on the front lines. He impressed the agent in charge of the New York office's labor desk with his "unusual physical courage in offering to go to Germany himself" to engage in espionage. Because Obermeier was still a German citizen, his offer was politely declined.[20]

In muted recognition of this work in support of the war, and as a subtle act of diplomacy, FDR commuted Earl Browder's prison sentence in May 1942. As quickly as he returned to leadership, Browder published a book, *Victory and After*, that attempted to synthesize the CP's seat-of-its-pants strategic compromises—vocal support for no-strike pledges and speed-ups in defense industries and a strict loyalty to the Roosevelt administration's war policies—into something approaching an ideology. Operating with the least direction from Moscow in his entire career (since the Comintern dissolved itself in June 1943 as an olive branch to the Allies), Browder was so convinced of a harmonious postwar future that he pressed the Communist Party to reconstitute itself as a new Communist Political Association that wrapped itself in the "traditions of Washington, Jefferson, Paine, Jackson and Lincoln."[21]

War Activities

In 1942, the *Hotel & Club Voice* added the slogan "A dime out of every dollar we earn IS OUR QUOTA for VICTORY with U.S. WAR BONDS" to its masthead, and huge banners hung outside the union headquarters' Eighth Avenue facade declaring, "We Cook, Serve, Work for Victory."[22] Victory for union leaders meant a home front that offered better jobs and more respect for women and minorities. Gertrude Lane advocated for child care for women in defense industries in the AFL's Labor Women's Defense Committee, Women's Division of the federal Department of Labor, and the Committee for the Care of Young Children in Wartime.[23] Martin Cody protested the Red Cross' practice of segregating the blood of Black donors.[24] Charles Collins editorialized against segregation in the "Jim Crow Army," lobbied the federal Manpower Commission to do more to fight racial discrimination in defense industries, and pressed the Hotel Association to hire Black workers to fill wartime job vacancies.[25]

Charlotte Stern, Local 6's Welfare Director, became "War Activities Director." The union raised substantial sums for Labor's War Chest, which made charitable contributions of food and clothing for Allied home fronts. So prodigious was Local 6's fundraising that AFL First Vice President Matthew Woll, an inveterate anti-Communist, commended them for contributing the second largest amount in 1944. The Local's $107,897 was only bested by the *entire* International Ladies Garment Workers Union.[26] In addition to ongoing blood and bond drives, union organizers were circulating petitions to President FDR to open a second front in Western Europe, coordinating collections of recyclable scrap metal (under the regrettably racist slogan "Slap a Jap with Scrap") and organizing classes in first aid and home nursing.[27]

The War Activities Committee sent care packages of cigarettes and the *Voice* to members serving overseas.[28] By D-Day, 2,000 Local 6 members were serving in the armed services. At least 150 had been wounded in combat and five had been killed.[29] After combat ended in Europe, Local 6 recruited cooks and stewards for the War Shipping Administration to staff the ships bringing soldiers home.[30]

The union organized several ethnic affinity groups to support home front activities. There was a Spanish-American Labor Committee, a Greek-American Labor Committee, an Italian-American Victory Committee, and a German-American Trade Union Victory Committee. The German-American Trade Union Victory Committee, in particular, was a joint effort of AFL and CIO union activists to appeal to the diaspora of the once robust network of German socialist and union activists to undermine the Nazi regime from within.

Ironically, this solidaristic trade union organizing on behalf of the Allied war effort—not his work for the OSS—put Obermeier in the U.S. government's

"We Cook, Serve, Work For Victory." Local 6 headquarters in 1942. (New York Hotel and Gaming Trades Council.)

crosshairs. The independent effort so alarmed the FBI that on April 20, 1942, J. Edgar Hoover personally ordered an investigation into the Committee's founding chairman and secretary, whom the FBI Director was aghast to learn was not on the Bureau's voluminous list of Communists who were to be "considered for custodial detention" depending on postwar geopolitical alliances.[31]

Agents' first report, filed in June 1943, contained intelligence from Ludwig Lore. While serving as a foreign newspaper correspondent, Lore had also become a National Defense informant providing intelligence on underground German leftists at home and abroad. Lore reported on Obermeier's speech at a March 1942 German-language rally. Lore saw the Party's attempt to "control as many German refugees as possible," which "would pay dividends if Hitler falls, and important refugees under Party influence trek back to take a hand in the government that follows." To underscore how dangerous he thought Obermeier was (and to settle a few old scores), he described Obermeier's role in the 1929 cafeteria strike's sabotage campaign. It would be his final act of revenge. Lore wrote his memo on April 20, 1942.[32] Less than three months later, he would die of a heart attack at the age of 67.[33]

This cursory report found plenty in the *New York Times* archives to document Obermeier's and Sam Kramberg's 1929 legal entanglements. The Bureau's own *Daily Worker* archive was probed. The Congressional record of the Dies Committee provided more fodder. A spy within the German-American Trade Union Victory Committee leaked the meeting minutes, but the Committee's own press releases possibly added more names to the FBI's security index. One informant, Otto Schatz of the erstwhile company union Geneva Society, dished on his quarter century of spying on the union organizer. He offered details of two trips—and one specific ocean liner, the S.S. Leviathan—he knew of Obermeier taking to Russia.

Detectives in the New York Police Department's anti-red "Special Squad 1" recommended that FBI agents interview Miguel Garriga, who eagerly cooperated.[34] A former member of the Party's National Committee who had been confidentially informing on his ex-comrades for some time was interviewed at length about Obermeier's Party assignments.[35] More creepily, a neighbor in Queens tattled that Mrs. Obermeier was familiar with the weather in Moscow.[36] Confidential informants ratted on his presumed Party membership and verifiable leadership in the TUUL, AFW, and FWIU as well as his many trips in and out of Russia. By May 1944, Obermeier was considered a "Key Figure" in the FBI's "Internal Security" index.[37]

The Bureau also opened a general investigation into "Communist Infiltration of Hotel and Restaurant Employees Unions" and specific investigations into Jay Rubin and Gertrude Lane. Because Rubin had become a naturalized citizen in 1929, agents had less of a case to pursue under the Smith Act. He was added to the Security Index, and agents continued to keep tabs on him.[38] Gertrude Lane was a natural-born citizen. Despite receiving (incorrect) evidence that she served on the CP's National Committee, she was dismissed as "not currently of sufficient importance" to add to the Bureau's Security Index. Instead, the New York office mildly collected her birth, education and voter records, known aliases, and whereabouts—and passively accepted tips from snitches.

Breaking the Ice

The union's renewed organizing drive faced an early setback when workers at the Warwick voted 74–88 against unionization on February 16, 1942. In the week before the election, two workers were fired. A "goon squad" of anti-union workers was whipped up to lead a whisper campaign of intimidation while the hotel's front service manager stationed himself outside the employees' entrance and spied on workers' interactions with union organizers. And the hotel's general manager Frank W. Kridel lied about employees' rights under the SLRB during a captive audience meeting. Although the SLRB permitted employers a free speech right to campaign against union certification, spying and lying about the process were violations of the law. The union filed objections.[39]

The experience at the Warwick caused the union to reevaluate its organizing staff. Many of the newer organizers deployed for the drive were rank-and-filers called up from their hotel jobs and relatively inexperienced in organizing (particularly in the face of employer opposition). The NYHTC Board, whose main motivation in employing rank-and-filers was to save money, resolved to pay higher salaries for experienced organizers in March, a process of staff professionalization that brought David Herman back to New York.[40]

Not that the bosses were effectively repelling the union organizing drive. The same week as the Warwick vote, workers at the Belvedere, a 20-story apartment hotel located downtown, voted 81–10 for the union.[41] Workers at the Drake, an all-suite Bing and Bing-managed residential hotel owned by Chase National Bank voted 92–15 for the union in February.[42] March brought a 31–6 SLRB win at the Knott chain's Bryant hotel, and two apartment hotels where the union had previously been certified, the Oliver Cromwell and the Russell, finally signed the IWA.[43]

The Plaza finally signed the IWA in March 1942. The sticking point was the across-the-board wage increases that management gave out in October to forestall the organizing drive. It brought one-third of the bargaining unit over the IWA's base wage. Since the IWA called for workers to get either the base wage or a $1 raise (or more—as much as $2.50 for the maintenance crafts), this would have increased the Plaza's payroll by 30% when the June 1, 1942, raises kicked in. Plaza management asked NYHTC to recognize the October raises as a part of the contractual wage package and delay the second wage increase. In shop committee meetings, workers expressed a willingness to swallow the bitter pill to get the contract. The 240 workers who were above the base rate would get a raise in September, but not when the IWA went into effect. Since many of that group were being asked to pay union dues for the first time with no wage increase to offset their payroll deductions, NYHTC decided to waive their local union dues until September. They would only be assessed the (far smaller) per capita fees to the Council and their respective international unions.[44]

Eight more hotels signed the IWA between March and May. Most were recently certified via SLRB elections.[45] In a report to the Council, Jay Rubin stated that "there is no question in any one's mind that we are breaking the ice among those employers who were organized for years to fight the collective agreement and to fight the HTC."[46]

In July, an organizing committee of employees in the engineering, housekeeping, and dining room departments of the Ritz-Carlton went public with their organizing drive.[47] The building, at 46th and Madison, was the first property to carry what is now a franchised luxury brand name. Its owner, Robert Walton Goelet, died the previous summer and bequeathed the building (estimated to be worth as much as $15 million) to his alma mater, Harvard University.[48] The absentee landlord left management to its own devices, which was mostly union-busting. When the hotel fired union activist Anthony D'Ambrosio during the drive, Charles Verillio, the organizer on staff, immediately recognized the name of the manager who fired the waiter. Charles Silvani had fired Verillio from Pierre's Restaurant in 1921 for his AFW membership. This time around, the ex-waiter served up a cold plate of revenge in the form of a ULP, which was later sustained, and the union won an SLRB election in September.[49]

July also saw management at the St. Moritz (where the union lost an August 1939 SLRB election) reenter negotiations with Jay Rubin. The hotel corporation's president, S. Gregory Taylor, was also an officer of the Hotel Association, which is why he agreed to meet with Rubin, who proposed a neutrality card check conducted by the Impartial Chairman. Taylor insisted upon a new election. The union retained majority support, but leaders doubted they could prevail in a new election if management campaigned against unionization. A few days after their meeting, Taylor gave his employees—some of the city's lowest-paid luxury hotel workers—raises of between $1 and $7 a week and tried to form a company union, offering a contract that would lock in the wage increases, promise no discrimination, and allow terminations to be appealed to his hand-picked representatives.

Union delegates circulated an open letter, stating "we'd never have received these increases without the union," and "we demand that Taylor negotiate with our shop committee, together with our union representatives, and sign the contract."[50] On July 3, the militants staged a work stoppage that tied up service in the hotel for a few hours until Taylor signed a stipulation that he would meet again with Rubin and either sign the IWA or lay the dispute before the Impartial Chairman. That session bore no fruit until Mulrooney joined and then it got slightly ridiculous. Taylor continued to insist upon a new SLRB election. Rubin argued that the stipulation Taylor signed the week before had the effect of granting formal union recognition, making an election moot. Incensed at the union's tricky play, Taylor accused the union of violating the no-strike clause of the IWA he refused to sign.[51] The parties met with the Hotel Association's full committee of hotel managers on the IWA bargaining team for hearings throughout July. Hotel Association representatives feared that forcing the union on the St. Moritz in this manner would spark another secession movement like the Hotel League debacle, which Taylor was agitating for. A compromise was finally worked out in which one more hearing was conducted in August for the union to establish, through worker testimony, that it enjoyed majority support. Meanwhile, Taylor was offered assurances that he could apply for Article 28 wage relief and receive a fair hearing if he signed the IWA, which he did on August 13.[52]

That summer saw the union reach the limit of the support it could muster among employees at the Waldorf-Astoria. Organizers had collected about 820 union authorization cards—a slim majority of the presumptive bargaining unit.[53] The Waldorf had been the union's top organizing priority since the union was founded, but management ran a constant anti-union campaign that was a sophisticated pioneer of operating within legal bounds. Its "Employer-Employee Relations" manual was updated and distributed every year. In addition to promising an "open door to management" and laying out a grievance procedure, the 39-page document emphasized that the law did not require employees to join a union. In a letter, Lucius Boomer explained his decision to pull out of the Hotel Association as not wanting to let a union be forced upon his employees without their consent.[54] In a velvet glove, management's iron fist handed workers an insurance program that mocked parity with the union shops.[55] Union supporters would occasionally disrupt captive audience meetings with needling questions about recognizing the union, events they cheekily described to organizers as "Boomerangers" because "when one of the employees got up and suggested to the boss that the Waldorf workers deserved a raise, you never saw such Boomer-anger."[56]

Management's campaign was most successful in the housekeeping and laundry departments, the predominantly female segments of the workforce, while the union garnered its best support in the dining rooms and kitchens where workers had been organizing for decades and in the maintenance crafts where union identity among workers was strong. Even still, when IBEW Local 3 grew impatient with organizers' slow progress with the rest of the workforce and filed for an SLRB election among the 17 electricians and helpers on payroll in 1940, it lost that election.[57]

In the renewed drive, the union held daily meetings by job class in its 3rd Avenue field office and touted a 100 percent sign-up rate in at least six departments. Management responded by firing one union activist, a houseman named Benito Tores, calling it a layoff. Tores was not a key leader of the effort, but he was seen as enough of a union supporter that the termination had its intended chilling effect. The union filed a ULP and publicized the case until it quietly stopped mentioning it.[58] Management followed up with discriminatory wage increases. Maids received raises of $1 a week; bartenders got $2.50. Employees in the dining rooms and kitchens, the front service staff, and the electricians got stiffed.[59] Even though the wage increases were clearly based on perceived union support (and lack thereof), the union didn't file a ULP lest it be accused of opposing the maids' raises.

Despite the uneven support, the union decided to risk an SLRB election. The stipulated bargaining unit consisted of 1,639 employees, and the election date was set for October 27.[60] It was a drubbing. Workers voted 935 to 473 against unionization.[61] The union filed objections, but as outrageous as Boomer's union-busting had been, it didn't run afoul of the law. The SLRB found "insufficient evidence" of management interference, within the definition of the law and rejected the union's case.[62]

The disappointment of the Waldorf loss was tempered a bit by the successful conclusion of the union's organizing drive focused on the luxury hotels clustered around the Plaza on Central Park South. Workers at the 700-room Pierre voted 151 to 76 for the union in November.[63] By the middle of January 1943, the union filed a representation petition at the swanky Sherry-Netherland, a 525-room hotel managed by Lucius Boomer. After a brief work stoppage forced owners to agree to an expedited SLRB election, 74 percent of eligible voters chose union representation, bringing another 271 members into the union. Management dragged their feet for two months before signing on to the IWA.[64] All told, NYHTC won twelve representation elections in 1942, another eleven in 1943, and 40 hotels would sign the IWA in those years.

Local 6 also continued to organize workers under its exclusive jurisdiction in private clubs and hotel restaurants, where, without a multiemployer framework, it was particularly dependent on the SLRB's machinery. In June 1942, 33 of 37 culinary employees at the Lawyers Club voted for Local 6.[65] The SLRB ordered a new election at the Cloud Club after finding that management committed ULPs at a captive audience meeting prior to its first election. The union won a January 1943 rerun election, 30–11, and the workers ratified a first contract within a month.[66] In October, 86 percent of workers at the University Club voted for Local 6, bringing another 170 members into the Club Dept.[67] In February 1943, the New York Athletic Club granted union recognition to nearly 250 workers—the largest bargaining unit of private club employees in the country while Local 6 won a rerun election at the Whitehall Club.[68] In 1943, Local 6 also won an SLRB election for the workers at La Guardia Airport's restaurants. Freestanding restaurants were slightly farther afield from the local's jurisdiction but justified by the fact that the airport restaurants were owned and managed by the New Yorker Hotel.[69]

By its fifth anniversary in February 1943, Local 6 had grown to 15,000 members.[70] NYHTC ended the year with 20,400 members at 127 hotels.[71] The pace of new organizing slowed for most of the war years, as the union turned its attention towards winning new wage increases, which would be complicated by federal wartime cost control measures.

War Labor

Hotel staff turnover was extremely high by the summer of 1942. Of those who didn't join the armed forces, many went into more lucrative employment in defense industries. Scheduled wage increases that went into effect on June 1 were already insufficient to maintain staffing levels. The union began circulating petitions to press for an immediate wage adjustment.[72] The current IWA was not set to expire until 1944 and only allowed for a June 1943 wage reopener. Amazingly, the Hotel Association agreed to enter direct negotiations and made a wage settlement without appealing to the Impartial Chairman. Tipped employees won a $1.50 a week raise, with all other bargaining unit members receiving $2.00, effective October 10, 1942.[73] The wage increases, however, had to be approved by the National War Labor Board, which enforced federal anti-inflation policies to limit wage increases to less than three percent in 1942.[74]

A tripartite federal agency with the authority to end work stoppages, mediate negotiations between unions and employers, and approve collective bargaining agreements, the NWLB was primarily concerned with maintaining production in the defense industries, where the CIO unions had recently completed a strike wave with little historical precedent. Nearly 2.4 million workers were involved in strikes in 1941. Only 1919 could boast more by that point.[75]

The leaders of the AFL and CIO who agreed to a "no lockout no-strike" pledge hoped for the NWLB to have wide authority—superseding that of the NLRB—to impose union shop standards on recalcitrant employers and to adjudicate reasonable pay standards.[76] Ed Flore endorsed both the NWLB and the no-strike pledge in "all war and defense material production industries."[77]

However, the NWLB soon applied its no-strike and contract approval provisions to the hotel and restaurant industries. Created by an executive order—by the commander-in-chief of the armed forces during a time of war—the NWLB was not limited by the definition of interstate commerce and soon regulated labor relations across the entire economy.

The NWLB was concerned with inflation driven by rapidly rising wages in the defense industries and limited availability of consumer goods. In July 1942, it settled on a three percent limit on wage increases in a pattern settlement in the steel industry. The "Little Steel" Formula would apply to all industries—including hospitality—as a *de jure* rule.[78] However, on October 3, 1942—one week before the wage increases in the new IWA were set to go into effect—FDR issued an executive order clarifying that raises would be allowed in limited circumstances to address inequality of pay or wages that lag industry standards.[79]

At the time that labor and management applied for NWLB approval, union leaders speculated that it would be the first, "or certainly one of the first," industry-wide cases brought before the new agency.[80] NWLB found it difficult to calculate the cost of living "due to the great number of hotels and employees." In its filings, the union encouraged the Board to think of the hotel workforce as three broad categories of workers—culinary, housekeeping, and maintenance—and filed copies of the hotel and restaurant minimum wage board decisions, the wage scales of HRE Locals 16 and 302, and the wage scales in the electrical and carpentry trades. The NWLB had just approved the wage increases in BSEIU Local 32B's industry-wide agreement with the Realty Advisory Board, which David Drechsler pointed to as justifying the hotel industry's wage increase. In addition, he submitted letters from several hotels attesting to their staff turnover.[81] As long as wage increases stayed within the NWLB's formulas, the Board approved them. On December 8, after several weeks of consideration, the NWLB approved the agreement on the grounds laid out in FDR's October order: that its wage increases served to eliminate inequalities both within the hotel industry and between comparable jobs in the city.[82]

Before the NWLB issued its decision, when it was clear that it would approve wage increases in the hotel industry, the Hotel Association asked for approval to give out raises at 33 non-signatory hotels. The union intervened in this new case. The union raised "no objection to the immediate granting" of the stingier wage increases that the Hotel Association was seeking, but reserved the union's right to "obtain the full amount of the wage increase obtained by the workers" in the IWA hotels should the workers vote for union representation. However, at four hotels that refused to sign the IWA, despite union certifications, it sought to block the increase. On February 1, NWLB Regional Director Theodore W. Kheel informed management at the Ambassador, Ritz-Carlton, Towers, and Warwick hotels that it was "not possible for this office to process your application as a voluntary wage adjustment without the Union."[83] Under such pressure, the Ritz-Carlton signed on February 15. The Warwick agreed to a snap SLRB rerun election two days later and signed on March 8. The Towers signed at the end of March, but immediately appealed for Article 28 relief from the full wage increases. The Ambassador held out until workers went on strike in November 1944, frustrated with management's intransigence as consumer prices continued to climb.[84]

The parties would continue to bargain on an annual basis throughout the war years with the next round starting not long after the 1942 retroactive wage increases went into members' bank accounts. Even with federal price and wage controls, inflation was running around six percent in the winter of 1943, eating up roughly half of the wage increase that workers had just won. Meanwhile, most hotels were making profits hand over fist. According to union estimates, hotel reservations increased 32 percent between 1942 and 1943, and hotel restaurant sales increased by as much as 33 percent.[85] The union asked for the contractual wage reopener on February 27, 1943. Before the parties could meet, President Roosevelt issued Executive Order 9328, a "hold the line" wage and price stabilization order that significantly restricted unions' wiggle room in contract bargaining. Bargaining dragged on into the summer, largely because of all parties' uncertainty about whether the NWLB would approve any wage deal.[86] Following a series of shop meetings and an almost ritualized membership rally at the Manhattan Center, the Hotel Association acceded to the union's wage demands in mid-July.[87] The raises were again targeted to reduce inequalities, with some workers gaining as much as $4.50 a week. The more in-demand mechanical and maintenance trades, along with cooks, bartenders, and housemen, got a general $3.00 a week raise while tipped waitstaff and bellmen got $1.50, with everyone else guaranteed $2.00 more.[88]

The parties signed the WLB-approved two-year contract extension on September 1, 1943, with raises retroactive to June 1. (The union immediately launched a "Back the Attack with Your Back Pay" war bonds campaign.[89]) The NWLB continued to aid the union's perennial challenge of getting hotels to sign on to the IWA. Hotels that dragged their feet on signing and implementing the wage increases were hauled before the NWLB as dispute cases, with the NWLB routinely ordering the employer to sign. Although hotels remained profitable, many still appealed to the NWLB for relief from the substantial wage increases, but the labor board rarely granted it—and only on back-pay awards—never on raises going forward.[90]

Because the 1939 IWA and its successor agreements set across-the-board percentage increases for all employees, and a wage floor for the lowest-paying hotels, rather than uniform wage scales across job classifications, the inflation and wage-control formula exacerbated inequalities within New York's hotel industry. The union was able to utilize NWLB machinery to bring the lower wage scales at stingier union houses closer to the median wages in the industry. Some of these were dispute cases, but often the individual hotels and the union jointly asked for permission to grant wage "adjustments" mid-contract.

This was a micro form of "industry-wide" collective bargaining. A typical round-up of NWLB adjustments reported raises "of $2 a week asked for 79 workers in the dining room, bar, front service and housekeeping departments and for a chef and two firemen" at the Greystone "were approved except that six in the housekeeping department were approved in part and denied for two workers"; "[A]sked for raises aggregating $666 a week for 305 union workers" at the Vanderbilt were downgraded to $475.40 when the NWLB approved the full wage increase for only 192 workers, "refused to do so for 35 employees, and okayed somewhat less increases than asked for 78 workers."[91]

In May 1944, the union again asked the Hotel Association for a formal wage reopener. Taking advantage of the recent NWLB revision of the Little Steel Formula that exempted fringe benefits from FDR's anti-inflation "hold the line" order, the union proposed an employer-paid, union-administered insurance plan.[92] Unions in HTC's orbit had been self-financing modest medical benefits for some time. Under Paul Coulcher, Local 16 opened a healthcare clinic financed by union dues in 1935.[93] BSEIU Local 144 also self-financed a free medical plan for members, and by 1943, it was operating a Medical Center with locations in Manhattan and Brooklyn.[94] Local 6's Sick and Death Benefit Committee had been exploring the union's options since 1940.[95]

The union's wage and social insurance demands were rejected by Hotel Association negotiators, mainly because they were afforded the luxury of kicking the matter to both the "3-Man" Commission and the NWLB.[96] Union organizers circulated a petition supporting the social insurance demand and condemning the "stubborn" bosses. Ten thousand members signed in just five days.[97] But this routine belied the fact that the social security plan—and the stability that would come with it—made sense. The union walked into the first session with the "3-Man" Commission on May 24 with a comprehensive plan for health and hospitalization insurance and a big vision of creating a union-operated healthcare clinic with doctors and nurses on staff.

The "3-Man" Commission awarded the union most of its demands after spending the summer studying the proposal. One month later, the WLB approved the wage increases in the contract, noting that the social security plan did not require review as it fit within the Little Steel formula. Payments to the fund were made retroactive to June 1.[98] Employers contributed an amount of money equal to six percent of payroll for the first six months to help build up a reserve to keep the fund solvent. After that, payments would be reduced to three percent.[99] While the fund was accruing its reserve, the union trustees invested $400,000 in the 7th War bond drive.[100]

Life and Times

During these years, Rubin and Obermeier somehow found time to write a book, *Growth of a Union: The Life and Times of Edward Flore*. Though their effort to curry favor with HRE leadership is obvious, the book, which served as both a biography of the HRE president and a comprehensive history of the international union, was a solid contribution to a growing field of labor history.

Obermeier long had an instinct for chronicling freshly made history, documenting anniversaries and notable achievements of both the AFW and FWIU in their publications. The authors were joined in researching the project by some of HRE's amateur documentarians—Ernst and two other longtime local leaders, Pittsburgh's John Bookjans and Detroit's Louis Koenig—who traveled the country in their youth producing reports about what they found regarding working conditions and organizing prospects amongst their sister locals.

Growth of a Union has been a touchstone for subsequent scholars of culinary unions—most notably HRE's officially commissioned historian Matthew Josephson in 1956's *Union House, Union Bar*—and so their interpretation of some events has carried forward to this day. The book disparaged Jere Sullivan and the "petty little ambitious men eager to ruin someone whom they wanted to supplant" on the GEB in its first decades, staking their claim that, "Many workers were dissatisfied and some of them had established an independent union in New York City's culinary industry which had more hotel, restaurant and tavern employees than any other two large cities combined."[101] On George McLane's misadventure in opposition, the authors injected more drama than was apparent in the staid convention minutes and lopsided vote count in Flore's favor, quoting Robert Kesketh, behind closed doors: "'I don't know why I did it, Ed,' he said finally, wiping tears from his eyes." They attempted to portray McLane as the absolute nadir of what they called "the red herring," strongly implying that red-baiting was the cynical provenance of racketeers that died with McLane's presidential prospects.[102] Thrown in for good measure is a line about how HRE members "who had been indifferent to the Soviet Union before, gave generously for Russian War Relief, partly in admiration for the fighting qualities not only of the Red Army but the Russian people" and an observation about the Panic of 1907: "Unrestricted production for profit instead of for use carries within it the seeds of its own ultimate destruction."[103]

Nevertheless, the book was largely greeted as a welcome addition to the growing library of labor history. AFL Secretary-Treasurer George Meany wrote, "The trade union movement should have a literature of its own and this book is a good start," for the book's dust jacket.[104] It was hyped for several issues of *Catering Industry Employee* and Flore was presented his copy at a banquet ceremony in Milwaukee during HRE's April 1944 General Executive Board meeting. Visibly moved, Flore called the book, "one of the greatest gifts to our international and to me." Others, including Emmanuel Kovaleski and BSEU President William McFetridge paid tribute to Flore and the book.[105] The praise was not universal, however. Aghast at its frank treatment of HRE's racketeering problems, as well as its subtle attempts to mainstream Communists in the union, District 1 Vice President John J. Kearny—a longtime antagonist of the New York radicals—was incensed enough to demand a review of recent issues of *Hotel Voice* and other New York locals' publications and to place the subject of their propriety on the agenda of the next day's GEB session. The discussion was not transcribed, but the GEB instructed Flore and Ernst to step up their efforts to keep local publications "within the scope of the principles of the American Federation of Labor and the International Union."[106]

Kearny went home and published a "review" of the book. To embarrass William Green, who also provided a blurb for the book, the *New York World-Telegram* published a story on the kerfuffle that heavily quoted Kearny's broadside. "You mention the extraordinary valor of the Russian army," he complained, "and omit to include the heroic efforts of other Allied armies," which Kearny deemed, "suspicious and alarming." Aware of efforts brewing to cleave the bartenders in Local 6 for the benefit of HRE's new citywide Bartenders Local 16, Kearny pointedly and repeatedly complained about the book's portrayal of HRE's bartending roots. "Frankly, dear Rubin," he concluded, "I cannot condescend to agree that 'strappy bartenders, barroom habitues, thick brogues, big beer-bellies, drooping moustaches, shiny bald domes, I.W.W., William Z. Foster, Trade Union Unity League, Food Workers Industrial Union, calling people Reds, the heroic struggle of the Russian army, Al Capone, the Mooney case, John L. Lewis, the Russian Revolution, racketeers, murders, suicides, exploitation and personal vilification' can be conjured in the most liberal mind as a history of our international union."[107]

Rubin and Obermeier published a four-page response to Kearny, saying his letter was "not a 'review' of the book but an attack on the integrity of the International President, whom, as many of our leaders know, you have previously tried to undermine ... so as to lay the groundwork for an attempt by you to step into his shoes." It reminded HRE leaders of Kearny's bungled intervention in the 1934 cafeteria chain bargaining, how Flore had to reverse his actions when he returned to the role, and of Kearny's vote *for* George

McLane to keep his seat on the GEB after Flore dropped him from his administration's slate as punishment for the Chicago leader's coup attempt. Finally, they savaged Kearny's dim-witted sense of history and his concluding philippic.

"Fifty-eight words," they challenged, "deliberately plucked out of their context, jumbled together and offered by you as an epitome of the book." They counterposed their own random list of 58 words: "Third degree, K.K.K., race riots, lynchings, attacks on pickets, lawlessness, civil war, secession, slavery, unemployment, bootlegging, corruption, assassination, bribery, miscarriage of justice, bank failures, muck-racking, Benedict Arnold, slums, child-labor, monopoly, sweat-shop, panic, frenzied finance, depression, 'whiskey ring,' fraud, graft, wilderness, Aaron Burr, alien and sedition laws, soup kitchens." Then, they wryly asked if these words would serve as the epitome of the "majesty and spirit and power and glory of our country" despite appearing in any general history of the United States.[108]

The First Public Declaration

As 1945 began, there was a widespread sense that the world war was ending, increasing the preparation for a postwar world. Unions feared that the end of defense production and the return of millions of soldiers to the workforce would swell the ranks of the unemployed, bringing back the Great Depression. Many looked forward to turning the wartime "united nations" rhetoric into a practical alliance for world peace. Others, particularly those connected to the burgeoning Allied military intelligence community, anticipated a reshuffle of world power alliances as nations formerly occupied by the Axis powers regained autonomy. Closer to home, liberals and conservatives harboring misgivings about the more than 100,000 Soviet sympathizers in the Communist Political Association began paying closer attention to its "Kremlinology."

Preparing for the post-war world, Soviet leaders also sought to restore influence over the CP. Without the Comintern, Soviet advice took a more circuitous route. "On The Dissolution of the American Communist Party" was a scathing indictment of Earl Browder's "notorious revision of Marxism." Published by the French Communist Party's theoretical journal *Cahiers du Communisme* and ostensibly written by a high-ranking officer there, Jacques Duclos, it was unmistakably a warning from Moscow that Browder had erroneously transfigured the diplomacy of the Tehran conference "into a political platform of class peace in the United States in the postwar period."[109] The article made its way to the U.S. in May and immediately created a crisis within the CPA's national board over how to conform to the Duclos line.

The resolution that the CPA national board passed repudiated Browder's "erroneous conclusions," credited William Z. Foster's skepticism of his "utopian economic perspectives" as having been correct, and vowed to restore the "independent, Marxist Party of the working class." In July, an emergency convention reconstituted the Communist Party of the United States of America and elected William Z. Foster its National Chairman. Browder was out, and Foster at long last found himself as the party's ideological leader—the role he had long coveted.[110]

Interested parties closely watched the Duclos affair and Browder's downfall. The anti-Communist tabloid *New York Star-Telegram* reported the existence of the Duclos article and its significance as a signal from Stalin.[111] *Catering Industry Employee* republished, without comment, a *Nation* report on the article and its fallout.[112] State Department officials saw it as a warning from Stalin that he intended to cause trouble in the United States and to press his sphere of influence as far west as possible. FDR, who had met Stalin and was familiar with his negotiating tactics, might have seen this as a slight provocation, but he died in office on April 12. His relatively inexperienced successor Harry S. Truman was more dependent on State Department intelligence and more credulous of their fears about Soviet ambitions for global conquest. Regardless of intentions, the Duclos affair came to be seen, in Browder's later words, as "the first *public* declaration of the Cold War."[113]

The AFL had been waging a cold war against communism for years. When labor leaders from the big three allied powers planned a new world labor body to provide workers formal representation in the planned United Nations and a strong voice in postwar rebuilding efforts, the AFL attempted to stop and then wreck the emerging World Federation of Trade Unions.[114] The AFL's formal objection was over the participation of Soviet labor unions. "The Russian trade movement is a government-controlled, government-fostered, and government-dominated labor front that denies to the workers the basic human freedoms," George Meany thundered in one speech.[115] The Local 6 Executive Board protested the AFL's decision to sit out the first "world labor parley," and sent an observer to London to report back on the February 1945 summit to which the CIO was the only formal U.S. participant.[116] New York's hotel workers took the lead in lobbying the AFL to change its policy in regard to the WFTU and join the fledgling world body. A "Committee of 100" AFL local leaders, representing more than 100,000 of the Federation's members, was formed in July 1945. Local 6 Business Agent Tom Wilson was its secretary-treasurer while the Painters' Louis Weinstock served as chairman. Rubin, Obermeier, Cody, and Steuben added their names to the list, which mostly served to give AFL leaders a map of their uncontained Communist insurgency.[117]

Back home in the realm of collective bargaining, NYHTC leaders decided the best way to prepare for the possibility of employer demands for wage reductions or other concessions was to organize the remaining non-union hotels and finally take wages completely out of competition. "We now can say that we have organized and represent the great majority of the workers in our industry in the city," Gertrude Lane reported in June. "But, among a few large hotels we have met with a strange resistance. The Waldorf and the Governor Clinton seem willing, for some reason, to do almost anything except sign a union contract. This stubbornness is a clue to their postwar wage plans. They wish a free hand and no holds barred for that period when the unemployed stand at their service entrances."[118] In the organizing drive that was kicked off in January, "organized and signed" were two apartment hotels near Central Park, the Stanhope and the Windsor, a downtown Knott hotel called the Van Rensselaer, and an Upper West Side apartment hotel called the Regent, where the union was first certified as the bargaining agent in a 1939 card check.

At the Governor Clinton, where the union lost a bitter strike in 1940, a team of six organizers led by Charles Martin leaflet ted and collected union cards outside the employee entrance for twelve hours a day, seven days a week.[119] By April, 260 employees—a clear majority—were dues-paying members. Organizers led a 45-minute work stoppage on April 25 in which they presented management with a stipulation that if the union could prove that 60% of the workers had union cards, then the hotel would sign the IWA.[120] Management refused, but the job action resulted in three days of conciliatory talks the following week. They reached an agreement for a consent election at the end of the second night. When they met the next morning at the SLRB's offices—ostensibly to sign the agreement and go over details—management pulled out of the deal, "categorically" refusing to enter into any form of union recognition.[121] In response to the union filing a representation petition at the SLRB, management dragged the workers through three weeks of hearings over the unit composition, while they hired a private detective agency and ran captive audience meetings. Even though white-collar clerical workers were excluded from the IWA, management fought for their inclusion in the hopes of flooding the voter list. The effort failed. When the election was held on June 22, the union won 166–144—a significant drop in union support but a win nonetheless.[122] Management sought to overturn the election results, complaining that union organizers "deceived, misled, over-awed, coerced and intimidated" voters on their way to the polls.[123] The meritless case dragged out the formal certification until late August. Management still refused to bargain, protesting the composition of the bargaining unit and the union's conduct in the election. Their lawyers' strategy was to draw a ULP charge from the union and, when the SLRB inevitably went into state court to gain enforcement powers to make the hotel bargain in good faith, to use the forum to relitigate the law, the union, and the IWA. Around the country and to this day, this would become a frustratingly common employer strategy at the NLRB, which could drag the process out for years.[124]

Deft use of labor board machinery would also come into play at the Waldorf-Astoria, although here it was the union getting creative about bargaining unit composition. After the 1942 election loss, the union retained a base of support—particularly in the dining rooms and kitchens where workers had been staunch union supporters going back as far as the 1912 strike. Hundreds of workers remained dues-paying members, even without the benefits of a contract. They participated in union meetings, sports leagues, and organizing events. In the fall of 1944, the bartenders even demanded and won a wage increase as a unit.[125]

The union decided that to demonstrate what Waldorf employees could win through the SLRB, it would establish a beachhead in the culinary departments. On January 19, Local 6 filed a petition for "all employees in the kitchen departments, steward's departments, miscellaneous kitchen employees, beverage departments, dining room departments, cafeteria, room service employees and chefs, and food and beverage checkers," 17 departments in all, employing approximately 650 workers. In hearing after hearing, the Waldorf's lawyers fought this attempt to certify smaller bargaining units. Once having fled the Hotel Association to avoid the reach of the Status Quo Agreement, the Waldorf now hid behind the Association and the IWA, insisting that the only appropriate bargaining unit was a wall-to-wall industrial bargaining unit as had become standard in nearly every other hotel in the city.[126] The hotel unions had already tested their ability to certify micro-units the previous year when a new HTC affiliate, Upholsterers Local 44, filed for and won a representation election for a little over a dozen upholsterers at the Waldorf. That, however, was a highly skilled craft unit, a distinction that was widely accepted in the short history of labor board decisions.[127] Despite the precedent, Waldorf lawyers managed to drag out hearings and deliberations over the propriety of the culinary unit for six months. During that time, Lucius Boomer inundated employees with letters warning about the unknowns of collective bargaining—what benefits could be lost, how work rules might change for the worse—while denigrating what unionized hotel workers had gained. Michael J. Obemeier debated Boomer in the pages of the *Hotel Voice*, which Boomer wryly noted easily reached most employees at the hotel.[128]

When the certification election was finally conducted on July 27, it was a smashing success for the union. Workers voted for Local 6 by a margin of 506–169. The win prompted workers in the engineering and maintenance departments to immediately push for their own election, which they won after Labor Day by a vote of 67–40.[129] Union leaders were now set on a course of bargaining a contract with Waldorf management with the goal of bringing all employees in all departments under the terms of the IWA. William Green, Hugo Ernst, Ed Flore, and leaders of the state AFL, CIO, and sister HRE locals in the city showered congratulations upon Local 6. Flore wrote, "This, to the International union and to me, is one of the greatest victories we have achieved in a long time."[130]

Flore dictated the note from his sick bed, where he had spent most of the summer getting progressively weaker and losing weight. He died on September 27, 1945. Meeting in Buffalo on the day of Flore's funeral, the GEB deadlocked on a vote to have Ernst serve out the remainder of Flore's term as president—work that he had already been doing for months. Some of the old-timers on the board nominated John Kearny against Ernst. Their motivation might have been as simple as thinking that the longest-serving vice president deserved to cap his union career in the president's office. It is also possible they thought Ernst had given the New York Communists too much rein and agreed with Kearny's vocal anti-Communism. The 6–6 tie vote left Ernst as secretary-treasurer and allowed him to keep the extra duties of acting president until the next convention could pick a new leader.[131]

The tensions between 1939 and 1941 would return with startling velocity and higher stakes. That convention, which could settle all kinds of lingering and emerging controversies, could not come soon enough in most parties' minds.

10

In Normal Order
1945–1947

On September 8, 1947, federal agents walked into Local 6's office and arrested Michael J. Obermeier for being an "undesirable alien." That same day, attorneys for the CIO's Transport Workers Union Local 100 were fighting an aggressive move to deport John Santo, the union's Romanian-born organizing director. Local press asked the Deputy Commissioner of Immigration and Naturalization, Thomas Shoemaker, if these actions were a part of a "new widespread drive against Communists by the Department of Justice." Shoemaker's mild denial was that the legal actions were "in normal order."[1] They were in fact part of a coordinated crackdown on foreign-born Communists led by the Attorney General. Tom C. Clark, picked by Truman from the ranks of his inherited intelligence bureaucracy, was a vehement anti-Communist who was particularly focused on foreign-born officials in the labor movement. By 1949, his dragnet would ensnare 135 immigrant activists in deportation proceedings while he lobbied Congress for a stronger law that would empower him to deport over 2,000 foreign Communists in the FBI's files.[2]

Obermeier's arrest escalated an anti-Communist drive that was already underway within HRE. Miguel Garriga, Obermeier's erstwhile comrade and the first president of Local 6, pressed for anti-Communist amendments to HRE's constitution so that Communist-led locals could be placed under trusteeship with their leaders expelled from the union. This threatened a split in the unions that had been brought together over the course of many years to organize the vast majority of workers in New York's hotel industry. Yet as the year 1947 drew to a close, an uneasy peace deal would be struck that had the potential to hold the union together.

Get Out of These Situations

After Local 6's SLRB election victory for a culinary bargaining unit at the Waldorf, maintenance and engineering workers voted 67–40 for union representation on September 14, 1945. Once again, NYHTC did not appear on the ballot for the narrow bargaining unit. Instead, workers selected a "Building Maintenance Organizing Committee" as their stop-gap representative while NYHTC wrangled with Lucius Boomer over items in the IWA. Boomer opposed the closed shop but was losing credibility with the Waldorf-Astoria Corporation. Its controlling interest, the New York Central Railroad, had made peace with the union at its other properties in 1939. The two SLRB election wins convinced executives that Boomer didn't speak for the employees.[3]

Edward P. Mulrooney came in as an impartial mediator (not as Impartial Chairman of the Hotel Industry), and, on December 10, he and Rubin broke the impasse with a proposal for a wall-to-wall union election for all IWA bargaining unit titles to be personally supervised by Mulrooney. Within the week, Waldorf workers voted 956–523 for NYHTC.[4]

After seven long years, six elections, dozens of SLRB hearings, 100,000 pieces of campaign literature, and over 300 organizing committee meetings, the largest non-union hotel was at long last bargaining on the same terms that the Hotel Association acceded to in 1938. Management signed the IWA in March 1946. Organizers commenced the urgent tasks of initiating new members and recruiting a full complement of union delegates and department committees.[5]

Another postwar union campaign was ensuring that members returning from military service returned to their old jobs or better ones. When the maître d' of the Algonquin would only offer an inferior position to a returning waiter and former shop chairman, his co-workers stopped work in the hotel to conduct a union meeting in the lobby while a delegation of union representatives convinced management to give the man his old job back.[6] One veteran was refused reemployment at the Plaza because his old job as head bartender was combined with the position of wine steward. After the union involved the Veterans Administration and the District Attorney's office, management backed down, split the merged job into its original two, and paid the grievant $100 in lost wages.[7]

The union also faced the challenge of finding jobs for their returning veterans on staff. Glen Stocks, a business agent who was one of the union's first to volunteer for combat, returned in October 1946 a disabled veteran, after three years recuperating from wounds suffered when he stepped on a landmine in Tunisia. Local 6 found a job for him in the secretary-treasurer's office.[8] *Voice* editor Jerry Fling returned from combat to find that the former *Daily Worker* foreign correspondent Sender Garlin had filled his old post. Happily, Fling was married to Obermeier's daughter, Marguerite, who had just earned a PhD, and the couple moved to California to support her academic career.[9]

These stories stand out because most veterans easily found work. Fears of a postwar depression were wiped away by workers' increased spending power and pent-up demand for nice things like vacations. The hotel industry boomed, and hotels needed help finding employees. The union saw its opportunity to finally put an end to the hotels' use of fee-charging employment agencies. By November 1945, the union's executive board mapped out a plan to revitalize the Employment Department it created a few years earlier to slay the "vampires."

Spearheaded by Antonio Lopez, the employment department included an expanded physical space for a hiring hall, classification of job applicants by experience, a renewed commitment to anti-discrimination with more Spanish-speaking staff, and a dedicated phone hotline.[10] The Employment Department placed 6,000 workers in a variety of steady and casual positions in the housekeeping, laundry, and food and beverage departments in the first five months of 1946. The banquets department, which was separated from the rest of the employment office, filled an average of over 4,000 extra banquet waiter spots a month during the same period.[11]

Making the Hotel Association fund the employment office became a key bargaining demand in 1945. Negotiations formally began at the beginning of the year, but summer passed with no settlement as the parties couldn't agree on the postwar framework for bargaining. The union demanded a 40-hour workweek, more paid vacation time, and wage increases of between 33 percent and 47 percent. During the war, most wage gains were made through special adjustments approved by the NWLB so the contractual minimums lagged prevailing wages. This "stabilization of wages" was a prime concern of unions in postwar bargaining.[12]

The Hotel Association viewed the NWLB wage adjustments as a temporary expedient that would go away as wartime inflation subsided. Hotel Association President Fred O. Cosgrove "would not hear of" a reduction in hours on top of rolling the NWLB wage increases into the IWA. Politically, the Association was once again struggling with a schism in its ranks as many of the banks and the insurance companies were looking to sell their holdings and were not much interested in buying labor peace for an industry they were leaving. Cosgrove insisted the hotels could not afford the union's demands until wartime rent controls were relaxed, allowing them to raise new revenue.[13]

Rent and wage controls eased enough by December 19 for a settlement. In addition to an agreement—in principle—on a Joint Industry Employment Office, the IWA increased base wage rates by up to 25 percent. The union didn't win a reduction in the workweek but did get time and a half for overtime to be paid by the day to incentivize steadier scheduling. Workers gained an extra week of vacation and four paid holidays with double overtime for holiday work. Retroactive to June 1, 1945, the agreement covered 25,000 workers in 144 hotels, once signed by the individual hotels.[14]

The union rushed to get every union house to sign the successor IWA in January so it could trigger the 1946 wage reopener in February.[15] Union leadership was under pressure from members—nearly half of whom were already earning the IWA's base wage rates and therefore received no raise in the December settlement—to win new wage increases to combat rising consumer prices. Nearly every union that bargained new contracts after the war faced similar issues, sparking a strike wave that was larger than the one that followed the First World War. Over four and a half million workers went on strike in 1946.[16] As Josh Freeman documented in *Working Class New York*, over a quarter of a million New Yorkers joined the strike wave, shutting down commercial landlords, harbor traffic, and more. It also left grocery store shelves bare and contributed to a fuel shortage that curtailed school days.[17]

NYHTC joined this strike wave in a series of wildcat job actions at individual hotels. Although the union retained a "self-help" right to strike against employers that refused to comply with Impartial Chairman decisions, shop delegates were abusing the privilege by launching job actions—often a simple matter of shutting down the elevators—over routine grievances. "Up to the present we have been able to get out of these situations without making public statements," Rubin reported to his board. Faced with employers seeking fines through the Impartial Chairman's office and the risk that the employers would seek to close the "self-help" loophole in negotiations, NYHTC made it clear to shop delegates that they lacked authority under the union bylaws to initiate job actions.[18] At the same time, Rubin used the rank-and-file pressure to advance the wage reopener to the "3 Man" commission in April. Because the industry was still subject to rent control, Mulrooney urged the parties to focus on reducing hours instead of raising wages. His award, issued in July, granted most employees a 40-hour, five-day workweek with no loss in pay. Tipped employees had their hours reduced to 45, but also received wage increases of up to $3.50, and the base wage rate for all employees was raised by $2.[19] It was a remarkably amicable settlement in the context of one of the most acrimonious years of labor politics in the country's history. "The Commission," Mulrooney said, "found that both sides were interested in a 'square deal' and we hope that we gave both sides that."[20]

Fast-Dwindling Small Group

In Local 6, Michael Obermeier, Martin Cody, and Gertrude Lane were reelected without opposition at the start of 1946. Miguel Garriga and Helen Blanchard, the only two non-Communist officers, were dropped from the ticket.[21] Antonio Lopez and Charles Martin replaced them, joining Charles Collins as the local's three vice presidents.

At their inauguration, Obermeier declared that 95% of hotel workers in the city were now organized, adding that "we will not rest until 100 percent are organized."[22] There were no signs of rest. A few weeks after the Waldorf maintenance workers' vote, the union won a 78–13 election victory at the Olcott on West 72nd Street on September 28, 1945.[23] The union focused on uptown apartment hotels throughout the fall, with quick wins at the Park Royal and Regent and protracted struggles at the Ansonia, Standish Hall, and Hamilton. Owned by a truculently anti-union member of the Stokes family during the 1913 strike, Ansonia management remained stubbornly anti-union, but they finally recognized the union voluntarily after a brief strike and an SLRB petition in May 1946.[24]

Many remaining non-union hotels were smaller and farther afield, requiring more worker self-organization. One example walked into the union's office in February 1946. Waiter Patrick Kincaid complained about understaffing at the Duane. Probed about the number of likely bargaining unit employees, Charles Martin handed the new on-the-spot shop chairman 60 union pledge cards. Three weeks later, Kincaid returned to union headquarters with 58 signed cards. Martin walked the cards over to the East Side apartment hotel, and, after a brief conference with the General Manager, Martin walked out with a signed IWA.[25]

By May, the "fast-dwindling small group of non-union hotels still remaining" was further reduced when the Martinique became the 145th hotel to sign the IWA after voluntary card check recognition.[26] All told, workers at 25 hotels won the IWA in 1946, five of them through card check or voluntary recognition and the rest through SLRB elections.[27] The ease with which some hotels signed belies just how long others dragged out the fight.

One of the earliest SLRB certifications, workers at the Hampshire House voted in 1939, but management refused to bargain a closed shop. The union spent years picketing the hotel; once incurring the wrath of actress Joan Crawford who had scheduled a day of interviews and was dismayed when confronted by a picket line. The Screen Actors Guild vice president chewed out management, following up with an angry letter of protest.[28] A change in management inspired a renewed drive. A scheduled SLRB recertification election was called off at the last moment when management, convinced that

Local 6 officers are sworn in on February 4, 1946. Emanuel Kovaleski (center) congratulates Michael J. Obermeier (right) while Martin Cody, holding the union charter, looks on. (New York Hotel and Gaming Trades Council.)

the vast majority of its 200 employees supported the union, finally signed the IWA on September 20, 1946.[29]

The Governor Clinton would hold out even longer. Management continued to appeal the June 1945 election, refusing to bargain, claiming that the unit was inappropriate for not including white-collar employees.[30] The union was sustained in a ULP in December 1945, and the SLRB initiated a lawsuit to gain enforcement powers in April 1946. Yet the hotel would continue to resist signing the IWA for years.[31]

Residential hotels under BSEIU's jurisdiction also saw organizing action. Former HTC affiliate Local 32-A continued to mismanage its affairs and negotiate substandard contracts. Ordered to merge into Local 144, the local's renegade leaders got a charter from the CIO's Retail, Wholesale, and Department Store Union (RWDSU), sparking a brief jurisdictional war. Local 144 began raiding the CIO breakaway as contracts expired and they could file decertification petitions.[32] In January 1946, RWDSU Local 32-A went on a brief jurisdictional strike at 30 shops, taking 400 workers out.[33] Within a month, they sued for peace. Former officers, led by business agent Peter Ottley, called for members to "cooperate wholeheartedly with the officers and members of Local 144 in order to build a united, militant organization that would be able to win more benefits for the membership." John Goodman, now an international Vice President of BSEIU, and John Steuben, now Local 144's

Secretary-Treasurer, committed to a rank-and-file committee at all conferences with the employers in upcoming "Division A" negotiations.[34] By the summer, they reported ten new shops under that contract and another 14 in progress.[35]

Local 6 forged ahead with the clubs. For instance, shortly after the staff at Columbia University's tiny campus hotel voted 13–10 for NYHTC, employees of the Columbia University Club joined the union on October 30, 1946.[36] It was a crowning victory in the local's drive to organize the "outstanding" clubs of New York, which included wins at the Bankers, Colony, Harvard, Metropolitan, and Yale clubs.

The political clubs demonstrated a partisan difference. When the union probed the National Democratic Club in the summer of 1945, "within two and a half hours after the business agents walked into the club for the first time," their organizing contact triumphantly returned to union headquarters with 30 union pledge cards representing 90 percent of the workers.[37] Management agreed to a card check two months later.[38] However, when the SLRB conducted an election at the National Republican Club, the union lost 12–36 after management organized a rank-and-file anti-union committee.[39] The union appealed the election and filed a ULP because management made employees sign a pledge to "not become affiliated, as a member or otherwise, with the 'International Hotel Workers Union,' or any other kindred organization, nor promote, aid, or participate, either directly or indirectly, in any strike against the Club." Such "yellow dog" contracts were outlawed by 1932's Norris–La Guardia Act and state law. So old-fashioned was this kind of union-busting that the pledge cards named the independent union that hadn't existed for 31 years![40] Local 6 won the rerun election 9–5 on November 15.[41]

The clubs all had separate collective bargaining agreements, but leaders planned to bring them into an industry-wide framework. Heading into the summer of 1945, as the union bargained for successor agreements in all 34 clubs under contract, business agents led by Theodore Mageau proposed common language across all the agreements and presented them as a master contract framework.[42]

Almost Entirely Free

The unity of the New Deal coalition was broken with dizzying speed by geopolitical controversies. Tensions rose as Soviet-style governments arose throughout Eastern Europe. President Truman escalated this new Cold War in March 1947, declaring the foreign policy goal of containing the geographic expansion of Communist countries at a joint session of Congress.

The AFL also embraced containment. In 1946, 50,000 people marched in the first May Day parade since 1941. The AFL forbade its affiliates from participating, on pain of suspension or worse. Local 6 got around the dictate by having its members march as individuals, without union banners. This small rebellion did not go unnoticed.[43] In October 1946, at the AFL's annual convention, President William Green implicitly denounced its rival "Communist-dominated" CIO before delegates passed a strongly worded anti-Communist resolution.[44] Green's and the AFL's attacks on the CIO, plus internal pressure, forced CIO President Phil Murray to take a harder anti-Communist line while denying the pervasiveness of Communist influence in his "patriotic American organization." "The AFL on its part, is almost entirely free of Communist influence," the *New York Times* noted when covering the inter-federation rivalry. "Where it does exist it is found mainly among New York painters, hotel, restaurant, cafeteria workers and service trades."[45]

That by-product of the AFL's premature anti-Communism, the House Un-American Activities Committee, won greater powers that came with permanent standing in January 1945.[46] Its first investigative target was an organization called the Joint Anti-Fascist Refugee Committee (JAFRC), which fundraised for refugees from Francisco Franco's Spanish regime. Local 6's Education Director Charlotte Stern served on the group's Executive Board.

A controversial speech denouncing the Catholic Church for its support of Franco's regime at a JAFRC rally at Madison Square Garden led to a HUAC subpoena for "all books, ledgers, records, and papers relating to the receipt and disbursement of money." Convinced that names submitted to HUAC would be vulnerable to Spanish fascist *and* FBI retaliation and that HUAC's probe was unconstitutional, JAFRC's Board unanimously refused to cooperate. They were cited for contempt of Congress and 17 members, including Stern, were indicted on March 31, 1946.[47]

In the midterm elections, the American Labor Party nominated Charles Collins to run for State Senate.[48] Collins' Harlem district overlapped with Adam Clayton Powell's Congressional district. Powell endorsed Collins, calling it "imperative that a half million Negro people have a representative in the New York State Senate. Otherwise, it is taxation without representation."[49] Rep. Vito Marcantonio also endorsed Collins, who borrowed Marcantonio's modus operandi by petitioning for the Democratic and Republican nomination. Operatives from each party challenged Collins' petitions on a myriad of technicalities, as was *their* m.o., and successfully had him knocked off the ballot. He continued as a write-in candidate in the Democratic primary but would only appear on the ALP ballot line in the general election, where he polled 15,219 votes (a little over one-fifth of the electorate).[50]

Election Day brought worse news as voter reaction against Truman's handling of the postwar economy and the ongoing strike wave led to a Republican sweep in the House and Senate. The Chamber of Commerce and other business interests blamed the strikes on Communist subversion. High on the agenda of the incoming Congress was a rollback of the Wagner Act's right to strike and a ban on Communists in union leadership.[51]

Noise about Communists in unions encouraged a member of Local 144's Executive Board to team with former 32-A officers, Edison hotel managers, and something calling itself the "National Foundation" to start an anti-Communist caucus. They were censured by Steuben's administration and repeatedly denounced in the union's newspaper as a clear warning to anyone else who might step out of line against the administration.[52]

At HRE's State Culinary Alliance's annual convention in August 1946, Obermeier was denied reelection as secretary-treasurer, a post he held for four years. Garriga was seen as the floor manager for the effort that gave Local 302's William Mesevich a 75–56 victory. Just before the meeting, the conservative *New York Journal-American* tabloid published a negative article about Obermeier, which he blamed, along with a switch from secret ballot elections to an on-the-record delegate tally, for the election result. "I want to make it emphatically clear," Obermeier declared in the presence of acting president Ernst, "that the membership of our Union demands that a halt be called to this campaign that tends to lead to the destruction of our union," concluding with a warning that the GEB "cannot continue to condone such acts without assuming the responsibility for the results which may follow."[53]

In this political environment, Obermeier tried to secure his citizenship, appearing before an INS hearing examiner for the third time in June 1946.[54] At his previous interview in 1945, immigration officials grilled him on his Party membership, involvement in the TUUL, friendship with William Z. Foster, and employment by the Soviet firm Intourist during his year in Moscow.[55] However, in a decision that helped Harry Bridges gain his citizenship, the Supreme Court narrowed the Smith Act's deportation powers to require active adherence to an organization's goal of overthrowing the government and not "mere cooperation with it in lawful activities" such as union organizing.[56] Obermeier understood the risks of both continuing and abandoning his application and picked this moment as his best chance of settling his legal status to prepare for retirement.

As it turns out, the INS had already flagged him and requested that J. Edgar Hoover share a copy of his FBI file with immigration investigators. The FBI complied and started its own "prosecutive summary report," seeing him as a candidate for prosecution under the Smith Act.[57]

Not a Witch Hunt

What cooperation existed within the LJEB when the war began was gone before it ended. In local union elections, opposing Communist and anti-Communist slates reordered the political alignment of the LJEB. In Local 302, William Mesevich united the anti-Stalinist left and defeated Sam Kramberg in 1942.[58] Around the same time, Communists voted incumbents Sam Friedman and Benny Gottesman out of leadership in Local 1. Local 16 President

David Siegal dumped William Albertson and purged all Communists from leadership at the end of the war.[59]

At the LJEB's annual elections in January 1946, the Communist locals used their numerical voting strength to purge the board of many of its "conservative" representatives. After a "sharp fight," the new board installed Local 89's Harry Reich as its Executive Manager, joining Kramberg, who was acting as the LJEB's Organizing Director.[60]

Locked out of LJEB decision-making, the anti-Communists appealed to the GEB to expand their jurisdictions, jealous of Local 6's wall-to-wall claim on hotel workers. Local 16 wanted waiters in street-level restaurants operating under separate leases within hotels and was briefly sustained, outraging Local 6 leaders.[61] Local 15 demanded jurisdiction for all bartenders across the city.[62] It was not the first time they'd proposed it, but previous efforts were quashed. Now, however, Local 15 President Jack Townsend made common cause with Miguel Garriga, marrying his dream of one big bartenders union with Garriga's wish to reduce the power of the Communists.

"Quite often in the past, unions which for years failed to organize the workers in their territory, have laid jurisdictional claim to them when other unions succeeded in unionizing them through greater activity or more effective organizational methods," Local 6 howled when the GEB agreed to study the matter. Although hotel bartenders would have continued to be covered by the IWA no matter what local was assigned jurisdiction, Local 6 leaders stoked fear about the 1948 contract expiration and upcoming wage reopeners in order to rally their bartenders: "What could the wrecking of our union's structure do but seriously jeopardize these negotiations?"[63] The NYHTC Executive Board viewed HRE's actions as an attack and resolved that "we will not permit an investigation of the Council" and vowed that the other seven international unions with affiliated locals "will not permit any one international to come in and destroy our Council."[64]

This statement followed an action that the GEB took earlier in the year to investigate the extent of Communist influence within the New York locals. A commission chaired by Ed S. Miller, a young vice-president soon to be selected by the GEB to serve as secretary-treasurer until the 1947 convention, set up an office in the Hotel Pennsylvania on March 20, 1946, and spent weeks conducting interviews and compiling dossiers on the accused Communists. The city and state AFL bodies took part, and lawyers were hired to take sworn affidavits.[65] Disgruntled members hurled accusations of dubious veracity, but a number of ex-Communists provided details about how the Party's culinary industry fraction caucused before union elections to ensure that Party members or allies—although a minority of union membership—would retain the most important leadership posts, claiming Jay Rubin directed the Party activists in every LJEB local. Others complained about how Locals 1 and 6 used their extra waiter hiring halls to reward comrades with good jobs and punish dissidents with bad jobs or no jobs, as the case may be. One member of Local 302 reported meeting Obermeier in Moscow in 1930.[66]

Although unclear on the commission's legal authority, officers from the LJEB and Locals 1, 42, and 89 participated.[67] They provided local union auditing reports and other financial records that were requested. When auditors showed up at NYHTC's office, Jay Rubin "impressed" upon them that it was "not under the supervision of, or chartered by our International Union" but that he "would try to comply" by producing the previous year's bookkeeping records.[68] A small group of Local 6's officers, including Rubin, huddled for weeks to get their stories straight in the face of potentially hostile questioning.[69]

Obermeier went first, on April 22. Ed Miller grilled him regarding his immigration status. Obermeier produced dated and signed letters from Edward Flore waiving HRE's constitutional prohibition on non-citizens serving in union office, and Hugo Ernst, who had not attended any session to that point, traveled to New York to personally vouch for Obermeier. Cody, Collins, and Lane also appeared before the commission. All of them were interrogated about how they first obtained their membership cards and whether they had ever worked in a hotel or restaurant. They produced reasonable backstories. Collins was challenged over the many front groups that he had lent his name and union title to. Those were "for identification purposes only," he coolly responded. They were mostly forthcoming about the causes and campaigns they took part in that could be called "Communist fronts." Most claimed to be sympathetic to the causes that Communists championed, but either denied membership in the Party or refused to answer the question. Of all the Communists, only Sam Kramberg forthrightly declared, "Yes, I have been a member for many years" and defended the Party as a legal organization that had two elected members serving on the New York City Council. Since Rubin held no elected office in an HRE affiliate, he was not compelled to interview. The commission wrapped up its investigation on May 3, after sticking around long enough to observe that no HRE banners could be seen at the May Day parade.[70]

The commission's report stated the obvious—that "substantial Communist sympathy and influence exists among some part of the leadership and some of the membership of our New York locals, notably in locals 1, 6 and 89." Insisting that its report was "not a witch hunt," and armed with no clear powers, the commission encouraged locals "to clean house themselves" before constitutional amendments would "be instituted to eradicate the evil practices above set forth and discipline the violators."[71] Anti-Communists on the GEB, Miguel Garriga and John Kearny most prominently, began formulating language that would give future investigations enforcement powers. Someone, meanwhile, put some of the commission's sworn affidavits to immediate use by handing them over to the FBI.[72]

A Red Baiter . . . A Red Hater, A Red Fighter

HRE had not held a convention during the war, deferring to governmental rationing on oil and travel. The GEB read its constitution as not allowing a new convention until 1948. Cold War controversies impelled a national referendum to speed the process by a full year.[73] HRE's Thirty-First General Convention was scheduled for April 1947 in Milwaukee, Wisconsin.

Communist controversies would dominate. Anti-Communists objected to the use of union resources—staff jobs and in-kind contributions of flyers, meeting halls, and more—to support Communist campaigns and "front" groups. They increasingly bought into State Department accusations that Communists represented a fifth column of potential spies and saboteurs whose ultimate loyalty lay with a hostile foreign power. And, finally, they were embarrassed with their guilt by association as the AFL's crimson rogue. Just the week prior to the convention, *Life* magazine ran a five-page spread featuring a gallery of mug shot-style portraits of union officials who "have helped spread the Communist doctrine in labor circles." For its millions of readers, the magazine featured Obermeier's picture under the banner, "These 16 Are Openly Communist or So Sympathetic As To Leave Little Doubt." Along with the red-baiting press' usual *bête noires* like TWU President Mike Quill and CIO General Counsel Lee Pressman, the Painters' Louis Weinstock was the only other AFL representative featured.[74]

The Communists and their allies, on the other hand, felt that the attacks on them were being manipulated by capitalist reactionaries. Their track record was routing corrupt elements from the New York locals, organizing the largest bargaining units on an industry-wide basis, and generally running a clean, democratic union. Their critics consistently misunderstood and disorganized the city's multicultural and genuinely left-wing hotel workforce. Finally, they were tired of being represented by a vice-president who sowed mischief within their ranks and threatened to trustee or split up locals whose members simply did not support him.

Caucusing commenced soon after the convention call. In late December, Garriga organized a "Conference of the Local Unions of the 2nd District" in Wilkes-Barre, PA.[75] By then, Garriga's support base was largely in the Pennsylvania locals, the New York Bartenders, and Locals 16 and 302. The conference proposed constitutional amendments aimed squarely at the left-wing New York locals, the gist of which was: "No local union or Local Joint Executive Board or State Culinary Alliance shall join any organization inimical to the best interest of our International or to the A. F. of L., nor shall any Union Official use his Union office title for furthering the interest of such organizations. Further, no individual, member or group of members shall undertake to represent the Local Union at any gathering, organization, group, etc., without proper authorization from the Local Union."[76]

In response, Local 6 hosted its own semi-official caucus in January, joined by Locals 1 and 89 and a smattering of allies from Chicago and the West Coast, at the Park Central. Purporting to represent 70,000 members with a unity agenda, this "Eastern States Conference" endorsed Ernst's election as president but pushed another young GEB member, C. T. McDonough, to challenge Ed Miller for secretary-treasurer.[77]

What followed were embarrassing echoes of the violence at the 1936 Rochester convention. On March 17, James Crowley, the president of Chicago Bartenders Local 278 who led his delegation in the Park Central meeting, was wounded in a drive-by shooting outside of his home. His wife bore the brunt of the fusillade of "shotgun pellets and large caliber bullets" and died at the scene. "I can't think of any reason for shooting me except I was trying to clean up the International union," Crowley explained to the press.[78] A few weeks later, Dennis Kelly, a business agent for Bartenders Local 714 in Joliet, Illinois, was wounded in a similar drive-by shooting.[79] Police connected that with Kelly's brother, who owned a jukebox business and had been murdered in a similar manner the prior October. Though no one was ever prosecuted for the shootings, police suspected a Chicago Outfit turf war.[80] The terrible optics didn't stop Local 6 from insinuating Crowley's initial claim that the violent campaign had something to do with the upcoming convention. That brave trade unionists who had on no fewer than three occasions routed gangster elements from the labor movement now found themselves in open alliance with ethically compromised sister locals smacked of desperation.

This coalition of convenience also settled on a candidate to run against Garriga. Obermeier's diabetes had become severe enough that it was costing him his eyesight. He spent the early part of 1947 convalescing, but even when he returned to work, he was not well enough to travel. He would miss the convention. For that reason, and with hopes that a candidate from outside New York might have a better shot at defeating Garriga, the opposition supported John Kenny, the president of a Pittsburgh hotel workers local, as the "unity" candidate.

Local 6 organizers conducted a union-wide campaign to elect the full allotment of delegates. In addition to 18 officers and staff members, they took pains to ensure that rank-and-file members with no apparent CP connections filled the remaining 29 seats. Whatever happened in Milwaukee, the Communists needed witnesses to bring the story home that the convention majority's anticipated aggression towards the local was unfair.[81]

"This is the largest convention in the history of our International Union," Ernst proudly declared as he addressed the 1,138 delegates in the convention hall at the opening session, "and rightfully so, because we now have the largest number of members in our history." With over 400,000 members, HRE was the fifth largest affiliate of the AFL—and growing![82] Despite impressive reports on the union's growth and activities, the atmosphere was notably tense. The officer elections, which would precede the vote on the anti-Communist amendment, were seen by some as a proxy for the looming fight. "I have been accused of being Communist or Communist-dominated. I am not," C. T. McDonough said at a caucus. "My only question to my supporters is, 'Are you a good trade unionist?' If you are, then you are good enough for me. I'm not concerned with your creed, color or politics."[83]

Indeed, the McDonough campaign was a far stranger coalition than just Communists and Chicago Bartenders as John Kearny also endorsed him. Still smarting from being denied the union's presidency for himself, the co-author of the anti-Communist amendment decided to oppose Ernst's chosen running mate. Although Ernst was unopposed for his first proper election as president, he was furious at the disloyalty of the GEB's longest-serving vice president, whom he privately considered "an intemperate man who exhibited the spirit of racial and religious intolerance calculated to arouse factitious strife," and dropped Kearny from the administration ticket.[84]

The Eastern States Conference's proposed amendments, many aimed squarely at Garriga (vice presidents should not serve on HRE payroll as organizers, "must be members and represent the local" from their district; shrinking District 2 to just New York and New Jersey, expanding the size of the GEB), were all killed in committee, as the anti-Communist resolution worked its way toward a showdown.[85]

On Thursday morning, James Crowley emerged from his Chicago hospital bed and dramatically entered the convention—greeted by a hero's welcome of cheers—to nominate C. T. McDonough. Shouts of "communists" and "racketeers" were traded from the floor. "Boo and be damned," Ernst reportedly snapped at McDonough supporters who protested the time limit on nominating speeches. The administration won this vote handily, with the weighted vote favoring Miller by 2,446 to McDonough's 1,744.[86]

Moments later, Jack Townsend nominated Miguel Garriga, who by then owed his delegate credentials to a membership card in Bartenders Local 15. "He is not a Red baiter, he is a Red hater, a Red fighter. He doesn't stop at hating them, he actually goes out and fights them," went Townsend's pugnacious endorsement. Harry Reich gave a slightly bumbling speech to nominate Garriga's opponent. "Sure, there is factionalism in New York; sure, there are splits," he said. That was because, he argued, "we have not had a representative who could keep himself above petty politics and factionalism." Ernst, still chairing, interrupted, "Cut it short, Harry. Your time is almost up." Charles Collins, acting president of Local 6 in Obermeier's absence, seconded Kenny's nomination on behalf of "6,500 Negro Americans and 17,000 united, progressive, militant and unified white brothers and sisters in this spirit of our great International Union." When the votes were cast, Garriga won by roughly the same margin as all the candidates on the administration ticket: 2,554 to 1,279. He only did slightly worse among the delegates representing the locals in the Second District—63 percent—with Bronx Bartenders Local 29, New York Chains Local 42, and Kenny's own Pittsburgh local joining the three Communist-led locals in opposing Garriga.[87]

The Communist controversy took center stage on the final Friday morning of the convention. First was a resolution protesting reports in the press that HRE was a "Communist penetrated" organization. Delegates speaking in favor of the resolution complained of the long history of "sudden and contradictory changes in the Communist party line," of how "Communists have now become the agents and emissaries of a great nationalistic foreign power," and of the pre-war "unholy alliance between the Communist dictatorship of Russia and the Nazi dictatorship of Germany." Reich spoke against the measure, arguing that "temporary expedients" of denouncing Communists were "dangerous paths" that could lead to new anti-labor legislation and open genuine "liberals and progressives" up to similar persecution. "It is not my position to defend any political party," he declared. "However, I will defend with all the strength at my command, and prompted by my own convictions, the right of any political party whose constitution conforms with the American Constitution to survive and to exist."

Before the vote, Ernst noted, "I am going to carry out the instructions of this convention to the best of my ability. But I plead with you to let good sense rule your decisions and not hysteria or hatred." After the motion was carried, a number of delegates paraded around the convention hall waving American flags and singing "God Bless America."[88]

Finally, the delegates turned to Local 15's amendment to ban Communists from "any elective or appointive position—paid or unpaid" at any level of the union, accompanied by strong enforcement powers: "If the above section has not been complied with in principle and intent by the local unions or its executive officers, the General President shall be empowered to take jurisdiction."

Rubin led the charge against "the most dangerous and disastrous step that the convention will take." The proposal, he warned, "does not only affect Communists, but it will affect anyone with an independent point of view in our International Union." He singled out the section that demanded loyalty to the "principles and ideals expressed by the American Federation of Labor." He reminded delegates that the AFL in 1930 was on record as being against the establishment of unemployment insurance. "If the convention had been held during that particular period I can assure you that you, under this law, would have been expelled."

Rubin reminded delegates when the New York locals were dominated by Paul Coulcher and Dutch Schultz that "members were expelled for daring to challenge racketeering in that particular union on the excuse that they were Communists." He cautioned, "[those] who introduced this amendment feel that now is the time, we have won, let's go out and make a job on them. I tell you, gentlemen, you are losing yourselves, you are forgetting yourselves, and I tell you that the workers in the industry will not let you utilize this amendment to destroy the Union." He then issued his most stark warning yet: "If you want us to we will call a membership meeting in Madison Square Garden and you will see what we will do and we will see what the response to that will be." He offered a minority report proposing to leave the 1946 investigation report in the president's hands.

"I am sick and tired of hearing so much about democracy," Garriga retorted on a discordant note. "Democracy brought Napoleon to France, brought Cromwell to England, brought Hitler to Germany and it brought Stalin to Russia, and for God's sake, don't let it bring a totalitarian government to us." A delegate from John Kenny's Pittsburgh Local 237, claiming to "hate Communism," sided with Rubin. He noted that the morning's papers reported that a House version of the long-dreaded anti-labor bill had been introduced, implying on the one hand that the union had bigger external enemies to fight while in the same breath insinuating that Kearny, whose chairmanship of the Committee on Law produced the majority report "is the same man who only a few years back was connected with the German Bund." Shaken by the previous speakers, Fourth District Vice President Clyde Foster proposed sending both reports back to the committee, effectively tabling them. His motion failed. More speakers followed, most of them in opposition to the resolution. "I am not worried about the so-called theory of Communism," Charles Collins said. "What I am fearful of is the perpetration of Fascism in the United States and the dissension of the labor movement and the demobilization of the workers in order to give the boss a free ride."

Before voting, Ernst took the privilege of speaking on the motion from the chair, criticizing it as "drastic," for placing too much power in the hands of the president, who could be a less "broadminded" person than he. He continued to praise "the officers of Local 6 for the splendid work they have done in the hotels in New York, which we tried unsuccessfully to organize a good many years ago." He attributed their success not to their being Communists ("probably in spite of that") and lamented that the current controversy was "entirely their own fault, because they did not heed friendly advices that were given to them by me and some others" to refrain "from using their official position for other than trade union principles, probably we would not be confronted with this issue that is before us now."[89]

By a voice vote, the proposed amendment was carried, and the convention recessed for lunch.

Sufficient Potential Dangerousness

After the convention adjourned, the GEB voted unanimously to direct Ernst to place New York's Local Joint Executive Board under trusteeship. They also referred Local 16's request for more of Local 6's jurisdiction in hotel restaurants to him, and in response to Local 15's incessant lobbying, directed him to supervise a referendum among the bartenders in all Manhattan locals.[90] There was no move to place Local 6 under a trusteeship. Garriga and the anti-Communists hoped to break HRE's largest local down to a manageable size. Ernst hoped that local leadership would stop toeing the CP line quite so obviously, and reshuffle its officers to demote some of the most flamboyantly public Communists.

One of those was Charles A. Collins. As soon as he got home, Collins charged in Harlem's *Amsterdam News* that if the anti-Communist amendment "is carried out there will be practically no Negroes in the union except those who are handpicked by the Administration" and "that the attempt would be made to "clean out' the Negro leaders in Local 6 and other locals throughout the country."[91] Offended by the accusation, Ernst chastised Collins.[92] Jack Townsend penned a letter to the *Amsterdam News* objecting to the "most vicious article." Feebly objecting to Collins' charges of discrimination, he attached a photograph of the induction ceremony for Local 15's first—and possibly only—Black member, way back in March 1946. "We do," he added, "discriminate against any member, black or white, who because of membership in any subversive group tries to undermine the principles of honest American Trade Unionism."[93]

The kerfuffle was a warning of how Local 6 would fight back against a *theoretical* trusteeship of it. The LJEB fought back against its *actual* trusteeship by HRE by obtaining an injunction, arguing that the 81(a) trusteeship authority was vested in the president—not the GEB—and still required him to present charges and conduct a hearing. The action was taken by LJEB President Sam Spitzer and Secretary-Treasurer Obermeier, after a tense meeting with Ernst, who traveled to New York to deliver the news. Mesevich, Siegal, and Townsend briefly suspended their months-long boycott of the LJEB to bring a motion to censure Spitzer and "withdraw and discontinue" the lawsuit. The vote, following a testy debate, revealed what Ernst already knew: five anti-Communist locals supported the trusteeship, and six locals representing two-thirds of the membership opposed it.[94]

Garriga had other schemes to vex his ex-comrades. In early May, three Local 6 business agents—Victor Brown, Vincent Aragno, and Theodore Mageau—were caught circulating petitions to split the members of the club division off into a chartered local of their own. Because Brown, Aragno, and Mageau were business agents talking about gaining power, members reported feeling duped into signing, saying they were under the impression that the initiative was coming from Local 6 leadership. Obermeier immediately suspended the business agents from office, and organizers scrambled to arrange membership meetings in the clubs. Within a week, more than 1,000 club division members attended emergency union meetings to denounce and sign counter petitions against the secessionists.[95]

The power struggle extended across New York in a minimum wage fight. Back in the fall of 1946, in response to the end of wartime price controls and rising inflation, the union pressed the state to reconvene the Hotel Minimum Wage Board. Gertrude Lane and Miguel Garriga were among the appointed labor representatives.[96] After months of testimony and deliberation, the Wage Board voted on June 4 to recommend a weekly wage of $26.55 for a 45-hour week. All the labor representatives objected that the minimum rate did not achieve parity with an order from the Restaurant Minimum Wage Board for similar workers. But Lane, wanting to show up Garriga, cast a dissenting vote and refused to sign the recommendation.[97] At the Wage Board hearings around the state, the union mobilized hundreds of hotel workers to testify that the proposed wage was inadequate and should be revised.[98] The HRE State Culinary Alliance, at its annual summer meeting, endorsed Lane's minority report and called on the Wage Board to reconvene to raise wages and lower hours in the hotel industry.[99] It didn't and voted on July 26, to approve the substandard minimum for hotels, further diminishing Garriga's reputation.[100]

Meanwhile, the LJEB's legal challenge to its trusteeship was sustained on July 14 when the New York State Supreme Court ruled that the HRE constitution only granted the GEB authority to hear appeals—not to initiate punitive actions.[101] One week later, Jay Rubin and Harry Reich, with lawyers in tow, traveled to Milwaukee to meet with Ernst, Garriga, and their lawyers to discuss a resolution. Ernst continued to want the locals to resolve the controversies on their own. Rubin and Reich agreed to submit their own proposal for a jurisdictional reorganization of bartenders and a political reshuffling of the Board and its officers.[102]

While the union was fighting with itself, Republicans and conservative Democrats were working together to roll back labor rights. The Hartley bill that was introduced during the HRE convention was combined with a Senate version and passed as the veto-proof Taft-Hartley Act on June 23, 1947.[103] Among its provisions was a "ban" on Communists in union leadership. It accomplished this by denying access to the administrative machinery of the NLRB to any union whose leaders didn't sign an affidavit swearing that they were not Communists, not only making organizing more difficult but also opening such unions up to the possibility of a decertification election with their name not even on the ballot.[104]

Hotels, restaurants, and clubs were not affected by Taft-Hartley—at least not yet. HRE attorneys' best guess was that the new law only applied to its locals in Washington, DC, and the territories of Alaska and Hawaii, and the bargaining units in food manufacturing plants that did business across state lines. The GEB spent the months waiting for Truman's performative veto and Congress' override deciding whether to comply with the anti-Communist requirements. It was one thing for a union to impose its own internal standard on members and leaders. It was another entirely to have that imposed by the federal government in what seemed to be a blatant violation of free speech rights. By the end of the summer, on advice from the AFL, the officers of the HRE GEB all signed non-Communist affidavits to protect their affected locals' ability to utilize NLRB.[105]

NYHTC responded to Taft-Hartley by creating a "Fighting Defense Fund," ostensibly to "meet any possible emergency or action that may be needed in connection with the wage-hour demands" in its negotiations with the Hotel Association. They asked members to voluntarily assess themselves a full day's pay to contribute.[106] The campaign to raise a $100,000 war chest sent a message that Garriga read loud and clear. "I assume you have received a copy of the *Hotel and Club Voice*," he wrote Ernst and continued, "We know they do not contemplate, neither do they even talk about, possible strikes where such amounts of money would be needed." He saw it as a planned "fight against the International Union."[107] He was proven right when a three-year extension of the IWA was settled on August 21—a full year before its expiration date.

The agreement raised wages by $2 to $4 a week and strengthened non-tipped employees' five-day, 40-hour week. At the same time, a separate agreement was signed whereby funds were set aside to establish a free medical clinic for union members. The agreement, the fruits of a mature and stable bargaining relationship, included the standard clause providing for an annual reopening on wages and hours on March 1, 1949, and it would remain in effect until the expiration date of May 31, 1950.[108]

Just prior to the IWA settlement, after many deliberate delays, Rubin, Obermeier, and their attorneys met with Garriga at his office to present their counterproposal to "the agreement of Milwaukee." They conceded that HRE could appoint a representative to serve as the LJEB's executive director but fought for the current representatives to maintain their seats on an expanded "provisional committee of eleven," tasked with drafting new bylaws "in accord with the spirit and intent of the International constitution governing local joint boards." Further, they ceded—pending membership ratification—the bartenders in Waiters Local 16, Chain Service Local 42, and Cafeteria Employees Local 302 to Townsend's Local 15 while insisting upon the structural integrity of Bronx Bartenders Local 29, Cooks Local 89, and, of course, Local 6.[109] Garriga reported to Ernst, "The only thing I could do in order to hide my disgust was to laugh as heartily as I could." He called it "a brazen misinterpretation of the agreement reached at Milwaukee" and terminated the parlay at once.[110]

Garriga chose this moment to prepare for the bartenders' referendum. The GEB had not informed Local 6 leaders of its April decision to conduct a plebiscite on the question of "one bartenders local for all." They received his letter on October 9 demanding they provide a list of their bartenders members within five days and raged at what seemed like another of Garriga's provocations.[111]

Pressure was mounting from higher authorities than the vice president of the Second District of the union. On June 27, the sixteen conscientious objectors of the JAFRC were convicted of contempt of Congress for their defiance of HUAC. Five of them immediately resigned from the board and recanted their refusals to testify before HUAC in an attempt to "purge" their convictions. Charlotte Stern, who was among the eleven who stuck to their principles, received a three-month sentence and a $500 fine for her role. She remained free while the convictions were appealed.[112]

Obermeier was in greater jeopardy as the Department of Justice was preparing to launch its deportation drive. FBI agents had recommended to their superiors in March that Obermeier's Communist activities were not "of sufficient potential dangerousness to be classified as a Key Figure." Key figures were the Party leaders to be arrested en masse if the government ordered a Smith Act crackdown. No sooner had they reprieved Obermeier than, on May 2, the INS sent the Bureau a list of individuals that *it* was considering for Smith Act deportations. Obermeier was the second name on the list. The FBI sent the INS nearly 200 pages of interviews with confidential informants, with names, dates, addresses, and sworn affidavits from the March 1946 HRE investigation with stories of real or rumored trips in and out of the country and especially to Moscow.[113]

Within a year, the INS would order 41 foreigners deported for past or present affiliation with the Communist Party.[114] The first was John Santo, the Hungarian-born organizing director of the CIO's left-led Transport Workers Union, who was summoned over the weekend to appear at an 11:00 AM hearing on Monday, September 8, on charges of being a subversive alien.[115] Obermeier was not given the courtesy of advance notice. Agents entered the 44th Street entrance of Local 6's headquarters at the same hour as Santo's hearing and took him into custody. He was released on $1,000 bond. The following day, Obermeier's arrest was front page news across the city's newspapers with headlines screaming, "Waiters Chief Arrested As Alien Red," "2d Labor Leader Arrested Here As Radical Alien," and "Obermeier, Hotel Union Head, Called Subversive."[116] Anti-Communists within HRE saw their opportunity to ramp up their drive.

A Full Vote of Confidence in All Past and Present Actions

The LJEB's regularly scheduled monthly meeting happened to fall on September 8. Obermeier was released from custody in time to participate.

The LJEB issued a vote of confidence in Obermeier and pledged to "defeat government plans to deport him." With five locals continuing to boycott the LJEB, the *Voice* offered a glass-half-full account: "Officers and delegates of locals present at the meeting, representing a membership of 42,000 out of 60,000 that are affiliated with the Board, each individually expressed their respect and administration for Obermeier as a leader of the organized Hotel and Restaurant workers."[117] An observer appeared unannounced at the evening's meeting. Joseph Steclen, a business agent from Soda Fountain Employees Local 254, announced that Garriga had appointed him to represent the "Hotel and Restaurant Committee for Democracy." A "Local 6 Committee for Democracy" also appeared, distributing anti-Communist leaflets among the membership.[118]

The "Committee for Democracy" caucuses suddenly had their own midtown office and staff and were spending over $10,000, funneled through the Second District Conference.[119] The nominal leader of the Local 6 group was Tom Passan, a waiter at the Astor and occasional opposition candidate. Passan would invent situations of implied repression. In one, he and 13 members of his Committee appeared—unannounced—at a Local 6 Executive Board meeting, to either announce or ask permission to form a caucus. Prepared to give them the floor, Obermeier asked for their names. Passan, the designated spokesman, refused to let anyone else give their names. The group then walked out and told waiting reporters that they were being prevented from running for office.[120] In another incident, he tried to have Astor security kick union business agent Carl Schutt out of the hotel when he quizzed Passan on who was paying his expenses. He then produced a leaflet accusing the administration of thuggery.[121] An unsigned leaflet from the "Anti Communist Committee, Local 144" was also circulating, accusing Jay Rubin of traveling to Switzerland in 1934 "under a forged passport for the Communist Party." NYHTC denounced it as "a bare faced lie and brazen libel."[122] There was also a bizarre instance of a forged telegram sent to President Ernst, purportedly coming from a group of members at the Waldorf-Astoria recommending that the hotel's shop chairman, Stanley Scott, take over as acting president. Scott had no involvement and even HRE officials recognized it as an obvious forgery.[123]

On October 15, Garriga headlined a Committee for Trade Union Democracy press conference at the Times Square Hotel. He endorsed Passan's opposition slate and warned that if Local 6 members didn't "clean house," HRE would place it under trusteeship.[124] Furious at the misuse of HRE resources on internal opposition efforts, LJEB leaders fired "the only anti-Communist official" of the LJEB, a business agent hailing from Local 15 named Charles Cresser. Jack Townsend went to the press charging that Obermeier was behind the action, which was made "without cause or hearing."[125]

Local 6 leaders took all of this together—Garriga's new demand for names and addresses of the bartenders, Brown, Aragno, and Mageau's effort to break off the club employees, the "Local 6 Committee for Democracy" and even Obermeier's arrest—and saw Garriga's hand. They charged that their ex-president had organized a vast conspiracy "to rob Local 6 of its democracy, to splinter it off section by section and eventually wreck it."[126]

Local 6 held a bartenders membership meeting on October 21 to agitate against the merger. David Herman criticized Local 15's inferior contracts and its more expensive dues, and he insinuated that Local 15's stated goal to "standardize drinks all over town" could lead to orders from above to only use certain "connected" brands of alcohol. Early in the meeting, Miguel Garriga dramatically entered the room, at the apparent invitation of some members who wanted to hear his side. Some in the crowd jeered at him. Obermeier put to the membership whether the meeting should be closed to members of Local 6 only, which the bartenders decided with "hardly any dissenting votes." Obermeier then asked the vice president for the Second District whether he was at the meeting "in any other capacity" than the invitation he received from the dissenting members. Garriga walked out of the room to boos and cries of "get out." At the end of the meeting, the bartenders voted 489 to 9 to boycott the referendum.[127]

The Local 6 executive board drew up charges against Garriga to submit to the GEB. They accused him of using dues money "to build up a political machine of his own" within the local, interfering with its local autonomy and injecting outsiders into the union's internal politics. They charged him with incompetence and argued that his "complete failure as an organizer" warranted suspension from membership.[128] They also accused David Siegal of complicity, claiming evidence of a deal in which he only agreed to the bartenders' merger if Local 16 would gain Local 6's banquet division afterward.[129]

Meanwhile, Obermeier was dealing with his own charges. His comrades formed a "Michael J. Obermeier Defense Committee" to raise the funds necessary to pay his legal bills. Chaired by NYHTC Secretary-Treasurer Peter J. Moroney, who hailed from IBEW Local 3, the executive board was made up of representatives of every local affiliated with NYHTC and most of the LJEB.[130] In a show of how integrated Obermeier was in New York City's mainstream left-liberal alliance, Paul O'Dwyer, the mayor's brother, joined Obermeier's legal team, which included NYHTC attorney Sidney E. Cohn. Presiding Inspector Arthur J. Phelan conducted Obermeier's first hearing on November 1. Obermeier's attorneys stipulated to the government's charge that he had been a member of the Communist Party from 1930 until 1939, but that the admission was "irrelevant," because "the questions the defense will raise are whether any law forbids membership in the Communist Party and, if so, whether such a law is constitutional."

Obermeier's was to be a test case for the CP, which was not mentioned by name in the Smith Act. If the government could not prove that the Party advocated the violent overthrow of the government, then proceedings against

Members demonstrate outside Local 6 offices against Michael J. Obermeier's deportation. (New York Hotel and Gaming Trades Council.)

individuals who were "affiliated" with it while they engaged in legal activities like union organizing and collective bargaining would violate the First Amendment. O'Dwyer moved to have the entire proceedings dismissed as a violation of Obermeier's due process rights under the Fifth Amendment and because Phelan was not appointed to his post in accordance with the Federal Administration Act. The hearing was adjourned for several weeks for motions or objections to be submitted.[131]

While the hearing was being conducted, Garriga hosted a two-day meeting of the Second District Conference across the street at the Empire Hotel. The assembled delegates endorsed a permanent organization—not a factional caucus but an official body to carry out anti-Communist activities. The body also cast a "full vote of confidence in all past and present actions of Brother Garriga." At a press conference, Garriga exulted in Obermeier's Communist confession, predicting the Local 6 president would "be sick at the union elections next February and will not run."[132]

The HRE bartenders' referendum took place on Election Day, November 4, when bars were traditionally closed to ensure higher turnout. Ballots were printed in five colors so that in addition to the citywide count, Garriga and Ernst could determine the sentiments within each local. The results were a washout. Only 3,000 bartenders across five HRE locals—a minority of affected members—cast ballots on the proposed amalgamation.[133]

The bartenders of Local 6 "virtually to a man" refused to participate, attending a union rally at the Manhattan Center instead. Voter turnout was low in general. Even in Local 15, which threatened $10 fines for members who did not attend a union meeting in conjunction with the vote, no more than half the membership cast ballots.[134]

Such Defiance

The repudiation of Garriga and the GEB as seen in the bartender's referendum, the NYHTC's "fighting defense fund," and the general acrimony had all become too much for Ernst, who called a peace conference on November 17. Representatives of each of the eleven NYC locals, Garriga, Ernst, and a whole lot of lawyers met at the LJEB office and hammered out an acceptable deal. The LJEB agreed to withdraw its injunction. Garriga, as Ernst's chosen trustee, would assume control of the LJEB. However, he and all international representatives "will not sponsor or aid any opposition movements in any of the local unions." The bylaws were to be suspended, but present officers would serve out the remainder of their term. Most encouragingly, the agreement promised that Ernst would waive the constitution's requirement that only U.S. citizens can be local officers for "any one now an officer, whose right to run for office is challenged because of non-citizenship but who has made application for citizenship."[135]

The LJEB deal also gave Charlie Cresser back his job as business agent with back pay. The following week, Ernst ruled on Victor Brown, Vincent Aragno, and Theodore Mageau's appeal against their suspensions as Local 6 business agents. Ernst upheld the suspensions but reduced them to two weeks, and he ordered Local 6 to put them back on payroll and give them back pay for the rest.[136] The relatively amicable settlement of the LJEB controversies prompted Local 6's officers to withdraw their censure resolution against Garriga.[137]

In December, Ernst declared his support for Obermeier at Local 6's fifth biennial convention. "I will do all I possibly can, morally and financially, if necessary, to see that all these deportation proceedings are aborted and that Mike Obermeier will stay with us," he told the assembled delegates. "They are not born out of Americanism but out of spite and I cannot subscribe to them."[138]

Despite improved relations, and Ernst's commitment that he would approve his candidacy, Obermeier decided not to run for reelection. The time demands that his legal case would place on him and his poor health made a move into semi-retirement desirable, but Obermeier claimed that his reelection would give Garriga and his allies on the GEB further justifications to break up or put Local 6 under trusteeship. "They believe that such defiance and my election would then give them the opportunity of using technicalities to proceed with the plans for seizing control of our union."[139]

Martin Cody, age 38, became the administration ticket's candidate to replace Obermeier. Gertrude Lane was nominated for secretary-treasurer and Tom Wilson for general organizer. In response to the craft-based agitation to split the local, the constitution was amended to provide for more proportional representation. Each craft department—kitchen, dining room, housekeeping, clubs, banquet, bar, and laundry—would have one vice president, in addition to a proportion of the union's 17 business agents.[140] Tom Passan headed up the opposition slate "Trade Union Committee for Democracy." The three censured club business agents joined the ticket, with Victor Brown running for Club Department vice president and Vincent Aragno and Theodore Mageau for business agent. Nine more candidates filled spots in the Dining Room, Banquet, and Bar departments.[141]

The January 28 election saw the largest turnout in the local's history, with over 16,000 votes cast. The administration ticket won a commanding victory, with Cody claiming 12,972 votes. His opponent, Tom Passan, garnered just 1,725 and the highest vote-getter of the three renegade club business agents only 406 votes.[142] "Let it sink well into the minds of our union's enemies that our membership has given unmistakable proof that it will not be misled, regardless of false or demagogic issues that may be raised," Cody gloated at the next Shop Delegates Council, which voted by acclamation to name Obermeier to the staff position of general manager.[143]

The Communists in Local 6 ended the year 1947 feeling battle-tested and vindicated in their ability to stand up to political enemies and keep the union together. They were not about to keep a low profile or act contritely.

Ernst's brokered settlement raised the possibility that the Communist leaders of New York's hotel workers unions could continue to operate in an open coalition within the AFL's Hotel & Restaurant Employees union. The balance of power would be tested, early and often. The next few years would determine the labor movement's postwar paradigm.

11

The Crack
1947–1950

Charles Collins addressed a closed-door meeting of the Communist Party section in the hotel trades, sometime in the autumn of 1949. "The struggle that we went through," Collins explained, "was a struggle between the policies of class collaboration and capitulation as represented by Jay, and the policies of militant defense of the interests of the workers and of class struggle as represented by the progressive leadership and the rank and file in the union." The context was the recently settled IWA, but it was also basic policy disagreements with NYHTC President Jay Rubin, going back at least as far as the 1948 Henry Wallace campaign. In Collins' account, the left had stayed too loyal to the union's leadership, blind to the "fact that a deep rooted crack had developed in the administration of the union," and he blamed "Jay, who persisted in drifting ... away from the basic united policy, who was responsible for the crack."

The left-wing leadership of Local 6 entered 1948 in a tenuous peace deal with their friends and enemies in the international union. That they immediately strained the bonds of their fragile alliances and cracked up a united front is, with decades of hindsight, almost incomprehensible—even more so because by the time Collins was speaking, the CIO was preparing to purge its rebellious Communist-led unions. In addition, the CP had experienced, in the Transport Workers Union, a break with President Michael J. Quill over the Wallace campaign, followed by rejecting his offer of a sizable minority on the union's executive board and losing a winner-take-all confrontation at the union's 1948 convention.[1] At that point, the Party was choosing to wage another high-stakes fratricidal battle—another self-inflicted error.

To be clear, Communists were facing state repression that only intensified as relations between the United States and the Soviet Union worsened and public opinion turned against them. Hundreds more foreign-born

Communists would be rounded up in the government's deportation drive, and by decade's end, the Party's national leadership itself would be prosecuted and jailed under the Smith Act.

It was the very expectation of a new world war that caused Communist leaders—particularly William Z. Foster—to take a hard line within labor unions over controversial pro-Soviet political issues, hastening the ostracization and expulsion of Communists and the fracturing of alliances. In Local 6's case, it resulted in HRE assuming control of the local, with fateful consequences for its leadership team.

The Michael J. Obermeier Defense Committee

On March 2, 1948, Charles Collins led a delegation of 50 union activists—mostly from CIO unions, aside from the members of Local 6 who participated—to picket the Department of Justice building calling for an end to the "deportation hysteria against union leaders."[2] A steady stream of foreign-born union activists continued to be persecuted under the Smith Act. Cooks Local 89's secretary-treasurer, Arduilio Susi, was ensnared in the witch hunt when the Department of Justice began deportation proceedings against him on June 28, 1948. A native of Italy, 14-year-old Susi came to America after his parental guardian, a Socialist member of Parliament, was shot by Mussolini's brownshirts. Susi was a reliable leftwinger and voted with the Communists at LJEB. Like Obermeier, his application for citizenship put him in the Justice Department's crosshairs. Unlike Obermeier, he received vigorous support from local HRE anti-Communists like Siegal, Mesevich, and even Townsend.[3] The NYS Culinary Alliance unanimously passed a resolution supporting Susi in his citizenship fight, and the HRE GEB gave him approval to run for reelection despite his challenged citizenship status.[4] Susi, Reich, and the entire incumbent leftwing slate in Local 89 were handily reelected.[5]

Local 6 allied with the American Committee for the Protection of the Foreign Born (ACPFB) for a campaign to stop, slow, or reverse the 500 new deportation proceedings the Justice Department announced as imminent.[6] (Obermeier was a guest of honor at the Committee's "Bill of Rights" dinner at its 15th annual conference in December 1948.[7]) The Justice Department soon suppressed the ACPFB as a "Communist-front" organization.[8]

The Michael J. Obermeier Defense Committee continued to raise funds to pay his legal bills. In December 1948, the union organized an Old Timers Committee to aid Obermeier's legal defense. The purpose was as much to round up character witnesses who could speak to his long-term track record of working for legitimate trade union causes as it was to remind current members how much had been won in a 35-year movement that Obermeier had been at the center of. At one meeting, participants reminisced about split shifts and blacklists from "the old days," noting that in the room were "enough leaders of the old Amalgamated Food Workers Union to have made up an executive board quorum."[9] The Old Timers' Committee eventually became a permanent social club in the union.[10] In May, it hosted a large testimonial dinner and dance in tribute to Obermeier. Over 1,600 union members and hotel executives attended the Astor event.[11] The FBI also attended, snagging a copy of the evening's program for its list of guests and sponsors.[12] By the end of September 1949, the Obermeier Defense Committee spent $24,958.72 on legal expenses.[13]

Local 6's leadership team remained on the defensive as well. The administration reorganized assignments to prevent craft-based intrigue and disunity. Local business agents, previously assigned to geographic districts, concentrated on the members and grievances of a particular craft. This meant that multiple officers would gain familiarity with the issues of each shop, making it harder to miss unauthorized petitions or leaflets.[14] NYHTC, meanwhile, assumed responsibility for a five-district geographic structure, in which business agents from all affiliated locals would report to a regional director to coordinate union-wide activities like re-signing contracts, filing grievances, raising money for the defense fund, and organizing shop committees.[15]

Tensions with HRE, meanwhile, relaxed. Since the bartenders referendum "did not clearly and sufficiently indicate the desire of the bartenders in all of the local unions that presently have bartenders in their ranks," the GEB tabled the matter, effectively killing it.[16] The LJEB's autonomy was restored after less than a year with a curious peace deal that saw the vociferously anti-Communist Jack Townsend elected president, openly Communist Harry Reich elected secretary-treasurer, and Sam Kramberg leaving the LJEB staff to join Local 6's as its Labor Chief, running the union's hiring hall.[17] Local 302's Joseph Fox fumed that he did "not fight for two years to exchange Obermeier for Reich." He blamed Garriga for "crying on our shoulders whenever someone hurt his feelings," creating the "fight against the Communists," and dropping it "whenever it suited his convenience."[18] Garriga—who spent the trusteeship trying to consolidate the bartenders locals, merge the waiters locals, and amalgamate the Brooklyn and New York Joint Boards while cranking out Local 89 opposition campaign literature on Local 302's mimeograph machine—alienated all factions. He would focus his energies on Pennsylvania for the remainder of his tenure.

Gideon's Army

Despite the Smith Act and deportation drive, 1947 was "the high tide of Communist strength in the postwar period." The CP had 73,000 dues-paying members, had over 100,000 subscribers to the Sunday *Daily Worker*, and could raise a quarter of a million dollars in a matter of days.[19] The 1948 election year would begin an abrupt decline that cannot merely be explained by state repression as the Party pushed a pro-Soviet political line—at a time of rising global tensions between the USSR and U.S. governments—within unions and other coalitions, even to the point of pushing allies away.[20]

Unions were dissatisfied with Harry S. Truman in his first two years in office because he let wartime price controls exacerbate inflation, was cool-to-hostile to the resulting strike wave, and even tried to draft strikers into the armed forces. This revived interest in a labor party, or at least a primary challenge. Truman's hawkish foreign policy convinced the CP that there should be an anti-war, pro-worker third-party presidential campaign featuring former vice president Henry Wallace. "Russian ideals of social-economic justice are going to govern nearly a third of the world. Our ideas of free-enterprise democracy will govern much of the rest," he said in a September 1946 speech that got him kicked out of Truman's cabinet and kick-started speculation about Wallace's presidential ambitions.[21]

On December 18, 1947, HRE Communists played a timely role in delivering a petition to Wallace signed by 45 leaders of both AFL and CIO unions, purportedly representing over 263,000 New York workers, urging an ambivalent Wallace to run. With their union affiliations listed "for identification purposes only," Martin Cody, Sal Gentile, Harry Reich, and John Steuben lent the ploy a great deal of credibility.[22]

"We have assembled a Gideon's Army, small in number, powerful in conviction, ready for action," Wallace announced, acknowledging that winning the presidency wasn't his campaign's real goal. "The bigger the peace vote in 1948, the more definitely the world will know that the United States is not behind the bipartisan reactionary war policy that is dividing the world into two armed camps and making inevitable the day when American soldiers will be lying in their Arctic suits in the Russian snow."[23]

By the time of Wallace's announcement, Truman had vetoed the Taft-Hartley Act, earning him and the Democratic Party most unions' continued loyalty. "I am against him," AFL President William Green declared of Wallace, warning that his candidacy "will help a reactionary Republican candidate," like Sen. Robert Taft. "To that extent it will help the Communists, too."[24] The CIO's Executive Board voted to repudiate the third-party movement. In New York, CIO unions disaffiliated from the American Labor Party over plans to lend Wallace its ballot line, hastening its demise.[25]

The Wallace campaign also produced the first crack in the Local 6 administration's unity. Jay Rubin shared the perspective that Wallace was a spoiler. Rubin resented efforts to pressure him to personally endorse the campaign, and responded by ceasing his involvement with the CP. Martin Cody's public identification of Local 6 with the Wallace campaign violated the spirit of the peace agreement with Hugo Ernst—and within just a few short weeks!—which must have frustrated Rubin and created tension between the comrades.[26] Neither NYHTC nor Local 6 would endorse Wallace, but the *Voice* devoted copious coverage to members' volunteer activities.

By summer, CP fraction meetings grew increasingly acrimonious and hostile to Rubin's administration. Charles Collins took the lead in hurling quibbling criticisms about bargaining strategies, grievance handling, and the administration of the employment office by Rubin and allies who had dropped out of the Party. The tenor of the meetings was so caustic that other business agents stopped attending or paying dues.[27] The fallout within Local 1 was more immediate. In May, Sam Spitzer and Sal Gentile's administration was rejected in local elections, which brought a new non-Communist leadership to HRE's oldest Waiters local, leaving Cooks Local 89 as the only other bastion of local Communist leadership.[28]

Because Wallace couldn't garner any union endorsements, Communist organizers created a thousand rank-and-file shop committees as a "united front from below."[29] Collins, Antonio Lopez, and business agents Joseph Flanagan and Don Tillman took the lead for Local 6 ("titles for identification only").[30] A little over a thousand members from across fourteen AFL locals attended the founding conference of the AFL Food, Restaurant and Hotel Workers Committee for Wallace, which had Vito Marcantonio as its star attraction.[31] Wallace-for-President committees were set up in nearly 70 hotels and clubs, which is a good deal less than organizers could usually muster for union campaigns, and gives a measure of the actual support for the Communist line—as opposed to support for union leadership—within Local 6. The die-hard members of the AFL Committee for Wallace operated a canteen for the staff and volunteers in Wallace's Park Avenue campaign headquarters.[32] Fifty Local 6 members anchored a delegation of 70 members of AFL food unions as voters and official observers at the founding convention of Wallace's Progressive Party in July.[33]

By October, Wallace was polling at half of the 7% that he started the year with.[34] Soviet maneuvers, like the West Berlin blockade and revelations of Soviet espionage in the U.S. State Department, created a significant public opinion backlash for all things Soviet and Communist.[35] Wallace, as a matter of principle, refused to engage in anything he considered "red-baiting," including distancing himself from the CP's efforts on his behalf. Worse, he unwittingly toed the Party line on matters like opposing the Marshall Plan by reading speeches that were written for him by Communist campaign staffers. All of it served to make him look like a sleeper agent, sank his campaign, and ostracized union leaders who supported him.

On Election Day, Wallace came in fourth place, behind Strom Thurmond's southern Dixiecrat ticket. Thirty-seven percent of his 1.1 million votes came from New York City on the American Labor Party ballot line.[36]

More and More Employers

The fight for better contracts and more organized shops still consumed most of the union's efforts during these years. The union nearly perfected its Employment Office in 1948. Particularly in the lucrative—but unsteady—banquet department, employers came to rely on the union to supply qualified workers. By union estimates, banquets brought in over $21 million in hotel revenue in 1947, but the work was largely seasonal and fluctuated daily. While the hotels that specialized in banquets had steady banquet waiters, captains, bussers, and bartenders on payroll, all needed help supplying extra workers in busy periods. The union maintained a "roll" of dues-paying members who satisfied an industry examination proving their fitness for luxury service. Some were looking for extra work after they clocked out of their regular jobs; others earned their entire living through the roll call.

Each member was assigned a number. At 3:30 PM every weekday, inside a packed hall on the union's second floor, the Labor Chief would read the orders that came in from the hotels and call out the numbers on the roll for workers' daily assignments. For hotel management, it was as easy as calling the union and asking for the number of waiters needed for each scheduled event. If a hotel's banquet manager found that any individual worker was not up to that house's standards, the worker would not be sent back.

In this way, as in all industry-wide collective bargaining arrangements that survive, the union brought order out of chaos. Banquet VP Fred Spinner negotiated to end the practice of having all workers show up at 5:00, regardless of an event's start time. "Today when we receive an order from a hotel it sounds something like this: 25 men at 5:30—2 men at 7:30 and 10 men at 10," he explained. The union negotiated 15 points of working conditions, including prompt payment of wages and tips, a standard number of guest "covers," and wage differentials for serving more patrons and for when a reduced menu would reduce gratuities.[37]

For non-banquet jobs the Joint Employment Office that was agreed upon in the 1945 contract had not yet become a reality by 1949. "However, more and more employers are calling the union when a vacancy occurs and finding that it pays to do so," reported the union's Labor Chief.[38] Hotels were apparently happy to see the union bear the burden of running its own Employment Office. In July of 1949, the union won an Impartial Chairman decision that directed employers to utilize the union's hiring hall under the terms of the IWA.[39]

Most of the new shops that were brought under the terms of the IWA continued to be far afield and mostly uptown. In February 1948, workers at an Upper West Side apartment hotel called the Windermere won a card check with 115 out of 132 eligible bargaining unit members signed up, and workers at the Lucerne voted 45–4 for the union.[40] On April 12, workers at the storied women's residential hotel, the Barbizon, voted for the union 64–26.[41]

BSEIU Local 144 worked to raise the standards of the residential hotels it had assumed responsibility for when Local 32-A was liquidated. On October 14, 1949, it went on a brief strike against 38 hotels affiliated with the Associated Hotels and Residence Clubs Association, aiming to match the 40-hour workweek that was won in the 1946 IWA.[42]

Although NYHTC's bargaining relationship with the Hotel Association was mature and stable, and most newly organized employers fell in line quickly and agreed to industry-wide terms, fights with two recalcitrant employers—the Harvard Club and Governor Clinton Hotel—revived some of the crusading spirit of the union's early days. On March 18, 1948, management at the Harvard Club locked out 140 members of Local 6 when bargaining over a successor agreement broke down. The union was seeking to align the club with the five-day, 40-hour week that most clubs had. The Harvard Club was one of only four holdouts among the twenty-nine union clubs.[43] The union filed a ULP and began paying out strike benefits. Fellow workers from the other organized clubs joined the picket line, as did the picketers' own children who carried lollipop-shaped picket signs that revealed what their parents earned ("THE HARVARD CLUB PAYS MY DAD $33.00 A WEEK AS A KITCHEN MAN") and exclaimed, "I can't go to Harvard on that!"[44]

The labor dispute was a minor cause celebre back in Cambridge, Massachusetts. Students in the Harvard Club for Wallace sent telegrams of protest, and the *Harvard Crimson* editorialized "that labor's side is much more justified in this dispute."[45] After six weeks, the Club ended the lockout and agreed to reenter negotiations after a 30-day "cooling off" period.[46] On June 4, management refused negotiations, claiming that a new company union called the "Employee Welfare Association of the Harvard Club" actually represented a majority of the workers. It didn't, but a few of the workers who suffered the temporary loss of their jobs during the lockout had little desire to repeat the experience and obediently signed whatever forms that management put in front of them.[47] Again, the union filed a ULP. In the face of management's intransigence, and deep divisions within the bargaining unit, the SLRB convinced Local 6 to agree to a new certification election, which they won decisively 79 to 48 on December 28, 1949. The Harvard Club finally signed a new contract in April 1950 that made modest improvements in holiday and overtime pay and wage increases of between $2 and $3 a week.[48]

At the Governor Clinton, the last great open shop holdout in the hotel industry, management continued to defy a ULP bargaining order from the SLRB well into 1949. Management's position was that they were willing to negotiate a contract, just not the IWA. NYHTC, however, maintained the Governor Clinton as a union shop, with an elected shop chairman and a full complement of delegates who raised grievances with department heads. Hotel management would occasionally deign to meet with the shop chairman only. Management tested this arrangement in the summer of 1947 when they fired a union delegate. Bellman Walter Cole was accused of being away from his station without approval. His co-workers saw the action as a "clear case of discrimination" and staged a brief walkout over the termination, only returning to work when the General Manager promised to "investigate."[49]

It took the SLRB two years to adjudicate Cole's termination and order the hotel to reinstate him to his old job.[50] The reinstatement kicked the organizing drive back into gear. Management finally recognized the shop committee and agreed to hear and resolve grievances.[51] Antonio Lopez chaired the rank-and-file bargaining team and spent several fruitless weeks trying to settle a contract. In September, management sent an open letter to employees stating their willingness to sign the IWA if only Lopez would agree to a few small modifications. Those changes, the *Voice* retorted, were only the deletion of "all the clauses relating to wage increases, overtime pay, job and union security and other benefits for the employees!"[52] The union responded in October by opening up bargaining. In the hotel's Governor's Room, union attorney Sidney Cohn debated Vice President William J. Cullen before an audience of hundreds of employees about what the hotel had and had not left on the table, to humiliating effect. The union insisted on more bargaining sessions in the large room to accommodate its expanded bargaining team.[53]

On November 10, the hotel's owners, the Meyer Hotel chain, finally bowed out of the fight by selling a controlling interest to the Carter Hotels Operating Corporation. The Carter chain also owned the Hotel Dixie and George Washington, both IWA signatories.[54] As positive a sign as it was perceived at the time, the new owners still retained the executive staff—namely, Cullen—who had been stubbornly resisting the IWA terms. Cullen's impasse inspired union organizers to revive a decades-old tactic. On January 11, 1950, after an afternoon bargaining session stalled over the same old issues, bargaining team members staged a union meeting in the lobby at 6:45, abruptly suspending dinner service.[55] That action steeled the resolve of the workers, who began preparations for a real strike, with a March 3 deadline to get back to the table.[56] The strike threat alarmed the owners. The last time the union took the Governor Clinton's workers out on strike, it lasted over a year. Although the 1939–40 strike did not result in union recognition, it had a devastating effect on the hotel's finances and reputation. The Carter chain directed Cullen to meet the union's ultimatum for a new bargaining date, but they also found a trusted intermediary to work on a settlement with Jay Rubin.[57]

The March 3 meeting showed the strategic value of opening bargaining up and letting the boss embarrass himself in front of his employees. Forty workers joined David Herman and Antonio Lopez on the union team, sitting across from Cullen and his attorney. Cullen ranted about how the union shop, payroll deduction of dues, and employer-funded healthcare were "un-American." When asked what difference it made to him to deduct union dues from members who voluntarily sign an authorization form, Cullen "sneered" that many of the workers were foreign-born and didn't understand "America and its traditions." Herman exploded at the xenophobic statement, "The workers are every bit as loyal as you are!" The meeting ended with the workers preparing to strike and with Cullen meekly saying he would "lay the union before the board of directors."[58] By March 29, Rubin reported to the Council's executive board that an MOU had been approved by a majority of the hotel's board of directors, granting them relief from wage increases but otherwise signing on to the terms of the IWA. The owners requested that no announcement be made until at least April 15 in deference to Cullen's sensitive ego.[59] On April 27, after twelve years of continued stubborn refusal, the workers of the Governor Clinton finally won the IWA.[60]

We May Lose the First Few Rounds

Winning Obermeier's freedom would prove trickier than beating the hotel bosses. Because of Obermeier's stipulation, the government based its deportation case entirely on the fact of his CP membership from 1930 until 1939 and his TUUL leadership role from 1930 to 1935. Obermeier's lawyers still called plenty of character witnesses, with a particular focus on Hotel Association executives who maintained "that Obermeier's activities during the periods of greatest economic distress and turmoil" were "always a stabilizing force in maintaining peace between employers and employees."[61] They also submitted a 1934 statement from the Department of Labor that the TUUL did not teach "the overthrow of the government by force and violence."[62]

The defense argued that the INS failed to prove that Obermeier was a member of an organization that advocated the overthrow of the government by force; that there was a distinction between advocating change, versus overthrow, of the government and capitalist system; that Obermeier was entitled to constitutional rights of free speech and due process; that the process was ex post facto as the Nationality Act was amended after Obermeier immigrated to the U.S.; that the Smith Act itself was "unconstitutional on its face and as a whole"; and finally that Presiding Inspector Arthur J. Phelan was improperly appointed under the Administrative Powers Act.[63]

Obermeier's attorneys put over 20 exhibits of published Communist materials from the 1930s—Party platforms and constitutions and books by Earl Browder and William Z. Foster—on the record. Informed via memo of Obermeier's legal team's plans, FBI Director J. Edgar Hoover scribbled a note to the special agent coordinating the case with the INS, "Shouldn't we make certain even though it is an immigration case that record is complete as it would appear the commies are trying to get U.S. Supreme Ct. ruling on character of communist party."[64]

Presiding Inspector Phelan ordered Obermeier's deportation on September 20, 1948.[65] "Though we may lose the first few rounds," Peter Moroney declared on behalf of the Obermeier Defense Committee, "we are certain that the courts will uphold Obermeier's right to American citizenship." He vowed Obermeier would appeal for his constitutional rights "all the way to the U.S. Supreme Court, if that becomes necessary."[66]

The government opened a new front in its battle with Obermeier on September 28, 1948, indicting him on three counts of perjury. Obermeier's on-the-record stipulation of his CP membership was cited as directly contradicting statements that he made in three separate INS interviews in 1945 and 1946.[67] The government announced plans to try the perjury case sometime in February 1949.[68] Not coincidentally, Phelan's recommendation to deport Obermeier was affirmed by the chief examiner of the INS on February 17, 1949, although all charges related to the TUUL were dropped. Obermeier's attorneys elevated the case to the Board of Immigration Appeals.[69]

The hearing before that Immigration Appeals board took place on June 8 and lasted two hours. Famed political columnist I. F. Stone "dropped in" for the proceedings. "Tom Dewey broke into the public eye in 1935 by smashing the Dutch Schultz mob in the restaurant industry of New York, which then controlled, terrorized and plundered both the employers and the unions," he wrote, recounting Obermeier's role. "Obermeier was then a Communist, a leader in the Food Workers Industrial Union. By all the current rules, Dewey should have used Dutch Schultz against Obermeier, and pinned a medal on the racketeer for patriotism."[70] On September 24, the Board of Immigration Appeals upheld Obermeier's deportation. His lawyers issued a statement reveling in their ability at long last to take their appeal on the constitutional issues at stake directly into federal court for the first time.[71]

They Are Through

Obermeier's appeal stressed that his past membership in the Party, having ended in 1939, was unconnected to the government's Smith Act trial of the CP leadership. On July 20, 1948, the Department of Justice indicted William Z. Foster and eleven other members of its Executive Committee on Smith Act charges. They were convicted a few weeks after Obermeier filed his District Court appeal.[72]

The political environment continued to worsen for Communists, with plenty of guilt-by-association for anyone who stood by them. The weeks that followed the Soviet Union's first successful test of a nuclear bomb in September 1949 were marked by societal paranoia about a fifth column of Soviet supporters that gave them the secrets of the atomic bomb. Wisconsin senator Joseph McCarthy used the bizarre case of Alger Hiss to announce

Despite leading the AFL's third largest affiliate, Hugo Ernst was passed over for six consecutive vacancies on the Federation's Executive Council. Seen here, seated between George Meany (on his right) and William Green (on his left), Ernst discusses a jurisdictional dispute at the 1949 AFL convention. (HERE Historical Photographs, 6199/013 P, Kheel Center for Labor-Management Documentation and Archives, Cornell University Library.)

that he had a list, "here in my hand," of hundreds of concealed Communists working in the State Department. The era of McCarthyism had begun.[73]

AFL leaders escalated pressure on suspected Communists. The red herring was raised at the New York State Federation of Labor's annual convention in August 1948 as the credentials of 27 delegates—most from HRE Local 6 and BSEIU Local 144—were challenged for violating a Communist ban.[74] The Credentials Committee grilled them with the question, "Are you now or have you ever been a Communist?" Seven, including Local 144's Peter Ottley, answered "no" and were seated. John Goodman, an international vice president of a major AFL affiliate, and Jay Rubin, who represented over 30,000 members in six AFL affiliates, were seated, but the committee urged continuing investigations into their political affiliations even after they answered in the negative. Obermeier was refused a seat on account of his lack of citizenship. The rest, including Martin Cody, Gertrude Lane, John Steuben, and Charles Collins, were barred; their 33 sponsored resolutions, including those calling for anti-lynching legislation and a renewed Fair Employment Practices Administration, were thrown out, and Collins' campaign to be the State Federation's first Black vice president was over before it began.[75]

Similar tensions within the World Federation of Trade Unions—over Cold War politics, the Marshall Act, and the role of the state in Soviet bloc unions—ultimately fractured the ambitious attempt to create a worldwide forum for labor within the United Nations. In January 1949, western labor groups including the CIO disaffiliated, leaving the rump organization as an essentially Communist-oriented labor federation. "So the CIO and the British Trade Union Congress felt that they would try an experiment," George Meany stated. He spoke at length about it at HRE's 1949 convention, perhaps because the New York locals had so publicly championed the creation of the WFTU. "Well, they have had four years of it, and they are through."[76]

By 1950, Hugo Ernst was nearly through with Meany and Green's guilt-by-association handling of Communists in the AFL when he was passed up for a sixth time by the AFL Executive Council. While not technically representative of every affiliate, the Council was a measure of esteem and power. When Edward Flore died in 1945, his seat went to the ILGWU's David Dubinsky, a prodigal son who had briefly joined the CIO in the 1930s and slowly earned his old seat back. When BSEIU's William McFetridge was picked in February 1950—despite the fact that HRE was by then the federation's third largest affiliate—Ernst found "ugly rumors" that his religious faith and "liberal outlook" were "not acceptable to the AFL council majority."[77] "We must therefore conclude," *Catering Industry Employee* reported, "the Council is 'punishing' our union for its progressive point of view."[78]

Periodic Health

During all this political tumult, the union maintained a relatively cooperative relationship with the Hotel Association, and, together, they pioneered what would become a crown jewel of the union-negotiated benefits enjoyed by New York's hotel workers: a wholly owned and operated medical health center. The union won insurance benefits in the 1945 contract that paid out nearly $780,000 by July 1947.[79] But insurance did not cover comprehensive medicine like routine check-ups and ambulatory care. The insurance fund trustees had ambitions to create an in-house health center from the beginning. To bring the project to fruition, the trustees hired the consulting and actuarial firm led by Martin Segal, who was trusted by several left-led unions to pioneer the burgeoning private-sector welfare state borne from collective bargaining.[80] By Segal's math the Health Center would require a $500,000 annual operating budget, which would be funded by employer contributions equivalent to 3% of their overall payroll. On June 18, 1949, the HTC-HA Insurance Fund announced the purchase of a five-story building at 50th Street and 10th Avenue to be the Health Center's future home.[81]

A gut renovation would take over a year. It would be outfitted with rooms for X-ray, bloodwork, and electrocardiograph equipment; a small surgery suite for minor procedures; a pharmacy; equipment for specialists such as ophthalmologists, urologists, and ear, nose, and throat doctors; and medical examination and consultation rooms.[82]

Martin Segal explained one innovative aspect of the Health Center: "Group practice means a lot more than just a number of doctors and their nurses sharing one large suite of offices. It means that the doctors can get together and consult with each other about the needs of the patient."[83] Routine check-ups were also relatively innovative at a time when most people only saw a doctor when they were sick. The trustees hired Dr. Frank P. Guidotti to be the medical director of the Health Center. Dr. Guidotti delighted in studying and publishing on the public health outcomes of routine periodic examinations of hotel workers. In its first five years, the Health Center conducted 4,224 check-ups that consisted of 93 diagnostic procedures. Thirty-five percent of the exams resulted in one or more new diagnoses and 35% of those were asymptomatic, allowing for better treatment in the early stages of a condition.[84]

This miniature system of socialized medicine—expanded to locations across the boroughs, covering family, retirees, and dental care—has remained the pride of NYHTC to this day, although, as socialists, its pioneers' ambition was for the benefits they won to be a part of a wider public system.[85] The Truman administration pushed to add universal health insurance to the country's Social Security benefits in 1949, an effort that HRE strongly supported.[86] It failed largely because of the organized opposition of the American Medical Association, who scare-mongered about doctors losing autonomy and professional judgment and "creeping socialism." It is a bitter irony that most doctors lost much of the independence they previously enjoyed to the powerful health insurance industry—an industry that barely existed until unions began negotiating health insurance benefits as a stopgap measure in light of the failure to pass national health insurance.

Healthcare politics remained a major issue for Jay Rubin, as he became a policy expert through his role as a trustee for the HTC-HA Insurance Fund. The union was heavily involved in lobbying for the passage of Medicare in the 1960s. Rubin was instrumental in an ultimately unsuccessful attempt to create a universal health insurance program in New York in the 1970s, and, for years when Blue Cross and Blue Shield rates were regulated by the state, Rubin was an expert witness offering testimony that punched holes in the insurance company's justifications of proposed rate hikes.

The Issues Involved Could Be Straightened Out in Conferences

In June 1949, the union found itself fighting jurisdiction under Taft-Hartley when Local 153 of the Office Employees International Union (OEIU) filed an NLRB petition for administrative employees at the Park Sheraton. Those employees had previously voted 65–13 for NYHTC representation under the SLRB. They were covered by the IWA and members of Local 6.[87]

Front desk employees and other white-collar workers were left out of the first IWA in 1939. At the time, these workers tended to identify more with management and oppose unionization by a narrow majority. But as they saw the wages and benefits accrue to their unionized colleagues, white-collar workers showed a newfound interest in organizing. Probing for interest in white-collar bargaining units had been David Herman's first union assignment in 1943, but it was put on hold when he joined the army.[88] NYHTC returned in earnest to organizing white collar workers late in 1946. Lee Candea, a Local 144 business agent who was close to John Steuben, was put in charge of the effort. The Hotel Association agreed to add them to IWA bargaining units, on a shop-by-shop basis, as workers voted their way into the union. White-collar workers at the Beaux Arts, Bossert, Commodore, Dixie, and Park Central were the first to do so.[89] In deference to the professional employees' aloofness towards the hoi polloi, the Council initially created a new Hotel Administrative Department Employees Local 7 for the workers, which had no international union affiliation. It was NYHTC's intention that Local 7 "be chartered by the appropriate body in the A.F. of L. having jurisdiction." Amazingly, leadership debated affiliating the CIO's United Office and Professional Workers of America (UOPWA) instead, even though such an action would violate AFL leaders' every deeply held bias against consorting with the enemy labor league.[90]

OEIU was a relatively new AFL affiliate, chartered in 1945. It was explicitly denied jurisdiction over white-collar hotel workers thanks to Hugo Ernst's lobbying. Like Ed Flore before him, Ernst jealously guarded HRE's jurisdiction over most hotel employees, and, having defended its right to represent administrative hotel employees, he insisted that NYHTC transfer the members into Local 6. Lee Candea, briefly only the second woman president of an NYHTC local, became vice president for Local 6's Administrative Employees Department.[91]

When UOPWA's leaders refused to sign non-Communist affidavits under the Taft-Hartley Act, OEIU jumped at the opportunity to grow at their expense, utilizing the process of NLRB decertification elections in which only OEIU was named on the ballot as the workers' union option. When OEIU petitioned for jurisdiction at three hotels, NYHTC leaders nervously watched but did not intervene. OEIU's petition at the Park Sheraton, however, was a raid. Challenging jurisdiction at the NLRB would have required NYHTC leaders to sign non-Communist affidavits. NYHTC negotiators weighed on Local 153 business agent Howard Coughlin to withdraw his NLRB petition so that "the issues involved could be straightened out in conferences."[92]

To avoid the NLRB, NYHTC allowed Local 153 to affiliate and claim jurisdiction over clerical and administrative employees in IWA signatory hotels. OEIU committed to join the Council in an SLRB drive to organize the estimated 3,000 remaining non-union office professionals in otherwise unionized hotels while Local 6 had one year to evaluate the partnership before transferring the administrative employees it represented (1,500 in 40 different hotels) into Local 153.[93]

Even though NYHTC was not subject to Taft-Hartley, the mere threat of its anti-Communist provisions was enough to make Local 6 cede a significant slice of its jurisdiction.

So Long as We Are United

New York's hotel industry consolidated and grew more complex in the postwar years. All the banks and insurance companies that had purchased hotel properties during the Great Depression had sold them off by 1949. Many new owners made plans to demolish the properties—particularly hotels that predated the 1920s building boom—to make way for skyscraper office buildings. Other real estate traders bought into new local chains, like Carter Management. As this was happening, national chains were also accumulating. One industry directory listed 128 chain management systems in 1940, operating 990 hotels. By 1948, that number increased to 186 chains owning or managing 1,592 properties. Industry publications cheered on the "ever-increasing emphasis on cost-cutting and cost-control."[94]

These national chains also began buying their way into the New York market. The Sheraton corporation purchased the Park Central in December 1948 and began operating it as the Park Sheraton. At the time, the company owned twenty-eight hotels in twenty-two cities, but it would go on a shopping spree for dozens of new properties throughout the 1950s.[95] That same year, the Statler corporation purchased the Hotel Pennsylvania from its namesake railroad company. The company had managed the city's third-largest hotel for decades. It was one of nearly a dozen in a growing portfolio of properties around the country. The renamed Statler Hotel was its first foray into ownership.[96] Late in the war years, an up-and-coming western hotel magnate made a splash by purchasing and refurbishing the Plaza. Conrad Hilton already owned the Roosevelt as he built up his nationwide chain. In 1949, the publishers of Hilton's new biography, *The Man Who Bought the Plaza*, halted production when his purchase of the Waldorf-Astoria necessitated a flashier book title.[97] Within a few years, he would initiate a hostile takeover of the Statler corporation.[98]

Sheraton, Statler, and Hilton traded on their brand names as an indication of quality. Other hotel moguls operated through subcontractors and franchisees. One "hotel trader," Louis Schleifer, would spend the early 1950s buying and selling dozens of properties in New York and around the world. The complexity of his arrangements could be exemplified by his purchase of the Cornish Arms from the Knott corporation in 1951. Schleifer promptly leased it to another entrepreneur who turned around and hired Knott to continue managing the hotel.[99]

Most of the "Hotel Men" whose egos drove the industry's collective bargaining strategy had faded from the scene. Frank Case died at the age of 76 in 1946. Lucius Boomer was felled by a heart attack at the age of 68 in 1947. S. Gregory Taylor also died of a heart attack in 1948. He was 59 years old.[100] Hotel management became a standardized profession with an increasingly faceless corporate management. Nevertheless, the 1949 IWA negotiations would prove to be one of the most difficult and would further divide the Local 6 administration. The year saw the first economic recession since before the war. Citing a statistical decline in the consumer price index, management demanded a general wage *reduction*.[101]

Union leaders had two basic demands: a 15 percent wage increase and time and a half for sixth day overtime for the non-tipped employees. They debated whether to follow the existing pattern of negotiating a new three-year deal instead of utilizing the arbitration process for a wage adjustment in this, the contract's final year. David Herman argued that the economic downturn meant that arbitration was the union's only decent chance at winning a wage increase in 1949. He thought the union should let the contract expire in 1950 and prepare for a strike. Others—including Cody and Steuben as well as Obermeier and Lane—were unsure they could win a strike vote. Many members were recent hires who inherited their union from struggles that preceded them, or who won their union through forms of neutrality that, even with a year to prepare, made an industry-wide strike seem risky.[102]

Bargaining began in early March, and by May, the union asked Mulrooney to convene the "3-Man" Commission.[103] Management's giveback demands dominated the "3-Man" sessions, which proved to be fruitless. Rubin would never agree to wage concessions and Mulrooney, as the tie-breaking third vote, couldn't sign off on a 2-1 decision under the circumstances without damaging his reputation for impartiality. Besides, it was past practice for management and the union to directly negotiate a new IWA in odd-numbered years. If they could come to an agreement on wages, a direct settlement in 1949 could provide the union and management security and stability until 1953.[104]

The Crack

As a result of the impasse, Rubin developed a "7 Point Program" of contract demands that would "strengthen the hand" of negotiators for long-term collective bargaining wins. They included: extending the 5-day, 40-hour week to tipped employees; providing time and a half for overtime after 8 hours in any one day; improving the administration of the joint employment agency; including special seniority rights and layoff protections for union delegates; adding minimum wage rates for administrative employees and a specific work schedule for banquet waiters to the contract; adjusting wage differentials between old and new employees; and requesting a new three-year IWA with yearly reopening on wages and hours.[105]

By summer, Rubin had a tentative agreement with the Hotel Association to extend the 40-hour week to tipped employees. So that dining room workers would be compensated for the tips they wouldn't earn in the hours they didn't work, Rubin extracted raises of between $2.20 and $5 for them, but it would increase the hotels' payroll by a million dollars annually, and it left no money for a general wage increase for the rest of the workforce. Deeming it a big win for a major union principle and a long sought-after goal, NYHTC leaders accepted the framework. Martin Cody, who was on several weeks' vacation as these negotiations developed, learned of it when he returned and intrigued with John Steuben. They saw agitating for an across-the-board wage increase as an opportunity to undermine Rubin's leadership. Even Charles Collins was blindsided when Cody tried to go back on the "7 Point Program" at a weekly meeting of staff and leaders. "Do you think we are children?" Collins snapped at his comrade. "We have lived with this all summer. We have discussed it and acted upon it. And you come in here on this late date?" Leaders polled the room and voted unanimously to reapprove the 7 Point Program and recommend it to the membership.[106]

The Wage Policy Committee, the union's extended bargaining team, met the following Monday at the Park Sheraton. As the Committee reviewed the progress of the seven points, Cody again broke the unity of the leadership by declaring, "I want an eighth point. There must be a wage increase."[107] Naturally, there was a lot of sentiment in the room for winning the 15 percent across-the-board increase that had been the union's initial demand. Committee members were ultimately convinced that it was not impossible and that negotiators were making enough gains on the seven points to endorse the plan, but the seeds of discontent had been sown.

The next night 1,200 members filled the Manhattan Center. It was a long meeting. From the floor, members continued to push for across-the-board wage increases. Rubin and Obermeier emphasized the gains that could only be made through direct negotiations. Charging that the fix was in, a group of dissidents loudly disrupted and walked out of the hall. "Some of us may feel certain actions would have made the proposals unnecessary," Charles Collins addressed the disruptors. "We will carry on the fight for wage increases, for better conditions of the hotel workers," concluding, "We have honest leaders. Above all, so long as we are united, we will keep building our democratic union, we will help in building democratic America."[108]

The new IWA, as Rubin had settled it, was signed on September 28.[109] By then, the Communist Party was directly challenging Rubin's leadership. "There is no security in a contract alone," Charles Collins declared at a CP fraction meeting. "What makes the difference is whether the contract is won in militant struggle and contains substantial gains for the workers." He carped that the "7 Point Program" was "in the bag," that the wage demand was "a tactic to strengthen the hand of the negotiators" and that, as such, no job actions were ever seriously proposed.[110] To underline the importance of worker militancy, Local 144 led a brief strike against 38 Associated Hotel Residence properties on October 13.

It was then that Collins warned that a "deep rooted crack had developed in the administration of the union." Whether he proposed spackle or a ballpeen hammer to address the crack, Collins himself seemed unclear. "Our job is to resume the initiative, to raise fundamental issues, to establish the independent role of the Party firmly, to capitalize on the new respect won by our Party among the workers, to rally them for the line, and in the process to help consolidate the union and build the party," he concluded. "Our attitude towards Jay will depend on how he reacts to issues."[111]

Unity Has to Have a Unity of Purpose

Local 6 leadership split into Rubin-Lane and Cody-Collins factions, and staff meetings frequently devolved into petty bickering. At one, Herman threw down the gauntlet and declared that Cody's reelection as president would be unacceptable to him and his allies.[112] Afterward, Rubin hit upon the idea of restoring Michael J. Obermeier to the Local 6 presidency. Obermeier was the only Rubin ally the Communists would not dare oppose in the upcoming local elections. He was, moreover, the only possible president capable of reunifying the Local 6 administration. Assured that Ernst would grant permission, Rubin convinced Obermeier to allow himself to be nominated for his old office, and Cody agreed to step aside for Local 6's once and future president.

Local 6 held its annual convention in the second week of December. The misgivings and disagreements over the Manhattan Center rally and the contract settlement that followed were the hot topics. Delegates endorsed an organizing plan and made a wage increase the central goal of 1950. "Unity has to have a unity of purpose," Obermeier declared in the main speech. "It has to center around principles that we are fighting for." He was greeted with a standing ovation, and Martin Cody took the opportunity to make the motion that Local 6 ask the HRE GEB permission for Obermeier to run once again for president, which passed by acclamation.[113]

In caucus, Gertrude Lane was picked to "succeed herself" as secretary-treasurer.[114] Only after "a long argument," in which he was threatened with being dropped from the slate entirely, did Cody accept his demotion to Lane's old position as general organizer.[115] The Communists insisted that an African American be nominated for the fourth-top officer position, recording secretary. Collins wanted the position for himself, but the two factions compromised on Daisy George, a business agent from the housekeeping department who was a less divisive CP member. The administration won without significant opposition, but there was a note of dissent. Over 15,000 members voted; a couple thousand of them abstained from voting for the top officers. Obermeier's 10,234 votes were only slightly better than the new recording secretary Daisy George's 10,203. Martin Cody got the most votes at 10,799. An opposition slate in the Bar Department lost by a 2–1 margin.[116]

At the February 8 installation ceremony, Arduilio Susi, who had won his citizenship fight the prior September, swore in the officers and symbolically handed the gavel to Obermeier.[117] A few weeks after resuming office, Obermeier was handed a reprieve when the Supreme Court paused the government's deportation drive on procedural grounds. In its rush to deport hundreds of alien Communists, immigration authorities failed to comply with the Administrative Procedure Act, under which immigration inspectors like Arthur J. Phelan could not also serve as final arbiters of the case. The Court's 6–1 decision voided every case that the INS had pursued since June 4, 1947.[118]

While Obermeier's restoration forestalled a crack-up in Local 6's leadership administration, Local 144's elections in April were a permanent break. John Goodman, the former local president and a BSEIU vice president, formed an opposition "New Deal" slate to challenge John Steuben's administration. "Our membership must have a new deal," Goodman's campaign literature implored. "We must unite our ranks. We must eliminate anyone who causes division, who tries to set up one-man rule in our local union."[119] Jay Rubin tacitly supported Goodman. Although Local 6 was by far the largest NYHTC affiliate, accounting for about 70 percent of membership and a clear majority of delegates to the Council, Local 144 was the second largest bloc of votes.[120] If Cody and Collins' faction of loyalist Communists ever decided to challenge Council Rubin's leadership, his support among the maintenance and engineering locals combined with new leadership in Local 144 that was loyal to his administration could be the margin of victory if Local 6's delegation split over the CP's direction.

Peter Ottley, the former Local 32-A business agent who swore allegiance to the Goodman-Steuben administration in 1945, saw his own opportunity and announced an anti-Communist "Save the Union" slate to run against Steuben for secretary-treasurer.[121] Goodman garnered just 790 votes, but it was the margin of difference to sink Steuben's administration. Ottley polled a plurality of 2,094 votes to Stueben's 1,512 in the November 21 election.[122]

"Two years ago Steuben told me that white workers would never vote for a Negro," Ottley gloated, showing "the falsity of the Communists' claim that they are the sole fighters against discrimination." Ottley concluded his post-election statement with a rebuke of Jay Rubin: "We are going out to get the things the Commies failed to get in 1949 and in years past."[123]

Also in April, NYHTC began publishing a new monthly magazine called *Hotel*. Although most members in the engineering, maintenance, and white-collar locals could easily find copies of *Hotel & Club Voice* in the shops, it contained relatively little coverage of those crafts' workplace issues, and some of the other local leaders began to chafe against Party line content of Local 6's tabloid. Plus, Rubin needed a direct line to all union members during bargaining, without partisan slant or factional interference.[124] The small-format glossy contained industry analysis, general economic forecasting, basic education on labor law and the union contract, labor history, "labor notes" on relevant news from other unions, and a thorough review of union services and legislative activities.[125]

Born Itzok Rijok, John Steuben and his family emigrated from Ukraine in 1923. Just 16 years old, he was already affiliated with the Communist International and immediately became a prominent organizer for the Young Communist League in Pennsylvania. He spent the early 1930s in the Soviet Union receiving an advanced Marxist education. He spent the latter 1930s on the staff of the Steel Workers Organizing Committee, in Youngstown, Ohio, working on the campaign to win a union for the workers at the "Little Steel" factories. Organizers were arrested on trumped-up charges of rioting and sabotage to remove them from the field; prosecutors added criminal syndicalism for Steuben, adding to his notoriety. By the end of 1937, he was purged along with the other Communists on the Steel Workers' payroll.[126] (New York Hotel and Gaming Trades Council. Located in Hotel Trades Council Photographs PHOTOS.097, Box 5, Folder 5; Tamiment Library and Robert F. Wagner Labor Archive, New York University.)

Another internal conflict arose in late May when the eleven board members of the JAFRC—including Charlotte Stern—lost their final appeal before the Supreme Court, in a ruling that paved the way for jailing the more famous "Hollywood 10" screenwriters. Stern began serving her three-month jail sentence on June 8.[127] Cody and Collins fought not only to retain her but to place her on paid leave while in prison; Rubin and Lane argued that her further employment invited a new trusteeship threat. They won the majority of Local 6's administrative board. It was only after Hugo Ernst telegrammed his opinion that it would be "to the best interests of the organization if Miss Stern is taken off the payroll of Local 6" that they joined the rest of the leadership in asking Stern to submit her resignation.[128]

By that point, Cody, who as general organizer was responsible for assisting and supervising business agents in their handling of grievances and approving cases to be advanced to the Impartial Chairman, was freezing out staff who weren't CP loyalists. Grievances at shops represented by Rubin loyalists languished unless Herman intervened as NYHTC administrative director to file them with the Impartial Chairman. Cody "devoted all of his time and energy taking up problems in the Waldorf-Astoria Hotel on every level" in order to show up Fred Spinner and rebuild a base of support in the city's largest hotel.[129]

The only point of unity heading into the summer of 1950 was the IWA wage reopener and the all-important need to win a wage increase after the controversial 1949 contract. The union's Wage Negotiations Policy Committee was demanding a 20 percent wage increase for members earning less than $40 a week, and 15 percent for everyone else. The union's demand to bargain had gone unanswered by management well into April. At first, the union staged a large rally of 7,000 members at St. Nicholas Arena to "ratify" the negotiators' demands. Rallies of this sort had become routine, and the Hotel Association was unmoved.[130] Hotel owners were also divided on their own wage policy, with one faction seeing the union's clear internal divisions as an opportunity to have another year of no or low wage increases, and another seeing wages as key to continued labor peace.

On June 9, the union began singling out hotels with on-the-clock job actions. Starting at the Statler, organizers called all 700 bargaining unit employees on duty down to the hotel's lobby for a "meeting" to discuss the Hotel Association's inaction on wages and to loudly demand that the hotel's general manager come to meet them and explain why the Hotel Association was not negotiating. The 90-minute "flash" strike was repeated at the St. Moritz and Park Sheraton days later. At other shops and the management offices of the Bing and Bing, Kirkeby, and Spencer-Taylor chains—where organizers couldn't get all workers to engage in a job action—large groups of union delegates marched on management offices, demanding to meet with executives. Before the week was over, Edward P. Mulrooney scheduled a meeting of the "3-Man" Commission for June 27.[131]

While this was occurring, Obermeier's perjury trial began. After a month of testimony, mostly from character witnesses, the defense rested.[132] On July 17, he was convicted on three counts of perjury. "Citizenship is not a right," the judge decreed, "but a precious privilege which our government confers upon aliens only under certain indispensable conditions."[133] His lawyers planned an appeal, but as a freshly convicted felon, he now posed a greater threat than Charlotte Stern ever did to Local 6's reputation and autonomy.[134] It was clear that Obermeier would have to resign as president. Less clear was what would happen to the tenuous unity of the Local 6 administration.

Highly Irregular

The following day was a previously scheduled membership rally to put pressure on the "3 Man" Commission. Obermeier's conviction added more pressure. The Commission announced wage increases of $3 and $4 at the end of the week, which was basically half of the increases the union was seeking.[135] For the first time ever, it was not a unanimous decision. The Hotel Association voted against the award. It appears that the Impartial Chairman feared the instability of the union's internal politics and recognized the *political* need for a wage increase. However, without the Hotel Association's approval, he had to cut the union's wage demand down to size. Rubin could have also rejected the decision, but then the union would enter direct negotiations with the Hotel Association at a moment of dangerous disunity. As an arbitrator's award in a wage reopener during an otherwise settled contract, the less-than-sought-after wage increase did not require ratification. Most members greeted the wage increase as a win; it was hard to call a 10 percent wage increase anything else.

On July 26, Obermeier announced his resignation to the Local 6 Shop Delegates Council (SDC). In a chaotic scene, delegates refused to accept it. From the chair, Obermeier began to appraise the relative strengths of his potential successors, intending to endorse David Herman. From the floor, a CP loyalist nominated Martin Cody. Before Cody could be declared the new president by acclamation, Herman was also nominated. The voice vote was inconclusive. With people shouting for paper ballots, Obermeier ordered a division of the house. Delegates supporting Cody lined up on one side of the room, Herman supporters on the other, while tellers from both factions counted. Accusations about repeat voters and uncounted delegates swirled. "Mike, I think you had better call this thing off," Herman intoned to Obermeier, watching the scene with him from the stage. "It cannot just go on with this state of confusion."[136] The tellers' count revealed Cody as having slightly more support than Herman, by a margin of 265–256. The rowdy meeting ended inconclusively.

Herman formally protested the "highly irregular" procedure the next day. Both sides of the looming civil war hid behind the fact that the SDC had not accepted Obermeier's resignation to acknowledge Obermeier as continuing to be president while they figured out the next steps.[137] Meanwhile, on July 31, Obermeier returned to court, was sentenced to a $1,000 fine and two years in a federal penitentiary, and was freed on bond pending appeal.[138]

While Local 6 considered its next steps, outside pressure continued to build. The following weekend was the New York State Federation of Labor's annual convention. Local 6 leadership had previously decided to participate again, although Cody and Collins objected and maintained their own boycott. Lane and Herman headed up the delegation. When they got to Albany, they once again found their credentials challenged. Even though most were willing to swear that they were no longer members of the Communist Party, the entire delegation found itself guilty by way of association with Charles Collins, whose activity in the Labor Conference for Peace was particularly offensive. Because Collins remained a vice president of the union, the credentials committee was "not convinced that there has been a change, but, rather is of the definite opinion that their activities previously aided and abetted the enemies of organized labor, and a mere statement by these delegates of change of heart will not suffice."[139] (Rubin, who attended as an NYHTC representative, was seated as he had been in 1949.) Ten of the delegates—headed by Lane and Herman—published an open letter denouncing the "injustice" done to the union. "The report of the credentials committee can only bring aid and comfort to those disruptive elements in Local 6 who would hamper the progress of our Local Union." The credentials committee singled out Lee Candea, who had married John Steuben earlier in the year, as having "no place in the councils of the State Federation of Labor." She issued her own statement denouncing the state AFL and accusing Lane and Herman of a red-baiting "frame-up," that also managed to jam in praise for Cody and Collins' "tireless fight" for wage increases in 1949.[140]

On August 10, Obermeier submitted his resignation in writing. "At this moment in history, I am faced with the likelihood of being deprived of my liberty as well as the prospect of exile," he wrote to the local's officers. "I am confident that eventually, my fight to become a citizen of this, my adopted land, which I chose in preference to any other country in the world, will be a successful one." The statement, which was widely circulated among the members, concluded, "I feel strongly, however, that while this fight is going on, that it should not give the enemies of our Union an opportunity to attack the Union because of my own problems."[141]

The Administrative Board accepted the resignation on the following day and scheduled a Shop Delegates Council meeting for August 17. It recommended that the election to fill Obermeier's vacancy be conducted via secret ballot membership vote on October 2.[142] With Cody's faction spreading slanderous innuendo about David Herman's attempt to "capture" the presidency "by hook or by crook," it was decided that he would not run in the election. Rubin instead tapped Richard Sirch, a club business agent who was never a member of the Party.[143] Martin Cody ran as the standard-bearer for the loyalist Communists and William Raymond, a dissident bartender who ran on Tom Passan's "Local 6 Committee for Democracy" slate in 1947, played the role of anti-Communist gadfly.[144]

In Cincinnati, Hugo Ernst received a flurry of petitions and telegrams from rank-and-file members complaining about the organizational dysfunction of the ongoing faction fight. Charles Betts, a club business agent and "former participant in the Rubin caucus," wrote him, "I must inform you that Jay Rubin is planning to make a bolt and defy the International."[145] Ernst dispatched Ed Miller to New York to assess the situation. He walked past members of the Association of Catholic Trade Unionists (ACTU) picketing the union office, protesting Communist domination. He met, privately and in groups, with officers from both factions. Each side, naturally, blamed the other for the discord, but insisted that it would be resolved by the election. After getting Miller's report, Ernst called Rubin on the phone.[146]

They discussed the current state of the local's politics. Martin Cody was popular with the members and likely to win. He was also a Communist and subject to investigation and expulsion under the HRE constitution. All of Local 6's officers had been spared that fate by Ernst's now-ruptured peace deal. Both men agreed that it was time to enforce the constitution's Communist ban. On September 15, Ernst ordered the local to be placed under trusteeship. "For months now the local has been split into various factions and the Communist issue has been the cause of the dissension. As a result of this fight grievances of members have been neglected, the true functioning of the local for the benefit of the membership has been disregarded, and a struggle for power has been taking place among several factions at the expense of the rank and file membership," he justified.[147]

The attempt to maintain a leadership coalition with Party-line Communists was over. The trusteeship would determine the future course of the union. Would the union remain militant? Could it hold on to its contract gains? Would it stay on a progressive course? And, in a Cold War environment of trials and investigations, could anyone who was now or ever had been a member of the Communist Party remain in leadership? The next year would be decisive.

12

Trusteeship
1950–1953

Sam Kramberg was summoned to the president's office sometime before lunch on Friday, October 6, 1950. The office was occupied by the trustee whom HRE President Hugo Ernst appointed to root out Communists in Local 6. Kramberg never hid his Party membership. He joined when it was founded in 1919, and for all those years, he was an organizer of food workers. He was a leader of citywide strikes staged by independent unions in 1918 and 1929. When HRE needed militant organizers, he and his comrades brought their thousands of members into the union, and he personally supervised organizing drives that extended collective bargaining to tens of thousands of restaurant and cafeteria workers at chain systems across the city.

This brought him into leadership of Local 302 and the LJEB, before anti-Communists drove him from office. Now, he was just a Local 6 staffer. There would be no trial or appeal. He was fired. The news was plastered across the front page of the *Hotel & Club Voice*, which had transformed into an anti-Communist rag. Instead of his forthright defense of the Communist Party as a legal organization and legitimate representative of New York voters, the paper recalled him as "a picture of insolence" during HRE's 1946 investigation. When Ed Miller asked if he was a Communist, he allegedly replied, with a smirk, "Yes. What are you—Republican or Democrat?"[1]

Although HRE's history of trusteeships was relatively young in 1950, Local 6's remaining loyal Communists knew they were in the trustee's crosshairs. Could they have remained concealed Communists, recommitted themselves to trade union unity, and remained a part of the administration that would emerge when local autonomy was restored? William Z. Foster, who trusted Michael J. Obermeier but had seen Jay Rubin as an unreliable ally, fostered a crack in the unity of New York's hotel employees unions and a decisive break with Rubin. Once a genius union organizing strategist, Foster had spent the

1920s pushing Trade Union Education League activists to endure all manner of attacks from entrenched union leadership to maintain unity in the fight to win collective bargaining. With the practice of collective bargaining stable and well-established by the 1950s, Foster concluded that unity was no longer existential for unions. *His* biggest existential concern was the defense of the Soviet Union. Remaining part of union leadership coalitions wasn't worth it to him if union leaders wouldn't use their power and platform to advance causes in the interest of the survival of the Soviet Union. Time and again, rather than come to an understanding with Party "influentials" in the labor movement, Foster counseled a clean break in the previous unity—at the risk of isolation, ostracization, or worse. Perhaps his plan was to return to the days of militant minorities, scoring points at the expense of "conservative" union functionaries by raising bigger bargaining demands and organizing more disruptive job actions. But the trusteeship, with its potential for charges, trials, suspensions, and expulsions, could decapitate the Party organization within the union.

Not that ex-Communists had a "get out of jail free" card, as Obermeier was literally heading to jail for his years of labor activism as a member and fellow traveler of the Party. If the fine distinction between member and "fellow traveler" seemed to make little difference to Party leadership, and even less to federal authorities, what more difference would adding the categories of "dissident Communist" or "ex-Communist" make to union trustees and rank-and-file voters once the testimony of bitter recrimination and campaign literature began flowing? No one was immune to the trustee's disciplinary power or his control of staff, union communications, and the election machinery.

Meanwhile, the anti-Communist opposition caucus—already the beneficiary of significant outside support and resources from the Association of Catholic Trade Unionists (ACTU)—certainly saw its opportunity to "clean house" and elect a new leadership that was more focused on negotiations and grievances and less on social and political issues.

The next three years would set the union on its course as a left-liberal (or "progressive") post-war union within the mainstream labor movement and New York's Democratic coalition.

Full Cooperation

Bert H. Ross arrived in New York on September 19, 1950. An HRE staffer who had just finished a successful trusteeship of a Miami local to clear up financial irregularities, he had a reputation for fairness and an even-keeled disposition. He now carried with him credentials from Hugo Ernst to take over the affairs of Local 6. He showed these to Obermeier and Cody, and they agreed to call a meeting first thing the following morning.[2]

At the meeting, Ross explained his charge to investigate and eliminate Communists from leadership. He declared the special election for president "suspended indefinitely," vacated all officer positions, and then reappointed everyone "temporarily pending investigation," while he assumed the office of president. All fifteen members of Local 6's Administrative Board voted "to concur with the actions of General President Hugo Ernst in ordering international supervision of Local 6."[3] Ross's meeting with the staff later in the day was slightly more tense. Someone mentioned a "reception committee" that was prepared to physically escort the trustee out of the building. Ross took a firmer tone, warning any Communists "would do well to resign from office now because it is only a matter of time before I would catch up to them." Before adjourning, Ross asked, "Are there any opposed to the policies of the International as announced?" Cody stated that he didn't like the idea of a trusteeship but "saw no alternative, due to the situation in Local 6, to go along with it." Ross recorded this as a "unanimous expression of approval and pledge of cooperation to the Trustee."[4]

Ross also met with a delegation of William Raymond's anti-Communist opposition. Whatever assurances Ross gave them were enough to win their endorsement. Their "Save the Union" committee, headquartered at the Beverly Hotel and supported by the Association of Catholic Trade Unionists, distributed a press release praising "the first step in a long hoped for and long awaited purge of Communists, Communist dissidents and fellow travelers." It called for the ouster of the "Obermeier-Rubin-Herman-Lane faction" and "an early general election."[5]

Around the same time, Rubin's faction distributed a leaflet, in the form of a statement from its candidate in the suspended election, Richard Sirch: "There is, as we know, a division in the ranks of our Local 6 administration." Sirch named and blamed the Communists—specifically Cody, Collins, and Antonio Lopez—for "the division and the fight in our ranks."[6] Simultaneously, Rubin instructed hotel managers to not permit Collins, Lopez, and Lee Candea to enter hotel properties and claim to represent the workers. When engraved invitations to the Health Center's ribbon-cutting ceremony went out to officers, those who didn't get one got the message.[7]

The *Daily Worker* punched back. An article headlined "Union Dictators Grab Hotel Local 6" denounced Jay Rubin for surrendering to "redbaiting hysteria," called the trusteeship "a desperate last-minute move" to keep Cody ("long a leader in the wage struggles for hotel workers") out of the presidency and accused Ross of exercising "dictatorial powers." The article was motivated by rumors that Ross would fire Sender Garlin, the former *Daily Worker* foreign correspondent who edited the *Hotel & Club Voice*.[8]

At an Executive Board meeting, Ross sensed the changed Party line. Members aligned with Cody tried to discredit the trusteeship, disparaged

Rubin, and tried to rehash the 1949 IWA negotiations. "I have said before and I repeat that persons who over the years have formed convictions against other members won't sway my judgment unless they present evidence to support those convictions," Ross replied. He won applause when he declared that "men and women belong to Local 6 because they are employed in hotels and clubs, *not* because they go to certain churches, or belong to certain political parties" and that no member "regardless of his rank need feel obligated to anyone in order to hold his job." The Executive Board voted unanimously to offer "full cooperation" in the trusteeship.[9]

As expected, Ross did fire Garlin on Friday so that Herb McCusker, another HRE staffer, could edit the next day's weekly *Voice*, which, of course, reported approvingly of the ongoing actions of the trustee.[10] Ross and McCusker also fired Garlin's assistant as well as the *Voice*'s printing press, the left-aligned Trade Union Service, which was bankrolled by Frederick Vanderbilt Field, an eccentric member of the Vanderbilt family who was disowned for his class treachery.[11]

The terminations prompted "A Message from Martin Cody," a protest leaflet circulated in the shops early the next week. Cody accused Ross of "embarking on a policy of firings" that would lead to the destruction of the union. Thirteen officers—four of the local's eight vice presidents and eight of its seventeen business agents—were seen distributing the leaflet. Ross summoned them all to his office on October 6. Martin Cody, vice presidents Lee Candea, Charles Collins, George Kyriages, and Antonio Lopez, and business agents Joe Bullard, Andrew Casalvolone, Patsy Edwards, Anne Finn, Joseph Flanagan, Gil Gerena, Mildred Parker, and Don Tillman all admitted to distributing the leaflet, claiming it as their right.

"I want to know why a question is raised pertaining to one statement," Cody challenged Ross, "and not raised for the balance of the staff." Richard Sirch was the first to distribute a factional leaflet circulated, Cody reminded Ross, and he faced no repercussions for it. Cody and Ross went back and forth for a few minutes about Cody's complaints of unequal treatment and of secret meetings between Ross and Rubin. "Can you name the particular times or incidents that you refer to?" Ross mildly inquired. "What I am trying to point out is that there was no attempt to sit down with me as elected representative of the workers, to see how we could create harmony and solve the problems of the workers," Cody replied.

"Anybody else want to speak?" Ross asked the room. "Obviously you are experienced enough to know that there is no point in discussion because of your action," Collins calmly responded, adding, "We will of course avail ourselves of all opportunity" to challenge their suspension from office and the decisions of the trusteeship. The thirteen were escorted out of the building and taken off payroll.[12]

Afterwards, Ross summarily fired Sam Kramberg, along with "the office manager, four confidential secretaries, the chief switchboard telephone operator and several other minor employees."[13] Later that day, Ross met with the Local 6 Executive Board, a body composed of the remaining officers—Gertrude Lane and Daisy George and vice presidents James Bohan, Charles Martin, Angel Santibanez, and Fred Spinner—and about seventy members who still worked in the shops. A vocal minority protested his actions. They were shut down, accused of trying to physically disrupt the meeting, and removed from the building. The remaining Executive Board cast yet another "unanimous" vote to support the Trustee.[14]

The cover of the October 7 issue of the *Hotel & Club Voice* carried a prominent warning: "All members are cautioned not to participate in any way in rebellious activities which may be attempted by Martin Cody and the suspended business agents. Any member who assists them or cooperates with them is subject to a trial by the Grievance Committee of Local 6."[15] In some shops, a business agent named James Marley underscored the terms of the IWA's closed shop clause which meant that a suspension from union membership could result in termination from hotel employment.

Ross charged the thirteen officers with violating Article 11, Section 18—the anti-Communist amendment passed at the 1947 convention—and scheduled a hearing.[16] Watching the controversy, industry publication *Trade Union Courier* reached the union for comment. Rubin called Ross's actions "a relief," and David Herman candidly admitted, "If we could have won [the special election] there wouldn't have been a trusteeship."[17]

On Monday, October 9, the Cody faction held meetings in shifts at Casa Galacia, a Spanish community center on West 59th Street with a legal capacity of 400.[18] Regrouped, twenty-five executive board members signed an open letter protesting the "harsh and prejudicial" treatment of the thirteen officers and calling for their "prompt reinstatement."[19] While some signers were Communists, others just sympathized with activists who had worked so hard for the union and remained loyal to people with whom they worked. Scotty Eckford, whose John Hancock headlined the petition, later explained, "We are here to fight the bosses. We are not here to have controversies with each other, whether you are a Democrat, whether you are a Republican, or whether you are a Socialist, or whether you are a Communist, or whether you are anything else."[20]

Legal and Unambiguous

Rather than rent a large hall for the full Shop Delegates Council, and give oppositionists a venue for disruption and protests, Ross met with the SDC on a department-by-department basis. Ross's first two meetings, with the housekeeping and kitchen departments on October 18, were marred by a vociferous minority who opposed the trusteeship and suspensions, but the majority of both groups voted to approve the trustee's actions.[21] By the first week of November, 91 percent of shop delegates approved of the trusteeship and suspensions.[22] The work of the union continued undramatically. On October 25, Jay Rubin cut the ribbon at the grand opening of the Health Center, a gala event attended by Hotel Association executives.[23] Ross ordered more grievances to be filed to demonstrate a union administration that was attentive to members' issues. He promoted ten rank-and-file union delegates to business agents to keep up with the work.[24]

Across the street from Local 6, in a makeshift office at 45th and Eighth, the suspended officials conducted a grievance intake, seeking to undermine members' confidence in Ross's leadership at key shops like the Waldorf. Someone stole files from the clubs department, giving them greater access to workers in shops that were theoretically easier to decertify Local 6 than in NYHTC's multi-union framework. They also began publishing their own newspaper, *Voice of the Membership*, to assail the trusteeship and publicize the "resistance growing" against Ross and Rubin, and they organized a dance party at the Manhattan Center to raise funds for their legal case.[25]

On November 17, the state judge enjoined Ross and Local 6 officers from "intimidating, threatening, suspending or otherwise disciplining any member of Local 6 upon the ground of his protest against the trusteeship or his support of the plaintiffs." However, the court denied Cody's team a full restraining order, finding that HRE's constitution gave Ernst trusteeship authority and that the union's internal procedures offered the plaintiffs opportunities to state their cases. The court would only hear a procedural appeal after HRE issued a decision on the thirteen officers' suspensions.[26]

Following union procedures, Cody formally protested the trusteeship, backed by a petition signed by 1,500 members. HRE officials, "in the light of the protest from a small minority," scheduled a hearing. Walter Cowan, leader of the Los Angeles Joint Board, flew to New York and began conducting the hearing at the LJEB office on November 13.[27] The subject: "Shall the Trusteeship Established for Hotel & Club Employees Union, Local 6, Be Continued Or Dissolved?" The trial of the suspended officers was delayed to first settle the appropriateness of the trusteeship.

David Herman represented "the membership majority supporting the trusteeship."[28] Gertrude Lane and Tom Wilson gave the picture of a local union in which staff meetings had almost completely stopped, with grievances "piling up," embarrassing controversies like Charlotte Stern's prison sentence and delegates' banishment from the State AFL convention playing out in the tabloid press, and a disunity that imperiled the 1950 wage negotiations. "Officers of the Union were devoting more time to circulating Stockholm Peace petitions than to the solution of the workers' problems," charged Lane.[29]

Martin Cody complained about the process. The union would not use release time so that members could testify during working hours, leaving his side overly reliant on vacation time and evening sessions. The transcription service company charged fifty cents a page if he wanted a copy of the proceedings, which would ultimately run to 1,915 pages and was prohibitively expensive for the unemployed officers. Cody tried in his day-and-half opportunity to question Ross to find evidence of collusion between Rubin, Ernst, and Ross. Ross gave him none. For the over-capacity audience in the tiny conference room, Cody grandstanded with insinuating questions about union expenses Ross had authorized and the length of his apartment lease—suggesting the trusteeship was the beginning of a long-term takeover.

None of the 13 officers testified, lest they subject themselves to a transcript of direct questioning about their Communist activities. Instead, their supporters testified. All of them argued that the matter should be put to the membership in either a referendum or a local election. David Herman, who aggressively cross-examined most witnesses to get them to prove or withdraw vague accusations about undemocratic actions or financial mismanagement, displayed a personal warmth towards Scotty Eckford and let him go with only a few soft questions. ("That's all? No more questions, Dave?" Eckford asked. "Do you want some more, Scotty?"[30])

Cody dragged the hearing out for weeks, seemingly trying to get all 1,100 petitioners to testify, even though it delayed his own trial and ability to appeal the court decision on the trusteeship. Most of these members were simply disgruntled, unhappy with the status of their particular grievance and forum-shopping for what they thought was better representation. Ed Simidaris, a banquet waiter at the Waldorf-Astoria, charged that the trusteeship "didn't eliminate this so-called bickering. Instead, they helped it." Simidaris complained about the direction of a grievance that would increase the automatic gratuity that workers received because he personally wanted to inspect all receipts.[31] Ruby Dorsey, also of the Waldorf, didn't even file her grievance. "We would rather go to management because we can get better results . . . than going to you." Asked if she knew her union representatives, she replied, "I don't know that because I was never too deep in the union to find that out. In fact, I was not too keen to join the union, in the first place. But I had to join the union because you can't work unless you join the union."[32] Mary Collins, a housekeeper at the Savoy Plaza, had been fired for union activity. The union won her job back, but she still complained about the business agents who worked on her case getting swapped out because of the trusteeship. She declared herself a Catholic, a Republican, and a supporter of Sen. Robert A. Taft, and she complained about the cost of union dues.[33]

Cody's difficulty with members' work schedules occasionally left him begging for postponements. After two weeks, Ross's *Voice* reported that Cody asked that the hearings be postponed indefinitely.[34] When no members showed up for the December 4 session, Cody lost his temper. "This lying filthy sheet here states without question that this was postponed indefinitely."[35]

As the hearings entered their fifth week, Walter Cowan, who had already missed celebrating Thanksgiving at home, instituted new rules to prevent the trial from dragging out beyond New Year's. He would hold two sessions daily, with no delays. If Cody or Herman were not available, somebody else from their team would have to handle the direct and cross-examinations, and he would not allow any more repetitive testimony from witnesses.[36] The hearings finally came to an end on December 14. Not surprisingly, he recommended to Hugo Ernst that the trusteeship continue.

Cowan stuck around for the week-long trial of the thirteen officers that began on December 16. Martin Cody spoke on behalf of all the accused. "I appear here solely for the purpose of challenging the authority and jurisdiction of this body." He charged that the proceedings violated the HRE constitution, the laws of the state of New York, and Judge Nathan's injunction against retaliation against opponents of the trusteeship. All but one of the suspended officers proceeded to walk out, and, for the duration of the trial, they rotated the duty of observing the proceedings.[37] Ross argued his case solely on the issue of their violation of the union constitution's anti-Communist clause. Daisy George, three Local 6 business agents (Joe Aluffo, Betty Bentz, and Louis Saulnier), and an NYHTC staffer named Howard Rohr all testified to their own past membership in the Party and provided ample evidence of the Communist activity of the accused.[38] The suspensions were sustained, and Hugo Ernst sentenced the thirteen to three years of probation.[39]

Cody went back to court, seeking an order to lift the trusteeship and reinstate the suspended officers. By this point, only five officers were seeking reinstatement. Lea Candea, Charles Collins, George Kyriages, and Antonio Lopez joined Cody in the lawsuit. Only Cody and an SDC member in whose name the suit was filed, appeared for the January 11 court date.[40] The judge dismissed the case, finding no irregularities and "adequate legal and unambiguous constitutional provisions."[41] HRE leaders celebrated "the very important legal victory" and a validation of the union's constitution.[42] Only after both the suspensions of the officers and the trusteeship itself were upheld did Bert Ross move to terminate Glen Stocks, the former business agent who was disabled in WWII combat and found a soft landing in Cody's secretary-treasurer's office.[43]

What seems odd is that few of the purged Communists fought particularly hard to get back into the union or to get their jobs back. Many seemed to have moved on with their lives. Charles Collins, for example, busied himself with the World Peace Congress in Warsaw and by November 26, he was in Moscow as part of a "large and representative" American peace delegation.[44] Ordered by Party leaders to make the fateful break with Jay Rubin and his loyalists and then to violate and fruitlessly challenge the trusteeship, the castaways just faded from the union.

How much longer they remained loyal to the Communist Party is unclear. Life in the Party was growing grimmer. Shortly after the United States turned the Cold War hot in Korea, Congress passed the McCarran Internal Security Act, which compelled Communist organizations to register with the government and provide membership lists. The Act also denied passports to registered Communists.[45] These two developments—the war and the McCarran Act—convinced the paranoid William Z. Foster that the country was taking a turn towards fascism. He ordered roughly half of the Party's cadre membership to go underground. Those activists who did were separated from their families and many of their comrades. They lived under assumed identities in new cities and communicated with each other in code for years, until the Korean War ended in a negotiated stalemate and it became clearer that it was not actually the beginning of a new World War. Many of those who went underground emerged between 1955 and 1956—just in time to learn of Soviet Premier Nikita Khrushchev's revelations about Stalin's terrible lies in the Great Purge that sent so many loyal Communists to their doom.[46] John Steuben, who stayed "above-ground" and spent a half-decade writing about organizing strategy for the Party's *March of Labor* magazine, declared that he would live out the remainder of his life "in agony and silence" when he finally quit the Party in 1956.[47]

The Whole Truth

Members who quit the Party before the witch hunts remained in legal jeopardy. The FBI noticed the *Daily Worker*'s attacks on Jay Rubin and began feeling out his willingness to sit for an interview. This offered Rubin a chance to stay free, but it was not without risks. The Department of Justice was beginning to prosecute lower-level Communist functionaries under the Smith Act and to denaturalize citizens who concealed their Communist affiliations. Rubin's old friend, Painters union leader Louis Weinstock, would be rounded up in one such sweep in 1951 along with Elizabeth Gurley Flynn, Si Gerson, and a dozen others.[48] Weinstock would serve 24 months, but not before the government also tried (unsuccessfully) to strip him of his citizenship and imprison him for perjury.[49]

Rubin was a Communist when he gained his citizenship in 1929—a fact that he surely did not disclose—leaving him vulnerable to perjury charges and deportation proceedings like those plaguing Obermeier. Rubin met with agents in the Bureau's New York office on November 28. They asked the extent of Communist influence in HRE. Rubin told them about the in-progress hearings that would sustain the suspensions of the staffers who were purged in Local 6, and he told them that the other locals had, one after another, voted their Communist leaders out of office. He gave them sixty names of Communists who had been involved in the union. Of his own past activities, he disclosed just enough to maintain credibility but withheld much. He made clear that he quit the Party in 1939, over the Nazi-Soviet Pact, and described a mutually beneficial relationship with the Party until 1947. The agents knew that he was not completely forthcoming about his own activities but decided "not to endeavor to force the subject to tell the whole truth concerning his connection to the Communist Party." They removed Rubin from the List of Key Individuals.[50]

Obermeier had a steeper hill to climb to get out of his legal problems. On October 20, 1950, his attorneys argued his appeal to the perjury conviction before a panel that included Judge Learned Hand. Two of the three counts related to interviews that took place in 1945, and his attorneys argued that, therefore, they fell outside of the statute of limitations. His June 6, 1946, interview, they argued, did not take place under oath and was "not yet a petition for the court."[51]

On November 29, the federal government began a new attempt to deport Obermeier, under the McCarran Act.[52] On December 20, the Second Circuit Court overturned the first two perjury convictions for being outside the statute of limitations but ruled against him on the third. The only practical effect of the ruling was to spare Obermeier the $1,000 fine. The Supreme Court declined to hear his appeal on March 26, 1951.[53] His lawyers sought to delay or commute his prison sentence on account of his poor health, but U.S. attorneys argued that federal penitentiaries "have the best of medical care" and on April 10, Obermeier was taken to the United States Penitentiary in Lewisburg, Pennsylvania, to begin his sentence.[54]

Old-Fashioned Four-Flushers

Next came the challenge of regaining autonomy with the remaining leadership group in control. Throughout their fight against the trusteeship, Cody's faction charged that it would continue indefinitely or result in a permanent takeover by HRE. At the January 31 meeting of the local Executive Board, Ross repeated President Ernst's assurances that the trusteeship would last no longer than one year and likely a good deal shorter.[55] For the trusteeship to end with an ally of Jay Rubin elected president of Local 6, much would depend on the results of bargaining with the Hotel Association. Responding to wartime inflation, the Council voted on December 7 to press for immediate wage negotiations with the Hotel Association.[56]

Rubin's goal was to "beat the gun" of a rumored wage freeze associated with the Korean War, which ultimately was announced on January 25, 1951.[57]

The federal order was that retroactive wage increases covering the period of May 24, 1950, to December 15, 1950, could go no higher than ten percent, with future increases in doubt.[58] Similar to its position during World War II, the union needed to get whatever gains it could wrest from management approved by the government. The Hotel Association was divided about giving much at all. The same strategic disagreement within its own ranks on what its wage policy *should be* remained from the prior year—whether the hotels should take advantage of the union's disunity to hold the line on new wage increases or whether to support the stability of the union and its leadership with raises for the workers.

Union representatives held a series of district meetings, receiving strong majorities of support for the wage reopener in January. Members of the opposing "Save the Union" committee leafletted outside, calling for a $16 a week wage increase. Inside the meetings, they peppered union leaders with questions about the Communist Party. Rumors were rampant that Jay Rubin pulled a fast one by having Cody's faction take the fall while the surviving leaders remained concealed Communists. "Save the Union" planned to run against the Communist Party in the canceled 1950 election, and they were going to stick with that strategy in 1951. Bert Ross would not treat any oppositionists with kid gloves. He had the *Voice* tarnish oppositionists with their own strategy, calling their disruptions "a procedure strangely similar to tactics usually employed by the pro-Communist faction which the 'Save the Union' group PROFESSES to oppose."[59]

On February 6, the union threatened to hold "lobby meetings" if the Hotel Association did not agree to a wage reopener. Within 48 hours, the bosses began bargaining.[60] After two weeks, they reached a deal that aligned with the ten percent cap, retroactive to February 1. Following the usual pattern of bargaining, even though this was a wage reopener in an IWA that was not set to expire for another year, the parties hammered out a tentative agreement on a new IWA that would last until 1954.

Local 144's Peter Ottley opposed the deal because he wanted changes in the Section 14(a) language on employee terminations that gave management wide discretion—at least on paper—to "lay off, promote, transfer or discharge any employee." To employers, it was an essential component of management's rights that made recognizing the union in 1939 palatable.

The other locals argued that they had "little to no difficulty getting discharged members reinstated" through "proper shop activity" and insisted on getting a wage increase quickly, before the wage freeze. Ottley's relatively young administration was relying on formal grievances more than job actions and losing. The argument dragged on for five hours, until the representatives of all the other NYHTC locals outvoted BSEIU and approved the wage increase.[61]

A few weeks later, NYHTC reelected its officers. Local 144 leaders continued to harbor resentments about the IWA settlement and ran one of their own, Stephen O'Donnell, against Jay Rubin. He received only Local 144's five votes (out of a total of 33).[62] The obvious irony is that Rubin maneuvered to oust John Steuben in 1950 to shore up his support within the Council, and instead saddled himself with persistent critics in its second-largest affiliate.

Local 144's complaints about the IWA's "company union clause" were picked up by the "Save the Union" committee, which loudly advocated against ratification. Incredibly, they argued that it would be better to let the IWA expire than to ratify it with core contract language they suddenly found offensive. Although members ratified the contract, hard-liners in the Hotel Association took advantage of the obvious disagreement within the union to walk back their wage commitments. Labor and management had to agree to submit their tentative agreement to a federal Wage Stabilization Board for approval before it could go into effect. The Hotel Association was waiting to see what kind of leadership emerged from the Local 6 trusteeship.

"Save the Union" had unwittingly painted themselves into a corner: a vote for their candidates was a vote against a ten percent wage increase. Rubin ridiculed the "self-styled spokesmen for the workers" who agreed with the hard-liner hotel managers. "Both oppose the wage plan in its present form."[63] To show activity on behalf of members to win their raise, union organizers circulated a petition to President Truman calling for the IWA settlement to be approved and implemented, and, in June, Ross and Herman testified before the Wage Stabilization Board that industries not bound by wartime price controls—like hotels and restaurants—should not be bound by wage controls.[64]

To begin the transition out of trusteeship, Ross issued a call for a special convention of Local 6. Delegate nominations began on April 11 at a series of nearly 100 shop meetings around the city.[65] Rubin circulated a loyalty pledge with a blank signature line for every business agent to "repudiate and condemn" the opposition and swear "complete accord with general aims and purposes of the present leadership."[66] Although "Save the Union" ran a slate of delegates, they were solidly voted down, so they couldn't hear the recurrent criticism of them by the trustee and the officers for their disruptive tactics and the delayed pay increases. The convention voted to ask Hugo Ernst for permission to schedule local officer elections and end the trusteeship, which served to elevate the profile of David Herman.[67]

While nominations were in process, the *Hotel & Club Voice*—responding to "several letters from members"—profiled Local 6's new General Organizer. Emphasizing Herman's four years on HRE staff and two years in the army, it presented him as a long-time presence in Local 6. As with all the ex-Communists in leadership, his past was rewritten. His origin story now placed him as a busboy at Klein's restaurant in 1935 who helped organize his bargaining unit.[68]

Herman topped the Administration ticket as its candidate for president, with Lane running for re-election as secretary-treasurer. Daisy George insisted she deserved the promotion to general organizer, but in the workaholic environment of Local 6, she was viewed by some as a malingerer because she took sick days, and her ultimatum was resented. She jumped ship for the "Save the Union" slate.[69] James Marley was nominated instead. Scotty Eckford was the administration's choice to replace Daisy George as recording secretary. Eckford was the epitome of a dedicated union activist who previously would have been passed up for higher office in favor of a Communist. Not only was he forgiven for opposing the trusteeship, but his heterodoxy was also considered an asset for an administration striving to prove that things had changed.

William Raymond once again led "Save the Union," with Daisy George as their candidate for General Organizer. "Clean Them All Out!," one campaign leaflet declared, accusing the Herman-Lane faction of a history of "slavish obedience to party orders" and calling the IWA's weak job security language a "Communist Company Union Contract."[70] "Save the Union" spread lurid innuendo about the secret identities and relationships of the "commisaars [sic] of Local 6" and punched holes in the identities they had carefully constructed. Of David Herman, they charged, "No one knows what his real name is!"[71] His brother, they accused, was Maurice Forge, a Communist who worked with John Steuben on *March of Labor*.[72] Of Rubin, they alleged that Party orders led to a forced merger of the old FWIU with "Dutch Schultz racketeers," accusing him of both Communism *and* gangsterism. After Max Pincus "fell or was pushed out the window," they claimed, "Only Rubin survives."[73]

Innuendo was one thing. "Save the Union" also had resources, backed up by the Association of Catholic Trade Unionists, led by AFL Retail Clerks' George Donohue. ACTU was founded in 1937 to provide training and resources, independently of the organized left, for workers to form new unions. Actists, as they called themselves, soon focused on encouraging anti-Communist caucuses within CIO unions. The advent of Taft-Hartley's anti-Communist affidavits inspired them to refocus on the AFL. By the 1950s, ACTU rivaled the CP in size and influence as outside organizations that intervened in internal union matters.[74]

The Administration candidates would harp on ACTU as just "another behind-the-scenes boss." One campaign circular, listing six "$64 Questions" for "Save the Union" made two of them about ACTU's George Donohue and his funding. Donohue handed the administration a gift when he dared Rubin's allies "to say a word against Russia and communism." Gertrude Lane had more than a few words and shared them in Nelson Frank's "Labor Today" column in William Randolph Hearst's right-wing *World-Telegram*. "Today I am against communism anywhere in the world," Lane averred. "And as for the American Communists," she continued, "I consider them a menace to the trade union movement in addition to being old-fashioned four-flushers." She pointed to stacks of care packages that the union was shipping to U.S. soldiers in Korea. After the article was published, the Local 6 leaders circulated it widely as a piece of campaign literature.[75]

Five "Save the Union" candidates dropped out after Ross leaked Daisy George's affidavit, admitting to past Party membership. Everyone on the Administration slate who had been a CP member—including Herman, Lane, and Marley—signed similar documents, but those remained under lock and key. In her caucus' campaign newspaper, the *Local 6 Liberator*, George told a tale of being pressured to join the Party to keep her job in 1943 (when "the Soviet Union was America's ally"). She claimed her place on the ballot's Row B was "an opportunity to throw off the Rubin-Lane-Herman-Cody yoke of Communism which I have been resisting and rejecting the past six years."[76] One of the newer business agents appointed by Ross the previous fall, Michael Reilly, issued a circular endorsing "Row B." He claimed to be disillusioned with the Administration's claims of "ridding the union of all Communists," seeing it all as a matter of them holding on to power. "I am not against COMMUNISM," he claimed Herman told him. Reilly continued, "The issue is MARTIN CODY."[77] Bert Ross swiftly fired Reilly. Herman's slate was always going to win the most votes, but Ross was not above putting his thumb on the scale.[78]

A third slate, "Voice of the Membership," was led by Martin Cody's allies, Walter Garcia and Gus Contes. The two had been the plaintiffs in the lawsuit to end the trusteeship. Ed Simidaris was "Voice of the Membership's" pick for banquets department vice president. Both slates failed to find enough candidates for business agent or executive board in some of the departments.[79] Because the "Voice" candidates were so obviously connected to Martin Cody, it was easy for the Administration candidates to red-bait them and portray a vote for them as a vote to return to the chaos and factionalism of the period before the trusteeship. But "Save the Union" was a threat because it would red-bait the administration and portray a vote for *them* as a vote for continuing dysfunction.

The "Voice of the Membership" caucus went to court to block the election. They pressed for a court-appointed monitor to conduct a rescheduled vote after a period of time in which the union was enjoined from publishing "any story, editorial, picture, comment or any other matter supporting one candidate or slate or opposing" any other, and from making any threats regarding the election campaign.[80] "Save the Union" joined them in the court proceeding on June 8—which the Administration pointed to as final evidence of collusion between the Communists and the "saintly flock" of disingenuous anti-Communists.[81]

Federal labor law would be amended in 1959 to set rules for inappropriate conduct in union elections. Under those rules, the Local 6 leadership election *would* likely have been overturned and a new election ordered with rules set and enforced by the Department of Labor. However, under New York state law in 1951, all a judge cared about was whether the election conformed with the union's bylaws (which it did).

When the votes were counted on June 13, the administration slate prevailed by a 2–1 margin. David Herman garnered 7,432 votes. The top of the "Save the Union" slate picked up 3,450 votes while "Voice of the Membership" eked out just 703.[82] Ross swore in the new and reelected officers at the Shop Delegates Council meeting on June 20 in a celebratory environment. Cameras flashed as Ross handed Herman Local 6's framed charter. The trusteeship was officially over.

At the swearing-in ceremony, with Impartial Chairman Mulrooney in attendance, Herman called for Hotel Association action on the long-delayed February raises.[83] It took a month of pressure—from the union, the Impartial Chairman, and the hotel employers who favored labor peace—on the minority of recalcitrant owners to get the Hotel Association to join the union in formally asking the WSB for approval. The application was submitted on August 1, and the wage increase was granted four days later.[84]

To Be Without Quarrels

The 1951 wage increases sparked another rebellion against the Hotel Association by the smaller hotels, who either didn't understand or didn't agree that the settlement included seven months' back pay. Many applied for relief, and almost all were rejected. Calling the promise of Section 28 relief a "fake," they looked to constrain the authority of the Hotel Association negotiating committee. They looked longingly at the Division "A" contract that the Associated Hotels and Residence Clubs negotiated with Local 144. That agreement had wage increases that were a dollar or two less than the IWA, and those were only effective June 1—not February 15. Switching employer associations—which a few hotels had done in recent years—would require closing food and beverage operations and BSEIU and HRE signing off on the jurisdictional switch. Some hotel owners argued that the Hotel Association should let the contract expire in 1953 and stare down the threat of a strike, and some decided to test their ability to withstand a work stoppage by refusing to implement the retroactive raises in 1951.[85]

Things came to a head at the Hotel Fourteen on January 10, 1952. Management *received* partial relief from the Impartial Chairman but appealed *that* decision *and* refused to pay its workers what they were owed. When one week's paychecks bounced, workers staged a sit-down strike in the lobby. Management responded by locking the bargaining unit out the next day.[86] This was hardly Hotel Fourteen's first experience with service disruptions. It took a 24-hour strike for the hotel to recognize the union in March 1950, and another four-day strike that September for management to pay retroactive increases under the contract.[87] An Impartial Chairman's order ended this lockout after one day.

An employer's refusal to comply with an arbitration decision freed the union from its obligations under the "no strike" provision of the IWA. The union took "aggressive action" against seventeen employers during the week of January 20, resulting in prompt settlements at each one. On January 30, the union went back on strike at the Hotel Fourteen, finally winning back wages after three days of picketing.[88]

By February 1952, all employers were finally paying February 1951's wages—just in time to begin bargaining all over again. The new wage reopener brought the potential for the union to win another landmark benefit: an old age pension. The Truman administration continued to enforce the January 1951 wage freeze but finally relented to lobbying by the AFL and CIO that pension payments should not count towards the wage ceiling, much like "fringe" health insurance benefits were exempted from World War II's "Little Steel" formula.[89] Many unions made employer-funded pension plans their main bargaining demand in 1952 and 1953.

Among the hotel owners, an anonymous "call to arms" circulated, demanding that Association negotiators take a hard line on no wage increases and even prepare to lock the union out.

On April 1, NYHTC "voted unanimously for sweeping improvements in the contract" including the pension and more vacation and holidays. Rubin warned that with the smaller hotels tightly organized within the Hotel Association, it would be a difficult round of negotiations. He predicted employer demands for a lower wage scale for the smaller hotels and their refusal to bargain over pensions in the wage reopener. "They'll say it isn't part of wages. But we will be prepared to prove that retirement benefit plans are part of wages."[90]

Sure enough, the Hotel Association's response to the union's demands was a flat "no." The war party in the Association was Morton Wolf, owner of the Spencer-Taylor chain.[91] Charging that the 25 largest hotels dominated the Association's industrial relations division at the expense of smaller properties, Spencer-Taylor managers fought for and won the principle that their bargaining team should be composed of an equal number of representatives of three types of hotels: residential hotels, transient hotels that exclusively served short-term rental guests, and semi-transient hotels that did a little of both types of business. Under fire was Charles L. Ornstein, who served as the Hotel Association's lead representative in both the 1951 and 1952 bargaining rounds. Ornstein was the general manager of the Paramount, a 700-guest-room hotel in midtown that was on the lower end of the 25 largest. After two sessions of direct negotiations were fruitless and the union kicked the dispute to the "3-Man" Commission, Ornstein became the sole employer representative. Behind closed doors, Wolf challenged Ornstein, arguing that he "had no right to bring up issues such as pensions, vacations and holidays."[92] The Spencer-Taylor group even went to court seeking an injunction preventing the commission from making any decision on those items and was rewarded with a temporary restraining order preventing any compensation award from being applied to its Beaux Arts, Belvedere, Madison, Mayflower, One Fifth Avenue, Surrey, and Towers hotels.[93]

Throughout the negotiations and the "3-Man" meetings, the union did not engage in any of its typical contract campaign tactics like circulating petitions or staging lobby meetings. The truth is that the small hotels were correct that the larger hotels wanted labor peace and were willing to pay for it. They would leave it to the union to discipline the smaller hotels. After only a handful of sessions, Ornstein gave in to the union's demands: an extra vacation day, an extra week of vacations for employees with three years' seniority, and an employer-funded defined benefit pension plan. The parties agreed to establish a new benefit fund, with an equal number of trustees from each side, and to collect 2 percent payroll contributions from each signatory hotel to endow a fund while continuing to discuss the exact terms of retirement benefits for qualified employees. Because of Wolf's injunction, and to thwart any other employers that would try to do the same, the settlement was *not* a wage order from the commission. Instead, it was a directly negotiated supplemental agreement that would require the union to make each individual hotel or chain sign on the dotted line. "This means it's only the beginning of the fight rather than the end of it," James Marley warned shop delegates.[94]

That fight was over pretty quickly. The Hotel Association immediately joined the union in submitting the agreement to the Wage Stabilization Board for approval. Fred Ornstein made a point of making the Paramount the first hotel to sign, and the big chains like Hilton and Statler promptly signed as well.[95] Three-fourths of the hotels had signed by August (including Hotel Fourteen).[96] Faced with the possibility of being singled out for job actions, the Spencer-Taylor chain reversed course and withdrew its injunction. Morton Wolf signed on behalf of his properties at a ceremony with the shop delegates from his hotels. He likened the IWA to a marriage that, "for better or for worse," he had to live with. "You don't expect every marriage to be without quarrels."[97]

Additional Facts

A pension for hotel workers was a landmark victory for the union. It was, Obermeier noted ruefully in a letter to Rubin, a demand that he placed in the *Hotel Worker* platform in 1917, but one that he would not benefit from.[98] HRE recently created a national pension for leaders and staff at all levels of the union, but he had been disqualified, or his benefits downgraded, because of his time in prison. Obermeier was released six months early as part of a deal to cooperate with his deportation. He was offered better deals if he cooperated with the government's anti-Communist investigations. He chose to protect his comrades and return to his native Germany on December 10, 1952. He was seen off on the ocean liner Stockholm by Rubin, Lane, and a handful of remaining comrades, providing some cash and emotional support.

As Obermeier was leaving the country, one of his principal antagonists was getting pushed out of HRE leadership. Miguel Garriga's political fortunes never recovered from his tenure as LJEB trustee, and Jack Townsend smelled blood in the water. He apparently worked out a deal with David Siegal, who headed what was by then—thanks to Garriga's needling—Consolidated Dining Room Employees Union Local 1-16-219. Townsend would support Siegal, taking his place as president of the LJEB in exchange for Siegal's support for Townsend's planned run for vice president of the Second District at the following year's HRE convention.[99] In September, Townsend had a group of members charge that Garriga "conspired to bring the Local Union into disrepute" and bring other trumped-up charges to suspend him from membership in Local 15 and, by extension, from holding office in HRE.[100] Garriga attempted to transfer his membership to Bartenders Local 666 in upstate Kingston, New York, but seemed resigned to his fate. He asked Hugo Ernst for a leave of absence. When Ernst paid him a visit in November, he found Garriga running a management-side consulting firm as a "Labor Relations Director." Putting it mildly, Ernst informed Garriga that "these functions are incompatible with active membership in our International Union" and directed him to resign.[101] The LJEB and State Culinary Alliance both declared their support for Bert Ross to fill Garriga's anticipated vacancy as vice president, despite Townsend's plotting.[102] Garriga tendered his resignation on February 5, 1953, taking a pension, and the GEB unanimously selected Ross to serve the remainder of his term.[103]

The early 1950s were a period of significant transition and institutionalization in the labor movement. AFL President William Green and CIO President Philip Murphy died within weeks of each other in November 1952. The rival labor groups' new presidents, George Meany and Walter Reuther, respectively, lacked strong personal resentments about the bitter 1935 split and the years of raids and counterraids that followed. Most AFL affiliates had long ago joined HRE in practicing the kind of industrial unionism that was the younger federation's *raison d'etre*, and without the red herring of Communism to divide them, the erstwhile antagonists began negotiating an agreement to respect each other's jurisdictions and stop the practice of turf raiding in April 1953. That agreement evolved into a framework for the merger of the AFL-CIO in 1955.[104]

The Republicans finally won the White House in 1952—for the first time in a quarter century—and left labor laws mostly in a status quo. In many parts of the country collective bargaining became a routine marked by lengthy contracts settled peacefully more often than through strikes. Unions added services and benefits for their members. The AFL-CIO became a people's lobby within the Democratic Party, advocating for increased social spending at home, and a firm supporter of Cold War foreign policy abroad. Unions invested their healthy treasuries in purchasing stately office buildings to serve as headquarters befitting of many union leaders' new status as power brokers.

Local 6 and the Hotel Trades Council broadly fit this pattern. Union leadership retained a progressive political outlook—championing, for example, the Black civil rights movement earlier than many other unions—but cloaked in the era's liberalism. Beginning in 1951, Local 6 began winning health insurance in the club contracts—initially through the city's non-profit Health Insurance Program but eventually through the union's system of Health Centers.[105] The Joint Employment Office became an arm of the state Department of Labor. The union purchased the building it had been renting, as well as the two adjacent buildings running the length of Eighth Avenue between 44th and 45th Streets. They had them converted into one continuous suite of offices for Local 6, NYHTC, and the Benefit Funds. In December 1952, David Herman announced plans to build an auditorium large enough to host meetings of the Shop Delegates Council and the daily roll call of banquet waiters.[106]

Although the union's leaders were once again deemed respectable members of the labor movement, their Communist pasts continued to dog them. HUAC spent a few weeks in July 1953 probing Communist influence in New York unions. Two members of upstate HRE locals who used to vote with the Communist-led locals at conventions named the names of about a dozen current and former HRE members they knew were Communists. Included among them were Herman, Lane, and Rubin (although they said they heard the three had quit the Party).[107] At a staff meeting after the hearings, Rubin warned union officials not to discuss their past membership and activities in the Party and not to cooperate with any government investigation. Someone who was in the room promptly reported Rubin's remarks to the FBI. Although he was no longer of much interest to the Bureau, the Justice Department's Immigration agency was still secretly considering him for a potential denaturalization proceeding and wouldn't drop it until the end of the decade. Rubin may not have known how close he ever came to deportation, but he likely felt a cloud over his head.[108]

It was a particularly ugly period for holding people's distant pasts and personal associations against them. One small but representative example is the author whom HRE chose to write the official history of the international union that it commissioned with Random House to honor Hugo Ernst. No sooner was Matthew Josephson picked—on the strength of his long repertoire of magazine articles and books, including his recently published biography of Sidney Hillman—than a tawdry mimeographed newsletter called *Counterattack* published a story detailing a handful of open letters and petitions that he had signed during the Popular Front era, accusing him of being a concealed Communist. "I personally believe every word about every person they mention, because the journal is run by ex-FBI agents," Jack Townsend wrote to Ed Miller, flagging the story and trying to get Josephson fired from the project that he had already spent months researching. Townsend helpfully ended his missive: "If you want additional facts on Matthew Josephson, I understand that for a nominal fee *Counterattack* will give you a complete history on the individual."[109] HRE hired a private investigator who spent months—and several hundred pages—to prove that Josephson's activities were well within the mainstream of liberal thought at the time. Ernst passed away before the book, *Union House, Union Bar*, could be published. The union's new secretary-treasurer, Jack Weinberger, told Townsend that they were sticking with Josephson because the entire inquiry into the author's free speech activity would have offended Ernst's liberal sensibilities.

The union experienced one more tragedy in its leadership in 1953. On November 2, the usually indefatigable Gertrude Lane came to work too exhausted to get much done. Herman persuaded her to accept a ride home while Rubin arranged for a doctor from the Health Center to examine her. The diagnosis was that Lane was suffering from "complete physical and nervous exhaustion." A blood clot had entered her heart and was causing partial paralysis on her left side. She was taken to a hospital in New Jersey and ordered to spend three weeks in its care. The hospital discharged her after only two weeks. Lane returned to her intense schedule, only allowing herself a day off on Sunday, when she collapsed at home and died of a heart attack on November 22. She was 44 years old.[110]

The union went through a period of deep grief. Two thousand mourners filled the Manhattan Center for her wake. Hundreds of telegrams of condolences poured in from labor federations, joint boards, sister locals, rank-and-file members, and the international union. The new auditorium, still under construction at union headquarters, was named for her, as was a new college scholarship fund. Her death cast a pall over the union's planned anniversary

The union went through a period of deep grief following Gertrude Lane's death. Two thousand mourners filled the Manhattan Center for her wake. (New York Hotel and Gaming Trades Council. Located in Hotel Employees and Restaurant Employees International Union, Local 6 Photographs PHOTOS.098, Box 2, Folder 12; Tamiment Library and Robert F. Wagner Labor Archive, New York University.)

celebrations. Local 6 was chartered in 1938, and a few weeks hence would be the 15th anniversary of the founding of the Hotel Trades Council. In preparing the summary of accomplishments and reminiscences of past battles, it was clear how essential she was in all of those 15 years. "It is hard to visualize a Local 6 without Gertrude Lane," mourned the *Voice*.[111]

Until the End

The month of May in 1960 found some of the union pioneers who had been cast out looking back wistfully on their time in the movement for hotel workers. May Day fell on a Sunday that year. The large parades through Union Square were a thing of the past, but weekends—thanks to years of struggle by veteran labor organizers—were still respected and remained a fine time for a "real bang up party," offering entertainment and a buffet supper, organized by veteran leftwing food workers to honor Sam Kramberg and William Albertson.[112]

It might have been the last good time. Kramberg passed away in 1966. Albertson suffered a worse fate before his 1972 death. As a part of the FBI's illegal 1960s surveillance and sabotage of left-wing organizations, agents forged and leaked a document to make it look like Albertson was snitching in order to distract Party leadership from their *actual* snitches. Albertson was expelled from the Communist Party in 1964, leaving him cast out of the organization that was so much a part of his life and to which his loyalty cost him years in prison under a Smith Act conviction.[113]

On May 9, 1960, 1,200 hotel and club workers danced through the night at the Commodore Hotel, in a gala ballroom benefit party for Michael J. Obermeier. The event helped raise $2,000 with which organizers hoped to purchase an annuity to provide Local 6's past president with some reliable monthly income.[114] The loss of his promised pension was a source of great bitterness to Obermeier. His primary income was $82.50 a month in rent from his old house in Flushing, Queens. He settled into a spare room in his brother's house in Munich, and he raised chickens and tended a garden to get by.[115] At the time of the benefit dance, Obermeier's health was failing and he had moved to a cousin's home in Alicante, Spain, where he could receive better in-home nursing care. He died on May 20 at the age of 68.[116] In and out of consciousness the night before, his mind slipped to the past and he announced to his wife, Georgette, "I just settled to everyone's satisfaction. The management agreed to good wage increases."

"He was with Local 6 until the end," she wrote.[117]

Afterword

It was a hot August day in 2003. It was check-in time at the Grand Hyatt hotel, and guests were waiting in long lines that only grew longer, while, curbside, the Baltimore Orioles waited for their luggage to get unloaded from their tour buses. The workers were in the lobby, gathered around Local 6 Vice President Hazel Hazzard.

Short and usually soft-spoken, an immigrant from Trinidad and Tobago and a former room attendant who helped unionize her co-workers at the Four Seasons, Hazzard stood up on the edge of a fountain and in her best rally voice explained why union leaders had called this impromptu lobby meeting. The hotel's air conditioning was toxic. "No safety! No work!" chanted the crowd. OSHA investigators found that the cooling tower was in such a state of disrepair that it could breed legionnaires disease, and the Impartial Chairman ordered the air conditioning shut off until repairs were made. If management didn't comply, Hazzard explained, then the lobby meeting would become a full-blown strike. "This type of tactic by the union is inappropriate and will not be tolerated," a Hyatt executive complained to the press, charging that the walkout was really a negotiating tactic to score concessions on the union contract.[1]

The issue *was* health and safety, but the background was a decades-long dispute about the contract. The history is that the glorious Commodore Hotel went out of business in 1976. A young real estate developer used his dad's money to purchase the "blighted eyesore" two years later. He stripped the building to its steel beams to construct the tasteless glass mediocrity that is the Grand Hyatt. Of course, this was Donald Trump, and of course, he secured a 40-year tax abatement from the city to finance the project.[2] One of the strings attached, however, was a neutrality agreement with NYHTC. Unfortunately, the union could only prove a narrow majority of worker support, and Trump's managers exploited the union's weakened position to negotiate its own version of the IWA that gave them more leeway over work rules. This arrangement lasted for decades because Hyatt management would sign a "Me Too" agreement before every round of bargaining. This was essentially a "no strike/no lockout" agreement to abide by the economic terms of the IWA before it was even negotiated. It is valuable for the union that some unionized hotels would remain staffed and open for business in the event of an industry-wide strike (as, it turns out, there would be in 1985) so that the targeted employers feel a disproportionate economic impact and so that the union still has some dues revenue coming in and fewer strike benefits to pay out.

In 2003, union leaders decided to target the Grand Hyatt in the middle of a five-year agreement with a complex campaign of work-to-rule job actions in the housekeeping department and grievances before the Impartial Chairman over the work rules and health and safety issues over the hotel's air conditioning system.

Within hours of the lobby meeting and Impartial Chairman's order, Hyatt management not only tore up their contract (with three years left) to sign on to the full terms of the IWA, but they also signed a "Me Too" for the 2006 round of bargaining *while* affiliating with the Hotel Association. Not only that, but the union also compelled them to fire their lawyers, the notorious anti-union firm Proskauer Rose, and accept the counsel of David Drechsler's firm.

• • •

Today, New York's hotel workers unions have a conservative reputation, but it's belied by their militant track record of quickie strikes, work-to-rule job actions, and marches on the boss—while the Industry Wide Agreement is in effect—and long-term strikes to win the IWA for new properties. The syndicalist influence on the union—the Wobbly genes in its DNA—is remarkable, but shouldn't be surprising. Many unions that haven't been merged or taken over have a degree of historical memory that fosters a culture—almost a personality—that guides their actions.

In NYHTC and Local 6, it's partly physical. Union leaders and staff still walk through the doors that federal agents did to arrest Michael J. Obermeier. Shop delegates still convene in the Gertrude Lane Memorial Auditorium.

But there's also been a continuity in leadership. Michael J. Obermeier and Sam Kramberg worked alongside and organized with veterans of the 1912 and 1913 strikes. Jay Rubin, in turn, learned from those men and led the union until his retirement in 1979. Vito Pitta was a business agent under Rubin before taking the reins from him. Peter Ward, whose tenure overlapped with Rubin's presidency and with many of Rubin's proteges, restarted the union's organizing department in the 1980s, learning a little (loathe as he would be to admit it) from Vinny Sirabella but more from the union's history. Richard Maroko, who—among a great many accomplishments—masterminded the 2003 Grand Hyatt campaign with Ward, became only the fourth president of the Trades Council in 2020.

The legacy of influence from the Communist Party can be detected in two major ways: one, structural, and the other, cultural. William Z. Foster's brainchild, the trades council structure, is still fully operational. It remains fundamental to the unions' effectiveness. Quietly, it is Foster's longest-lasting influence on AFL-CIO trade unions. It cries out to be revived as an organizational model to get unions to stop squabbling over "who will get the members" and pool their resources to organize on a larger scale in non-union sectors.

Today, the union calls itself the New York and New Jersey Hotel and Gaming Trades Council, after its jurisdiction expanded to the areas surrounding New York City and the new casinos that have developed. Its eight affiliates are mostly the same as in the period of this book, with changes reflecting a mix of growth and decline of job crafts in the hotels, and consolidation and mergers, during a period of dynamic change in the economy since the 1970s.

Local 144 went on to become a pioneer in healthcare worker organizing in 1959, a major reason BSEIU dropped the "B" from its name. After the formerly independent District 1199 affiliated with SEIU in the late 1980s, the local was restructured, and its hotel workers became SEIU Local 758. When SEIU and UNITE HERE left the AFL-CIO to form Change to Win—ostensibly to renew focus on organizing within "core jurisdictions"—SEIU made a show of finally ceding its hotel workers to the Hotel Employees Union, and Local 758 was merged into Local 6. Its industry-wide contract with the residence clubs and no-frills hotels became the Trades Council's "Division A," and, at long last, the doormen and bellmen—natural workplace leaders given their strategic locations in the workplace—could become activists within the Trades Council's largest local.

Hotel and Club Employees Local 6's name also expanded along with its jurisdiction. The Hotel, Gaming, Restaurant & Club Employees & Bartenders Local 6 has occasionally organized free-standing restaurants, like Tavern on the Green and the Rainbow Room, but its core work is strikingly similar to that of 1953.

IBEW consolidated its New York locals, and Local 1005B was merged into Local 3. Upholsterers Local 44 became Steelworkers Local 43 when its international union merged out of existence. The Firemen and Oilers international union became a "national conference" of SEIU, and its Trades Council affiliate is now Local 56 IBFOMM, 32 BJ, SEIU. The other locals remain the same (aside from adding the word "Professionals" in Local 153's case and dropping the word "Brotherhood" in the Painters'), except that members in miscellaneous jobs who were never claimed by a craft union now have their own Hotel Maintenance, Carpenters, Valet & Utility Workers Local 1 whose only affiliation is to the Trades Council.

As of this writing, none of these affiliates are listed on the unions' hotelworkers.org website. In explaining its "Affiliated Locals," the website advises, "Neither the local unions affiliated with HTC nor any of the other affiliated organizations to which they belong have authority of any kind over HTC. HTC is not a subordinate body of any other organization or entity. HTC answers only to its own members."[3]

That disclaimer points to the other lasting influence of New York's hotel workers unions' experience in the Communist Party. The union's leadership has been marked by a deep-seated paranoia—about internal opposition, about meddling from affiliated bodies, about the bosses trying to break the union. This feeling has been passed down from Jay Rubin and his comrades to generations of successors and can be traced to the intense postwar period when the union was threatened from all sides.

It is the combination of the organizing strategies and tactics that were passed down through oral tradition from the Wobblies and the Communists and the paranoia that has made the union remain an effective powerhouse well into the 21st century.

While other Hotel Employees locals resisted involving their immigrant members (particularly undocumented immigrants) for decades before finally embracing their role as a union of immigrants, Local 6 and NYHTC could not afford to shun any significant membership group, lest they form an opposition. Each successive wave of immigrants who found their way into New York hotel employment from Latin America, the Caribbean, Africa, Eastern Europe, and all corners of the world was organized into membership, recruited into shop delegate leadership, hired on as business agents and organizers and was added to the administration's reelection slate—as Hazel Hazzard had been. What began as a union of immigrants has remained proudly so, and the membership unity that transcends race, religion, and national origin has kept the union strong.

Paranoia about the international unions and other parent bodies has, paradoxically, made Local 6 and NYHTC generous allies. The unions have often donated staff and release-time member activists to Central Labor Council campaigns and sister locals' contract fights and strike preparations to maintain goodwill for the times they build walls around themselves and jealously defend their prerogatives.

Paranoia about the bosses has inspired union leaders to almost always be waging a "war" against a singled-out employer, like the Grand Hyatt in 2003. In strikes for recognition at non-union boutique hotels, NYHTC will make a show of employing the kinds of resources—dozens of staff organizers, millions of dollars in the fighting defense fund, strategic corporate research, and political leverage—that await any faction of the Hotel Association that might try to evade or degrade the IWA.

In that way, one sees a clear through-line from the first uprising at the Belmont Hotel in 1912 to the "militant spirit of 1918," the Amalgamated Food Workers' wage-and-hour drive of 1923, the repeated targeting of the Waldorf-Astoria's business operations during the 1934 strike, and the singling out of the Governor Clinton during the first drive for the IWA in 1939.

New York's hotel workers always have a union, and its culture, structure, and militancy are an inherited legacy that each new generation continues to build upon.

Notes

Introduction

1. "Munich, June 12, 1953," WAG 123; Box 3; Folder 5, Tamiment/Wagner.

2. Melvyn Dubofsky, *When Workers Organize: New York City in the Progressive Era*, (University of Massachusetts Press, 1968), 121–124.

3. Dorothy Sue Cobble, *Dishing It Out: Waitresses and Their Unions in the Twentieth Century* (University of Illinois Press, 1991), xii.

4. Priscilla Murolo and A.B. Chitty, *From the Folks Who Brought You the Weekend: A Short, Illustrated History of Labor in the United States* (The New Press, 2001), 215.

5. Julius G. Getman, *Restoring the Power of Unions* (Yale University Press, 2010), 106.

6. Howard Kimeldorf, *Battling for American Labor: Wobblies, Craft Workers, and the Making of the Union Movement* (University of California Press, 1999), 157.

7. Theodore Draper, *The Roots of American Communism* (Viking, 1957), 198.

8. Theodore Draper, *American Communism & Soviet Russia: The Formative Period* (Viking, 1960).

9. Edward P. Johanningsmeier, *Forging American Communism: The Life of William Z. Foster* (Princeton, 1994); James R. Barrett, *William Z. Foster and the Tragedy of American Radicalism* (University of Illinois Press, 1999); Bryan D. Palmer, *James P. Cannon and the Origins of the American Revolutionary Left 1890–1928* (University of Illinois Press, 2007).

10. *Reds* (1981) Script, Transcript DB (website), https://transcripts.thedealr.net/script.php/reds-1981-LaN (accessed June 10, 2022).

11. Draper, *Roots of American Communism*, 77.

12. Draper, *American Communism & Soviet Russia*, 106–135.

13. James P. Cannon, *History of American Trotskyism* (Pathfinder, 1972).

14. Harvey Klehr, *The Heyday of American Communism: The Depression Decade* (Basic Books, 1984), 132–133, 238.

15. Maurice Isserman, *Which Side Were You On? The American Communist Party During the Second World War* (Wesleyan University Press, 1982).

16. David A. Shannon, *The Decline of American Communism: A History of the Communist Party of the United States Since 1945* (Harcourt, Brace and Company, 1959).

17. Joseph Starobin, *American Communism in Crisis, 1943–1957* (Harvard University Press, 1972).

18. Toni Gilpin, *The Long Deep Grudge: A Story of Big Capital, Radical Labor, and Class War in the American Heartland* (Haymarket, 2020), 282–300.

19. Mary M. Stolberg, *Fighting Organized Crime: Politics, Justice, and the Legacy of Thomas E. Dewey* (Northeastern University Press, 1995).

20. Jennifer Luff, *Commonsense Anticommunism: Labor and Civil Liberties Between the World Wars* (University of North Carolina Press, 2012).

21. Julia Rose Kraut, *Threat of Dissent* (Harvard University Press, 2020).

Chapter 1. The Unsafest Proposition in the World

1. Kimeldorf, *Battling for American Labor*, 98.

2. Karl Schriftgeisser, *Oscar of the Waldorf* (E.P. Dutton & Co., 1943), 52, 81–90; Stanley Turkel, *Hotel Mavens* (AuthorHouse, 2014), 3, 20–37, 44, 51.

3. *Sun*, October 2, 1904; *NYTr*, September 4, 1904; *NYT*, September 4, 1904; *NYT*, April 26, 1905; Chase, *Wonder City*, 136.

4. *NYT*, October 24, 1906; *New York Hotel Record* 8, no. 4 (November 6, 1909): 4.

5. *NYT*, May 8, 1906; *NYTr*, May 8, 1906; *New York Hotel Record* 8, no. 4 (November 6, 1909): 4; *NYT*, March 10, 1929; Benjamin Waldman, "From Forge to Skyscraper: The Story of 120 Park Ave.," *Untapped New York*, https://untappedcities.com/2012/06/25/from-forge-to-skyscraper-the-story-of-120-park-avenue/ (accessed May 19, 2022).

6. Fremont Rider, *Rider's New York City and Vicinity, including Newark, Yonkers and New Jersey* (Henry Holt & Company, 1916), 171.

7. Julie Satow, *The Plaza: The Secret Life of America's Most Famous Hotel* (Hachette Book Group [Twelve], 2019), 19–34.

8. *NYT*, December 22, 1910; Chase, *Wonder City*, 148.

9. Chase, *Wonder City*, 148; Corsa Hotel Files, New-York Historical Society.

10. *NYT*, October 10, 1912; *New York Hotel Record* 10, no. 20 (June 25, 1912): 12.

11. *NYT*, January 10, 1912; Chase, *Wonder City*, 127.

12. *NYT*, December 13, 1912.

13. Josephson, *Union House*, 51.

14. *NYT*, June 3, 1869.

15. Kimeldorf, *Battling for American Labor*, 89.

16. Murolo and Chitty, *From the Folks*, 123.

17. Josephson, *Union House*, 11.

18. Josephson, *Union House*, 12, 14, 17, 31.

19. *Mixer & Server* 22, no. 2 (February 1913); Josephson, *Union House*, 17, 36, 82–83.

20. Josephson, *Union House*, 37–42, 53, 93.

21. Josephson, *Union House*, 51.

22. Josephson, *Union House*, 86–91.

23. Josephson, *Union House*, 13.

24. Schriftgeisser, *Oscar of the Waldorf*, 104–105.

25. *Mixer & Server* 13, no. 1 (January 1904), 52; Josephson, *Union House*, 58.

26. Kimeldorf, *Battling for American Labor*, 96–97.

27. Patrick Renshaw, *The Wobblies: The Story of Syndicalism in the United States* (Doubleday, 1967), 3.

28. David J. Saposs, *Left Wing Unionism: A Study of Radical Policies and Tactics* (International Publishers, 1926), 153.
29. *International Hotel Work* 1, no. 1 (November 13, 1911).
30. *Sun*, June 2, 1912.
31. Kimeldorf, *Battling for American Labor*, 97–98.
32. *Call*, May 8, 1912.
33. *Call*, May 9, 1912; *Call*, May 11, 1912.
34. *NYTr*, May 12, 1912.
35. *NYTr*, May 16, 1912.
36. *NYTr*, May 13, 1912.
37. *NYT*, May 14, 1912.
38. *NYT*, May 15, 1912.
39. *NYTr*, May 14, 1912.
40. *NYTr*, May 13, 1912.
41. *NYTr*, May 15, 1912; *NYTr*, May 14, 1912; *NYT*, May 14, 1912; *NYT*, May 15, 1912.
42. *NYT*, May 16, 1912.
43. *Call*, May 16, 1912.
44. *NYTr*, May 16, 1912.
45. *NYT*, May 16, 1912.
46. Adam Hochschild, *Rebel Cinderella* (Houghton Mifflin Harcourt, 2020).
47. *NYT*, May 16, 1912.
48. *Call*, May 20, 1912; *NYTr*, May 20, 1912.
49. *NYTr*, May 24, 1912.
50. *Call*, May 24, 1912; *NYTr*. May 25, 1912.
51. *Call*, May 23, 1912; *NYTr*. May 26, 1912.
52. *NYTr*, May 28, 1912.
53. *NYEW*, May 29, 1912.
54. *NYT*, May 30, 1912.
55. *NYTr*, May 29, 1912; *NYT*, May 30, 1912.
56. *Boston Daily Globe*, May 31, 1912.
57. *NYEW*, June 1, 1912; *NYTr*, June 1, 1912; *Sun*, June 3, 1912.
58. *Atlanta Constitution*, June 2, 1912.
59. Stephen H. Norwood, "The Student as Strikebreaker: College Youth and the Crisis of Masculinity in the Early Twentieth Century," *Journal of Social History* 28, no. 2 (Winter 1994), 331–349.
60. *NYTr*, May 31, 1912.
61. *Sun*, June 1, 1912.
62. *NYTr*, June 1, 1912.
63. *NYTr*, June 2, 1912.
64. *NYTr*, June 2, 1912.
65. *Sun*, June 2, 1912.
66. *Mixer & Server* 21, no. 8: 28–30; *NYT*, June 1, 1912.
67. *NYTr*, June 2, 1912.
68. *NYTr*, June 6, 1912; *NYTr*, June 8, 1912.
69. *Call*, June 5, 1912.
70. *NYTr*, June 4, 1912; *NYEW*, June 3, 1912.
71. *NYEW*, June 4, 1912.
72. *Sun*, June 4, 1912.

Notes to Chapter 1

73. *Call*, June 6, 1912.
74. *NYTr*, June 8, 1912; *Sun*, June 7, 1912.
75. *NYEW*, June 8, 1912; *Sun*, June 10, 1912; *NYT*, June 9, 1912.
76. Hochschild, *Rebel Cinderella*, 121.
77. Kimeldorf, *Battling for American Labor*, 104.
78. *Call*, June 12, 1912.
79. Hochschild, *Rebel Cinderella*, 121.
80. *Sun*, June 11, 1912.
81. *NYT*, June 12, 1912.
82. *NYEW*, June 13, 1912.
83. *Call*, June 15, 1912; *Call*, June 18, 1912; *Call*, June 19, 1912.
84. *NYTr*, June 19, 1912.
85. *New York Evening Post*, June 22, 1912.
86. *NYT*, July 3, 1912.
87. *NYTr*, June 26, 1912.
88. *NYTr*, June 26, 1912.
89. *NYEW*, June 26, 1912.
90. Kimeldorf, *Battling for American Labor*, 106.
91. *NYTr*, September 17, 1912.
92. *NYT*, October 23, 1912.
93. Frank Bohn, "The Strike of the New York Hotel and Restaurant Workers," *International Socialist Review*, February 1913.
94. *Sun*, October 25, 1912.
95. *NYTr*, October 26, 1912.
96. *NYEW*, August 27, 1912; *NY Post*, October 25, 1912; *Sun*, November 3, 1912.
97. *NY Post*, December 31, 1912.
98. Frank Bohn, "The Strike of the New York Hotel and Restaurant Workers," *International Socialist Review*, February 1913.
99. *NYTr*, January 9, 1913.
100. *NYT*, January 1, 1913.
101. *NYTr*, January 2, 1913.
102. *NYTr*, January 4, 1913.
103. *Sun*, January 1, 1913; *NYTr*, January 1, 1913; Kimeldorf, *Battling for American Labor*, 106.
104. Elizabeth Gurley Flynn, *The Rebel Girl: An Autobiography* (International Publishers, 1955; republished 1994), 152.
105. Flynn, *Rebel Girl,* 153
106. *Call*, January 3, 1913; *Call*, January 4, 1913.
107. *Call*, January 5, 1913.
108. *Call*, January 7, 1913.
109. *Sun*, January 8, 1913; *Call*, January 8, 1913.
110. *NYT*, January 9, 1913; *NYTr*, January 9, 1913; *Call*, January 9, 1913.
111. Frank Bohn, "The Strike of the New York Hotel and Restaurant Workers," *International Socialist Review*, February 1913.
112. *NYTr*, January 15, 1913.
113. *NYTr*, January 10, 1913.
114. *NYT*, January 12, 1913.
115. *NYTr*, January 13, 1913.

116. *NYT*, January 13, 1913.
117. Hochschild, *Rebel Cinderella*, 125–127.
118. *NYT*, January 14, 1913.
119. *Sun*, January 16, 1913.
120. *NYTr*, January 19, 1913.
121. *Call*, January 23, 1913.
122. *Call*, January 24, 1913.
123. *NYT*, January 24, 1913; *NYTr*, January 24, 1913.
124. *Sun*, January 25, 1913; *NYTr*, January 25, 1913.
125. *NY Post*, January 27, 1913.
126. *NYTr*, January 27, 1913.
127. *NYTr*, January 28, 1913.
128. *NYTr*, February 1, 1913.

Chapter 2. Bolsheviki Methods

1. *NYTr*, November 29, 1918; *Sun*, November 29, 1918.
2. Kimeldorf, *Battling for American Labor*, 114.
3. *NYTr*, October 19, 1913.
4. *NYTr*, November 9, 1913.
5. Kimeldorf, *Battling for American Labor*, 117.
6. *NYTr*, January 3, 1913.
7. *NYTr*, January 20, 1913.
8. *NYT*, January 2, 1913.
9. "Proceedings of the Eighteenth General Convention Hotel and Restaurant Employees' International Alliance and Bartenders International League of America," June 14–19, 1915: 40.
10. *NYT*, February 5, 1913.
11. Kimeldorf, *Battling for American Labor*, 117.
12. Flynn, *Rebel Girl*, 183.
13. *NYT*, March 31, 1915.
14. *NYTr*, December 18, 1915.
15. *NYT*, December 21, 1915.
16. *NYT*, December 20, 1915.
17. *NYTr*, January 2, 1916.
18. *Catering Industry Employee* 50, no. 3 (March 1941): 26; *NYTr*, October 28, 1903, 14.
19. *NYHT*, March 12, 1937; *NYT*, March 26, 1937.
20. "Application for Transfer to the Soviet Union," RGASPI 495-261-625.
21. Josephson, *Union House*, 58.
22. "A German Lad Arrives in New York," Hotel Employees and Restaurant Employees International Union, Local 6 Records; WAG.148; Box 15; Folder 13, Tamiment/Wagner.
23. "Interview with Otto Wagner," David J. Saposs Papers, Box 21, Folder 5, Wisconsin Historical Society.
24. *NYTr*, February 28, 1917.
25. *NYTr*, March 7, 1917.
26. *Sun*, August 23, 1917.

27. David Freeland, *Automats, Taxi Dances and Vaudeville* (New York University Press, 2009), 176.
28. *NYTr*, December 1, 1917.
29. *NYEW*, December 7, 1917; *NYT*, December 8, 1917; *NYTr*, December 8, 1917.
30. *NYTr*, December 21, 1917; *Call*, December 21, 1917.
31. *Mixer & Server* 26, no. 2 (February 1918): 28; *Call*, December 17, 1917.
32. *M&S* 27, no. 7 (June 1918), 9–12.
33. For the IWW's entreaties, see the 38-page pamphlet, credited to L.S. Chumley, "Hotel, Restaurant and Domestic Workers; How They Work and How They Live." For IFWHR's discomfort, see David J. Saposs's 1919 interview with Otto Wagner: David J. Saposs Papers, Box 21, Folder 5, Wisconsin Historical Society.
34. Jeffery B. Perry, *Hubert Harrison: The Voice of Harlem Radicalism, 1883–1918* (Columbia University Press, 2010), 369.
35. Kimeldorf, *Battling for American Labor*, 119.
36. *NYT*, May 25, 1918.
37. *NYT*, June 7, 2019.
38. *NYTr*, June 19, 1918.
39. *Sun*, June 19, 1918.
40. *NYT*, June 12, 1917; *Call*, May 30, 1918.
41. Willard Marakle, "New York Anti-Loafing Law in Effect," *State Service: An Illustrated Monthly Magazine Devoted to the Government of the State of New York and Its Affairs* 2, no. 6 (June 1918).
42. *M&S* 27, no. 6 (June 1918): 28.
43. *NYT*, August 22, 1918.
44. *NYT*, October 29, 1918.
45. "Wages of Women in Hotels and Restaurants in Massachusetts," *Bulletin # 17*, Minimum Wage Commission of the Commonwealth of Massachusetts, September 1918.
46. *Sun*, October 29, 1918.
47. Turkel, *Hotel Mavens*, 89–90.
48. James Wyatt Woodall, "From 'Servant' to 'Hotel Worker': Class Warfare, Hotel Workers, and Wobblies in New York City, 1893–1913" (undergraduate thesis, Columbia University, April 4, 2018), 23.
49. *Call*, October 29, 1918.
50. *Call*, November 1, 1918.
51. *M&S* 35, no. 11 (October 1925): 17; *M&S* 33, no. 10 (October 1923): 13; *M&S* 37, no. 9 (September 1926): 15.
52. *M&S* 27, no. 12 (December 1918): 20.
53. *NYT*, November 2, 1918.
54. *NYTr*, November 13, 1918.
55. *NYT*, November 10, 1918; *Call*, November 11, 1918.
56. *NYT*, November 2, 1918.
57. *NYT*, November 12, 1918; *Sun*, November 12, 1918.
58. *NYEW*, November 14, 1918.
59. *NYTr*, October 29, 1918.
60. *NYTr*, November 8, 1918.
61. Cobble, *Dishing It Out*, 2–3.
62. *NYT*, October 31, 1918.

63. *NYTr*, November 22, 1918.
64. *NYEW*, December 20, 1918.
65. Cobble, *Dishing It Out,* 63–68.
66. Cobble, *Dishing It Out*, 72.
67. *NYTr*, October 30, 1918.
68. *NYT*, October 31, 1918.
69. *NYTr*, November 13, 1918; *NYTr*, January 14, 1919.
70. *NYTr*, November 22, 1918.
71. *NYTr*, November 17, 1918.
72. Thomas Kessner, *Fiorello H. La Guardia and the Making of Modern New York*, (McGraw-Hill, 1989), 30–66.
73. *NYTr*, November 19, 1918.
74. *Sun*, November 23, 1918.
75. *NYTr*, November 21, 1918; *Call*, November 21, 1918.
76. *NYTr*, November 24, 1918; *Call*, November 27, 1918.
77. *NYT*, November 19, 1918.
78. *NYT*, November 29, 1918.
79. *Sun*, November 29, 1918.
80. *NYTr*, November 30, 1918.
81. *Sun*, December 3, 1918.
82. *Call*, December 6, 1918.
83. *Call*, December 9, 1918.
84. *Sun*, December 4, 1918.
85. *Call*, December 16, 1918.
86. *Call*, December 23, 1918.
87. *M&S* 28, no. 1 (January 15, 1919): 10.
88. Kimeldorf, *Battling for American Labor*, 88; Josephson, *Union House,* 82–83, 95.
89. *FW*, October 1935.
90. Jay Rubin and Michael J. Obermeier, *Growth of a Union: The Life and Times of Edward Flore* (The Historical Union Association, Inc., 1943), vii.
91. *NYEW*, December 10, 1918.
92. *M&S* 28, no. 1 (January 1919): 11.
93. *Call*, December 20, 1918.
94. *NYTr*, December 26, 1918.
95. *Sun*, January 2, 1919.
96. *Call*, January 2, 1919.
97. *Sun*, January 2, 1919.
98. *NYTr*, February 5, 1919.
99. Jeremy Brecher, *Strike!* (South End Press, 1972), 121–122.
100. James R. Barrett, *William Z. Foster and the Tragedy of American Radicalism* (University of Illinois Press, 1999), 11; William Z. Foster, *Pages from a Worker's Life* (International Publishers, 1939 [1978 edition]).
101. Barrett, *Tragedy of American Radicalism*, 44.
102. Edward P. Johanningsmeier, *Forging American Communism: The Life of William Z. Foster* (Princeton University Press, 1994), 44.
103. William Z. Foster, *From Bryan to Stalin* (International Publishers, 1937), 55–56,
104. Barrett, *Tragedy of American Radicalism*, 1999, 58.

105. Melvyn Dubofsky, *The State and Labor in Modern America* (University of North Carolina Press, 1994), 75.
106. Barrett, *Tragedy of American Radicalism*, 83–101.
107. Vladimir I. Lenin, *"Left-Wing Communism," An Infantile Disorder,* New Translation (International Publishers, 1940), 38.
108. Barrett, *Tragedy of American Radicalism*, 7.
109. David J. Saposs, *Communism in American Unions* (McGraw-Hill, 1959), 10.

Chapter 3. Practical Trade Union Tactics

1. *NYTr*, May 24, 1923.
2. Barrett, *Tragedy of American Radicalism*, 2–3.
3. This number is gleaned from details of a union subscription drive in *Hotel Worker* 1, no. 8 (May 24, 1919).
4. *Hotel Worker* 1, no. 12 (August 16, 1919).
5. Kimeldorf, *Battling for American Labor*, 129–130.
6. "Interview with Otto Wagner," David J. Saposs Papers, Box 21, Folder 5, Wisconsin Historical Society.
7. *Hotel Worker* 1, no. 12 (August 16, 1919).
8. *Hotel Record* 18, no. 1 (September 23, 1919).
9. *Hotel Worker* 2, no. 10 (May 8, 1920).
10. Marion Dutton Savage, *Industrial Unionism in America* (The Ronald Press Company, 1922), 287.
11. *Hotel Worker* 2, no. 12 (June 15, 1920).
12. Constitution of the International Workers in the Amalgamated Food Industries adopted at the joint convention of the International Federation of Workers in the Hotel, Restaurant, Club and Catering Industry, and the Journeymen Bakers' and Confectioners' International Union of America, held in New York City, May 24–29, 1920; "Notice To Branches," *FV* 2, no. 3 (February 1, 1921).
13. *Hotel Worker* 1, no. 15 (November 15, 1919).
14. *NYTr*, November 6, 1918.
15. Simon De Leon, *The American Labor's Who's Who* (Stratford Press, 1925), 33.
16. David Lore, *Firebrand: Journalist Ludwig Lore's Lifelong Struggle Against Capitalism, Stalinism and the Rise of Nazism* (Lulu, 2017), 18.
17. Draper, *Roots of American Communism*, 76–77.
18. Saposs, *Left Wing Unionism*, 153–155.
19. Marion Dutton Savage, in her dissertation from four years prior to Saposs's book, used the word "amalgamation" to refer to the slow process of some AFL craft unions converting to industrial forms of organizing. *Industrial Unionism in America*, 28.
20. *FV* 8, no. 6 (June 1, 1927).
21. Saposs, *Left Wing Unionism*, 155.
22. As Saposs explained in 1926, "The boring from within element has also appropriated the word as their symbol for structural, tactical and ideological union adaptations. It is no longer 'industrial unionism' popularised by the socialists and I.W.W., but 'Amalgamation' that the revolutionists demand. From the 'seventies through the 'nineties the word 'Progressive' was in vogue as designating radicalism in union matters. Now it is being replaced by the words 'Amalgamated' and 'Amalgamation'" (155).

23. Lore, *Firebrand,* 18; "United Labor Council of America," *The Toiler,* December 3, 1921.
24. "Application for Transfer to the Soviet Union," RGASPI 495–261–6072; "Questionnaire," RGASPI 495–261–625.
25. "Early American Marxism: Communist Party of America History Page." *Marxist Internet Archive,* https://www.marxists.org/history/usa/eam/cpa/communistparty.html (accessed September 10, 2019).
26. *FV* 3, no. 2 (January 15, 1922).
27. *NYT,* July 7, 1920.
28. *FV* 3, no. 2 (January 15, 1922).
29. *The Toiler,* December 3, 1921; *FV* 3, no. 2 (January 15, 1922).
30. *LH* 1, no. 7 (September 1922); *FV* 3, no. 16 (December 15, 1922).
31. "Resolutions and Decisions of the First International Congress of Revolutionary Trade and Industrial Unions," The American Labor Union Educational Society, 1922, 62.
32. *FV* 4, no. 4 (February 15, 1923).
33. *FV* 4, no. 4 (February 15, 1923).
34. *LH,* January 1923.
35. *LH,* April 1923.
36. *LH,* October 1923; *LH,* April 1923.
37. *LH,* October 1923.
38. *FV* 4, no. 4 (February 15, 1923).
39. *FV* 4, no. 6 (March 15, 1923).
40. *FV* 4, no. 5 (March 1, 1923).
41. *FV* 4, no. 10 (May 15, 1923).
42. *FV* 4, no. 7 (April 1, 1923).
43. Cobble, *Dishing It Out,* 39.
44. "Behind the Scenes In a Hotel," *Consumer League of New York,* 1922.
45. Flynn, *Rebel Girl,* 281.
46. *FV* 4, no. 12 (June 15, 1923).
47. *FV* 4, no. 10 (May 15, 1923).
48. *NYT,* May 22, 1923.
49. *FV* 4, no. 11 (June 1, 1923).
50. Josephson, *Union House,* 144.
51. *FV* 4, no. 21 (November 1, 1923).
52. *FV* 5, no. 7 (April 1, 1924).
53. *FV* 5, no. 10 (May 15, 1924).

Chapter 4. Strange as It May Seem

1. *DW,* June 1, 1929.
2. Klehr, *Heyday of American Communism,* 13.
3. Draper, *American Communism & Soviet Russia,* 134–135, 357.
4. Benjamin Gitlow, *I Confess: The Truth About American Communism* (E.P. Dutton & Co., 1940), 248.
5. *NYHT,* March 12, 1937; *NYT,* March 26, 1937.
6. Josephson, *Union House,* 129.
7. *M&S* 28, no. 11 (November 1919): 62; Proceedings, 748.
8. Proceedings, 748, 754.

9. *M&S* 29, no. 1 (January 1920): 22.

10. *M&S* 31, no. 2 (February 1922): 18; Proceedings of the Twenty-Third General Convention. Hotel and Restaurant Employees' International Alliance and Bartenders' International League of America. Held at Montreal, Quebec, Canada, August 10, 11, 12, 13, 14, and 15, 1925, 96–97.

11. Josephson, *Union House,* 110–112, 250, 344.

12. Josephson, *Union House,* 143–144.

13. *M&S* 32, no. 7 (July 1923): 24–36.

14. *M&S* 35, no. 11 (October 1925): 17; *M&S* 33, no 10 (October 15, 1923): 13; *M&S* 37, no. 9 (September 15, 1926): 15.

15. *M&S* 36, no. 2 (February 1926): 16.

16. Martel found Local 5 running an illegal gambling room and speakeasy out of its union hall for its last 40 dues-paying members and had its charter revoked. Proceedings of the Twenty-fourth General Convention, 119.

17. *M&S* 36, no. 2 (February 1926): 62.

18. *M&S* 36, no. 1 (January 1926): 16.

19. *FV* 6, no. 23 (December 1, 1925).

20. *M&S* 36, no. 4 (April 1926): 46.

21. *FV* 7, no. 1 (January 1, 1926).

22. *M&S* 35, no. 3 (March 1926): 15, 46.

23. *M&S* 35, no. 8 (August 1926): 11

24. All these membership figures come from Proceedings of the Twenty-Fourth General Convention, 67.

25. *M&S* 37, no. 4 (April 1927): 14.

26. *M&S* 37, no. 7 (July 1927): 19–20; Proceedings of the Twenty-Fourth General Convention, 67.

27. Proceedings of the Twenty-Fourth General Convention, 284.

28. Josephson, *Union House,* 158.

29. *FV* 6, no. 23 (December 1, 1925).

30. *FV* 7, no. 1 (January 1, 1926).

31. *FV* 7, no. 9 (May 1, 1926).

32. *FV* 7, no. 10 (May 15, 1926).

33. *FV* 7, no. 11 (June 1, 1926).

34. *FV* 7, no. 12 (July 15, 1926).

35. *FV* 8, no. 14 (September 1, 1927).

36. *FV* 8, no. 18 (November 1, 1927).

37. *DW*, May 24, 1929.

38. *M&S* 35, no. 3 (March 1927): 18; *M&S* 37, no. 3 (March 1929): 42–43.

39. *FV* 9, no. 18 (November 1, 1928).

40. *FV* 10, no. 1 (January 1, 1929).

41. Proceedings of the Twenty-Fifth General Convention, 109.

42. "Questionnaire," RGASPI 495-261-625.

43. *FV* 10, no. 5 (March 1, 1929).

44. *DW*, March 18, 1929.

45. *DW*, February 8, 1929.

46. *NYT*, April 4, 1929.

47. *NYT*, April 5, 1929.

48. *FV*, April 1, 1929.

49. *NYT*, April 5, 1929.
50. *NYT*, April 6, 1929.
51. *NYHT*, April 11, 1929.
52. *NYT*, April 12, 1929.
53. *NYHT*, April 9, 1929.
54. *NYT*, April 10, 1929.
55. *NYT*, April 13, 1929.
56. *NYT*, May 5, 1929.
57. *NYT*, May 25, 1929.
58. *NYHT*, April 17, 1929.
59. *NYT*, April 15, 1929.
60. *NYT*, April 20, 1929.
61. *NYT*, April 21, 1929.
62. *NYT*, May 25, 1929.
63. *NYHT*, April 30, 1929.
64. *NYT*, May 7, 1929.
65. *NYHT*, April 23, 1929.
66. *NYT*, April 21, 1929.
67. *NYT*, May 3, 1929.
68. *NYT*, May 9, 1929.
69. *NYT*, May 18, 1929.
70. *NYT*, June 2, 1929.
71. *FV*, July 1, 1929.
72. *NYT*, June 15, 1929; *FV* 10, no. 6 (June 1, 1929).
73. *FV* 10, no. 7 (July 1, 1929).
74. *NYT*, May 5, 1929.
75. *FV* 10, no. 6 (June 1, 1929).
76. *DW*, May 28, 1929; *DW*, July 27, 1929.
77. Proceedings of the Twenty-Fifth General Convention, 106–115.

Chapter 5. Political Sentimental Giddiness

1. *NYHT*, January 25, 1934.
2. *DW*, January 29, 1934.
3. Klehr, *Heyday of American Communism*, 118.
4. Philip S. Foner, *History of the Labor Movement in the United States, Volume 11: The Great Depression, 1929–1932* (International Publishers, 2022); Ahmed White, *The Last Great Strike: Little Steel, the CIO, and the Struggle for Labor Rights in New Deal America* (University of California Press, 2016), 78–79, 81, 85, 96, 139; Victor G. Devinatz, "A Reevaluation of the Trade Union Unity League, 1929–1934," *Science & Society* 71, no. 1 (January 2007): 33–58.
5. *LU* 3, no. 2 (March 1929).
6. Harvey Klehr, John Earl Haynes, and Kyrill M. Anderson, *The Soviet World of American Communism* (Yale University Press, 1998), 50–51, 58.
7. *LU*, June 8, 1929.
8. *LU*, September 14, 1929.
9. *LU*, September 14, 1929.
10. *LU*, October 5, 1929.

Notes to Chapter 5

11. *FV* 10, no. 11 (November 1, 1929).
12. *Party Organizer* 2, nos. 5–6 (May–June 1928).
13. *FV* 10, no. 12 (December 1, 1929).
14. *FW,* December 1931.
15. *FW,* March 1934.
16. *FW,* April 1933.
17. Josephson, *Union House,* 174.
18. *DW,* January 28, 1935.
19. *DW,* January 26, 1932.
20. *FW,* March 1933.
21. Howard Zinn, *A People's History of the United States* (Harper Perennial Modern Classics, 2015), 387.
22. Foster, *From Bryan to Stalin,* 238–244; Victor Devinatz, "A Reevaluation of the Trade Union Unity League, 1929–1934," *Science & Society* 71, no. 1: 36–38.
23. "Minutes of TUUL Bure, March 14, 1932," RGASPI 515-1-3341.
24. Debra E. Bernhardt and Rachel Bernstein, *Ordinary People, Extraordinary Lives: A Pictorial History of Working People in New York City* (New York University Press, 2000), 132–134; "Jay Rubin, 100-HQ-52865," FBI, https://archive.org/details/JayRubinFBI, 7.
25. "Jay Rubin, 100-HQ-52865," FBI, https://archive.org/details/JayRubinFBI, 129.
26. "Jay Rubin, 100-HQ-52865," FBI, https://archive.org/details/JayRubinFBI, 47, 103.
27. "Michael J. Obermeier, 100-HQ-96104," FBI, https://archive.org/details/MichaelJObermeierFBI1, 59.
28. "Michael J. Obermeier, 100-HQ-96104," FBI, https://archive.org/details/MichaelJObermeier, FBI, 1, 59.
29. Foster, *Pages From a Worker's Life,* 283.
30. Barrett, *Tragedy of American Radicalism,* 183–188.
31. Foster, *Pages From a Worker's Life,* 282.
32. Barrett, *Tragedy of American Radicalism,* 183–188.
33. *LU* 3, no. 1 (February 1929).
34. Johanningsmeier, *Forging American Communism,* 255.
35. *FV* 11, no. 1 (January 1, 1930).
36. *FV* 11, no. 6 (June 1, 1930).
37. *FV* 11, no. 5 (May 1, 1930).
38. *Revolutionary Age* 1, no. 18 (August 1, 1930).
39. *FV* 11, no. 8 (August 1, 1930).
40. *NYT,* June 8, 1928.
41. Satow, *The Plaza,* 77.
42. Herbert Solow, "The New York Hotel Strike," *The Nation,* February 28, 1934.
43. *FV* 12, no. 4 (April 1, 1931).
44. *Revolutionary Age* 1, no. 3 (December 1, 1929); *Revolutionary Age* 1, no. 5 (January 1, 1930).
45. Leilah Danielson, *American Gandhi: A. J. Muste and the History of Radicalism in the Twentieth Century* (University of Pennsylvania Press, 2014), 179.
46. Bryan D. Palmer, *James P. Cannon and the Origins of the American Revolutionary Left 1890–1928* (University of Illinois Press, 2007), 323–331.

47. James P. Cannon, *The History of American Trotskyism* (Pathfinder Press, 1972), 126–127.
48. *FV* 12, no. 2 (February 1, 1931).
49. *FV* 12, no. 6 (June 1, 1931).
50. *NYHT,* December 6, 1931.
51. *FV* 13, no. 8 (August 1, 1932).
52. 29 U.S. Code § 102. Public policy in labor matters declared.
53. Dubofsky, *The State and Labor in Modern America,* 111–119.
54. Fraser, *Labor Will Rule,* 290.
55. Josephson, *Union House,* 180–189.
56. Josephson, *Union House,* 195.
57. Dubofsky, *The State and Labor in Modern America,* 111–119.
58. *FW,* October 1, 1933.
59. *FV* 14, no. 10 (October 1, 1933).
60. *FW,* October 1, 1933.
61. Josephson, *Union House,* 195–196.
62. *NYHT,* January 30, 1937.
63. *NYHT,* April 28, 1935.
64. *CIE* 38, no. 11 (November 15, 1929): 39.
65. Proceedings of the Twenty-sixth General Convention Hotel and Restaurant Employees' and Beverage Dispensers' International Alliance, Held at Boston, Mass., U.S.A., August 8, 9, 10, 11 and 12, 1932, 53.
66. *CIE* 40, no. 1 (January 1931): 38.
67. *CIE* 40, no. 2 (February 1931): 41.
68. *CIE* 40, no. 4 (April 1931): 11.
69. *CIE* 40, no. 6 (June 1931): 15.
70. Oliver E. Allen, *The Tiger: The Rise and Fall of Tammany Hall,* Addison-Wesley Publishing Company, 1993, 256–259.
71. *CIE* 40, no. 11 (November 1931): 21; Proceedings of the Twenty-sixth General Convention, 15.
72. *People of the State of New York v. James J. Hines, et al.,* 1938; New York County District Attorney indictments, 1883–1951; ACC-2015–012; Box 1014; Folder: Williams, John; Coulcher, et al.; Municipal Archives, City of New York; *NYT,* January 29, 1937.
73. *NYT,* January 29, 1937; *NYT,* February 2, 1937; *NYT,* January 24, 1937; *NYHT.* November 13, 1936.
74. *CIE* 41, no. 6 (June 15, 1932): 31; *NYT,* March 11, 1937.
75. *NYHT,* March 13, 1937.
76. *NYHT,* February 21, 1937.
77. *NYHT,* February 21, 1937.
78. *NYHT,* October 29, 1933.
79. Alan Block, *East Side–West Side: Organizing Crime in New York 1930–1950* (Routledge, 1983), 154.
80. *People of the State of New York v. James J. Hines, et al.,* 1938; New York County District Attorney indictments, 1883–1951; ACC-2015–012; Box 1014; Folder: Williams, John; Coulcher, et al.; Municipal Archives, City of New York.
81. *NYHT,* November 13, 1933.
82. *CIE* 42, no. 12 (December 1933): 9, 19.
83. Josephson, *Union House,* 212.

84. "Analysis of Strikes and Lockouts in 1934," Bureau of Labor Statistics.
85. *NYT,* January 24, 1934.
86. *FV* 15, no. 1 (January 1, 1934).
87. *DW,* January 29, 1934.
88. *DW,* January 27, 1934.
89. *NYHT,* January 24, 1934.
90. *NYT,* January 25, 1934.
91. *DW,* January 25, 1934.
92. *NYHT,* January 25, 1934.
93. *DW,* January 26, 1934; *DW,* January 27, 1934.
94. *NYT,* January 26, 1934.
95. *NYHT,* January 26, 1934.
96. *NYHT,* January 27, 1934.
97. *NYT,* January 26, 1934.
98. Walter Galenson and Marjorie Spector, "The New York Labor-Injunction Statute and the Courts," *Columbia Law Review* 42, no. 1 (January 1942): 51–88.
99. *NYHT,* January 26, 1934; *NYT,* January 27, 1934.
100. *NYT,* January 28, 1934.
101. *NYT,* January 29, 1934.
102. *NYHT,* January 29, 1934.
103. *NYT,* January 29, 1934.
104. *DW,* January 30, 1934; *DW,* January 29, 1934.
105. The photograph appeared on the cover of the January 31, 1934, issue of the *DW.*
106. *NYHT,* January 30, 1934.
107. *NYT,* January 8, 1993.
108. *NYHT,* February 7, 1934.
109. *NYT,* January 30, 1934; *NYHT,* January 31, 1934.
110. *NYT,* January 29, 1934.
111. *NYHT,* January 31, 1934.
112. *DW,* January 31, 1934.
113. *NYT,* January 31, 1934.
114. *NYHT,* February 1, 1934.
115. *DW,* January 30, 1934.
116. *DW,* February 1, 1934.
117. *The Militant,* February 2, 1934.
118. *DW,* February 2, 1934.
119. Cannon, *History of American Trotskyism,* 130–131.
120. *NYT,* January 29, 1934.
121. *NYHT,* February 1, 1934.
122. *NYHT,* February 2, 1934.
123. *NYT,* February 2, 1934.
124. *The Militant,* February 2, 1934.
125. *NYT,* February 4, 1934.
126. *NYT,* February 6, 1934.
127. *DW,* February 7, 1934.
128. *NYHT,* February 6, 1934.
129. *DW,* February 7, 1934; Chase, *Wonder City,* 124, 133.

130. *NYT,* February 6, 1934.
131. *DW,* February 5, 1934.
132. *NYT,* February 4, 1934.
133. *DW,* February 3, 1934.
134. *NYT,* February 7, 1934.
135. The 1,100-room hotel, opened in 1924, was not named for the current President but for his cousin Theodore Roosevelt. *NYHT,* February 11, 1934; Chase, *Wonder City,* 126.
136. *NYHT,* February 8, 1934.
137. *NYT,* February 8, 1934.
138. *NYHT,* February 9, 1934.
139. *NYT,* February 8, 1934.
140. *NYT,* February 10, 1934.
141. *NYHT,* February 11, 1934.
142. *NYT,* February 14, 1934.
143. *NYT,* February 15, 1934.
144. Cannon, *History of American Trotskyism,* 132–133.
145. *The Militant,* February 17, 1934.
146. *NYT,* February 16, 1934.
147. *DW,* February 16, 1934.
148. *NYHT,* February 16, 1934.
149. *DW,* February 12, 1934.
150. *NYHT,* February 17, 1934.
151. *NYT,* February 17, 1934.
152. *NYT,* February 18, 1934.
153. *DW,* February 19, 1934; *DW,* February 21, 1934.
154. *NYT,* February 20, 1934.
155. *DW,* February 21, 1934.
156. *NYT,* February 21, 1934.
157. *NYHT,* February 23, 1934.
158. *NYHT,* February 24, 1934.
159. *NYHT,* February 23, 1934.
160. *NYT,* February 22, 1934.
161. *NYT,* February 24, 1934.
162. *NYT,* February 23, 1934.
163. *NYT,* February 22, 1934.
164. *NYT,* February 23, 1934.
165. *NYT,* February 24, 1934.
166. *NYT,* February 27, 1934.
167. *NYT,* February 24, 1934.
168. *NYHT,* March 1, 1934.
169. *NYT,* March 1, 1934.
170. *DW,* March 5, 1934.
171. *FV* 15, no. 5 (May 1, 1934).
172. *FV* 15, no. 4 (April 1, 1934).
173. *FV* 15, no. 5 (May 1, 1934).
174. *FV* 11, no. 7 (July 1, 1930).
175. *FW,* April 1934.

176. *FW,* May 1934.
177. *FW,* May 1934.
178. *FW,* June 1934.
179. *FV* 15, no. 6 (June 1, 1934).
180. *FV* 15, no. 8 (August 1, 1934).
181. *FV* 15, no. 8 (August 1, 1934).
182. Stuart Bruce Kaufman, *A Vision of Unity: The History of the Bakery and Confectionary Workers International Union* (University of Illinois Press, 1987), 114.
183. *FW,* September 1934; *FV* 15, no. 8 (August 1, 1934).
184. *FW,* October–November 1934.
185. "Letter from M.M. Borodin to Comrade Sherman," RGASPI 495-261-373.
186. Jonathan Haslam, "The Comintern and the Origins of the Popular Front 1934–1935," *The Historical Journal* 22, no. 3 (1979), 673–691.
187. Victor G. Devinatz, "A Reevaluation of the Trade Unity League, 1929–1934," *Science & Society* 71, no. 1 (January 2007): 53.
188. *FV* 16, no. 1 (January 1, 1935).
189. The action was reported in the February issue, and the Hotel Branch ceased to appear in March.
190. Kaufman, *A Vision of Unity,* 114.
191. *FV* 16, no. 4 (April 1, 1935).

Chapter 6. An Industry Has Been Freed

1. *FW,* December 1936.
2. The Comintern's personnel files on Party activists mainly contain the paperwork related to his initial application to travel abroad but does not systematically keep track of each specific trip. Rubin's earlier 1934 trip was documented because M. M. Borodin, Editor-in-Chief of the *Moscow Daily News,* sent a letter to the American representative to the Comintern, requesting that Rubin's stay be extended by one year. "Questionnaire" and "Letter from M.M. Borodin to Comrade Sherman," RGASPI 495-261-373.
3. Howard Kimeldorf, *Reds or Rackets? The Making of Radical and Conservative Unions on the Waterfront* (University of California Press, 1988).
4. Josephson, *Union House,* 208.
5. Josephson, *Union House,* 200–201.
6. *Chicago Tribune,* December 1, 1922; Josephson, *Union House,* 212.
7. Josephson, *Union House,* 213.
8. Proceedings of the Twenty-Seventh General Convention. Hotel and Restaurant Employees' and Beverage Dispensers' International Alliance, Held at Minneapolis, Minn., Monday, August 13, 1934, 113–114.
9. *CIE* 43, no. 10 (October 12, 1934): 6.
10. David J. Saposs, *Communism in American Unions* (McGraw-Hill, 1959), 83; *CIE* 44, no. 10 (March 12, 1934): 29; *CIE* 45, no. 7 (July 12, 1936): 24–25; *CIE* 45, no. 10 (September 12, 1936): 17.
11. Rubin and Obermeier, *Growth of a Union,* 232.
12. *FW,* October–November 1934.
13. *NYT,* August 11, 1934.
14. Josephson, *Union House,* 219–221.

15. Jay Rubin, "Food Workers Strike and Unity Movement," Fond 515, Delo 3657, CPUSA Microfilm, Reel 284; Rubin and Obermeier, *Growth of a Union*, 232–233.

16. Josephson, *Union House*, 219–221.

17. *LU* 1, no. 9 (November 1934).

18. *FW*, December 1934.

19. *FW*, January 1935.

20. *FW*, May 1935; Rubin and Obermeier, *Growth of a Union*, 233.

21. Josephson, *Union House*, 1956, 221.

22. Stephen Kotkin, *Stalin: Waiting For Hitler, 1929–1941* (Penguin Press, 2017), 259–263.

23. Josephson, *Union House*, 206–207.

24. *DW*, July 27, 1929; *DW*, September 12, 1929.

25. Josephson, *Union House*, 176–179.

26. Rubin and Obermeier, *Growth of a Union*, 238.

27. *CIE* 45, no. 5 (June 12, 1935), 9–10.

28. *NYHT*, September 11, 1935.

29. Rubin and Obermeier, *Growth of a Union*, 240.

30. *FW*, September 1935.

31. "Shall the Trusteeship . . .," HERE General Office Legal Files on Microfilm, 1892–1984, Collection Number: 6199/010 mf, Reel 3, Cornell, 1534–1535.

32. *FW*, February 1935.

33. It was Volume 4, Issue 21, dated February–March 1936.

34. *NYHT*, July 2, 1935.

35. *NYT*, October 24, 1935; Stolberg, *Fighting Organized Crime*, 94–95.

36. Rubin and Obermeier, *Growth of a Union*, 240–241.

37. Rubin and Obermeier, *Growth of a Union*, 244.

38. Josephson, *Union House*, 226–227.

39. *CIE* 45, no. 7 (July 12, 1936): 24–25; Proceedings of the Twenty-Eighth General Convention of the Hotel and Restaurant Employees' International Alliance and Bartenders' International League of America, Held at Rochester, N.Y., Monday, August 10–15, 1936, 107–108.

40. Josephson, *Union House*, 229–230.

41. *NYT*, August 17, 1936.

42. *NYHT*, December 30, 1936.

43. *NYT*, October 24, 1935.

44. *NYHT*, March 7, 1935.

45. *NYHT*, November 13, 1933.

46. *NYHT*, October 21, 1936.

47. *NYT*, October 22, 1936.

48. *NYT*, October 24, 1936.

49. *NYT*, October 31, 1936.

50. *NYT*, December 12, 1936.

51. *NYT*, October 27, 1936.

52. WAG 148; Box 12; Folders 9 and 10, Tamiment/Wagner.

53. *NYHT*, December 30, 1936.

54. *NYHT*, January 18, 1937.

55. *NYHT*, January 19, 1937.

56. *NYT*, January 24, 1937; Stolberg, *Fighting Organized Crime*, 176–179.

57. Stolberg, *Fighting Organized Crime*, 180.
58. *NYT*, February 16, 1937.
59. Stolberg, *Fighting Organized Crime*, 182.
60. *NYT*, March 14, 1937.
61. Stolberg, *Fighting Organized Crime*, 183.
62. *NYT*, February 27, 1937.
63. Because Folsom confessed, there was no trial and therefore little surviving legal record. His story was recounted by the *Daily News'* "Justice Story" series a few weeks after Borson's name was raised in the trial. The main sources for that story were both self-aggrandizing fantasists; Folsom's story simply couldn't be trusted, and Lt. William Sullivan told a tale of pure copaganda. In it, Borson was "quoted" begging and praying for his life on his knees and spent a day or two in the hospital refusing to cooperate with police questioning, even though contemporaneous newspaper accounts of his slaying noted that he never regained consciousness in the hospital. *NYT*, February 17, 1937; *NYDN*, March 7, 1937.
64. *NYHT*, March 26, 1937.
65. *NYHT*, April 8, 1937.
66. *People of the State of New York v. James J. Hines, et al.*, 1938; New York County District Attorney indictments, 1883–1951; ACC-2015–012; Box 1014; Folder: Williams, John; Coulcher, et al.; Municipal Archives, City of New York.
67. *NYHT*, October 10, 1937.
68. *NYT*, April 17, 1937.
69. "Report of the Investigation Committee of Local 16," WAG.148; Box 4b; Folder 13, Tamiment/Wagner.
70. Horowitz, *New York Hotel Industry*, 28–29.
71. *NYT*, May 15, 1937.
72. *NYT*, June 27, 1937.
73. *NYT*, April 2, 1937.
74. "Statement of Jay Rubin, July 8, 1937," WAG.148; Box 33 Folder 14, Tamiment/Wagner.
75. Undated Press Release, WAG.148; Box 33 Folder 13, Tamiment/Wagner.
76. *HCV* 19, no. 9 (May 1959): 3.
77. 1940 Census record found on Ancestry.com.
78. *Amsterdam News*, February 19, 1938; *PM*, October 11, 1942; "Michael J. Obermeier, 100-NY-25590," FBI, 176.
79. DW, November 24, 1936; Jenny Carson, *A Matter of Moral Justice: Black Women Laundry Workers and the Fight for Justice* (University of Illinois Press, 2021), 38–40, 111.
80. *DW*, September 3, 1934; "Gertrude Lane, NY-100–51123," FBI, https://archive.org/details/GertrudeLaneFBI.
81. "Donald Frederic Tillman, 1912–2003," Ancestry.com, https://www.ancestrylibrary.com/family-tree/person/tree/78740913/person/77021286571/facts?_phsrc=CCg48&_phstart=successSource (accessed June 15, 2022).
82. "Martin Cody, 1910–1985," Ancestry.com. https://www.ancestrylibrary.com/family-tree/person/tree/6673565/person/210182172882/story (accessed June 15, 2022).
83. *The Hotel Worker* 1, no. 1 (April 1937), WAG 148; Box 33 Folder 13, Tamiment/Wagner.

84. "To All Shanty Employees,", "Independence," "To All Hotel Employees," "To All Hotel Bartenders and Bar Boys," "To All Hotel New Yorker Employees," "To All Pennsylvania Hotel Employees," "To All Employees of the Roosevelt," "To All Waldorf-Astoria Hotel Employees," WAG.148; Box 33, Folder 13, Tamiment/Wagner.

85. *NYT,* September 2, 1937.

86. *NYT,* September 23, 1937.

87. Josephson, *Union House,* 278.

88. Assorted flyers, WAG.148; Box 33, Folder 13, Tamiment/Wagner.

89. *NYT,* January 6, 1938.

90. Gene Ruffini, *Harry Van Arsdale Jr.: Labor's Champion* (M.E. Sharpe, 2003), 46–65; Debra E. Bernhardt and Rachel Bernstein, *Ordinary People, Extraordinary Lives: A Pictorial History of Working People in New York City* (New York University Press, 2000), 132–134.

91. "General Membership Meetings," WAG.148; Box 33, Folder 13, Tamiment/Wagner.

92. Horowitz, *The New York Hotel Industry,* 28–29.

93. David Witwer, "The Scandal of George Scalise: A Case Study in the Rise of Labor Racketeering in the 1930s," *Journal of Social History* 36, no. 4 (Summer 2003): 922–923.

94. David Witwer, "The Scandal of George Scalise," *Journal of Social History* 36, no. 4 (Summer 2003): 930.

95. *NYT,* February 8, 1936.

96. *NYT,* October 3, 1937.

97. David Witwer, "The Scandal of George Scalise," *Journal of Social History* 36, no. 4 (Summer 2003): 930–931.

98. *CIE* 46, no. 8 (August 1937): 4–5.

99. *CIE* 46, no. 10 (October 1937): 4–5.

100. "Meeting of the Board of Directors, October 15, 1937," WAG.148; Box 5; Folder 29, Tamiment/Wagner.

101. "Hotel, Restaurant and Cafeteria Employees Organization Committee Press Release," dated 10/21, WAG.148; Box 33, Folder 14, Tamiment/Wagner.

102. Horowitz, *New York Hotel Industry,* 29–30.

103. Corsa Hotel Files, New-York Historical Society.

104. Brecher, *Strike!,* 206.

105. Horowitz, *New York Hotel Industry,* 30.

106. Kessner, *La Guardia and the Making of Modern New York,* 398.

107. *NYT,* June 6, 1937.

108. Stanley Applebaum, *The New York World's Fair 1939/1940 in 155 Photographs by Richard Wurts and Others* (Dover Publications, 1977), ix.

109. "Meeting of the Board of Directors, December 10, 1937," 148; Box 5; Folder 29, Tamiment/Wagner.

110. *HCV* 6, no. 3 (June 23, 1945): 2.

111. Horowitz, *New York Hotel Industry,* 33.

112. This information is pieced together from factional campaign literature from later elections in Local 16. WAG 123; Box 7; Folder 15, Tamiment/Wagner.

113. Horowitz, *New York Hotel Industry,* 31.

114. Horowitz, *New York Hotel Industry,* 33.

Chapter 7. Status Quo

1. *NYHT,* March 21, 1939.
2. *NYT,* March 28, 1938; Horowitz, *New York Hotel Industry,* 241–242.
3. Horowitz, *New York Hotel Industry,* 33–34.
4. Horowitz, *New York Hotel Industry,* 241.
5. *DW,* January 20, 1938.
6. Proceedings of the Thirtieth General Convention of Hotel and Restaurant Employees' International Alliance and Bartenders' International League of America Held at Cincinnati, OH, U.S.A., April 21–26, 1941, 31–32.
7. "AGREEMENT made between Building Service Employees of America Local 32-A and Hotel and Club Employees Union Local 6," WAG.148; Box 5; Folder 29, Tamiment/Wagner.
8. Minutes, July 5, 1938, WAG 123; Box 1; Folder 1, Tamiment/Wagner.
9. Louis Budenz, *Men Without Faces* (Harper, 1948), 196–197.
10. *NYT,* June 8, 1938; *DW,* July 1, 1940.
11. Horowitz, *New York Hotel Industry,* 66–69.
12. Minutes, May 2, 1938, WAG 123; Box 1; Folder 1, Tamiment/Wagner.
13. Press Releases dated January 27, 1938, and May 19, WAG 123; Box 28; Folder 38, Tamiment/Wagner.
14. "Follow the Lead," WAG.148; Box 33; Folder 13; "To you workers of the above mentioned buildings," WAG 123; Box 25; Folder 35; "TO ALL FIFTH AVENUE HOTEL EMPLOYEES," WAG 123; Box 24; Folder 33, Tamiment/Wagner.
15. "Hotel Unions Certified," *NYT,* June 24, 1938.
16. Minutes, June 16, 1938, WAG 123; Box 1; Folder 1, Tamiment/Wagner.
17. *DW,* July 25, 1938.
18. Minutes, June 16, 1938; Minutes, July 18, 1938; Minutes, September 9, 1938," WAG 123; Box 1; Folder 1, Tamiment/Wagner.
19. *DW,* July 21, 1938.
20. *DW,* July 25, 1938.
21. Horowitz, *New York Hotel Industry,* 34.
22. July 7, 1938, circular, WAG.148; Box 11; Folder 2, Tamiment/Wagner.
23. Report of the Proceedings of the Twenty-Ninth General Convention of the Hotel and Restaurant Employees' International Alliance and Bartenders International League of America, Held at San Francisco, Calif., August 15–21, 1938; "Eckford Goes to Union Meet," *Amsterdam News,* August 6, 1938.
24. Cobble, *Dishing It Out,* 176–177.
25. Josephson, *Union House,* 250.
26. Proceedings of the Twenty-Ninth General Convention, 38, 42, 56–58; "Miguel Garriga, 62-HQ-60527 serial 30530," FBI, https://ia601506.us.archive.org/26/items/080103-miguel-garriga-foipa-1091412-000/080103MiguelGarriga_FOIPA 1091412-000.pdf; "Garriga, Miguel, 1938–1951," J. B. Matthews papers, 1862–1986 and undated, Box 606, Duke University Libraries Archives and Manuscripts.
27. Josephson, *Union House,* 253.
28. The whiskey ads were for the American Distilling Company of Illinois. *CIE* 46, no. 5 (May 1937): 57; *CIE* 46, no. 8 (August 1937): 34.
29. James Mishra, "The Dark History of the Jukebox," *Click Track: Music Industry Analysis,* May 15, 2020. https://www.clicktrack.fm/p/the-dark-history-of-the-jukebox-how?s=r (accessed March 17, 2022).

30. "How Gangsters Seized Union of Bartenders," *Chicago Tribune,* March 24, 1943; Josephson, *Union House,* 245.

31. Rubin and Obermeier, *Growth of a Union,* 276–277, 283.

32. Josephson, *Union House,* 245–254; Report of the Proceedings of the Twenty-Ninth General Convention, 114.

33. Josephson, *Union House,* 255.

34. Report of the Proceedings of the Twenty-Ninth General Convention, 142–143.

35. Josephson, *Union House,* 257–259.

36. Report of the Proceedings of the Twenty-Ninth General Convention, 143–147.

37. *CIE* 48, no. 7 (October 1938): 40.

38. *Chicago Tribune,* May 30, 1940.

39. *Chicago Tribune,* March 24, 1943; *Chicago Tribune,* August 26, 1959.

40. Minutes, June 16, 1938, WAG 123; Box 1; Folder 1, Tamiment/Wagner; Chase, *Wonder City,* 133.

41. Minutes, July 5, 1938, WAG 123; Box 1; Folder 1, Tamiment/Wagner; Horowitz, *New York Hotel Industry,* 36.

42. *NYT,* November 2, 1938.

43. *NYT,* November 27, 1938.

44. *NYT,* December 2, 1938.

45. *NYT,* December 28, 1938; *NYHT,* December 28, 1938.

46. *NYT,* December 29, 1938; *NYHT,* December 29, 1938; Horowitz, *New York Hotel Industry,* 36–37.

47. *NYT,* December 30, 1938.

48. *NYT,* December 28, 1938.

49. Horowitz, *New York Hotel Industry*, 45.

50. Horowitz, *New York Hotel Industry*, 38.

51. "Agreement made this 18th day of Jan., 1939," WAG.148; Box 33; Folder 21, Tamiment/Wagner.

52. "For Release Friday Jan. 27," WAG 123; Box 27; Folder 31, Tamiment/Wagner; Corsa Hotel Files, New-York Historical Society and Hotel Files in Hotel Trades Council files.

53. "Shop Delegates Class, March 4, 1943," WAG 123, Box 3, Folder 5.

54. *NYHT,* March 4, 1939.

55. *NYT,* March 4, 1939; Corsa Hotel Files, New-York Historical Society.

56. *NYHT,* March 5, 1939; *NYHT,* March 6, 1939; March 6, 1939, Press Release, WAG 123; Box 25; Folder 54, Tamiment/Wagner.

57. *NYHT,* March 22, 1939.

58. April 5 Press Release, WAG 123; Box 25; Folder 8; Minutes, March 30, 1939, WAG 123; Box 1; Folder 2, Tamiment/Wagner.

59. Ruffini, *Harry Van Arsdale Jr,* 73; Minutes, April 8, 1939, WAG 123; Box 1; Folder 2, Tamiment/Wagner.

60. *HCV* 12, no. 39 (March 8, 1952).

61. Horowitz, *New York Hotel Industry*, 81.

62. Carson, *A Matter of Moral Justice.*

63. Minutes, March 30, 1939, and April 8, 1939, WAG 123; Box 1; Folder 2, Tamiment/Wagner.

64. Horowitz, *New York Hotel Industry,* 70–71; *Local 6 News* 1, no. 4 (January 29, 1941): 4; *DW,* January 13, 1940; September 6, 1939, Telegram, The Records of Mayor

Fiorello H. La Guardia, 1934–1945, Collection No. 0028, New York City Municipal Archives, Box 253, Folder 8, Reel 116.

65. *DW,* October 30, 1940; Horowitz, *New York Hotel Industry,* 70–71.
66. Press Release April 7, WAG 123; Box 29; Folder 12, Tamiment/Wagner.
67. Press Releases April 14 and June 15, WAG 123; Box 24; Folder 23, Tamiment/Wagner.
68. "Join the Big Parade!," WAG 123; Box 25; Folder 35, Tamiment/Wagner.
69. Report of the New York State Labor Relations Board For the Period From July 1, 1937 to December 31, 1939, 124–125.
70. *HCV* 1, no. 46 (April 28, 1941); Notes, WAG 123; Box 24; Folder 27, Tamiment/Wagner.
71. *NYHT,* February 28, 1948.
72. *NYT,* August 17, 1939.
73. Horowitz, *New York Hotel Industry,* 40–41.
74. *NYT,* August 6, 1939; Horowitz, *New York Hotel Industry,* 40.
75. *NYHT,* August 8, 1939.
76. *NYHT,* August 10, 1939.
77. Alexander Woollcott, August 9, 1939, and Orson Welles, August 10, 1939, WAG 123; Box 21; Folder 19, Tamiment/Wagner.
78. October 4, 1939, Press Release, WAG 123; Box 21; Folder 19, Tamiment/Wagner.
79. Horowitz, *New York Hotel Industry,* 36–37.
80. *CIE* 48, no. 7 (July 12, 1939): 22.
81. *CIE* 50, no. 3 (March 1941): 26.
82. *Local 6 News* 1, no. 1 (November 1939): 2.
83. *Local 6 News* 1, no. 2 (December 1939): 2.
84. "In re Mayflower Hotel, December 14, 1939," "In re Whitehall Hotel, January 3, 1940," WAG 123; Box 10; Folder 1, Tamiment/Wagner.
85. "In the Matter of Benito Huamani," WAG 123; Box 10; Folder 1, Tamiment/Wagner; "In re Park Central Hotel," WAG 123; Box 10; Folder 3, Tamiment/Wagner.
86. *HCV* 1, no. 4 (July 6, 1940): 8.
87. *NYT,* October 13, 1939.
88. WAG 123; Box 25; Folder 11, Tamiment/Wagner.
89. *Local 6 News* 1, no. 4 (January 29, 1940): 2.
90. *Local 6 News* 1, no. 3 (December 23, 1939).

Chapter 8. Only the Question of Final Alliances Remains

1. Proceedings of the Thirtieth General Convention of Hotel and Restaurant Employees' International Alliance and Bartenders' International League of America Held at Cincinnati, Ohio, U.S.A., April 21–26, 1941, 161, 163.
2. Maurice Isserman, *Which Side Were You On? The American Communist Party During the Second World War* (Wesleyan University Press, 1982), 37.
3. Lore, *Firebrand,* 199.
4. Kotkin, *Waiting For Hitler,* 659–663.
5. Irving Howe and Lewis Coser, *The American Communist Party: A Critical History* (Praeger, 1962), 387.
6. Isserman, *Which Side Were You On?,* 32–54.
7. *CIE* 49, no. 8 (August 1940): 25.

8. "Miguel Garriga, 62-HQ-60527 serial 30530," FBI, https://archive.org/details/MiguelGarrigaFBI; "Garriga, Miguel, 1938–1951," J. B. Matthews Papers, 1862–1985, Box 606, David M. Rubenstein Rare Book & Manuscript Library, Duke University; *DW,* June 7, 1939; *DW,* August 4, 1939.

9. *HCV* 1, no. 30 (January 4, 1941).

10. *Local 6 News* 1, no. 4 (January 29, 1940): 4.

11. *Socialist Appeal* 4, no. 26 (June 29, 1940); *CIE* 49, no. 8 (August 1940): 37.

12. *CIE* 50, no. 5 (May 1941): 42.

13. Minutes, January 13, 1940, WAG 148; Box 1; Folder 3.

14. Philip Taft, *The A.F. of L. From the Death of Gompers to the Merger* (Harper & Brothers, 1959), 207.

15. *HCV* 1, no. 1 (June 15, 1940).

16. *HCV* 1, no. 9 (August 10, 1940).

17. *HCV* 1, no. 15 (September 21, 1940): 3.

18. *American Federationist* 47, no. 4 (October 1940): 3.

19. "Jay Rubin, 100-HQ-52865," FBI, https://archive.org/details/JayRubinFBI, 166.

20. Joseph R. Starobin, *American Communism in Crisis,* 1943–1957 (Harvard University Press, 1972), 40–41.

21. *HCV* 1, no. 11 (August 24, 1940); *HCV* 1, no. 42 (March 29, 1941).

22. Isidor Lubin and Charles Pearce, "New York's Minimum Wage Law: The First Twenty Years," *Industrial and Labor Relations Review* 11, no. 2 (January 1958): 203–219.

23. *HCV* 1, no. 1 (June 15, 1940); *HCV* 1, no. 13 (September 7, 1940); "Hotel Wage Minimum," *NYT,* November 23, 1940.

24. *Local 6 News* 1, no. 4 (January 1940); *HCV* 1, no. 30 (January 4, 1941).

25. *HCV* 2, no. 1 (June 14, 1941).

26. "First Annual Frolic," WAG 148; Box 34; Folder 14, Tamiment/Wagner; *Local 6 News* 1, no. 2 (December 1939); *HCV* 1, no. 22 (November 9, 1940).

27. *HCV* 1, no. 28 (December 21, 1940).

28. *HCV* 1, no. 8 (August 3, 1940); *HCV* 1, no. 9 (August 10, 1940).

29. *HCV* 1, no. 37 (February 22, 1941).

30. *HCV* 6, no. 7 (July 21, 1945).

31. *HCV* 1, no. 3 (June 29, 1940).

32. *CIE* 49, no. 6 (June 1940): 35.

33. *HCV* 1, no. 1 (June 15, 1940); *HCV* 1, no. 5 (July 13, 1940); *Amsterdam News,* June 8, 1940.

34. *HCV* 1, no. 6 (July 20, 1940).

35. *NYHT,* April 9, 1940.

36. *CIE* 49, no. 6 (June 1940): 35.

37. *HCV* 1, no. 34 (February 1, 1941).

38. Luff, *Commonsense Anticommunism,* 166–167.

39. *Chicago Tribune,* May 13, 1938.

40. *DW,* August 16, 1938.

41. Isserman, *Which Side Were You On?,* 48.

42. *NYT,* February 18, 1941.

43. U.S. Congress, House of Representatives, Special Committee on Un-American Activities. "Investigation of Un-American Propaganda Activities." September 7,

1939, p. 4715. https://archive.org/details/investigationofu194007unit/page/4714/mode/2up.

44. U.S. Congress, House of Representatives, Special Committee on Un-American Activities. "Investigation of Un-American Propaganda Activities." October 13, 1939, p. 5761. https://archive.org/details/investigationofu193909unit/page/5760/mode/2up.

45. *NYHT,* January 15, 1941; *NYT,* January 15, 1941.

46. *NYT,* November 17, 1940.

47. Kraut, *Threat of Dissent,* 108–110.

48. Westbrook Pegler, "Fair Enough," *The Atlanta Constitution,* January 20, 1940.

49. *NYT,* March 2, 1940; "Your Chance to Start the Parade," "To All Hotel St. George Employees," WAG 123; Box 29; Folder 1, Tamiment/Wagner.

50. May 2, 1940, Minutes, WAG 123; Box 1; Folder 2, Tamiment/Wagner.

51. *NYT,* March 10, 1940.

52. *NYT,* April 22, 1940.

53. *NYT,* August 13, 1940.

54. *NYT,* April 29, 1940.

55. *DW,* May 14, 1940.

56. *DW,* May 8, 1940.

57. Horowitz, *New York Hotel Industry,* 74–75.

58. *DW,* May 14, 1940.

59. *NYHT,* September 20, 1940.

60. *NYHT,* May 8, 1940.

61. *NYHT,* May 6, 1940.

62. *NYHT,* August 21, 1940.

63. *NYHT,* September 4, 1940.

64. *NYT,* September 15, 1940.

65. Horowitz, *New York Hotel Industry,* 75.

66. *DW,* January 18, 1941.

67. *CIE* 49, no. 4 (April 1940): 15.

68. Proceedings of the Thirtieth General Convention, 20.

69. "Central Trades and Labor Council Investigation of Hotel and Restaurant Union, Transcript," Board of Education Series 591 Subject Files, Municipal Archive, City of New York.

70. Proceedings of the Thirtieth General Convention, 205.

71. Proceedings of the Thirtieth General Convention, 106–108, 233–246.

72. Proceedings of the Thirtieth General Convention, 161.

73. Proceedings of the Thirtieth General Convention, 90–91.

74. Analysis based upon pages 5–8, 181–183, 253–264 of Proceedings of the Thirtieth General Convention.

75. Andrew E. Kersten, *Labor's Home Front: The American Federation of Labor During World War II* (New York University Press, 2006), 44.

76. *HCV* 2, no. 10 (August 16, 1941).

77. *CIE* 50, no. 9 (September 1941): 29.

78. 1943 Bylaws, WAG.148; Box 5; Folder 35; *HCV* 2, no. 24 (November 22, 1941).

79. *HCV* 2, no. 34 (January 31, 1942).

80. "Gertrude Lane, 100-NY-51123," FBI, https://archive.org/details/GertrudeLaneFBI, 10, 20.

81. Yes, this is the philanthropist Donald Rubin, founder of the Rubin Museum of Art. The information about Mollie Rubin is found in the 1940 census records and Jay Rubin's military draft card on Ancestry.com.

82. "Gertrude Lane, 100-NY-51123," FBI, 8; "Jay Rubin, 100-HQ-52865," FBI, https://archive.org/details/JayRubinFBI, 40–41.

83. *HCV* 2, no. 34 (January 31, 1942); *HCV* 2, no. 35 (February 7, 1942).

84. *HCV* 2, no. 3 (June 28, 1941); *HCV* 2, no. 4 (July 5, 1941).

85. *HCV* 2, no. 15 (September 20, 1941): 1.

86. *HCV* 2, no. 17 (October 4, 1941): 1; *HCV* 2, no. 18 (October 11, 1941): 1.

87. *HCV* 2, no. 9 (August 9, 1941); *HCV* 2, no. 10 (August 16, 1941); *HCV* 2, no. 12 (August 30, 1941).

88. *HCV* 2, no. 18 (October 11, 1941).

89. *HCV* 2, no. 15 (September 20, 1941): 1; *HCV* 2, no. 11 (August 23, 1941); *HCV* 2, no. 12 (August 30, 1941); *HCV* 2, no. 13 (September 6, 1941); *HCV* 2, no. 14 (September 13, 1941); *HCV* 2, no. 17 (October 4, 1941).

90. *HCV* 2, no. 18 (October 11, 1941).

91. *HCV* 2, no. 20 (October 25, 1941): 1; *CIE* 49, no. 8 (August 1940): 34.

92. *HCV* 2, no. 15 (September 20, 1941): 1.

93. *HCV* 2, no. 19 (October 18, 1941).

94. *HCV* 2, no. 20 (October 25, 1941).

95. *HCV* 2, no. 25 (November 29, 1941); *HCV* 2, no. 27 (December 13, 1941).

Chapter 9. We Cook, Serve, Work for Victory

1. *HCV* 5, no. 16 (September 23, 1944).

2. Nelson Lichtenstein, *Labor's War at Home: The CIO in World War II* (Cambridge University Press, 1982), x.

3. Nelson Lichtenstein, *The Most Dangerous Man in Detroit: Walter Reuther and the Fate of American Labor* (Basic Books, 1995), 282.

4. *CIE* 51, no. 1 (January 1942): 37.

5. *HCV* 2, no. 37 (February 21, 1942): 8.

6. *HCV* 2, no. 28 (December 20, 1941): 1.

7. *HCV* 2, no. 32 (January 17, 1942): 1.

8. *DW,* January 22, 1942.

9. *CIE* 51, no. 5 (May 1942): 25.

10. *HCV* 2, no. 29 (December 29, 1941).

11. *HCV* 2, no. 33 (January 24, 1942): 1.

12. Horowitz, *New York Hotel Industry*, 46–47.

13. January 15, 1942, Minutes, WAG 123; Box 1; Folder 5.

14. Isserman, *Which Side Were You On?*, 145–147, 180–181.

15. *HCV* 3, no. 22 (November 7, 1942); *HCV* 4, no. 31 (January 8, 1944); *CIE* 52, no. 7 (July 1943): 44.

16. "Shall the Trusteeship . . .," HERE General Office Legal Files on Microfilm, 1892–1984, Collection Number: 6199/010 mf, Reel 3, Cornell, 1546–1548.

17. "John Steuben, 100-HQ-21445," FBI, https://archive.org/details/200212john steuben1459221000, 18–23; "Application for Permission to Leave the United States," RGASPI 495-261-6022; WAG.148; Box 5; Folder 25, Tamiment/Wagner; White, *The Last Great Strike,* 3, 232–233, 246; "John Steuben, 50, Red Labor Leader," *NYT,* May 10, 1957.

18. *HCV* 4, no. 9 (August 7, 1943); *HCV* 11, no. 50 (May 26, 1951).
19. Isserman, *Which Side Were You On?*, 145–147, 182–183.
20. "Brief on Behalf of Michael J. Obermeier Before the Board of Immigration Appeals, Department of Justice of the United States," WAG 148, Box 14, Folder 4, Tamiment/Wagner.
21. Isserman, *Which Side Were You On?*, 127–133, 205, 145–147, 174–175.
22. *HCV* 3, no. 5 (July 11, 1942): 1; *CIE* 51, no. 11 (November 1942): 40.
23. *DW*, August 23, 1942; *NYHT*, November 23, 1953; *HCV* 3, no. 22 (November 7, 1942): 7.
24. *HCV* 3, no. 9 (August 8, 1942): 1.
25. *HCV* 1, no. 20 (October 26, 1940); *CIE* 51, no. 11 (November 1942): 22; *HCV* 3, no. 39 (March 6, 1943); *HCV* 2, no. 45 (April 18, 1942): 1.
26. *CIE* 54, no. 10 (October 1945): 18.
27. *HCV* 2, no. 50 (May 23, 1942): 1; *HCV* 3, no. 17 (October 3, 1942): 1.
28. *CIE* 51, no. 6 (August 1942): 41.
29. *HCV* 5, no. 1 (June 10, 1944).
30. *HCV* 6, no. 5 (July 7, 1945): 1.
31. "Michael J. Obermeier, 100-HQ-96104," FBI, https://archive.org/details/MichaelJObermeierFBI1, 7–8.
32. "Michael J. Obermeier, 100-HQ-96104," FBI, https://archive.org/details/MichaelJObermeierFBI1, 14–15.
33. "Ludwig Lore, Commentator, Columnist, Dies," *NYHT*, July 9, 1942.
34. "Michael J. Obermeier, 100-HQ-96104," FBI, https://archive.org/details/MichaelJObermeierFBI1, 88.
35. The name is redacted, but the description would match that of Louis Budenz who would not publicly break with the Party until 1945, suggesting that he was secretly informing on Party activists for at least two years prior.
36. "Michael J. Obermeier, 100-HQ-96104," FBI, https://archive.org/details/MichaelJObermeierFBI1, 15–27.
37. "Michael J. Obermeier, 100-HQ-96104," FBI, https://archive.org/details/MichaelJObermeierFBI1, 59–62.
38. "Jay Rubin, NY-100-52865," FBI, https://archive.org/details/JayRubinFBI, 7, 80.
39. *HCV* 2, no. 37 (February 21, 1942): 1; *HCV* 3, no. 11 (August 22, 1942).
40. March 6, 1942, Minutes, WAG 123; Box 1; Folder 6.
41. *HCV* 2, no. 33 (January 24, 1942): 1.
42. *HCV* 2, no. 37 (February 21, 1942): 1.
43. *HCV* 2, no. 41 (March 21, 1942): 1.
44. March 6, 1942, Minutes, April 22, 1942, Minutes, WAG 123; Box 1; Folder 6.
45. *HCV* 3, no. 41 (March 21, 1942); *HCV* 3, no. 42 (March 28, 1942).
46. April 23, 1942, Council Minutes, WAG 123; Box 1; Folder 6.
47. *HCV* 3, no. 7 (July 25, 1942).
48. *NYT*, July 12, 1941.
49. *HCV* 3, no. 8 (August 1, 1942): 1.
50. July 10, 1942, Minutes, WAG 123; Box 1; Folder 6; *HCV* 3, no. 4 (July 4, 1942).
51. July 10, 1942, Minutes, WAG 123; Box 1; Folder 6; *HCV* 3, no. 5 (July 11, 1942).
52. July 31, 1942, Minutes, July 10, 1942, Minutes, WAG 123; Box 1, Folder 6; *HCV* 3, no. 9 (August 8, 1942); *HCV* 3, no. 11 (August 22, 1942).

53. July 10, 1942, Minutes, WAG 123; Box 1, Folder 6.
54. "Employer-Employee Relations," Fourth Edition, revised and reprinted 1939 (The Waldorf-Astoria Corporation).
55. *HCV* 5, no. 30 (December 30, 1944).
56. *HCV* 2, no. 32 (January 17, 1942).
57. "In the Matter of Hotel Waldorf-Astoria Corporation and International Brotherhood of Electrical Workers, Local 3, A.F. of L., Decision No. 907—June 5, 1940," *Decisions and Orders of the New York State Labor Relations Board,* Vol. 3, March 1, 1940–December 31, 1941, 338–342.
58. *HCV* 2, no. 39 (March 7, 1942).
59. *HCV* 2, no. 44 (April 11, 1942).
60. October 22, 1942, Minutes, July 10, 1942, Minutes, WAG 123; Box 1, Folder 6.
61. *NYT,* October 28, 1942.
62. "In the Matter of Hotel Waldorf-Astoria Corporation and New York Hotel Trades Council, AFL, Decision No. 2301—December 30, 1942," *Decisions and Orders of the New York State Labor Relations Board,* Vol. 5, January 1, 1942–December 31, 1942, 1385–1386.
63. *HCV* 3, no. 35 (February 6, 1943); *HCV* 3, no. 32 (January 16, 1942); *HCV* 3, no. 25 (November 28, 1942); *HCV* 3, no. 25 (November 28, 1942).
64. *HCV* 3, no. 33 (January 23, 1943); *HCV* 3, no. 36 (February 13, 1943); *HCV* 3, no. 41 (March 20, 1943).
65. *HCV* 3, no. 3 (June 27, 1942).
66. *HCV* 3, no. 33 (January 23, 1943); *HCV* 3, no. 37 (February 20, 1943).
67. *HCV* 3, no. 20 (October 24, 1942).
68. *HCV* 3, no. 36 (February 13, 1943); *HCV* 3, no. 37 (February 20, 1943).
69. *HCV* 3, no. 40 (March 13, 1943).
70. *HCV* 3, no. 35 (February 6, 1943).
71. Horowitz, *New York Hotel Industry,* 46.
72. *HCV* 3, no. 6 (July 18, 1942): 1.
73. Horowitz, *New York Hotel Industry,* 50–51.
74. Lichtenstein, *Labor's War At Home,* 72.
75. Lichtenstein, *Labor's War At Home,* 46.
76. Joseph C. Goulden, *Meany: Unchallenged Strongman of American Labor* (Atheneum, 1972), 86.
77. *CIE* 51, no. 1 (January 1942): 2.
78. Lichtenstein, *Labor's War At Home,* 71–72.
79. *HCV* 3, no. 24 (November 21, 1942).
80. *HCV* 3, no. 13 (October 17, 1942): 1.
81. "Research Section Memorandum, November 17, 1942," Sidney Cohn letter October 29, 1942," "David Drechsler letter October 29, 1942," RG202/National War Labor Board (WW II), Dispute Case Files: File 4167 Hotel Assn. of New York-As Tabbed, National Archives at College Park, College Park, MD.
82. Horowitz, *New York Hotel Industry,* 52.
83. "Theodore W. Kheel letter, attached to Minutes of February 11, 1943," WAG 123; Box 1; Folder 5; "Sidney Cohn letter, December 4, 1942," RG202/National War Labor Board (WW II), Dispute Case Files: File 4167 Hotel Assn. of New York-As Tabbed, National Archives at College Park, College Park, MD; *HCV* 3, no. 36 (February 13, 1943).

84. *HCV* 3, no. 38 (February 27, 1943): 1; *HCV* 3, no. 43 (April 3, 1943); *HCV* 6, no. 1 (June 9, 1945).
85. *HCV* 3, no. 39 (March 6, 1943): 1.
86. Horowitz, *New York Hotel Industry*, 52.
87. *HCV* 4, no. 7 (July 24, 1943): 1.
88. Horowitz, *New York Hotel Industry*, 52.
89. *CIE* 52, no. 10 (October 1943): 42.
90. Horowitz, *New York Hotel Industry*, 53; *HCV* 4, no. 13 (September 4, 1943): 1.
91. *HCV* 5, no. 37 (February 17, 1945): 8.
92. *HCV* 4, no. 51 (May 27, 1944).
93. *CIE* 44, no. 6 (July 12, 1935): 29.
94. *HCV* 2, no. 40 (March 14, 1942): 3; *HCV* 4, no. 12 (August 28, 1943): 3.
95. *HCV* 1, no. 9 (August 10, 1940).
96. *HCV* 5, no. 3 (June 24, 1944).
97. *HCV* 5, no. 4 (July 1, 1944).
98. *HCV* 5, no. 16 (September 23, 1944); *HCV* 5, no. 19 (October 14, 1944).
99. Horowitz, *New York Hotel Industry*, 203.
100. *HCV* 6, no. 6 (July 14, 1945): 1.
101. Rubin and Obermeier, *Growth of a Union*, 122–123.
102. Rubin and Obermeier, *Growth of a Union*, 290–291.
103. Rubin and Obermeier, *Growth of a Union*, 81, 314.
104. *NY World-Telegram*, May 25, 1944.
105. *HCV* 4, no. 47 (April 29, 1944).
106. *CIE* 53, no. 5 (May 1944): 13.
107. *NY World-Telegram*, May 25, 1944.
108. "Copy of a Letter to John J. Kearny, April 29, 1944," WAG.148; Box 33; Folder 20, Tamiment/Wagner.
109. Isserman, *Which Side Were You On?*, 217–218.
110. Isserman, *Which Side Were You On?*, 226–229, 233–234.
111. Isserman, *Which Side Were You On?*, 221.
112. *CIE* 54, no. 7 (July 1945): 24.
113. Isserman, *Which Side Were You On?*, 218–220.
114. Jon V. Kofas, "U.S. Foreign Policy and the World Federation of Trade Unions, 1944–1948," *Diplomatic History* 26, no. 1 (Winter 2002).
115. Ted Morgan, *A Covert Life* (Random House, 1999), 152.
116. *HCV* 5, no. 34 (January 27, 1945); *HCV* 5, no. 35 (February 3, 1945).
117. *HCV* 6, no. 8 (July 28, 1945): 1.
118. *HCV* 6, no. 2 (June 16, 1945): 2.
119. *HCV* 5, no. 38 (February 24, 1945).
120. April 26, 1945, Minutes, WAG 123; Box 1; Folder 8.
121. *HCV* 5, no. 47 (April 28, 1945); *HCV* 5, no. 48 (May 5, 1945).
122. *HCV* 5, no. 50 (May 19, 1945); *HCV* 6, no. 4 (June 30, 1945).
123. *HCV* 6, no. 8 (July 28, 1945).
124. *HCV* 6, no. 12 (September 1, 1945); *HCV* 6, no. 14 (September 15, 1945).
125. *HCV* 5, no. 24 (November 18, 1944).
126. "In the Matter of Hotel Waldorf-Astoria Corporation and Hotel & Club Employees Union, Local 6, A.F. of L., Decision No. 3053—July 13, 1945," *Decisions and*

Orders of the New York State Labor Relations Board, Vol. 8, January 1, 1945–December 31, 1945, 315–321.

127. "In the Matter of Hotel Waldorf-Astoria Corporation and Upholsterers, Decorators & Allied Craftsmen, Local 44, Women Upholsterers Union, Local 45, A.F. of L., Decision No. 2898—December 21, 1944," *Decisions and Orders of the New York State Labor Relations Board,* Vol. 7, January 1, 1944–December 31, 1944, 273–280.

128. *HCV* 5, no. 37 (February 17, 1945).
129. *HCV* 6, no. 9 (August 4, 1945): 1; *HCV* 6, no. 15 (September 22, 1945): 1.
130. *CIE* 54, no. 8 (August 1945): 19.
131. *CIE* 54, no. 10 (October 1945): 2, 8.

Chapter 10. In Normal Order

1. *NYHT,* September 9, 1947.
2. Kraut, *Threat of Dissent,* 122–123.
3. *HCV* 6, no. 13 (September 8, 1945): 1; *HCV* 6, no. 15 (September 22, 1945): 1; *HCV* 6, no. 22 (November 17, 1945): 1; September 13, 1945, Minutes, WAG 123; Box 1; Folder 8, Tamiment/Wagner.
4. *HCV* 6, no. 27 (December 15, 1945): 1; *HCV* 6, no. 28 (December 22, 1945): 1.
5. *CIE* 55, no. 4 (April 1946): 18; *HCV* 6, no. 28 (December 22, 1945): 1; *HCV* 6, no. 42 (March 30, 1946): 1, 4.
6. *HCV* 6, no. 26 (December 8, 1945): 3.
7. *HCV* 7, no. 15 (September 21, 1946): 3.
8. *HCV* 7, no. 20 (October 26, 1946): 8.
9. *HCV* 6, no. 13 (September 8, 1945); *HCV* 6, no. 14 (September 15, 1945).
10. *HCV* 6, no. 24 (November 30, 1945).
11. *HCV* 7, no. 4 (July 6, 1946).
12. "The Stabilization of Wages in the Reconversion Period, May 1945-April 1946," National Wage Stabilization Board, Washington, DC, May 1, 1946.
13. July 19, 1945, Minutes; November 2, 1945, Minutes; WAG 123; Box 1; Folder 8, Tamiment/Wagner.
14. *CIE* 55, no. 1 (January 1946): 31–32; *HCV* 6, no. 28 (December 22, 1945): 1, 8; *HCV* 6, no. 30 (January 5, 1946): 1; *HCV* 6, no. 34 (February 2, 1946); Horowitz, *New York Hotel Industry,* 56–57.
15. Horowitz, *New York Hotel Industry,* 57.
16. Brecher, *Strike!,* 228.
17. Joshua B. Freeman, *Working Class New York: Life and Labor Since World War II* (The New Press, 2000), 4–7.
18. April 25, 1946, Minutes, WAG 123; Box 1; Folder 9, Tamiment/Wagner.
19. Horowitz, *New York Hotel Industry,* 57.
20. *HCV* 7, no. 7 (July 27, 1946).
21. Garriga transferred his membership to Bartenders Local 15 and Blanchard continued her work with the WTUL and became a legislative representative for the Amalgamated Clothing Workers.
22. *CIE* 55, no. 3 (March 1946), 29; *HCV* 6, no. 35 (February 9, 1946).
23. *HCV* 6, no. 17 (October 6, 1945): 8.
24. *HCV* 7, no. 5 (July 13, 1946): 8.
25. *HCV* 6, no. 37 (February 23, 1946): 1.

26. *HCV* 6, no. 49 (May 18, 1946): 1.

27. *HCV* 7, no. 29 (December 28, 1946): 4.

28. In an age when the fastest communication technology was landline telephones and telegrams, such meetings were nearly impossible to reschedule on short notice. NYHTC gave her special dispensation to proceed with her press interviews. Joan Crawford, April 29, 1940, Letter, WAG 123; Box 25; Folder 29, Tamiment/Wagner.

29. *HCV* 7, no. 16 (September 28, 1946): 1.

30. *HCV* 6, no. 14 (September 15, 1945): 1.

31. *HCV* 6, no. 25 (December 1, 1945): 1; May 13, 1946, Minutes, WAG 123; Box 1; Folder 9, Tamiment/Wagner.

32. *HCV* 6, no. 19 (October 27, 1945): 4; *HCV* 6, no. 27 (December 15, 1945): 7; *HCV* 6, no. 32 (January 19, 1946): 4; *HCV* 6, no. 31 (January 12, 1946): 4.

33. *NYHT,* January 22, 1946.

34. *HCV* 7, no. 37 (February 23, 1946): 4.

35. *HCV* 8, no. 7 (July 27, 1946): 2.

36. *HCV* 8, no. 20 (October 26, 1946): 1.

37. *HCV* 6, no. 9 (August 4, 1945): 3.

38. *HCV* 6, no. 17 (October 6, 1945): 3.

39. *HCV* 7, no. 2 (June 22, 1946): 2.

40. *HCV* 7, no. 21 (November 2, 1946): 1–2.

41. *HCV* 7, no. 24 (November 23, 1946): 1.

42. *HCV* 6, no. 45 (April 20, 1946): 1.

43. *Amsterdam News,* May 4, 1946.

44. *NYT,* October 8, 1946; *CIE* 55, no. 11 (November 1946): 29–31.

45. *NYT,* October 6, 1946.

46. Philip Dery, "'A Blot Upon Liberty': McCarthyism, Dr. Barsky and the Joint Anti-Fascist Refugee Committee," *American Communist History* 8, no. 2 (2009): fn 6.

47. *NYT,* December 21, 1945; *NYT,* March 29, 1946; *NYT,* April 1, 1947; Philip Dery, "'A Blot Upon Liberty': McCarthyism, Dr. Barsky and the Joint Anti-Fascist Refugee Committee," *American Communist History* 8, no. 2 (2009): 173–175.

48. *HCV* 7, no. 3 (June 15, 1946): 1.

49. *HCV* 7, no. 13 (September 7, 1946): 4.

50. *Amsterdam News,* August 3, 1946; *HCV* 7, no. 22 (November 9, 1946): 1.

51. Murolo and Chitty, *From the Folks Who Brought You the Weekend,* 231–240.

52. *HCV* 7, no. 23 (November 16, 1946): 4; *HCV* 7, no. 14 (September 14, 1946): 2.

53. *NYT,* August 19, 1946; *HCV* 7, no. 11 (August 24, 1946); *HCV* 7, no. 12 (August 31, 1946): 2.

54. *HCV* 9, no. 17 (October 2, 1948): 1; "Michael J. Obermeier, NY-100–25590," FBI, 62.

55. "Michael J. Obermeier, NY-100–25774," FBI, 23–26.

56. Kraut, *Threat of Dissent,* 107–116.

57. "Michael J. Obermeier, NY-100–25590," FBI, 129, 176.

58. *CIE* 52, no. 2 (January 1943): 42; *DW,* December 11, 1942; *DW,* December 31, 1942.

59. "William Albertson, 65-HQ-38100," FBI, https://archive.org/details/201221-william-albertson-foipa-148425-000_202012/mode/2up, 414–415, 421–423.

60. *CIE* 52, no. 8 (August 1943): 42–43; *CIE* 53, no. 12 (December 1944): 6; *CIE* 55, no. 4 (April 1946): 12–13; *CIE* 52, no. 10 (October 1943): 37; *CIE* 55, no. 6 (June 1946): 38–39.

61. *CIE* 53, no. 12 (December 1944): 6; *CIE* 54, no. 12 (December 1945): 6; *CIE* 55, no. 4 (April 1946): 12–13.

62. *CIE* 55, no. 3 (March 1946): 18.

63. *HCV* 6, no. 40 (March 16, 1946): 1, 8.

64. March 28, 1946, Minutes, WAG 123; Box 1; Folder 9, Tamiment/Wagner.

65. *HCV* 11, no. 18 (October 7, 1950): 1, 8.

66. "Michael J. Obermeier, 100-HQ-96104," FBI, https://archive.org/details/MichaelJObermeierFBI1, 209–220.

67. Proceedings of the Thirty-First General Convention Hotel and Restaurant Employees' International Alliance and Bartenders' International League of America, Milwaukee, Wis., April 4–11, 1947, 44–45.

68. "Central Trades and Labor Council Investigation of Hotel and Restaurant Union, transcript," Board of Education Series 591 Subject Files, Municipal Archive, City of New York.

69. "Shall the Trusteeship . . .," HERE General Office Legal Files on Microfilm, 1892–1984, Collection Number: 6199/010 mf, Reel 3, Cornell, 1553.

70. "Central Trades and Labor Council Investigation of Hotel and Restaurant Union, transcript," Board of Education Series 591 Subject Files, Municipal Archive, City of New York.

71. Proceedings of the Thirty-First General Convention, 44–45.

72. "Michael J. Obermeier, 100-HQ-96104," FBI, https://archive.org/details/MichaelJObermeierFBI1, 209–220.

73. *CIE* 55, no. 3 (March 1946): 4.

74. *Life* 22, no. 12 (March 24, 1947): 31–35.

75. *CIE* 55, no. 12 (December 1946): 15.

76. *CIE* 56, no. 3 (March 1947): 20.

77. *HCV* 7, no. 32 (January 18, 1947): 1, 8.

78. *Chicago Tribune,* March 18, 1947; *HCV* 7, no. 41 (March 22, 1947): 1.

79. *Chicago Tribune,* April 4, 1947; *HCV* 7, no. 43 (April 5, 1947): 1.

80. *Chicago Tribune,* October 15, 1946.

81. *HCV* 7, no. 36 (February 15, 1947); Profiles of the 29 delegates followed for several issues.

82. Josephson, *Union House,* 311.

83. *HCV* 7, no. 44 (April 12, 1947): 1.

84. "Letter to Random House from Weil, Gotshal & Manges. May 27, 1955," HERE Historical Files, 1892–1989, #6199/013, Box 2, Folder 2, Cornell; Josephson, *Union House,* 317.

85. Proceedings of the Thirty-First General Convention Hotel and Restaurant Employees' International Alliance and Bartenders International League of America, Milwaukee, Wisconsin, April 4–11, 1947, 65–66, 200, 225.

86. Josephson, *Union House,* 317; Proceedings of the Thirty-First General Convention, 116–121.

87. Based on analysis of the roll call: Proceedings of the Thirty-First General Convention, 77–84, 131–134.

88. Proceedings of the Thirty-First General Convention, 180–188.

89. Proceedings of the Thirty-First General Convention, 188–198.

90. *CIE* 56, no. 5 (May 1947): 11.

91. *Amsterdam News,* April 26, 1947.

92. *CIE* 56, no. 6 (June 1947): 4.

93. *CIE* 56, no. 6 (June 1947): 16.

94. The five anti-Communist locals, at this point, were Bartenders Local 15, Waiters Local 16, Delicatessen & Restaurant Countermen Local 60, Luncheonette & Soda Fountain Employees Local 254, and Cafeteria Employees Local 302. The locals that backed autonomy for the LJEB (not all of them led by Communists) were Waiters Local 1, Hotel & Club Employees Local 6, Bronx Bartenders Local 29, Chain Service Employees Local 42, Cooks Local 89, and Waiters Local 219. Source: Minutes of the Local Joint Executive Board, May 5, 1947, WAG.148; Box 1; Folder 8, Tamiment/Wagner.

95. *HCV* 7, no. 49 (May 17, 1947): 1–2; *HCV* 7, no. 49 (May 17, 1947): 8.

96. *HCV* 7, no. 19 (October 19, 1946): 1.

97. *HCV* 8, no. 1 (June 14, 1947): 1, 4.

98. *HCV* 8, no. 3 (June 28, 1947): 1, 3.

99. *HCV* 8, no. 5 (July 19, 1947): 1.

100. *HCV* 8, no. 7 (July 26, 1947): 1.

101. *NYHT,* July 15, 1947.

102. *HCV* 8, no. 19 (October 18, 1947): 1; Miguel Garriga, Letter to Hugo Ernst, August 6, 1947; Miguel Garriga, Letter to Hugo Ernst, August 12, 1947, HERE Historical Files, 1892–1989, #6199/013, Cornell.

103. *NYT,* August 22, 1947.

104. Dubofsky, *State and Labor in Modern America*, 201–204.

105. *CIE* 56, no. 10 (September 1947): 13; *CIE* 56, no. 9 (October 1947): 5.

106. *HCV* 8, no. 4 (July 5, 1947): 1.

107. *HCV* 8, no. 8 (August 2, 1947): 1; *HCV* 8, no. 10 (August 16, 1947): 1; Miguel Garriga, Letter to Hugo Ernst, August 6, 1947, HERE Historical Files, 1892–1989, #6199/013, Cornell.

108. *HCV* 8, no. 11 (August 23, 1947): 1, 8.

109. *HCV* 8, no. 19 (October 18, 1947): 2.

110. Miguel Garriga, Letter to Hugo Ernst, August 12, 1947, HERE Historical Files, 1892–1989, #6199/013. Kheel Center for Labor-Management Documentation and Archives, Cornell University Library.

111. *HCV* 8, no. 18 (October 11, 1947).

112. *NYT,* June 28, 1947; *NYT,* July 17, 1947.

113. "Michael J. Obermeier, 100-HQ-96104," FBI, https://archive.org/details/MichaelJObermeierFBI1, 200, 204.

114. Kraut, *Threat of Dissent*, 122–123.

115. *NYT,* September 7, 1947.

116. *HCV* 8, no. 17 (October 4, 1947): 1, 8; *NYHT,* September 9, 1947; *NY Daily News,* September 9, 1947.

117. *HCV* 8, no. 14 (September 13, 1947): 3.

118. *HCV* 8, no. 15 (September 13, 1947): 1, 4.

119. Minutes of the Official Second District Conference Held at the Empire Hotel, New York City, October 31 and November 1, 1947, HERE Historical Files, 1892–1989, #6199/012 mf Reel 10, Cornell.

120. *HCV* 8, no. 14 (September 13, 1947): 1, 4.

121. *HCV* 8, no. 18 (October 11, 1947): 2.

122. *HCV* 8, no. 18 (October 11, 1947): 8.
123. *HCV* 8, no. 16 (September 27, 1947); *HCV* 8, no. 17 (October 4, 1947).
124. *NYT,* October 16, 1947.
125. *NYT,* October 8, 1947.
126. *HCV* 8, no. 18 (October 11, 1947).
127. *HCV* 8, no. 20 (October 25, 1947): 1; Minutes of the Official Second District Conference Held at the Empire Hotel, New York City, October 31 and November 1, 1947, HERE Historical Files, 1892–1989, #6199/012 mf Reel 10, Cornell.
128. *HCV* 8, no. 20 (October 25, 1947): 1; *HCV* 8, no. 22 (November 8, 1947): 1.
129. *HCV* 8, no. 20 (October 25, 1947): 1.
130. *HCV* 8, no. 17 (October 4, 1947).
131. "Chronology in Obermeier Case," WAG.148; Box 14, Tamiment/Wagner; *HCV* 8, no. 20 (October 25, 1947), 1; *NYHT,* November 2, 1947.
132. Minutes of the Official Second District Conference Held at the Empire Hotel, New York City, October 31 and November 1, 1947, HERE Historical Files, 1892–1989, #6199/012 mf Reel 10, Cornell; *NYHT,* November 2, 1947.
133. *NYT,* November 5, 1947.
134. *HCV* 8, no. 22 (November 8, 1947): 1.
135. *CIE* 57, no. 5 (May 1948): 4–6.
136. *CIE* 56, no. 12 (December 1947): 9–10.
137. *HCV* 8, no. 24 (November 22, 1947): 7.
138. *CIE* 57, no. 1 (January 1948): 20, 36–37; *HCV* 8, no. 30 (January 3, 1948): 1.
139. *HCV* 8, no. 32 (January 17, 1948): 1, 8.
140. *HCV* 8, no. 30 (January 3, 1948): 1.
141. Forty other members ran against the administration slate for scattered vice president and business agent slots as independents out of a total of 157 slots up for election. *HCV* 8, no. 32 (January 17, 1948): 4–5.
142. *HCV* 8, no. 34 (January 31, 1948); *CIE* 57, no. 3 (March 1948): 32–33.
143. *HCV* 8, no. 35 (February 7, 1948).

Chapter 11. The Crack

1. Joshua Freeman, *In Transit: The Transport Workers Union in New York City, 1933–1966* (Oxford University Press, 1989), 286–317; David A. Shannon, *The Decline of American Communism* (Harcourt, Brace and Company, 1959), 214–215.
2. *HCV* 8, no. 39 (March 6, 1948).
3. *HCV* 9, no. 4 (July 3, 1948).
4. *HCV* 9, no. 10 (August 14, 1948); *CIE* 58, no. 3 (March 1949): 17.
5. *HCV* 9, no. 43 (April 2, 1949).
6. *HCV* 9, no. 33 (January 22, 1949): 7.
7. *HCV* 9, no. 24 (November 20, 1948): 2.
8. Michelle Chen, "Radical Defense," *Journal of Migration History* 9, no. 1 (2023): 106–134.
9. *HCV* 8, no. 28 (December 24, 1947): 1, 3.
10. *HCV* 9, no. 23 (November 13, 1948): 8.
11. *HCV* 8, no. 50 (May 22, 1948).
12. "Michael J. Obermeier, NY-100-257744," FBI, https://archive.org/details/MichaelJObermeierFBI2, 125–134.

13. Obermeier Defense Committee financial ledgers, WAG.148; Box 15; Folder 11, Tamiment/Wagner.

14. *HCV* 9, no. 39 (February 19, 1949): 8.

15. August 27, 1947, and September 25, 1947, Minutes, WAG 123; Box 1; Folder 10, Tamiment/Wagner.

16. *CIE* 57, no. 5 (May 1948): 12–13; *HCV* 8, no. 41 (March 20, 1948).

17. *HCV* 9, no. 19 (October 16, 1948): 4; *HCV* 9, no. 24 (November 20, 1948): 1, 7; Proceedings of the Thirty-Second General Convention of Hotel & Restaurant Employees' and Bartenders' International Union, Chicago, Ill., April 25–29, 1949, 18.

18. October 29, 1948, Letter from Joseph Fox to Hugo Ernst, HERE Joint Executive Board Files on Microfilm, 1941–1982, Collection Number: 6199/012 mf, Reel 10, Cornell.

19. Shannon, *Decline of American Communism*, 92–93.

20. Starobin, *American Communism in Crisis*, 51–70, 155–194.

21. Shannon, *Decline of American Communism*, 118–121.

22. *DW*, December 19, 1947; Thomas Devine, *Henry Wallace's 1948 Presidential Campaign and the Future of Postwar Liberalism* (University of North Carolina Press, 2013), 52–52.

23. Devine, *Wallace's 1948 Presidential Campaign*, 58–59.

24. *CIE* 57, no. 2 (February 1948): 30.

25. Devine, *Wallace's 1948 Presidential Campaign*, 62.

26. "Jay Rubin, NY-100–52865," FBI, https://archive.org/details/JayRubinFBI, 166.

27. "Affidavit of Betty Bentz in the Matter of Charges Preferred by Bro. Bert Ross Against Martin Cody, Lee Candea, et al.," WAG.148; Box 5; Folder 23, Tamiment/Wagner.

28. *CIE* 57, no. 7 (July 1948): 37.

29. Devine, *Wallace's 1948 Presidential Campaign*, 210.

30. *HCV* 8, no. 40 (March 13, 1948).

31. *HCV* 8, no. 45 (April 17, 1948).

32. *HCV* 8, no. 48 (May 8, 1948).

33. *HCV* 9, no. 7 (July 24, 1948).

34. Devine, *Wallace's 1948 Presidential Campaign*, 284.

35. Shannon, *Decline of American Communism*, 178–179.

36. *HCV* 9, no. 22 (November 6, 1948): 4.

37. *HCV* 8, no. 37 (February 21, 1948); *HCV* 9, no. 6 (July 17, 1948); *HCV* 9, no. 7 (July 24, 1948).

38. *HCV* 9, no. 8 (July 31, 1948).

39. *HCV* 9, no. 7 (July 24, 1948).

40. *HCV* 8, no. 35 (February 7, 1948); *HCV* 8, no. 36 (February 14, 1948).

41. *HCV* 8, no. 45 (April 17, 1948).

42. *HCV* 10, no. 19 (October 15, 1949); *NYHT,* October 14, 1949.

43. *HCV* 8, no. 42 (March 27, 1948).

44. *HCV* 8, no. 43 (April 3, 1948).

45. *HCV* 8, no. 44 (April 10, 1948); *HCV* 8, no. 44 (April 10, 1948).

46. *HCV* 8, no. 47 (May 1, 1948); *HCV* 8, no. 48 (May 8, 1948).

47. *HCV* 9, no. 1 (June 12, 1948).

48. *HCV* 10, no. 29 (December 24, 1949); *HCV* 11, no. 1 (June 10, 1950).

49. *HCV* 8, no. 7 (July 26, 1947): 1, 8.

50. *HCV* 9, no. 12 (August 28, 1948).
51. *HCV* 10, no. 8 (July 30, 1949); *HCV* 10, no. 9 (August 6, 1949).
52. *HCV* 10, no. 15 (September 17, 1949).
53. *HCV* 10, no. 18 (October 8, 1949).
54. *HCV* 10, no. 24 (November 19, 1949).
55. *HCV* 10, no. 32 (January 14, 1950).
56. *HCV* 10, no. 38 (February 25, 1950).
57. February 23, 1950, Minutes, WAG 123; Box 1; Folder 13, Tamiment/Wagner.
58. *HCV* 10, no. 40 (March 11, 1950).
59. March 29, 1950, Minutes, WAG 123; Box 1; Folder 13, Tamiment/Wagner; In re Hotel Governor Clinton March 7, 1950, WAG 123; Box 10; Folder 1, Tamiment/Wagner.
60. *HCV* 10, no. 47 (April 29, 1950).
61. "Brief on Behalf of Michael J. Obermeier Before the Board of Immigration Appeals," WAG.148, Box 14, Tamiment/Wagner.
62. *HCV* 9, no. 24 (November 20, 1948): 1, 8.
63. "Brief on Behalf of Michael J. Obermeier Before the Board of Immigration Appeals," WAG.148, Box 14, Tamiment/Wagner.
64. "Michael J. Obermeier, NY-100-257744," FBI, https://archive.org/details/MichaelJObermeierFBI2, 76.
65. "Chronology in Obermeier Case," WAG.148, Box 14, Tamiment/Wagner.
66. *HCV* 9, no. 15 (September 18, 1948).
67. "Obermeier Indicted In Citizenship Case," *NYT*, September 29, 1948; *HCV* 9, no. 17 (October 2, 1948): 1.
68. *HCV* 9, no. 24 (November 20, 1948): 1, 8.
69. "Brief on Behalf of Michael J. Obermeier Before the Board of Immigration Appeals," WAG.148, Box 14, Tamiment/Wagner; *HCV* 9, no. 42 (March 26, 1949).
70. *HCV* 10, no. 1 (June 11, 1949).
71. *HCV* 10, no. 16 (September 24, 1949).
72. Shannon, *Decline of American Communism*, 195–200.
73. Shannon, *Decline of American Communism*, 178–179, 185–189.
74. *NYT*, September 24, 1947.
75. *NYT*, August 5, 1948; *HCV* 9, no. 9 (August 7, 1948).
76. Proceedings of the Thirty-Second General Convention, 454–457.
77. Ernst was Jewish, but so was Dubinsky, and, while Ernst's relative tolerance of its Communist minority was likely the decisive cause for the snub, it is also hard to ignore—from a twenty-first-century perspective—the likelihood that the men of the AFL Executive Council may have been discomfited by the old San Francisco waiter's presentation of his masculinity. Philip Taft records HRE's relative size in *The A.F. of L. From the Death of Gompers to the Merger*, 207.
78. *CIE* 59, no. 3 (March 1950): 2–3, 5.
79. *HCV* 8, no. 7 (July 26, 1947).
80. James J. Bambrick, *The Building Service Story* (Labor History Press, 1948), 80.
81. *CIE* 57, no. 7 (July 1948): 19.
82. *HCV* 9, no. 47 (April 30, 1949); *HCV* 10, no. 27 (December 10, 1949).
83. "Report for the Year Ending May 31, 1965- and Review of Previous and Related Matters," Union Family Medical Fund of the Hotel Industry of New York City, November 9, 1965, WAG.123, Box 9, Tamiment/Wagner.

84. Frank P. Guidotti, "Periodic Health Examinations in the Hotel Industry," *Industrial Medicine and Surgery,* November 1957, 506–510.

85. Ralph Katz, "Hotel Industry, Workers Join in Unique Medical Care Pact," *Industrial Bulletin,* New York State Department of Labor, August 1961; "Report for the Year Ending May 31, 1965- and Review of Previous and Related Matters," Union Family Medical Fund of the Hotel Industry of New York City, November 9, 1965, WAG.123, Box 9, Tamiment/Wagner.

86. *CIE* 58, no. 1 (January 1949): 16–18.

87. *HCV* 10, no. 3 (June 25, 1949).

88. "Shall the Trusteeship . . .," HERE General Office Legal Files on Microfilm, 1892–1984, Collection Number: 6199/010 mf, Reel 3, Cornell, 1544.

89. *HCV* 7, no. 27 (December 14, 1946), 1; *HCV* 7, no. 29 (December 28, 1946): 1.

90. Memorandum 10/2/47, WAG 123; Box 12; Folder 47, Tamiment/Wagner.

91. February 19, 1948, Minutes, WAG 123; Box 1; Folder 11, Tamiment/Wagner.

92. *HCV* 10, no. 5 (July 9, 1949).

93. *HCV* 10, no. 24 (November 19, 1949); Horowitz, *New York Hotel Industry,* 79–82.

94. *Hotel* 1, no. 1 (May 1950): 15.

95. *NYT,* December 18, 1948.

96. *NYT,* July 1, 1948.

97. Satow, *The Plaza,* 105–113.

98. *NYT,* August 7, 1954.

99. *NYT,* June 24, 1951; *NYT,* April 24, 1955.

100. *NYT,* June 8, 1946; *NYT,* June 27, 1947; *NYT,* February 24, 1948.

101. Horowitz, *New York Hotel Industry,* 58; Benjamin Caplan, "A Case Study: The 1948–1949 Recession," *Policies to Combat Depression,* National Bureau of Economic Research, 1956.

102. "Shall the Trusteeship . . .," HERE General Office Legal Files on Microfilm, 1892–1984, Collection Number: 6199/010 mf, Reel 3, Cornell, 1578–1580.

103. *HCV* 9, no. 49 (May 14, 1949).

104. Horowitz, *New York Hotel Industry,* 142.

105. *HCV* 10, no. 13 (September 10, 1949); *HCV* 10, no. 14 (September 17, 1949).

106. "Shall the Trusteeship . . .," HERE General Office Legal Files on Microfilm, 1892–1984, Collection Number: 6199/010 mf, Reel 3, Cornell, 1611–1613.

107. "Shall the Trusteeship . . .," HERE General Office Legal Files on Microfilm, 1892–1984, Collection Number: 6199/010 mf, Reel 3, Cornell, 1615.

108. *HCV* 10, no. 11 (August 20, 1949); *CIE* 58, no. 9 (September 1949): 29–30.

109. *HCV* 10, no. 17 (October 1, 1949).

110. "Jay Rubin, NY-100–52865," FBI, https://archive.org/details/JayRubinFBI, 90–94.

111. The transcript of the speech was passed on to the FBI by a stool pigeon. The name of the person who delivered it was redacted. John Steuben was rarely in the city, due to ill health. For Martin Cody to have delivered the speech would have made the criticism seem personal or careerist. Only Collins had the stature to announce such a definite turn against Rubin, and Collins had been issuing warnings about Rubin's leadership to Party fraction meetings since the Wallace campaign. "Jay Rubin, NY-100–52865," FBI, https://archive.org/details/JayRubinFBI, 90–94.

112. "Shall the Trusteeship . . .," HERE General Office Legal Files on Microfilm, 1892–1984, Collection Number: 6199/010 mf, Reel 3, Cornell, 1651–1652.

113. *HCV* 10, no. 28 (December 17, 1949).

114. *HCV* 10, no. 31 (January 7, 1950); *HCV* 10, no. 32 (January 14, 1950); *HCV* 10, no. 33 (January 21, 1950).

115. *The Labor Leader* 8, no. 3 (February 21, 1950).

116. *HCV* 10, no. 34 (February 4, 1950).

117. *CIE* 58, no. 9 (September 1949): 18, 30; *HCV* 10, no. 13 (September 3, 1949); *HCV* 10, no. 34 (February 11, 1950).

118. *NYT*, February 22, 1950; *HCV* 10, no. 38 (February 25, 1950).

119. "Let's Get a New Deal!," WAG.148, Box 12, Folder 46, Tamiment/Wagner.

120. Horowitz, *New York Hotel Industry*, 82–82.

121. *NY World-Telegram*, April 20, 1950; *NY World-Telegram*, April 22, 1950.

122. John Steuben, 100-HQ-21445," FBI, 315–326. https://archive.org/details/200212johnsteuben1459221000/mode/2up; *HCV* 10, no. 47 (April 29, 1950): 8; "They Plotted Seizure of Hotel Union Since 1946," *DW,* October 31, 1950.

123. *The Labor Leader* 8, no. 8 (April 30, 1950).

124. *HCV* 10, no. 46 (April 22, 1950).

125. Based on a review of *Hotel,* Volume 1, Issue 1 (May 1950) through Volume 1, Issue 12 (June 1951).

126. "John Steuben, 100-HQ-21445," FBI, https://archive.org/details/200212johnsteuben1459221000, 18–23; "Application for Permission to Leave the United States," RGASPI 495–261–6022; WAG.148; Box 5; Folder 25, Tamiment/Wagner; White, *The Last Great Strike*, 3, 232–233, 246; "John Steuben, 50, Red Labor Leader," *NYT*, May 10, 1957.

127. *NYT,* May 30, 1950; *NYT,* June 8, 1950; *HCV* 11, no. 1 (June 10, 1950).

128. "Shall the Trusteeship . . .," HERE General Office Legal Files on Microfilm, 1892–1984, Collection Number: 6199/010 mf, Reel 3, Cornell, 39–40.

129. "Shall the Trusteeship . . .," HERE General Office Legal Files on Microfilm, 1892–1984, Collection Number: 6199/010 mf, Reel 3, Cornell, 1674–1677.

130. *HCV* 10, no. 48 (May 6, 1950).

131. *NYHT,* June 10, 1950; *HCV* 11, no. 2 (June 17, 1950).

132. *HCV* 11, no. 6 (July 15, 1950).

133. *NYT,* July 18, 1950.

134. *HCV* 11, no. 7 (July 22, 1950).

135. *HCV* 11, no. 7 (July 22, 1950).

136. "Shall the Trusteeship . . .," HERE General Office Legal Files on Microfilm, 1892–1984, Collection Number: 6199/010 mf, Reel 3, Cornell, 72.

137. *HCV* 11, no. 8 (July 29, 1950).

138. *NY Journal-American,* July 31, 1950; *HCV* 11, no. 9 (August 5, 1950).

139. "Shall the Trusteeship . . .," HERE General Office Legal Files on Microfilm, 1892–1984, Collection Number: 6199/010 mf, Reel 3, Cornell, 1091–1092.

140. *HCV* 11, no. 9 (August 5, 1950).

141. *HCV* 11, no. 10 (August 12, 1950).

142. *HCV* 11, no. 14 (September 9, 1950).

143. He was known to be a Norman Thomas Socialist. "Shall the Trusteeship . . .," HERE General Office Legal Files on Microfilm, 1892–1984, Collection Number: 6199/010 mf, Reel 3, Cornell, 1688–1689.

144. *HCV* 11, no. 15 (September 16, 1950).

145. "Charles Betts to Hugo Ernst, September 5, 1950, HERE General Office Legal Files on Microfilm, 1892–1984, Collection Number: 6199/010 mf, Reel 66, Cornell,

146. "Shall the Trusteeship . . .," HERE General Office Legal Files on Microfilm, 1892–1984, Collection Number: 6199/010 mf, Reel 3, Cornell, 1551.

147. "Shall the Trusteeship . . .," HERE General Office Legal Files on Microfilm, 1892–1984, Collection Number: 6199/010 mf, Reel 3, Cornell, 16–18.

Chapter 12. Trusteeship

1. *HCV* 11, no. 18 (October 7, 1950).

2. "Report of Trustee," Daisy George Papers, SCM 02–51, Manuscripts, Archives and Rare Books Division, New York Public Library.

3. *HCV* 11, no. 16 (September 23, 1950).

4. "Minutes of the Staff Meeting, September 20, 1950," HERE General Office Legal Files on Microfilm, 1892–1984, Collection Number: 6199/010 mf, Reel 65, Cornell; "Report of Trustee," Daisy George Papers, SCM 02–51, Manuscripts, Archives and Rare Books Division, New York Public Library.

5. "Clean Them All Out!" HERE General Office Legal Files on Microfilm, 1892–1984, Collection Number: 6199/010 mf, Reel 66, Cornell.

6. "A Statement to Local 6 Members by Richard Sirch," HERE General Office Legal Files on Microfilm, 1892–1984, Collection Number: 6199/010 mf, Reel 66, Cornell.

7. "Transcript of Conference Held on Friday, October 6, 1950," HERE General Office Legal Files on Microfilm, 1892–1984, Collection Number: 6199/010 mf, Reel 66, Cornell.

8. *DW*, September 22, 1950.

9. *HCV* 11, no. 17 (September 30, 1950).

10. *HCV* 11, no. 17 (September 30, 1950).

11. *HCV* 11, no. 41 (March 24, 1950); *NYT*, February 7, 2000; "Report of Trustee," Daisy George Papers, SCM 02–51, Manuscripts, Archives and Rare Books Division, New York Public Library.

12. "Transcript of Conference Held October 6, 1950," HERE General Office Legal Files on Microfilm, 1892–1984, Collection Number: 6199/010 mf, Reel 66, Cornell.

13. *HCV* 12, no. 3 (June 30, 1951).

14. *HCV* 11, no. 18 (October 7, 1950); *HCV* 11, no. 18 (October 7, 1950); *HCV* 11, no. 19 (October 14, 1950); *HCV* 11, no. 18 (October 7, 1950); "Report of Trustee," Daisy George Papers, SCM 02–51, Manuscripts, Archives and Rare Books Division, New York Public Library.

15. *HCV* 11, no. 18 (October 7, 1950).

16. *HCV* 11, no. 21 (October 28, 1950).

17. *DW*, October 9, 1950.

18. "Don't Let Your Union Be Wrecked," HERE General Office Legal Files on Microfilm, 1892–1984, Collection Number: 6199/010 mf, Reel 66, Cornell; "Shall the Trusteeship . . .," HERE General Office Legal Files on Microfilm, 1892–1984, Collection Number: 6199/010 mf, Reel 3, Cornell, 1678.

19. "A Message From 25 Members of the Executive Board," HERE General Office Legal Files on Microfilm, 1892–1984, Collection Number: 6199/010 mf, Reel 66, Cornell.

20. "Shall the Trusteeship . . .," HERE General Office Legal Files on Microfilm, 1892–1984, Collection Number: 6199/010 mf, Reel 3, Cornell, 1475.

21. *HCV* 11, no. 20 (October 21, 1950).

22. *HCV* 11, no. 22 (November 4, 1950).

23. *CIE* 59, no. 11 (November 1950): 22–24; *HCV* 11, no. 21 (October 28, 1950).

24. *HCV* 11, no. 22 (November 4, 1950).

25. *"Voice of the Membership,* November 11, 1950," HERE General Office Legal Files on Microfilm, 1892–1984, Collection Number: 6199/010 mf, Reel 66, Cornell.

26. *HCV* 11, no. 20 (October 21, 1950); "Union Trusteeship Continued By Judge," *NYT,* November 18, 1950; "Walter Garcia, et al., Plaintiff, against Hugo Ernst et al., Defendants," HERE General Office Legal Files on Microfilm, 1892–1984, Collection Number: 6199/010 mf, Reel 66, Cornell.

27. *HCV* 11, no. 21 (October 28, 1950).

28. *HCV* 11, no. 24 (November 18, 1950).

29. "Shall the Trusteeship . . .," HERE General Office Legal Files on Microfilm, 1892–1984, Collection Number: 6199/010 mf, Reel 3, Cornell, 45.

30. "Shall the Trusteeship . . .," HERE General Office Legal Files on Microfilm, 1892–1984, Collection Number: 6199/010 mf, Reel 3, Cornell, 1479.

31. "Shall the Trusteeship . . .," HERE General Office Legal Files on Microfilm, 1892–1984, Collection Number: 6199/010 mf, Reel 3, Cornell, 613–640.

32. "Shall the Trusteeship . . .," HERE General Office Legal Files on Microfilm, 1892–1984, Collection Number: 6199/010 mf, Reel 3, Cornell, 679–681.

33. "Shall the Trusteeship . . .," HERE General Office Legal Files on Microfilm, 1892–1984, Collection Number: 6199/010 mf, Reel 3, Cornell, 528–556.

34. *HCV* 11, no. 26 (December 2, 1950).

35. "Shall the Trusteeship . . .," HERE General Office Legal Files on Microfilm, 1892–1984, Collection Number: 6199/010 mf, Reel 3, Cornell, 1011.

36. "Shall the Trusteeship . . .," HERE General Office Legal Files on Microfilm, 1892–1984, Collection Number: 6199/010 mf, Reel 3, Cornell, 1395–1398.

37. "Report and Summation of Evidence to General President Hugo Ernst, Prepared by Walter Cowan, Hearing Officer, January 2, 1951," HERE General Office Legal Files on Microfilm, 1892–1984, Collection Number: 6199/010 mf, Reel 66, Cornell.

38. *HCV* 11, no. 28 (December 23, 1950); "Report and Summation of Evidence to General President Hugo Ernst, Prepared by Walter Cowan, Hearing Officer, January 2, 1951," HERE General Office Legal Files on Microfilm, 1892–1984, Collection Number: 6199/010 mf, Reel 66, Cornell.

39. "Hotel Union Puts 13 on 3-Year Probation," *NYT,* January 12, 1951; *HCV* 11, no. 31 (January 13, 1951); *CIE* 60, no. 2 (February 1951): 4–5.

40. *HCV* 11, no. 31 (January 13, 1951).

41. *NYT,* February 3, 1951; *HCV* 11, no. 34 (February 3, 1950).

42. *CIE* 60, no. 2 (February 1951): 16.

43. *HCV* 11, no. 35 (February 10, 1951); "Report of Trustee," Daisy George Papers, SCM 02-51, Manuscripts, Archives and Rare Books Division, New York Public Library.

44. *DW,* November 27, 1950.

45. Kraut, *Threat of Dissent,* 126–127.

46. Starobin, *American Communism in Crisis,* 219–223.

47. "John Steuben," *Prabook,* undated, https://prabook.com/web/john.steuben/3769098 (accessed September 14, 2022); Shannon, *Decline of American Communism,* 361.

48. *NYHT,* July 12, 1951.

49. *NYHT,* January 23, 1953; *NYT,* November 29, 1994.

50. "Jay Rubin. 100-HQ-52865," FBI, https://archive.org/details/JayRubinFBI, 106, 137, 166.

51. *United States v. Obermeier,* 186 F.2d 243 (2d Cir. 1950).

52. *NYT,* November 30, 1950.

53. *NYT,* March 27, 1951.

54. *NYT,* April 11, 1951.

55. *HCV* 11, no. 34 (February 3, 1951).

56. *HCV* 11, no. 31 (January 13, 1951).

57. *HCV* 11, no. 38 (March 3, 1951).

58. Larry Blomstadt, *Truman, Congress and Korea: The Politics of America's First Undeclared War* (University Press of Kentucky, 2016), 130–132.

59. *HCV* 11, no. 34 (January 20, 1951).

60. *HCV* 11, no. 35 (February 10, 1951).

61. *HCV* 11, no. 37 (February 24, 1951).

62. *HCV* 11, no. 49 (May 19, 1951).

63. *HCV* 11, no. 39 (March 10, 1951); *The Labor Leader,* January 24, 1951; "Communist Infiltration in the Hotel and Restaurant Employees Union, 100-HQ-92004," FBI, 106; Horowitz, *New York Hotel Industry,* 59.

64. *HCV* 11, no. 44 (April 14, 1951); *HCV* 11, no. 51 (June 2, 1951).

65. *HCV* 11, no. 43 (April 7, 1951).

66. *The Labor Leader*, April 30, 1951.

67. *HCV* 11, no. 48 (May 12, 1951); *HCV* 11, no. 46 (April 28, 1951).

68. *HCV* 11, no. 50 (May 26, 1951).

69. "The True Story of Double-Dealing Daisy George," Hotel Employees and Restaurant Employees International Union, Local 6 Records; WAG.148; Box 9; Folder 13, Tamiment/Wagner; "Shall the Trusteeship . . .," HERE General Office Legal Files on Microfilm, 1892–1984, Collection Number: 6199/010 mf, Reel 3, Cornell, 1024–1041.

70. "Clean Them All Out!," "Wage Raises? . . . YES!," HERE General Office Legal Files on Microfilm, 1892–1984, Collection Number: 6199/010 mf, Reel 66, Cornell.

71. "Reilly Purged in True Kremlin Fashion," WAG.148; Box 9; Folder 13, Tamiment/Wagner.

72. According to his self-published autobiography, Forge did have a brother named David, but, by the spring of 1951, he had grown disenchanted with *March of Labor* and the Party's direction under William Z. Foster.

73. *Local 6 Liberator* 1, no. 1 (June 9, 1951), WAG.148; Box 9; Folder 13, Tamiment/Wagner; *The Labor Leader* 9, no. 9 (September 30, 1951).

74. Douglas P. Seaton, *Catholics and Radicals: The Association of Catholic Trade Unionists and the American Labor Movement, from Depression to Cold War* (Bucknell University Press, 1981), 23, 60, 213, 221.

75. Nelson Frank, "'Dare' Accepted by Leaders of Hotel Union," *New York World-Telegram,* undated news clip used in a leaflet; "Dare Them to Give You True Answers to These $64 Questions," WAG.148; Box 9; Folder 13, Tamiment/Wagner.

76. *Local 6 Liberator* 1, no. 1 (June 9, 1951), WAG.148; Box 9; Folder 13, Tamiment/Wagner.

77. "A Statement by Michael Reilly," WAG.148; Box 9; Folder 13, Tamiment/Wagner.

78. *HCV* 11, no. 52 (June 9, 1951).

79. *HCV* 11, no. 49 (May 19, 1951); *HCV* 11, no. 51 (June 2, 1951).

80. "Gus Contes, Walter Garcia, Celia Scorda and Albert Jones, each suing on his own behalf and on behalf of others similarly situated, Plaintiffs, AGAINST Bert H. Ross . . .," HERE General Office Legal Files on Microfilm, 1892–1984, Collection Number: 6199/010 mf, Reel 66, Cornell.

81. "In the last minute scheme to defeat . . .," Hotel Employees and Restaurant Employees International Union, Local 6 Records; WAG.148; Box 9; Folder 13, Tamiment/Wagner.

82. *HCV* 12, no. 1 (June 16, 1951).

83. *HCV* 12, no. 2 (June 23, 1951); *CIE* 60, no. 7 (July 1951): 23–24.

84. Horowitz, *New York Hotel Industry*, 59.

85. Horowitz, *New York Hotel Industry*, 59–62.

86. *HCV* 12, no. 31 (January 12, 1952).

87. *HCV* 10, no. 42 (March 25, 1950); *HCV* 11, no. 13 (September 3, 1950).

88. *HCV* 12, no. 34 (February 2, 1952).

89. *NYT,* March 5, 1952; *HCV* 12, no. 39 (March 8, 1952).

90. *HCV* 12, no. 43 (April 5, 1952).

91. Formed after the death of S. Gregory Taylor, the merged management group divested itself of Taylor's larger properties like the St. Moritz and focused largely on residential hotels.

92. Horowitz, *New York Hotel Industry*, 127–129.

93. *HCV* 12, no. 51 (May 31, 1952).

94. *HCV* 13, no. 2 (June 21, 1952).

95. *HCV* 13, no. 4 (July 5, 1952).

96. *HCV* 13, no. 9 (August 9, 1952).

97. *HCV* 13, no. 5 (July 12, 1952).

98. "Munich, June 12, 1953," WAG 123; Box 3; Folder 5, Tamiment/Wagner.

99. *New York World-Telegram & Sun,* January 8, 1952.

100. Minutes, Regular Membership Meeting, September 10, 1952, WAG.148; Box 4; Folder 25, Tamiment/Wagner.

101. Minutes, Regular Membership Meeting, October 8, 1952, WAG.148; Box 4; Folder 25, Tamiment/Wagner.

102. *HCV* 13, no. 26 (December 6, 1952).

103. *CIE* 62, no. 10 (March 1953): 27.

104. Taft, *From the Death of Gompers to the Merger*, 483–486.

105. *HCV* 11, no. 43 (April 7, 1951).

106. *HCV* 13, no. 28 (December 20, 1952).

107. "Annual Report of the House Un-American Activities Committee for the Year 1953," U.S. House of Representatives Report No. 1192 (February 6, 1954), 80–91, https://archive.org/details/annualreportfory1953unit/page/n1/mode/2up.

108. "Jay Rubin. 100-HQ-253223," FBI, 139.

109. Letter from Jack Townsend to Ed Miller, November 16, 1953, HERE Historical Files, Collection Number: 6199/013, Box 2, Folder 6, Kheel Center for Labor-Management Documentation and Archives, Cornell University Library.

110. *HCV,* Special Edition (November 27, 1953); *NYHT,* November 23, 1953.

111. *HCV,* Special Edition (November 27, 1953); *HCV* 14, no. 15 (December 5, 1953).

112. *DW,* March 27, 1960; *DW,* April 10, 1960; *DW,* April 24, 1960.
113. John Earl Haynes and Harvey Klehr, "Framing William Albertson: The FBI's 'Solo' Operation and the Cold War," *Journal of Cold War Studies* 22, no. 3 (2020): 63–85.
114. *HCV* 20, no. 9 (May 14, 1960).
115. "Munich, June 12, 1953," WAG 123; Box 3; Folder 5, Tamiment/Wagner.
116. *NYT,* May 21, 1960.
117. *HCV* 20, no. 10 (June 1960): 13.

Afterword

1. *NYDN,* August 23, 2003.
2. *NYT,* May 12, 1976; *NYT,* September 18, 2015.
3. "Affiliated Locals," NY/NJ Hotel & Gaming Workers Union, https://hotelworkers.org/about/affiliated-locals (accessed July 7, 2023).

Sources

Archives

The archives of both the New York Hotel Trades Council and Hotel Employees Local 6 are housed in the Tamiment Library & Wagner Library Archives at New York University (Daniel Bell's papers, which had some helpful notes regarding the FWIU's merger negotiations with HRE, are also there). This was a primary source for this book and an essential resource for anyone seeking to expand on the story. The Hotel & Restaurant Employees historical files (1892–1989) are stored at the Kheel Center for Labor-Management Documentation and Archives at the Cornell University Library. Aside from two boxes of files accumulated during Matthew Josephson's work on *Union House, Union Bar*, everything is stored on microfilm. Unfortunately, there is no usable finding aid. Happily, the folks at Kheel have pioneered a system of remote access to their microfilm readers via Zoom! I searched through nearly 200 reels and found everything I was looking for except the transcripts of HRE's 1946 investigation into the influence of the Communist Party in its New York locals. I have to conclude that whatever copies in the HRE files weren't passed on to the FBI were destroyed after the trusteeship of Local 6. As it turns out, the New York Central Trades and Labor Council provided them to a witch hunt for Communist teachers conducted by the New York City Board of Education a few years later, and an original copy was preserved in the City's Municipal Archive. Prior to 1941, minutes of the HRE international conventions and General Executive Board meetings were published in the union's journal. Beginning with the 1941 convention and continuing beyond the time period of this book, all minutes were published in bound volumes that are digitally archived at HathiTrust.

SEIU's archives are housed at the Walter P. Reuther Library at Wayne State University. The union's archivist was immensely helpful with virtual consultations and finding and scanning relevant files. Similarly helpful was the Wisconsin

Historical Society with David J. Saposs's papers. Other archives that assisted long-distance research via e-mail and scanned PDFs were the Department of Rare Books, Special Collections, and Preservation at the University of Rochester—which is the caretaker of Thomas E. Dewey's papers, and Duke University's Rubenstein Library—whose J. B. Matthews papers contain scores of accusations of Communist affiliations submitted to HUAC.

The George B. Corsa Hotel Collection at the New-York Historical Society—a collection of news clippings, brochures, and ephemera—was useful for piecing together some information about the ownership, branding, and history of some of these long-gone hotels. I also consulted with the Daisy George papers at the NYPL's Schomburg Center for Research in Black Culture and with Martin Segal's papers in the Brooke Russell Astor Reading Room for Rare Books and Manuscripts at the NYPL's Main Branch (the one from *Ghostbusters*).

The staff at the New York City Municipal Archives searched high and low for trial transcripts from the *People of the State of New York v. Paul Coulcher et al.* They convinced me that Dewey's office did not transfer the files. It was not standard practice to retain such files after a convicted felon's appeals had been exhausted in those days. They did find a memo on a post-conviction interview in Dewey's case files for Jimmy Hines, which produced the closest thing to a smoking gun of Paul Coulcher's role in the racket. While I was working with them, I also consulted with the microfilm Records of Mayor Fiorello H. La Guardia, 1934–1945, which produced the closest thing to a paper trail to his obvious-but-not-obvious influence on the Status Quo agreement. Archivists also found the 1946 HRE commission's transcripts in the Board of Education's files.

The Reports of the National War Labor Board were published in bound volumes and can be found in many libraries. The dispute resolution files are archived by the National Archives and Research Administration (NARA) in College Park, Maryland. Nelson Lichtenstein's archival advice in *Labor's War at Home* is still the best for researching this Board's activity, although NARA has shifted some of its regional files as storage needs have dictated. I accessed the dispute case files regarding the New York Hotel Association via NARA's reproduction services, which provided a PDF scan roughly 150 days into their service commitment of 30–60 days.

The Reports of the House on Un-American Activities Committee were published in bound volumes and can be found in many libraries. They've also been scanned and saved to the Internet Archive (archive.org).

Finally, we have the archives of the Comintern and of the Communist Party of the United States, which are stored in Moscow. In 1998, John Earl Haynes facilitated a deal between the Library of Congress and the Russian Center for the Preservation and Study of Documents of Recent History (oft referred to in earlier scholarship by its Russian acronym, RTsKhIDNI) to put collection number 515 (often cited also by the Russian word for collection: fond) on microfilm. That collection contains the files that the Communist Party of the United States shipped to the USSR around the time of the Smith Act. It is the main archive of the Party covering the period between 1919–1944. Aside from the Library of

Congress, NYU possesses a complete copy of the microfilm. I was able to access it through NYPL's interlibrary loan service while NYU remained closed to outside scholars in early 2022. In 1999, RTsKhIDNI was merged with another library to become the Russian State Archive of Socio-Political History (often, and within here, referred to by its Russian acronym, RGASPI). Fond 495 contains the voluminous files of the Comintern, the most interesting of which for me were the "personnel files" on members who traveled globally on Comintern business. It is not available on microfilm; the paper files are exclusively in Moscow at RGASPI. As of this writing, the Google Chrome browser does a pretty reasonable job of translating the Russian RGASPI finding aid to English. In fact, I found this version of the finding aid for fond 515 more useful than Haynes', which reflects his particular research interests. A Moscow-based research assistant accessed and photographed my wish list of fond-opis-delo (or, collection, sub-collection-folder) numeric files for both the 495 and 515 fonds, and they are cited as such.

Newspapers

Volumes of the *Hotel & Club Voice* are deposited at various libraries, including NYU, Cornell, and the NYPL, and beginning with 1952, many years are digitally archived at HathiTrust. The NYPL's holdings are a combination of bound print copies and a few years of microfilm. The union has also scanned its own complete collection and shared with me the word-searchable PDF files. *Hotel*, the magazine of the HTC, seems to have been reformatted and renumbered in 1953. Everything gets a bit jumbled in WorldCat records since the two publications merged at some point by the 1960s and NYHTC became the publisher of the *Hotel Voice*. The union retains a volume of the first twelve issues of the glossy magazine, which they shared with me. The entire run of *Mixer & Server* and *Catering Industry Employee* are digitally archived, completely word-searchable and available via Creative Commons license at the HathiTrust website.

Paper copies of the handful of issues of *International Hotel Work* that were published between 1911 and 1912 are archived at the NYPL. A bound-volume, post-strike second year of *Hotel Worker* is saved at the Wirtz Labor Library of the U.S. Department of Labor. The first issues, which would have covered the preparation and conduct of the 1918 strike in the workers' own voices, do not seem to have survived. The entire run of the *Free Voice of the Amalgamated Food Workers* is saved as bound volumes at the NYPL. Most of *Food Worker* is also archived at the NYPL.

Digitization of local newspapers allowed for so much more research than time used to permit for a book like this. Dozens of titles are scanned and word-searchable on the NYS Historical Newspapers website. The materials available were particularly rich for the 1912–1923 portions of this story. *The New York Times* is also completely archived online on its own website and available to subscribers. The *New York Herald* and the *Herald-Tribune* are collected in a ProQuest database, which I was able to access online at home through the NYPL website. Other local papers that are cited for news from other parts of the country or for syndicated content, like the *Chicago Tribune* and the *Atlanta Constitution*, were similarly accessible. The *Daily Worker* and the *Toiler* are collected in a ProQuest database called the Communist Historical Newspaper Collection and, yes, the NYPL provides access for library cardholders.

The Militant, which covered the 1934 strike as well as some of the efforts to oust Stalinist leadership from HRE locals, has been scanned and archived at the Marxist Internet Archive. That archive, at marxists.org, also has scanned volumes of the *New York Call* newspaper from 1908 to 1912. The entire run of New York's old Socialist daily newspaper is archived on a master microfilm at the NYPL. The microfilm collection of Earl Browder's papers contains the most complete collection of *Labor Herald*, the TUEL's early newspaper. I accessed it at NYU, before the pandemic. *Labor Unity* began as a TUEL newspaper and became a TUUL magazine, which is why the issue numbering is idiosyncratic. Both are held on microfilm at NYPL. NYU has the magazine in print. An incomplete collection of *Party Organizer* is held on microfilm at NYPL. The Association of Catholic Trade Unionists' monthly newspaper, *The Labor Leader*, is collected on microfilm at NYU.

FBI Files

If journalism is the "first rough draft of history," then the Federal Bureau of Investigation files are the scattered notes and false leads of a story that gets cut for space. There's useful stuff in there, but you have to learn how to read them. They start out as sophomoric cage-rattling exercises of checking apartment directories and widely available union newspapers (to confirm that such-and-such person still lives *here* and works *there*) and soon branch out into quick check-ins with local cops and stool pigeons. But, if there's a *there* there (that J. Edgar Hoover cared about), they soon get deadly serious with reams of leaked documents, HUAC transcripts, and interviews with sworn enemies freely spilling the tea. Sometime in the last decade, the FBI began methodically transferring the case files of dead Communists to the National Archives and Records Administration. This is a disaster for scholarship on American Communism. If the FBI retains a file, they quickly review it to redact the names of agents and spies and then email you a PDF at no cost to you. If NARA possesses the file, they put you in a ridiculously long queue to meticulously review the file. Years later, they'll tell you that you can get a PDF copy of the file for 80 cents a page (and there are often hundreds, if not thousands, of pages). Alternatively, you can absurdly travel to College Park, Maryland, to view the files on one of their computers *and email them to yourself!* I'm lucky that I began researching this topic in 2006, but I regret that many of the names that I encountered during my research are in the dreaded "third tier of processing" with a decade-long backlog.

I have deviated from the established practice of footnoting FBI files by citing a FOIPA number and clumsily describing a particular redacted page. Instead, I digitally inserted page numbers into the PDF documents that the FBI and NARA created and then uploaded my files to the Internet Archive website. I footnote the case file, URL, and page number for my citations. The FBI files that I used as sources are as follows:

Albertson, William. My FOIPA #148425-000 to the FBI produced sections 1–2 of 65-HQ-38100. That consists of 487 pages and covers the period of 1941–1951. It is now archived at https://archive.org/details/201221-william-albertson-foipa-148425-000_202012/mode/2up. John Earl Haynes has archived sections 3–14 at https://www.governmentattic.org/8docs/FBIfile65-HQ-38100Albertson_2006-2010.pdf.

Garriga, Miguel. My FOIPA #1091412-000 to the FBI produced a response for a partial section, serial 30530 from file #62-HQ-60527. The file likely relates to supporters of the Spanish Civil War. Garriga's brief section, five pages in total, details some of his past left-wing affiliations. This section is now archived at https://archive.org/details/MiguelGarrigaFBI.

Lane, Gertrude. My FOIPA #51091 to NARA produced FBI file NY-100-51123. This 76-page report was produced by the New York field office. It is now archived at https://archive.org/details/GertrudeLaneFBI.

Obermeier, Michael J. My FOIPA #1034000-000 to the FBI produced two files. The first, 100-HQ-96104, consists of 244 pages. It began as an investigation into the German-American Trade Union Committee but soon focused on Obermeier and was only closed upon his death. It is now archived at https://archive.org/details/MichaelJObermeierFBI1. The other file, 100-NY-57744, was compiled by the New York office. It is 213 pages long and covers the period of 1947–1952 (right before he was arrested and until he left the country). It is archived at https://archive.org/details/MichaelJObermeierFBI2. Both files are apparently now in the possession of NARA.

Rubin, Jay. My FOIPA #1061113-000 to the FBI produced all 167 pages of 100-HQ-52865. It is apparently now in the possession of NARA. I archived it at https://archive.org/details/JayRubinFBI.

Steuben, John. My FOIPA #1459221-000 to the FBI produced all 895 pages of 100-HQ-1156. It was opened in 1941 and closed upon his death. It is archived at https://archive.org/details/200212johnsteuben1459221000/page/n895/mode/2up.

Books

Allen, Oliver E. *The Tiger: The Rise and Fall of Tammany Hall*. Addison-Wesley Publishing Company, 1993.

Applebaum, Stanley. *The New York World's Fair 1939/1940 in 155 Photographs by Richard Wurts and Others*. Dover Publications, 1977.

Barrett, James R. *William Z. Foster and the Tragedy of American Radicalism*. University of Illinois Press, 1999.

Block, Alan. *East Side-West Side: Organizing Crime in New York 1930–1950*. Routledge, 1983.

Blomstadt, Larry. *Truman, Congress and Korea: The Politics of America's First Undeclared War*. University Press of Kentucky, 2016.

Brecher, Jeremy. *Strike!* South End Press, 1972.

Budenz, Louis. *Men Without Faces*. Harper, 1948.

Cannon, James P. *The History of American Trotskyism*. Pathfinder, 1972.

Carson, Jenny. *A Matter of Moral Justice: Black Women Laundry Workers and the Fight for Justice*. University of Illinois Press, 2021.

Chase, W. Parker. *New York: The Wonder City*. Wonder City Publishing Co., 1932.

Cherny, Robert W. *Harry Bridges: Labor Radical, Labor Legend*. University of Illinois Press, 2022.

Cobble, Dorothy Sue. *Dishing It Out: Waitresses and Their Unions in the Twentieth Century*. University of Illinois Press, 1991.

Danielson, Leilah. *American Gandhi: A.J. Muste and the History of Radicalism in the Twentieth Century*. University of Pennsylvania Press, 2014.

De Leon, Simon. *The American Labor's Who's Who*. Stratford Press, 1925.

Deutscher, Isaac. *The Prophet Armed: Trotsky 1879–1921*. Verso, 2003.

Devine, Thomas. *Henry Wallace's 1948 Presidential Campaign and the Future of Postwar Liberalism*. University of North Carolina Press, 2013.

Draper, Theodore. *American Communism & Soviet Russia: The Formative Period*. Viking, 1960.

Draper, Theodore. *The Roots of American Communism*. Viking, 1957.

Dubofsky, Melvyn. *The State and Labor in Modern America*. University of North Carolina Press, 1994.

Dubofsky, Melvyn. *We Shall Be All: A History of the Industrial Workers of the World*. Abridged ed. University of Illinois Press, 2000.

Flynn, Elizabeth Gurley. *The Rebel Girl: An Autobiography*. 1955. International Publishers, 1994.

Foner, Philip S. *History of the Labor Movement in the United States, Vol. 8: Postwar Struggles 1918–1920*. International Publishers, 1988.

Foster, William Z. *From Bryan to Stalin*. International Publishers, 1937.

Foster, William Z. *Pages from a Worker's Life*. 1939. International Publishers, 1978.

Fraser, Steven. *Labor Will Rule: Sidney Hillman and the Rise of American Labor*. The Free Press, 1991.

Freeland, David. *Automats, Taxi Dances and Vaudeville*. New York University Press, 2009.

Freeman, Joshua B. *In Transit: The Transport Workers Union in New York City, 1933–1966*. Temple University Press, 1989.

Freeman, Joshua B. *Working Class New York: Life and Labor Since World War II*. The New Press, 2000.

Goulden, Joseph C. *Meany: Unchallenged Strongman of American Labor*. Atheneum, 1972.

Hochschild, Adam. *Rebel Cinderella*. Houghton Mifflin Harcourt, 2020.

Horowitz, Morris A. *The New York Hotel Industry: A Labor Relations Study*. Harvard University Press, 1960.

Isserman, Maurice. *Which Side Were You On? The American Communist Party During the Second World War*. Wesleyan University Press, 1982.

Johanningsmeier, Edward P. *Forging American Communism: The Life of William Z. Foster*. Princeton, 1994.
Josephson, Matthew. *Union House, Union Bar: The History of the Hotel & Restaurant Employees and Bartenders International Union, AFL-CIO*. Random House, 1956.
Kaufman, Stuart Bruce. *A Vision of Unity: The History of the Bakery and Confectionary Workers International Union*. University of Illinois Press, 1987.
Kersten, Andrew E. *Labor's Home Front: The American Federation of Labor During World War II*. New York University Press, 2006.
Kessner, Thomas. *Fiorello H. La Guardia and the Making of Modern New York*. McGraw-Hill, 1989.
Kimeldorf, Howard. *Battling for American Labor: Wobblies, Craft Workers, and the Making of the Union Movement*. University of California Press, 1999.
Klehr, Harvey. *Heyday of American Communism: The Depression Decade*. Basic Books, 1984.
Klehr, Harvey, John Earl Haynes, and Kyrill M. Anderson. *The Soviet World of American Communism*. Yale University Press, 1998.
Kotkin, Stephen. *Stalin: Waiting For Hitler, 1929–1941*. Penguin Press, 2017.
Kraut, Julia Rose. *Threat of Dissent*. Harvard University Press, 2020.
Leffler, Melvyn P. *The Spectre of Communism: The United States and the Origins of the Cold War, 1917–1953*. Hill and Wang, 1994.
Lenin, Vladimir I. *"Left-Wing" Communism, An Infantile Disorder*. New Translation. International Publishers, 1940.
Lichtenstein, Nelson. *Labor's War at Home: The CIO in World War II*. Cambridge University Press, 1982.
Lore, David. *Firebrand: Journalist Ludwig Lore's Lifelong Struggle against Capitalism. Stalinism and the Rise of Nazism*. Lulu, 2017.
Luff, Jennifer. *Commonsense Anticommunism: Labor and Civil Liberties Between the World Wars*. University of North Carolina Press, 2012.
Meyer, Gerald. *Vito Marcantonio: Radical Politician, 1903–1954*. SUNY Press, 1989.
Morgan, Ted. *A Covert Life: Jay Lovestone, Communist, Anti-Communist, and Spymaster*. Random House, 1999.
Murolo, Priscilla, and A. B. Chitty. *From the Folks Who Brought You the Weekend: A Short, Illustrated History of Labor in the United States*. The New Press, 2001.
Palmer, Bryan D. *James P. Cannon and the Origins of the American Revolutionary Left 1890–1928*. University of Illinois Press, 2007.
Raddock, Maxwell C. *Portrait of an American Labor Leader: William L. Hutcheson*. World Wide Press Syndicate, 1955.
Renshaw, Patrick. *The Wobblies: The Story of Syndicalism in the United States*. Doubleday, 1967.
Rider, Fremont. *Rider's New York City and Vicinity, including Newark, Yonkers and New Jersey*. Henry Holt & Company, 1916.
Ross, Jack. *The Socialist Party of America: A Complete History*. Potomac Books, 2015.
Rubin, Jay, and Michael J. Obermeier. *Growth of a Union: The Life and Times of Edward Flore*. The Historical Union Association, Inc., 1943.
Salvatore, Nick, *Eugene V. Debs: Citizen Socialist*. University of Illinois Press, 1982.

Saposs, David J. *Communism in American Unions*. McGraw-Hill, 1959.

Saposs, David J. *Left Wing Unionism: A Study of Radical Policies and Tactics*. International Publishers, 1926.

Satow, Julie. *The Plaza: The Secret Life of America's Most Famous Hotel*. Hachette Book Group (Twelve), 2019.

Savage, Marion Dutton. *Industrial Unionism in America*. The Ronald Press Company, 1922.

Schriftgeisser, Karl. *Oscar of the Waldorf*. E.P. Dutton & Co., 1943.

Shannon, David A. *The Decline of American Communism: A History of the Communist Party of the United States Since 1945*. Harcourt, Brace and Company, 1959.

Starobin, Joseph, *American Communism in Crisis, 1943–1957*. Harvard University Press, 1972.

Stolberg, Mary M. *Fighting Organized Crime: Politics, Justice, and the Legacy of Thomas E. Dewey*. Northeastern University Press, 1995.

Taft, Philip. *The A. F. of L. from the Death of Gompers to the Merger*. Harper, 1959.

Taylor, Nick. *American-Made*. Bantam-Dell, 2008.

Turkel, Stanley. *Hotel Mavens: Lucius M. Boomer, George C. Boldt and Oscar of the Waldorf*. AuthorHouse, 2014.

Vapnek, Laura. *Elizabeth Gurley Flynn: Modern American Revolutionary*. Taylor & Francis Group, 2015.

White, Ahmed. *The Last Great Strike: Little Steel, the CIO, and the Struggle for Labor Rights in New Deal America*. University of California Press, 2016.

Zinn, Howard. *A People's History of the United States*. Harper Perennial Modern Classics, 2015.

Index

Albertson, William, 75, 78, 85, 96, 108, 117, 126, 133, 152, 199, 259–60
Aluffo, Joe, 246
Amalgamated Association of Iron and Steel Workers, 47, 54
Amalgamated Clothing Workers, 53–54, 84, 119, 126, 295n21
Amalgamated Food Workers, 2, 6, 7, 49, 50–53, 55–60, 63–68, 70–73, 75–78, 80–84, 86–88, 90–93, 95–103, 108, 115, 132, 155, 174, 176, 183
Amalgamated Meat Cutters, 54
Amalgamated Metal Workers, 54, 55, 56, 79
Amalgamated Textile Workers, 55, 79
Amalgamated Tobacco Workers, 54, 79
Amalgamation, 50, 53–54, 57, 105, 117
American Committee for the Protection of the Foreign Born, 216
American Distilling Company, 286n28
American Federation of Labor, 1–8, 15–17, 24–25, 34, 40, 45–48, 50, 52–57, 62, 63, 68–71, 73, 74, 76, 77, 79, 82, 91, 94, 97, 102–3, 104–5, 107–10, 112, 117, 122–24, 128, 130, 133–35, 141–42, 149, 150, 152–53, 158, 161, 164, 169–70, 172–73, 179, 184, 186, 189, 196–98, 199, 201–2, 204, 208, 218, 219, 225–26, 237, 244, 251, 254, 256–57, 274n19
American Labor Party, 117, 197, 219
Amsterdam Opera House, 21, 24, 27, 43, 44, 45
Aragno, Vincent, 206, 210, 213, 214

Assel, John, 35, 50, 81, 145
Associated Hotels and Residence Clubs Association, 221
Association of Catholic Trade Unionists, 238, 240, 241, 251–52
Astor, John Jacob, 12
Astor, Vincent, 143
Astor, William Waldorf, 12, 13
Auto Workers Union, 79

Bakery & Confectionery Workers International Union, 50, 102, 103, 106
Bartenders Local 15, 199, 203–4, 206, 208, 210–13, 256, 295n21
Bartenders Local 278 (Chicago), 134, 136, 202
Bary, Arthur, 118
Baum, Charles B., 88, 113, 115, 117
Benchley, Robert, 93
Bentz, Betty, 246
Betts, Charles, 238
Bing and Bing, 148, 175, 235
Bingham, Alfred M., 93
Blochinger, Edward, 18, 20–21, 23–24, 27, 28, 34
Bohan, James, 243
Boland, Frank A. K., 100–101
Boland, John P., 117, 125–26, 130, 131, 137
Boldt, George C., 12, 17
Bookjans, John, 183
Boomer, Lucius, 39, 41–42, 75, 100, 120, 125, 131, 177–78, 188, 191, 230

Index

"boring from within," 5, 6, 46–48, 54–58, 62, 68–69, 73, 74, 79, 103, 158, 159
Borson, Abe, 65, 74, 85, 87–90, 106, 113, 116
Bridges, Harry, 159–60, 198
Broun, Heywood, 93
Browder, Earl, 80, 151, 158, 172, 185–86, 223
Brown, Victor, 206, 210, 213, 214, 216
Bryant Hall, 19, 20, 22, 27–31, 39, 91
Budenz, Louis, 292n35
Building Service Employees International Union, 122–25, 129, 130, 138, 141, 148, 161–62, 180, 182, 195–96, 221, 225, 226, 233, 249, 253, 263
Bullard, Joe, 242
Burkhardt, August, 52, 56, 68, 70, 77, 102

Candea, Lee, 228, 237, 241, 242, 246
Cannery & Agricultural Workers Industrial Union, 79
Cannon, James P., 5, 6, 82, 93, 95, 96, 98, 101
Carnegie Hall, 25, 137
Casa Galacia, 243
Casalvolone, Frank, 242
Case, Frank, 137, 140, 144, 230
Chambermaid's Union, 20, 21, 25, 26
Childs Restaurants, 37, 110, 121
Christenberry, Robert K., 157, 167
City Bank Farmers Trust, 149
Clark, Tom C., 190
clubs: Bankers Club, 36; Cloud Club, 178; Colony Club, 196; Columbia University Club, 196; Downtown Athletic Club, 118; Harvard Club, 132, 196, 221; Lawyers Club, 178; Metropolitan Club, 196; National Democratic Club, 196; National Republican Club, 196; New York Athletic Club, 179; Princeton Club, 132; Produce Exchange Club, 38; Racquet and Tennis Club, 132; Stock Exchange Luncheon Club, 25; University Club, 132, 179; Whitehall Club, 179; Yale Club, 196
Cody, Martin, 119, 127, 140, 155, 165–66, 172, 186, 194, 195, 200, 214, 218, 225, 230–33, 235–38, 240–43, 244–49, 252
Cohn, Sidney E., 211, 222
Cole, Walter, 222
Collins, Charles, 118, 172, 194, 197, 200, 203, 205, 206, 215, 216, 219, 225–26, 231–33, 235, 237, 241, 242, 246
Collins, Mary, 245

Comintern (Communist International), 5, 47, 48, 55, 61–62, 63, 68, 69, 80, 82, 102–3, 108, 159, 172, 185, 234
Communist Labor Party, 6, 54–55
Communist Party, 2, 5–9, 47–48, 49, 54–55, 60, 61–63, 66, 69, 70, 72–74, 75, 77, 79–82, 102–3, 105, 108, 118–19, 130, 145, 150–53, 155, 158–65, 168, 171, 172, 174, 185–86, 198, 199–200, 201–4, 206, 209–12, 215–19, 223, 224, 232, 233, 235–38, 239–41, 246–49, 251, 252, 259–60
company unions, 22, 25, 50, 75, 91, 92, 109, 131, 174, 176, 221
Congress of Industrial Organizations, 4, 5, 7, 8, 105, 109, 112, 117, 131, 133–34, 148, 155, 158–59, 164, 169, 170, 173, 179, 186, 189, 195, 197, 201, 215, 216, 218, 226, 251, 254, 256–57
Contes, Gus, 252
Cooks and Pastry Chefs Local 24, 25–26
Cooks Local 89, 108, 133, 150, 163, 168, 169, 206, 208, 216, 217, 219, 298n94
Cooks Local 719, 16, 17, 36, 64, 68
Cooks Syndicate, 36
Cosgrove, Fred, 169, 192
Cosmopolitan Hotel Waiters Local 94, 34
Coughlin, Howard, 229
Coulcher, Paul, 35, 63, 65, 68, 75, 88, 89, 91, 100, 104, 106, 107, 109–13, 115–17, 126, 182, 204
Counterattack, 258
Cowan, Walter, 244, 246
Cresser, Charles, 210, 213
Crowley, James, 202, 203

Daily Worker, 72, 92, 95, 97, 99, 101, 108, 158, 174, 192, 217–18, 241, 247
Delicatessen Countermen and Cafeteria Employees Local 302, 65, 67, 68, 71, 73, 74, 86–90, 104, 106–7, 110, 112, 114, 115, 121, 133, 155, 198, 200, 208, 217, 239
Delmonico's (restaurant), 12, 32
Dewey, Thomas E., 1, 8, 104–5, 111–17, 121, 122, 160–61, 224
Dies, Martin, 158, 174
Dies Committee. *See* House Un American Activities Committee
Dodge, William C., 90, 111
Donohue, George, 251
Dorsey, Ruby, 245
Drechsler, David, 126, 142, 180, 262
DuPont, Coleman T., 39, 41
DuPont, Pierre, 91

Index

Eckford, Scotty, 133, 140, 157, 243, 245, 251
Edwards, Patsy, 242
Elster, Joseph, 17, 18-19, 21-23, 25-29, 34, 45, 63
Epstein, Irving, 89, 113, 115, 116
Emigrant Industrial Savings Bank, 124, 143
employment in hotels, 14-15, 23, 25-26, 34-35, 37, 39, 41-43, 58-59, 68, 118-19, 138-39, 179, 192-93, 220-21, 231, 257
Ernst, Hugo, 4, 8, 64, 74, 84, 105, 109, 134-35, 155, 163, 183, 184, 189, 198, 200, 202-8, 210, 213, 214, 218, 225, 226, 228, 232, 235, 238, 239-41, 244-46, 248, 250, 256, 258
Ernst, Morris, 96
Ettor, Joseph, 29-31

Federal Bureau of Investigation, 5, 9, 174-75, 190, 197-98, 200, 209, 217, 223, 247, 257, 258, 259
Federation of Hotel Guilds, 91-92
Ferris, Charlotte, 154
Field, B. J., 75, 82, 91-93, 93-101
Field, Frank Vanderbilt, 242
Finn, Ann, 242
Firemen and Oilers union, 25, 40, 129, 141, 263
Flanagan, Joseph, 219, 242
Fling, Jerry, 171, 192
Flore, Edward, 44-45, 64, 65, 73, 84-85, 89, 105-12, 116, 123, 126, 133-35, 152, 162, 163, 165, 179, 183-85, 189, 200, 226, 228
Flynn, Elizabeth Gurley, 3, 29, 31-32, 34, 43, 59, 119, 247
Folsom Jr., Charles E., 116
Food Worker, 78, 101, 102, 111
Food Workers Industrial League, 77-78
Food Workers Industrial Union, 6, 7, 75, 76, 78-84, 91, 92, 94, 96-99, 101-3, 104, 105, 107, 108, 110-11, 159, 174, 183, 184, 224, 251
Forge, Maurice, 251
Foster, Clyde, 205
Foster, William Z., 46-48, 49, 56, 57, 59, 62, 69, 73, 77, 80, 82, 184, 186, 198, 216, 223, 224, 239-40, 247
Fournigault, Andre, 90-91, 96
Fox, Joseph, 217
Free Voice of the Amalgamated Food Workers, 51, 52, 55, 56, 58-60, 65, 67, 68, 73, 77, 81-83, 101, 103

Freiheit, 67
Frohman, Siegfried, 86
Furniture Workers Industrial Union, 79

Garriga, Miguel, 108-10, 113, 117, 118, 121, 124, 126, 133-35, 145, 150-52, 163-65, 170, 174, 190, 194, 198, 199-214, 217, 256
Gaynor, William J., 27
Geneva Society, 21, 22, 25, 28, 32, 50, 64-65, 75, 91, 108, 174
Gentile, Sal, 101, 103, 218, 219
George, Daisy, 233, 243, 246, 251, 252
Gerena, Gil, 242
German Waiters Union, 14-15, 35. *See also* Waiters Local 1
Gerson, Simon, 97, 247
Giovannitti, Arturo, 29, 30, 59
Gitlow, Benjamin, 63, 96, 101, 158
Golden, Ben, 99, 101
Gompers, Samuel, 45, 47, 48, 54, 97
Goodman, John, 162, 195, 225, 233
Gottesman, Benny, 85, 89, 115, 117, 198
Grecht, Rebecca, 67
Green, William, 73, 97, 110, 124, 160, 184, 189, 197, 218, 225, 256
Greeter's Association, 50
Growth of a Union, 3, 183-85
Grubb, Al, 118

Hand, Learned, 248
Hardart, Frank, Jr., 37
Harvard University, 176, 221
Henkel, Joseph, 77
Herrick, Eleanor, 93, 94, 96-101, 107
Herzog, Paul M., 117
Hesketh, Robert, 84, 134, 135
Hillquit, Morris, 25
Hilton, Conrad, 229
Hintz, Ralph, 131
Hiss, Alger, 224
Horn & Hardart, 36-37, 110, 127
Hotel & Club Employees Local 6, 1, 2, 4, 7-9, 126, 127, 129, 131-36, 141, 145, 149, 150, 152-54, 163-65, 170-73, 178-79, 182-84, 186, 188-89, 190-92, 194-97, 199, 200, 202, 203, 205-7, 209-14, 215-19, 221, 225, 228-29, 230, 232-36, 238, 239-48, 250-53, 257, 259, 260, 261-64; recreational activities, 155; welfare activities, 154-55, 172-73; women's activities, 153-55, 172

Index

Hotel and Restaurant Employees' International Alliance and Bartenders' International League, 15–17, 34–35, 40, 42, 44–45, 63–66, 67, 74, 84–89, 103, 105, 107–12, 123, 126, 130, 133–36, 151, 158, 162–64, 171, 190, 201–5, 210–12, 216–18, 226, 227, 238, 239–43, 244–46, 256–58; Genera; Executive Board (GEB), 17, 37, 42, 63, 86, 106, 109, 110, 118, 135, 163, 183–85, 189, 198–203, 206–9, 211, 213, 214, 216, 217, 232, 256; New York Local Joint Executive Board (LJEB), 68, 85–88, 113, 117, 118, 152, 165, 170, 199–201, 206–11, 213, 216, 217, 239, 244, 256

Hotel Association, 7, 19–21, 22, 24, 25, 27, 28, 30, 31, 40, 43–45, 58, 65–66, 91–92, 96, 98–101, 122, 124–26, 127–33, 136–40, 144, 157, 161, 166, 170, 177, 179–83, 188, 191, 192, 208, 223, 228

Hotel Captains and Waiters Local 16, 66, 68, 75, 86–89, 91, 92, 96, 100, 104, 106, 110–13, 117, 126, 152, 159, 163, 182, 184, 198–99, 206, 208, 211

Hotel Front Service Employees Local 144, 161–62, 171, 182, 195, 198, 210, 221, 225, 228, 232, 233, 249–50, 253, 263

hotel industry, 5, 11–14, 36, 81, 124–26, 179–80, 181, 229–30

Hotel League, 137, 140, 144, 177

Hotel Men's Association. *See* Hotel Association

Hotel, Restaurant and Cafeteria Workers Organizing Committee, 118–23, 129, 144–45, 161, 165

Hotel, Restaurant and Club Workers Industrial Union No. 110, 35

hotels: Adams, 148; Alamac, 143; Alden, 139; Algonquin, 22, 93, 137, 140, 144, 191; Ambassador, 157, 181; Ansonia, 31, 194; Astor, 13, 19, 22, 23, 29, 30, 40, 45, 91, 97, 98, 100, 131, 157, 166, 167, 210, 217; Beaux Arts, 228, 255; Belmont, 11, 12, 17–22, 29, 32, 41, 44, 81, 265; Belmont-Plaza, 143; Belvedere, 175, 255; Beverly, 241; Biltmore, 40, 92, 139; Bolivar, 157; Bossert, 228; Breevort, 92; Brewster, 148; Brittany, 132, 139; Breslin, 92, 133; Brewster, 148; Broadway-Central, 152; Bryant, 175; Buckingham, 143, 149; Cameron, 133, 139; Carlton Terrace, 24; Centre Arms, 89; Claridge, 13, 38, 39, 42; Commodore, 78, 139, 228, 260, 261; Cornish Arms, 167, 230; Drake, 175; Duane, 194; Dixie, 222, 228; Edison, 133, 140, 161, 198; Empire, 170, 212; Endicott, 29, 44; Essex House, 92, 143; Fifth Avenue, 14, 24, 32; Four Seasons, 261; Fourteen, 253–55; Gotham, 19, 23, 157; George Washington, 122; Governor Clinton, 98, 127–28, 133, 140, 141, 143, 148, 157, 187, 195, 221–23, 265; Gramercy Park, 148; Grand Hyatt, 261–64; Greystone, 92, 182; Hamilton, 194; Hampshire House, 149, 194; Hoffman House, 29; Holland House, 13, 22, 29, 35; Imperial, 23, 25, 26, 29, 32; Kimberly, 132, 143; Knickerbocker, 12, 18, 19, 22, 31, 32, 39, 40, 81; Lincoln, 92, 120, 133, 140, 141; Lombardy, 92; Madison, 225; Manhattan, 19, 22, 81; Martinique, 13, 31, 32, 44, 194; Mayflower, 146, 148, 149, 255; McAlpin, 14, 35, 39, 42, 66, 98, 118, 132, 136, 137, 139; Netherland, 24, 25 (*see also* Sherry-Netherland); New Weston, 92; New Yorker, 92, 97, 120, 131, 139, 143, 155, 179; Oliver Cromwell, 148, 175; Olcott, 194; One Fifth Avenue, 129, 255; Paramount, 255; Park Avenue, 38, 39; Park Central, 91, 92, 97, 100, 132, 139, 141, 147, 202, 228, 229 (*see also* Park Sheraton); Park Crescent, 132, 139; Park Royal, 194; Park Sheraton, 229 (*see also* Park Central); Pennsylvania, 92, 97, 120, 131, 132, 139, 142, 199, 229 (*see also* Statler); Piccadilly, 139; Pierre, 168, 178; Plaza, 13, 19, 22, 23, 39–41, 49, 59–60, 64, 92, 137, 149, 166–68, 171, 175–76, 178, 191, 229; Prince George, 23, 44; Raleigh, 149; Rector's, 13, 23 (*see also* Claridge); Regent, 148, 187, 194; Ritz-Carlton, 32, 38, 98, 137, 176, 181; Roosevelt, 97, 120, 131, 139, 229; Russell, 175; Savoy, 24, 25; Savoy-Plaza, 81, 137, 149, 157, 166, 168, 245; Seville, 29; Sherry-Netherland, 24, 25, 92, 166, 168, 178; Standish Hall, 194; Stanhope, 187; Statler, 229, 235; St. Moritz, 92, 143, 176, 177, 235; St. Regis, 12, 23, 27, 40, 100, 137, 143; Sulgrave, 143; Taft, 139, 142; Times Square, 133, 210; Towers, 181, 255; Van Rensselaer, 187; Vanderbilt, 13, 21, 22, 36, 40, 139, 182; Victoria, 132, 167; Waldorf-Astoria, 12–14, 17, 19, 20, 22, 23–25, 27, 29, 31, 32,

Index

39, 40, 64, 66, 75, 90, 91, 93, 97, 100, 120, 131, 144, 166, 177, 178, 187, 188, 191, 194, 210, 230, 235, 244, 245, 265; Warwick, 102, 175, 181; Wellington, 155; White, 133; Whitehall, 144, 146; Windsor, 187; Woodstock, 139

Hotel Trades Council, 1, 2, 4, 8, 129–33, 136, 137, 139–45, 148, 153, 157, 159–61, 166, 167, 169–71, 175–79, 180–82, 186–89, 191–93, 196, 199–200, 208, 210, 213, 215, 217, 219, 221, 227–29, 231, 233–35, 237, 249–50, 254, 261–65

Hotel Waiters Local 5, 16, 17, 18, 63, 163

House Un American Activities Committee, 9, 158–60, 174, 197, 209, 257

Huamani, Benito, 147

Hudson Shore Labor School, 154

Hylan, John F., 33, 43

IBEW Local 3, 104, 122, 130, 178, 211, 263, 293n57. *See also* International Brotherhood of Electrical Workers

IBEW Local 1005-B, 141, 263. *See also* International Brotherhood of Electrical Workers

Immigration & Naturalization Service (INS), 159, 198, 209, 223–24, 233, 257

Industrial Workers of the World, 2, 5, 6, 11, 18, 21, 24, 25, 27, 29–32, 33–35, 38, 36, 47, 48, 49, 51, 53, 55, 56, 59, 60, 69, 82, 184, 262

Industry Wide Agreement, 7, 136–39, 145–47, 154, 157, 166, 169–70, 191, 208, 215, 226–27, 230–32, 235, 236, 243, 249, 251, 253, 262, 265; Article 14a (hiring and firing), 138, 146, 249, 251; Article 28 ("Exceptional Cases"), 138, 146–47, 177, 181, 253; health insurance, 169–70, 182–83, 226–27; hours, 138; pensions, 254–56; union shop, 137, 177, 191, 194, 243; wages, 137–38, 145, 166, 168, 173, 179, 181, 192–93, 208, 230–32, 235, 236; injunctions, 37, 51, 60, 61, 71, 72, 73, 75, 77, 83, 86, 87, 91, 92, 97, 100, 107, 110, 157, 206, 213, 244, 252, 255

International Brotherhood of Electrical Workers, 24, 110, 129, 145, 161; Local 3, 104, 122, 130, 178, 211, 263, 293n57; Local 1005-B, 141, 263

International Federation of Workers in the Hotel and Restaurant Industry, 38–47, 49, 50, 52

International Hotel Workers Union, 18–20, 23–29, 34, 196

International Restaurant Employees Association, 37

Johnson, George, 90

Johnson, Hugh, 85

Johnstone, Jack, 56

Joint Anti-Fascist Refugee Committee, 197, 209, 235

Josephson, Matthew, 183, 258

Journeymen Bakers' and Confectioners' International Union of America, 50, 52

The Jungle, 26, 47

Karlin, William, 39, 52–53

Kearny, John J., 107, 109, 184–85, 189, 200, 203, 205

Kelly, Dennis, 202

Kenny, John, 202–5

Kheel, Theodore W., 180

Kincaid, Patrick, 194

Knispel, Julius, 68

Knott hotel chain, 167, 169, 175, 187, 230

Koenig, Harry, 109, 112, 113, 116

Koenig, Louis, 183

Kovaleski, Emmanuel, 68, 109, 184, 195

Kramberg, Sam, 35, 55, 61, 68, 70–73, 76–78, 101, 106–8, 110, 114, 133, 152, 159, 174, 198–200, 217, 239, 243, 259, 262

Krantz, Sam, 113–15

Kridel, Frank W., 175

Kronen, Al, 118, 135

Kyriages, George, 242, 246

Labor Unity Council of America. *See* United Labor Council

La Guardia, Fiorello, 1, 43, 77, 83, 98, 100, 110, 111, 117, 125, 142, 149, 157

Lane, Gertrude, 3, 119, 133, 147, 165, 172, 174, 175, 187, 194, 200, 207, 214, 225, 230, 232, 233, 235, 237, 241, 243, 244, 251, 252, 256, 257–59, 262

Lehman, Herbert H., 111, 117

Lehman, William, 35, 37, 63, 65, 73, 74, 106–8, 112

Lesino, Cesar, 17, 35, 36, 38, 39

Long, Robert, 68

Lopez, Antonio, 118, 157, 167, 192, 194, 219, 222, 241, 242, 246

Lore, Ludwig, 6, 9, 53, 54, 61–63, 77, 81, 82, 88, 151, 174
Losovsky, Solomon, 69
Lumber Workers Industrial Union, 79

Madison Square Garden, 93, 94, 96, 197, 205
Mageau, Theodore, 196
Malkin, Maurice, 159
Manhattan Center, 137, 155, 181, 213, 231, 232, 244, 258, 259
Manley, Joseph, 58
Marcantonio, Vito, 110, 197, 219
March of Labor, 247, 252, 306n72
Marine Transport Workers Industrial Union, 79
Marley, James, 243, 251, 252, 255
Martel, Albert, 39–40, 64–66
Martin, Charles, 118, 243
Martin, Jules, 85, 88, 89, 113–15
McCarthy, Joseph, 224–25
McCarthy, Leo, 171
McCarthy, Thomas D., 38
McCusker, Herb, 242
McDeavitt, John, 86, 89
McDonough, C. T., 202–3
McFetridge, William, 161, 162, 184, 226
McLane, George B., 106, 112, 134–36, 183–84
Meany, George, 110, 130, 184, 186, 225–26, 256
Mesevich, William, 114–15, 133, 152, 198, 206, 216
Miller, Ed, 135, 199–200, 202–3, 238–39, 258
Moore, John D., 117
Moroney, Peter J., 130, 211, 224
Mulrooney, Edward P., 92, 104, 142, 146–47, 157, 166, 169, 177, 191, 193, 230, 236, 253
Murphy, Philip, 256
Muste, A. J., 77, 81, 82, 84, 93

National Committee for Organizing the Iron and Steel Workers, 47
National Hotel Management Company, 131
National Labor Relations Board, 109, 117, 158, 179, 188, 207–8, 228–29
National Labor Union, 14
National Miners Union, 79
National Textile Workers Union, 79

National War Labor Board, 169, 179–82, 192
Needle Trades Workers Industrial Union, 70, 79
New York Club Employees Association, 36
Norris–La Guardia Act, 83, 92, 110, 144, 196
no-strike agreements, 5, 24, 28, 50, 166, 172, 177, 179–80, 193, 254, 262
Novy Mir, 67

Obermeier, Georgette, 173, 260
Obermeier, Marguerite, 192
Obermeier, Michael J., 1, 3, 4, 6, 9, 36, 45, 49, 52, 55, 58–59, 61–62, 70, 72–73, 76–78, 80, 101, 108, 111, 113, 118, 123–24, 126, 129, 133–34, 140, 145, 147, 150, 158–60, 163–65, 170–74, 183–84, 186, 190, 192, 194, 195, 198, 200–203, 206–14, 216–17, 223–25, 230–33, 236–41, 247–48, 256, 260, 262
O'Donnell, Stephen, 250
O'Dwyer, Paul, 211, 212
Office Employees International Union, 228–29
Operating Engineers, 15, 24, 25, 40, 110, 122, 129
Ornstein, Charles L., 255

Parker, Dorothy, 93
Parker, Mildred, 242
Passan, Tom, 210, 214, 238
Pearl, Victor, 18, 19, 20
"Pearlism," 20, 39
Pegler, Westbrook, 160
Phelan, Arthur J., 211, 212, 223, 224, 233
Pincus, Max, 89, 106, 107, 109–16, 251
Powell, Adam Clayton, 197
Pressman, Lee, 201
Profintern, 48, 55–56, 69, 76–77, 79

Quill, Mike, 201, 215

Raymond, William, 166, 238, 241, 251
Red International of Labor Unions. *See* Profintern
Reed, John, 6
Regan, James, 22, 31
Regan, Mary T., 141
Reich, Harry, 78, 110, 118, 124, 150, 163, 164, 199, 203, 204, 207, 216, 217, 218

Reilly, Michael, 252
Retek, Aladar, 88, 89, 113, 115, 116, 117
Rezac, Otto, 65
Richberg, Donald, 98
Rodman, Selden, 93
Roosevelt, Eleanor, 97
Roosevelt, Franklin D., 75, 83–84, 91, 93, 109, 153, 158, 159, 172, 173, 180–81, 182, 186
Ross, Bert H., 240–46, 248–50, 252, 253, 256
Rubin, Audrey J., 165
Rubin, Donald, 165
Rubin, Jay, 1, 3, 4, 7, 8, 79–80, 83, 102, 104–9, 112, 117, 118, 121, 123, 124, 126, 129, 130, 133, 134, 136, 138, 140, 142, 143, 148, 149, 153, 158–61, 163, 165, 166, 167, 169–71, 174, 176, 177, 183, 184, 186, 191, 193, 199, 200, 204, 205, 207, 208, 210, 215, 218, 219, 222, 223, 225, 227, 230–38, 239, 241–58, 262, 264
Rubin, Mollie, 165
Ryan, Joseph P., 89, 110

sabotage, 5, 30–31, 46, 55, 61, 72, 174
Salvin & Thompson restaurant group, 60
Santibanez, Angel, 243
Santo, John, 190, 209
Saulnier, Louis, 246
Scalise, George, 122, 123, 130, 140, 141, 148, 160–62
Schatz, Otto, 174
Schleifer, Louis, 230
Schutt, Carl, 210
Scott, Stanley, 210
Segal, Martin, 226–27
Sherman, Henry L., 72
Sherman cafeterias, 107
Shoe and Leather Workers Industrial Union, 79
Shoemaker, Thomas, 190
Siegal, David, 113, 152, 163, 199, 206, 211, 216, 256
Silvani, Charles, 176
Simidaris, Ed, 245, 252
Sirch, Richard, 155, 238, 241, 242
Smith Act, 159, 174, 198, 209, 211, 216, 217, 223, 224, 247, 260
Socialist Party, 19, 21, 25, 53, 54, 55, 70, 76, 96
Society of Restaurateurs, 44
Soda Fountain Employees Local 254, 210

Spinner, Fred, 220, 235, 243
Spitzer, Sam, 206, 219
Stachel, Jack, 80
Stalin, Joseph, 6, 60, 61, 69, 73, 80, 82, 122, 151, 160, 186, 205, 247
State Labor Relations Board (SLRB), 117, 120–21, 123, 125–26, 131–33, 136, 140, 143–45, 148–49, 157, 166–67, 170, 175–79, 181, 187–88, 191, 194–96, 221–22, 228–29
Statler chain, 64, 120, 125, 131, 229, 230, 255
Steclen, Joseph, 210
Steel and Metal Workers Industrial Union, 79
Stenzler, Leo, 117
Stern, Charlotte, 154, 172, 197, 209, 235, 236
Sterry, Fred, 23, 39
Steuben, John, 171, 186, 195, 198, 218, 225, 228, 230, 231, 233, 234, 237, 247, 250, 251, 302n111
Stocks, Glen, 171, 191, 246
Stockyards Labor Council, 47, 56, 129
Stokes, J. Graham Phelps, 21
Stokes, Rose Pastor, 3, 21, 22, 24–28, 119
Stokes, W. E. D., 31, 194
Stone, I. F., 224
Sullivan, Jere, 15–16, 37, 40, 44–45, 64, 66
Sullivan, John J., 161
Susi, Arduilio, 216
Syndicalist League of North America, 47
Syndicalist Militant Minority League, 46

Taft, Robert, 218
Taft, William Howard, 31
Tammany Hall, 8, 43, 73, 85–90, 98, 104, 111, 115, 116
Taylor, S. Gregory, 140, 143, 176, 177, 230, 307n91
telephone operators. *See* International Brotherhood of Electrical Workers
Thomas, Norman, 82, 94, 96, 303n143
Thurmond, Strom, 219
Tillman, Don, 119, 171, 219, 242
Tip Toe Inn, 107
Tobacco Workers Industrial Union, 54, 79
Todes, Charlotte. *See* Stern, Charlotte
Townsend, Jack, 199, 203, 206, 208, 210, 216, 217, 256, 258
Trade Union Education League, 54, 56–58, 68, 69, 73, 79, 80, 82

Trade Union Unity League, 3, 6, 7, 73, 75–82, 92, 102, 103, 108, 119, 142, 174, 184, 198, 223, 224
Tresca, Carlo, 30, 32, 34
Trotsky, Leon, 6, 7, 53, 54, 62, 80, 82, 88
Truman, Harry S., 186, 190, 196–97, 208, 218, 227, 250, 254
Tschirky, Oscar, 12, 17, 20, 23, 90

ULP. *See* Unfair Labor Practice
Unfair Labor Practice, 109, 117, 131, 141, 144, 149, 157, 167, 176, 178, 187, 195, 196, 221
Union House, Union Bar, 3, 64, 183, 258
United Amusement, Hotel and Restaurant Unions, 110, 122
United Office and Professional Workers of America–CIO, 228
United Labor Council, 6, 55–56, 57–58, 159
United Mine Workers, 84

Van Arsdale, Harry, Jr., 122, 141
Vatel Club, 65, 108
Vehling, Joseph, 18, 34
Vehling, Paul, 18, 34
Verillio, Charles, 176

Villard, Oswald Garrison, 96
Vladeck, B. C., 96

Waiters Local 1, 14–15, 16–17, 24, 34, 35, 37, 57, 60, 64
Waitresses Local 679, 16, 42
Wagner, Otto, 36, 38, 41, 44, 45, 50
Wagner, Robert, 100, 109
Waldman, Louis B., 114, 115
Ward, Peter, 4, 262, 263
Weilburg, Esther, 147, 154
Weinstock, Louis, 130, 142, 158, 186, 201, 247
Welles, Orson, 144
Williams, John J., 89, 106, 107, 113, 116
Wilson, Tom, 188, 214, 244
Wilson, Woodrow, 47
Wolf, Morton, 254–55
Woolcott, Alexander, 93, 144
Workers (Communist) Party. *See* Community Party
World Federation of Trade Unions, 186, 226
Wurlitzer-Simplex, 134

Zack, Joseph, 159
Zack, Paul, 148, 160

SHAUN RICHMAN teaches labor history at SUNY Empire State University. He is the author of *Tell the Bosses We're Coming: A New Action Plan for Workers in the Twenty-First Century.*

The University of Illinois Press
is a founding member of the
Association of University Presses.

———————————————

Composed in 10.5/13 Mercury Text G1
with Avenir LT Std display
by Kirsten Dennison
at the University of Illinois Press

University of Illinois Press
1325 South Oak Street
Champaign, IL 61820-6903
www.press.uillinois.edu